Many today substitute human se~~r~~
word of God, thinking that plurali~~s~~
exclusivism. Todd Miles demonstr~~a~~ ..... ~~e~~xegetically faithful and theologically profound work that the Scriptures teach that one must hear the gospel to
be saved. I found his discussion of the role of the Spirit in salvation particularly
helpful, for he shows that the Spirit does not bring salvation apart from the gospel
of the Son. Miles reminds us that faithfulness to Scripture is always the most loving position, for those who do not hear the gospel are perishing. I pray, therefore,
that this book will motivate the church to proclaim the gospel to the ends of the
earth.

Thomas R. Schreiner
James Buchanan Harrison Professor of New Testament Interpretation
The Southern Baptist Theological Seminary

Christians have historically held that the biblical gospel alone has the power to
deal with the root and fruit of human fallenness, and that its salvific benefits must
be appropriated by personal faith in Jesus Christ. This stance, known has "exclusivism," has been increasingly challenged by many both within and outside the
church as being arrogant and uncharitable. Dr. Miles' robust defense of the traditional Christian position is thus both timely and necessary. He gives special
attention to how the Trinitarian congruence taught in Scripture requires these
convictions, and urges us to even greater faithfulness in global mission as their
compelling consequence.

Dr. Randal Roberts
President and Professor of Spiritual Formation
Western Seminary

Like it or not, we all have a theology of religions, whether examined or unexamined. With sound exegesis and keen cultural analysis, Todd Miles reminds us
of the uniqueness of the Christian message, and why it matters today. Where I
live, the church engages daily with countless other worldviews and religions. The
sheikhs are actually inviting interfaith dialogue. But are we up to the challenge?
I'm grateful for this book, and I relish the opportunity to use it to equip our people
to proclaim Christ more faithfully in our cultural setting.

John Folmar
Senior Pastor
United Christian Church of Dubai
United Arab Emirates

The exclusivity of Christ is no small matter to the Christian faith. *Everything* hinges on the truth claims of the Scriptures that Jesus, the God-man, is the only Savior of sinners, and that his gospel is the only good news by which sinners, through faith in Christ, may be saved. Todd Miles's excellent defense of these central Christian convictions is both timely and prophetic. His scholarship is superb, his fairness to those with whom he differs is exemplary, and his argumentation is strong and compelling. May God be pleased to see *A God of Many Understandings?* read widely for the sake of the truth of Christ and the spread of his gospel.

Bruce A. Ware
Professor of Christian Theology
The Southern Baptist Theological Seminary

This book is Gospel clear and Gospel bold! Todd Miles weaves the contemporary, the global, the theological, and the practical in driving toward a biblical theology of religions. It is a must read for anyone seeking clarification of Christ and his message for the world.

Jeff Louie
Associate Professor of Theology at Western Seminary
Stakeholder of The Gospel Coalition
219 Anita Dr
Millbrae, CA 94030

The gospel is not merely one of God's warm-hearted attempts at negotiation with His mistaken, but adorable creation. It is His only and exclusive summons to defiant rebels—a summons from the universal Lord demanding compliance from all without exception. This is the Bible's message. This is orthodox Christianity. Nevertheless, familiar vampires have revived once again seeking to drain the gospel's lifeblood via the haggard heresies of inclusivism, pluralism, and universalism. Thankfully, Todd Miles has the courage to prize the exclusivity of the gospel over the political correctness of our culture—even our evangelical sub-culture. In *A God Of Many Understandings?* he articulates an authentically Christian "theology of religions," and in so doing helps us distinguish between the human richness of various religious traditions and their ultimate inability to effect salvation.

Art Azurdia, D. Min.
Associate Professor of Pastoral and Church Ministry
Director of Pastoral Mentoring Western Seminary

A God of Many Understandings?

A God of Many Understandings?

THE GOSPEL AND A THEOLOGY OF RELIGIONS

TODD L. MILES

ACADEMIC

NASHVILLE, TENNESSEE

Published by B&H Publishing Group
Nashville, Tennessee

Dewey Decimal Classification: 261.2

Subject Heading: RELIGIONS\CHRISTIANITY AND OTHER
RELIGIONS\THEOLOGY

Printed in the United States of America
1 2 3 4 5 6 7 8 9 10 11 12 • 17 16 15 14 13 12 11 10
VP

Contents

List of Abbreviations   x
Acknowledgments   xiii

Chapter One
The Exclusivity of Christ
and a Christian Theology of Religions   1

Chapter Two
The Bible and Religions   33

Chapter Three
Universalism, Hell, and Conditional Immortality   95

Chapter Four
Pluralism   137

Chapter Five
Inclusivism I: Nonevangelical Expressions   183

Chapter Six
Inclusivism II: Evangelical Expressions   210

Chapter Seven
The Starting Point for a Biblical Theology
of Religions—Christ or the Spirit?   247

Chapter Eight
Son and Spirit: The Christ-Glorifying Work
of the Holy Spirit   277

Chapter Nine
A Christian Theology of Religions and Mission   328

Bibliography   355
Name Index   363
Subject Index   369
Scripture Index   375

To Natalie, Ethan, and Levi,

May you always hold fast

to the gospel of Jesus Christ.

List of Abbreviations

AB	Anchor Bible
AH	*Against Heresies*
ANF	*The Ante-Nicene Fathers,* ed. A Roberts and J. Donaldson (Buffalo: Christian Literature, 1885–96; reprint, Grand Rapids: Eerdmans, 1975)
Ap.	*Josephus, Against Apion*
AUSS	*Andrews University Seminary Studies*
BDAG	*A Greek-English Lexicon of the New Testament and Other Early Christian Literature,* 3rd ed.
BSac	*Bibliotheca Sacra*
BTB	*Biblical Theology Bulletin*
CBQ	*Catholic Biblical Quarterly*
CD	*Current Dialogue*
CSR	*Christian Scholar's Review*
CT	*Christianity Today*
CTJ	*Calvin Theological Journal*
De Prin	*First Principles*
EBC	*The Expositor's Bible Commentary*
ECNT	Evangelical Commentary on the New Testament
EDT	*Evangelical Dictionary of Theology,* 2nd ed.
EMQ	*Evangelical Missions Quarterly*
ER	*Ecumenical Review*
ERT	*Evangelical Review of Theology*
ESV	English Standard Version
EvQ	*Evangelical Quarterly*
HCSB	Holman Christian Standard Bible
ICC	International Critical Commentary
JAAR	*Journal of the American Academy of Religion*
JBL	*Journal of Biblical Literature*
JES	*Journal of Ecumenical Studies*
JETS	*Journal of the Evangelical Theological Society*
JPT	*Journal of Pentecostal Theology*
JR	*Journal of Religion*
LXX	Septuagint
NAC	New American Commentary
NDBT	*The New Dictionary of Biblical Theology*

NIBC	New International Biblical Commentary
NICNT	The New International Commentary on the New Testament
NICOT	The New International Commentary on the Old Testament
NIGTC	New International Greek Testament Commentary
NIV	New International Version
NIVAC	NIV Application Commentary
NTS	*New Testament Studies*
OTL	Old Testament Library
PG	*Patrologia graeca* (Paris: J.-P. Migne, 1857–66)
PNTC	The Pillar New Testament Commentary
RTR	*Reformed Theological Review*
SBET	*Scottish Bulletin of Evangelical Theology*
SBJT	*The Southern Baptist Journal of Theology*
SJT	*Scottish Journal of Theology*
TOTC	Tyndale Old Testament Commentaries
TR	*Theological Review*
TS	*Theological Studies*
TynBul	*Tyndale Bulletin*
WBC	Word Biblical Commentary
WCC	World Council of Churches
WEC	*Wycliffe Exegetical Commentary*
WTJ	*Westminster Theological Journal*

Acknowledgements

As in all aspects of the Christian life, this book is a community effort. Work on this project began during my doctoral studies at The Southern Baptist Theological Seminary and continued through the first years of my teaching career at Western Seminary. Throughout that time, I have been encouraged by the generous assistance of others. I am grateful for Broadman and Holman's willingness to work with me and to publish a book on the necessity of faith in Jesus Christ for salvation. Dr. Ray Clendenen, the academic editor, has guided me through this project from the beginning. I thank him for his labors on my behalf.

I have been blessed by many teachers and colleagues who have guided me into greater understanding of the gospel and more faithful obedience to the Lord. Dr. Bruce Ware, Dr. Tom Schreiner, Dr. Steve Wellum, Dr. Gerry Breshears, Dr. Art Azurdia, and Ron Marrs have taught me, encouraged me, and consistently pointed me to Christ. I will always be grateful for their godly influence.

Western Seminary is committed to Gospel Transformation as its guiding principle. My leaders at Western Seminary, Dr. Randy Roberts and Dr. Marc Cortez, have created an environment that challenges me to think through the implications of the gospel in every class that I teach. They have also given enormous scheduling flexibility to me which has enabled the completion of this book. It is a joy and a privilege to work at an institution that is characterized by such faithfulness to the Lord Jesus Christ. I would also like to thank my graduate assistants, Andy Middlekauf, Allen Jones, JohnMark Beazley, and Brian LePort, for all of their legwork and diligent research.

Art and Laverne Denning, my wife's parents, have been a blessing to me since I married their daughter. Much of this book was written in their home, while they cared for my wife and children. I am thankful for their encouragement and the love that they lavish on my family.

I first heard the gospel of Jesus Christ from my parents. My mother, Barbara Miles, has been an essential source of every possible kind of support through my entire life and that was the case on this project as well. I am grateful to her and for her.

My children, Natalie, Ethan, and Levi, have sacrificed time and attention that was rightfully theirs for the sake of this project and they have done so without complaint. It is my privilege, joy, and a source of godly pride to be their father.

I cannot adequately express my gratitude to my wife, Camille. She has joyfully been my friend, my encourager, my editor (a difficult and often thankless task), my helper, and mother to my children. Because of her sacrificial care and the grace of God, we have flourished as a family. I adore her.

Finally, I am humbled to be loved and saved by our gracious God. I continue to be stunned by His desire to use individuals such as me to proclaim the gospel of Christ and to advance His Kingdom. I pray that the Holy Spirit would continually work in all those who confess Christ, to the end that He would always find willing participants in His task of bringing glory to the Lord Jesus Christ (John 16:14).

Soli Christo Gloria.

Todd Miles
Portland, Oregon
January 2010

Chapter One

The Exclusivity of Christ and a Christian Theology of Religions

Introduction

On Sunday morning, January 18, 2009, Gene Robinson, the Episcopal bishop of New Hampshire, stepped to a podium near the Lincoln Memorial in Washington, DC, to open the inauguration festivities for Barack Obama with an invocation and began his prayer, "O god of our many understandings, we pray that you will . . ."[1] Rather than national outrage at the blasphemous and nonsensical address of the One who controls the destinies of nations, the invocation was hailed by many as a demonstration of inclusiveness. Robinson, an openly homosexual Episcopal priest, had studied previous inaugural prayers and was "horrified" at how "specifically and aggressively Christian they were."[2] He promised that his prayer would not be overtly Christian, nor would he quote Scripture because he wanted "all people to feel that this is their prayer."[3]

Confusion over the identity of God is especially rampant among the younger generations. Lillian R. Mongeau, writer and blogger for

---

[1] A. Augustine, "Bishop Gene Robinson's Inaugural Invocation," *Concord Monitor*, 19 January 2009, http://www.concordmonitor.com/apps/pbcs.dll/article?AID=/20090119/FRONTPAGE/901190386/ (accessed 20 January 2009).

[2] L. Goodstein, "Gay Bishop Is Asked to Say Prayer at Inaugural Event," *New York Times*, 13 January 2009, http://www.nytimes.com/2009/01/13/us/13prayer.html (accessed 21 January 2009).

[3] Ibid.

the millennial generation, comments, "God, Allah, Yahweh, the Creator, the One, the Energies, goes by as many names in this country as ever. . . . I do believe that God is in everyone, though by what name he resides there seems to me to be up to the person in question." This is logical and theological nonsense, but she defends the oddity of her statements by explaining that for her generation believing such things "is simply considered good manners."[4]

Postmodernity's skepticism toward truth claims, the elevation of tolerance as the prevailing human virtue, and the shrinking of the world due to rapid advancements in transportation and communications technology have caused a radical alteration in the theological and missiological landscape. This is exemplified in Western Christianity's interaction with world religions. For the Western church, participants in the religions of the world other than Christianity, or "religious others," used to be overseas. Today religious others live next door. Western Christians used to learn of religious others primarily through Christian missionary presentations at their local churches or by reading *National Geographic*. Today they learn of religious others through personal encounters at their workplaces and schools. The reality of religious pluralism has occasioned a call for a renewed Christian theology of religions—an investigation into the biblical understanding of world religions and how they fit into the redemptive purposes of God.[5]

The purposes of this book are many, but all are related to the promotion of the proclamation of the gospel of Jesus Christ. First, I will defend the basic biblical assertion that there is one supreme God, the Creator, who is sovereign over all. He has revealed Himself as triune and has uniquely and finally revealed Himself in Jesus Christ, the incarnate Son of God, the second member of the Trinity. Humanity, due to its rebellion against God, stands justly condemned before God, under wrath and utterly without hope. God, in His rich mercy and love, has reached out to us in Jesus Christ, paving not just a way, but the only way, for relationship with Him through conscious and intentional repentance and faith in Christ. This assertion is of vital importance.

---

[4]L. R. Mongeau, "Diverse Generation Choosing Faith Paths on Its Own," *The Oregonian*, 8 March 2009, D2.

[5]H. Netland, *Encountering Religious Pluralism: The Challenge to Christian Faith & Mission* (Downers Grove, IL: InterVarsity, 2001), 12. Netland's book provides the best treatment that I have encountered of the issues surrounding religious pluralism.

The pluralistic world denies God's right and ability, uniquely and particularly, to reveal Himself, and in so doing, catastrophically denies the only means of salvation open to it.[6]

Second, I will maintain on biblical and theological grounds that conscious faith in the gospel, defined as the good news of the life, death, and resurrection of Jesus Christ as anticipated, developed, and presented in Holy Scripture, is necessary for salvation. This position is commonly referred to as *exclusivism*. Exclusivism is challenged by some evangelical Christians, who while remaining convinced that the only hope and basis of salvation is the work of Christ, question how God could justly condemn those who, through no fault of their own, were not recipients of the proclamation of the gospel. These well-meaning Christians, referred to as *inclusivists* throughout this book, speculate that perhaps some of the unevangelized who seek God will be saved on the basis of Christ's death even though they have not consciously repented and believed the gospel.[7] My goal is to demonstrate that not only is the reality of Christ's death and resurrection absolutely necessary for salvation, but it must also be proclaimed and believed. If any are saved, it is through conscious faith in Jesus Christ and His work on the cross.

Third, I will demonstrate that the ministry of the Holy Spirit has been and is focused on the glorification of Jesus Christ, the Son of

---

[6]The following is just a sample of the books written in the last 30 years: C. E. Braaten, *No Other Gospel: Christianity Among the World's Religions* (Minneapolis: Fortress, 1992); A. D. Clarke and B. W. Winter, eds., *One God, One Lord: Christianity in a World of Religious Pluralism*, 2nd ed. (Grand Rapids: Baker, 1992); D. B. Clendenin, *Many Gods, Many Lords: Christianity Encounters World Religions* (Grand Rapids: Baker, 1995); G. D'Costa, *The Meeting of Religions and the Trinity* (Maryknoll, NY: Orbis, 2000); id., *Theology and Religious Pluralism: The Challenge of Other Religions* (Oxford: Blackwell, 1986); J. A. DiNoia, *The Diversity of Religions: A Christian Perspective* (Washington, DC: Catholic University of America Press, 1992); A. Fernando, *The Christian's Attitude Toward World Religions* (Wheaton, IL: Tyndale, 1987); V. Kärkkäinen, *An Introduction to the Theology of Religions: Biblical, Historical and Contemporary Perspectives* (Downers Grove, IL: InterVarsity, 2003); G. R. McDermott, *Can Evangelicals Learn from World Religions? Jesus, Revelation & Religious Traditions* (Downers Grove, IL: InterVarsity, 2000); H. Netland, *Dissonant Voices: Religious Pluralism and the Question of Truth* (Grand Rapids: Eerdmans, 1991); id., *Encountering Religious Pluralism*; E. Rommen and H. Netland, eds., *Christianity and the Religions: A Biblical Theology of World Religions* (Pasadena, CA: William Carey Library, 1995); J. G. Stackhouse, ed., *No Other Gods Before Me? Evangelicals and the Challenge of World Religions* (Grand Rapids: Baker, 2001); and T. C. Tennent, *Christianity at the Religious Roundtable: Evangelicalism in Conversation with Hinduism, Buddhism, and Islam* (Grand Rapids: Baker, 2002).

[7]I will follow Daniel Strange, who defines the *unevangelized* as "any person in history who has lived and died without hearing the Gospel of Jesus Christ from a human messenger." D. Strange, *The Possibility of Salvation Among the Unevangelised: An Analysis of Inclusivism in Recent Evangelical Theology* (Waynesboro, GA: Paternoster, 2002), 35.

God. This goal is really a subcategory of the second goal. Currently, many inclusivists are speculating that the Spirit of God is at work in the world, perhaps in other religions, turning people to God and applying the atoning work of Christ to them, even though they have not believed the gospel. To make this claim, inclusivists have to postulate a relative independence of the Spirit from the Son. Contrary to those who assert either an independent work of the Holy Spirit apart from the Son or a work of the Son that is subordinate to the Spirit in world religions, I will argue that the roles of Jesus Christ and the Holy Spirit are inextricably linked: the Holy Spirit always seeks to glorify the Son. When Jesus said of the Holy Spirit, "He will glorify Me, because He will take from what is Mine and declare it to you" (John 16:14),[8] Christ was not merely defining one aspect of the work of the Holy Spirit. Rather, He was declaring the nature of the relationship between Himself and the Holy Spirit within the broad scope of trinitarian life and redemptive history. Therefore, those who posit an independent salvific work of the Holy Spirit in world religions are denying the Bible's own presentation of the relationship between the Son and the Spirit in the economic Trinity. Any proposal that seeks to sever or reverse this relationship fails on grounds of proper theological method, historical theology, biblical theology, and systematic theology.

Fourth, I want to present a positive model for how a Christian theology of religions should be developed. Many questions face the Christian living in the pluralistic world in general and in the post-Christian West in particular. How do the religions of the world fit into God's sovereign plan of redemption? Why is it that Christians are often no more neighborly than non-Christians? What is the fate of those who have never heard the gospel? Does general revelation convey enough truth to save? Is there truth in non-Christian religions? What role does conscience play in God's revelation in Christ Jesus? Though each of these questions will be addressed, changing contexts will demand that they be answered again and again. It is crucial for the mission of the Church that answers to these questions and others be developed in a biblically faithful way that communicate effectively to each culture and context that asks them. Indeed, because of the nature of God's revelation in Christ and Scripture, any answer to these questions that does not communicate to particular people and contexts is

---

[8]Unless indicated otherwise, all Scripture quotations are from the HCSB.

by definition not biblically faithful. To build a theology of religions that is true to Scripture and glorifying to Christ, we must build along the lines of the methodology and theology of the Son and Spirit that this book describes and defends.

Finally, I hope to convince the readers of the simple and necessary answer to the question, What about those who have never heard the gospel? The consistent biblical response is, "Go tell them!" In the revelation of God, there is no protracted philosophizing and conjecture over the fate of the unevangelized. There is, however, an urgent call to proclamation and a developed biblical theology of mission. Any theological construction that impedes zealous commitment to evangelism is unbiblical and unfaithful. Concurrent with the investigation of Christian interaction with world religions is a call for a review of the Christian missiological strategy. Doctrines that are being challenged and defended in light of that strategy include soteriology, Christology, and pneumatology.[9] Gerald Anderson, writing in 1993, stated, "No issue in missiology is more important, more difficult, more controversial, or more divisive for the days ahead than the theology of religions. . . . This is the theological issue for mission in the 1990s and into the twenty-first century."[10] I am concerned that if an inclusivist understanding of salvation in a pluralistic world wins the day, the heart will be cut out of the motivation to missions.[11]

---

[9]The following is just a sample of the evangelical challenge and response in the last 20 years to salvation in a world of religious pluralism: M. J. Erickson, *How Shall They Be Saved? The Destiny of Those Who Do Not Hear of Jesus* (Grand Rapids: Baker, 1996); C. W. Morgan and R. A. Peterson, eds., *Faith Comes by Hearing: A Response to Inclusivism* (Downers Grove, IL: InterVarsity, 2008); R. H. Nash, *Is Jesus the Only Savior?* (Grand Rapids: Zondervan, 1994); D. L. Okholm and T. R. Phillips, eds., *Four Views on Salvation in a Pluralistic World* (Grand Rapids: Zondervan, 1995, 1996); C. Pinnock, *A Wideness in God's Mercy: The Finality of Jesus Christ in a World of Religions* (Grand Rapids: Zondervan, 1992); J. Sanders, *No Other Name: An Investigation into the Destiny of the Unevangelized* (Grand Rapids: Eerdmans, 1992); Strange, *Possibility of Salvation Among the Unevangelised*; T. L. Tiessen, *Who Can Be Saved? Reassessing Salvation in Christ and World Religions* (Downers Grove, IL: InterVarsity, 2004); A. Yong, *Beyond the Impasse: Toward a Pneumatological Theology of Religions* (Grand Rapids: Baker Academic, 2003); and id., *Discerning the Spirit(s): A Pentecostal-Charismatic Contribution to Christian Theology of Religions* (Sheffield, UK: Sheffield Academic, 2000).

[10]G. H. Anderson, "Theology of Religions and Missiology: A Time of Testing," in *The Good News of the Kingdom: Mission Theology for the Third Millennium*, ed. C. Van Engen, D. S. Gilliland, and P. Pierson (Maryknoll, NY: Orbis Books, 2003), 201.

[11]Christian theologians who are currently working in the area of the possibility of salvation in world religions are conscious of this concern but deny that it is a valid refutation of their proposals. Valid, demonstrable implications of proposals, however, must be considered, particularly when these implications run contrary to the heart of the biblical message and mission. See, for example, Tiessen, *Who Can Be Saved?*, 259–94.

WHAT IS A CHRISTIAN THEOLOGY OF RELIGIONS?

Religious and philosophical pluralisms have been empirical realities since shortly after the fall of man.[12] The early chapters of Genesis chronicle the sad reality that the world has rarely been unified in acceptable worship of the one true and living God. Early in human history, there were multiple religions, the worship of different gods, and incompatible convictions on the nature of reality and the moral universe. The current cultural milieu shares much in common with that of previous generations. What has changed, however, is the public perception of religious pluralism. In the West, because of factors such as the rise of the global village, increased communications technology, and the relativistic mind-set of postmodernity, what was once a simple reality has been elevated or "cherished" in the Western value system.[13] That there are many religions in the world is no longer a simple statement of arithmetic reality. In our shrinking world it is a statement of how things "ought to be." The implications for Christianity and Christian mission are enormous.

The Church of Jesus Christ was birthed in the context of mission and gospel proclamation. Jesus ascended to the right hand of the Father leaving clear marching orders for His followers. They were to "make disciples of all nations, baptizing them in the name of the Father and of the Son and of the Holy Spirit" (Matt 28:19). To enable this mission, Jesus promised that His authoritative presence would always attend His disciples (Matt 28:20). He promised that He would send His Spirit to empower them to witness of Him to the ends of the earth (Acts 1:8). When Jesus fulfilled His promise by sending the Spirit at Pentecost, the first sermon preached, following the inauguration of the Church by the Spirit, resulted in 3,000 people repenting and believing the gospel (Acts 2:41). The Church exists for the glory of Christ and the sake of missions. When the Church ceases to proclaim, she denies the fundamental reality of who she is.

The purpose of the Church has not changed. Today, as in the first century, the Church is called to proclaim the gospel of Jesus Christ to people "blinded" by "the god of this age" so that "they cannot see the

---

[12] See D. A. Carson, *The Gagging of God* (Downers Grove, IL: InterVarsity, 1996), 13–22.

[13] Klaas Runia comments that the rise in pluralism is felt in our knowledge of other religions and the shift to a post-Christian America in the West. K. Runia, "The Gospel and Religious Pluralism," *ERT* 14 (1990): 341–42.

light of the gospel of the glory of Christ" (2 Cor 4:4). The message of the cross of Christ remains "foolishness" to those "who are perishing" (1 Cor 1:18). But today there is enormous cultural pressure, masquerading as a commitment to the "value" of tolerance, to reject any truth claim that assumes superiority to alternatives. The gospel makes just such a claim to superiority. Jesus commissioned the Church with a unique message of salvation. The Church has been motivated to herald that message out of love for and obedience to Christ and because apart from that message there is absolutely no hope for anyone, anywhere. When the prevailing wisdom of the world is that there ought to be religious diversity, then the gospel becomes suspect because the exclusive and necessary nature of its message threatens the way things ought to be. It is the Christian conviction that the world must hear and believe the particular message of Jesus Christ as "the way, the truth, and the life" that runs headlong into contemporary sensibilities. When the Church alters the gospel message into something more palatable to modern sensibilities, it might be respected and embraced by some religious others. But such a message would not be the gospel and would be a denial of who Jesus is and what He did to reconcile the world to God.

Evangelical Christian theologians have been slower to address religious pluralism than their mainline and liberal counterparts.[14] Responding to this cultural, social, religious, and epistemological shift is the responsibility of the Church. Evangelicals are beginning to wade into the discussion with their own proposals for how Christianity and other religions relate. It will not do to dismiss non-Christian religions as pagan without argument or comment. The Church needs a theology of religions that is at once Christ-honoring, biblically faithful, intellectually satisfying, compassionate, and that will encourage Spirit-empowered mission.[15]

A theology of religions seeks, in a coherent and consistent manner, to answer questions concerning the relationships among world religions, special revelation, general revelation, and salvation. A theology of religions is not a description of the doctrines and practices

---

[14]As recently as 2001, J. Stackhouse described the state of evangelical theology of religions as "rudimentary and fragmented." J. G. Stackhouse, "Preface," in *No Other Gods Before Me?*, 11. See also McDermott, *Can Evangelicals Learn from World Religions*, 40.

[15]See D. J. Bosch, *Transforming Mission: Paradigm Shifts in Theology of Mission* (Maryknoll, NY: Orbis, 1991), 483.

of the various religions of the world. It is not a comparative study of religions, nor is it a specific evangelistic or apologetic strategy tailored to reach any one particular non-Christian religion. Rather, a theology of religions is foundational to those descriptive and apologetic tasks. Because each particular religion has different, often incompatible, convictions on the nature of God, revelation, the human dilemma, and salvation, each particular religion will have a different theology of religions. A Christian theology of religions addresses the reality and significance of religious others from a distinctly Christian perspective. It is the attempt to "think theologically about what it means for Christians to live with people of other faiths and about the relationship of Christianity to other religions."[16] Of primary consequence, a Christian theology of religions seeks to answer these questions: Is there salvation outside conscious faith in the gospel of Jesus Christ?[17] If so, how is it appropriated? Why are people incurably religious, and where do their religious impulses and convictions arise? Are there salvific elements or truths of God and redemption outside "the faith that was delivered to the saints once for all" (Jude 3)? How are Christians to relate to religious others as they bring the gospel of truth to them? The formulation of a Christian theology of religions is not peculiar to the current setting. Chapter 2 will demonstrate that from the earliest missionary endeavors of the Church recorded in Acts, Christians have consciously and strategically thought of the gospel's implications for religious others.[18]

---

[16]Kärkkäinen, *Introduction to the Theology of Religions*, 20. See also A. Race, *Christians and Religious Pluralism: Patterns in the Christian Theology of Religions* (Maryknoll, NY: Orbis Books, 1982), 3; Braaten, *No Other Gospel*, 93.

[17]Harold Netland laments that most evangelical attempts at a Christian theology of religions result in a mere analysis of what is the fate of the unevangelized. Netland suggests that three issues demand attention in a theology of religions: "(1) the soteriological question of the destiny of the unevangelized; (2) a theological explanation for the phenomena of human religiosity; and (3) the missiological question of the extent to which we can adapt and build upon aspects of other religious traditions in establishing the church in various cultural contexts." Netland, *Encountering Religious Pluralism*, 310.

[18]Perhaps the first attempt to articulate intentionally a robust theology of religions came from Justin Martyr during the second century with his doctrine of *Logos Spermatikos*. Justin's writings were not primarily an attempt to formulate a Christian theology of religions. His apologetic work was an attempt to stop the persecution of Christians by making the case that Christianity was not treasonous but was the true religion. In making this case, he argued that Christ is the true *Logos* and that the seed of God's universal *Logos* is present in all people groups. Therefore, all people have some divine revelation though Jesus Christ is the full *Logos* and revelation of God. On this basis Justin argued that those who have lived reasonably, like Socrates, were actually Christians because they had responded to the *Logos* of God even though it was only in seed form. Justin Martyr, *First Apology*, ANF, 1:178. Following Justin, the church became progressively

This work will be distinctly and unashamedly Christian. It will reflect a Christian perspective, based upon Christian presuppositions, submitted to the authority of the Christian Scriptures, while seeking to honor the Christ of Christianity with a call to Christian mission. This call to Christian mission is rooted in the unique nature of God as revealed in Scripture and the exclusive claims of Jesus based on His life and work. In order to understand all that a Christian theology of religions entails, it is necessary to understand clearly the nature of Christianity and the gospel. All the conclusions presented in this book flow from my understanding of the gospel.

What Is It to Be Christian?

Historically, the term *Christian* was first applied to the disciples of Jesus, those who were committed to the teaching ministry and fellowship of the Church (Acts 11:26). They had confessed faith in the resurrected Lord, Jesus Christ (Acts 2:32–36). That confession was not a mere attraction to the teachings of Jesus but was a commitment to the totality of His person and work. Simply put, Christians were those who believed His claims and submitted to His lordship.

The claims and lordship of Jesus are part of the story that began at creation; it includes the fall of mankind and God's promise to rescue His people through the offspring of Abraham (Gen 12:1–3; 48:9–10) and the heir to the Davidic throne (2 Sam 7:12–13; Isa 9:6–7; 11:1–5; Jer 23:5; Ezek 34:23–24; 37:24–25; Zech 12:10). This story was orchestrated by God in history and revealed to humanity through the prophets and other biblical writers. The redemptive narrative, anchored in history, focuses on Jesus as the Savior of mankind and the Lord of all and is inscripturated in the Bible.[19] Jesus put Himself at the center of the biblical story (Luke 24:25–27,44–47). He is the fulfillment of the Law, the Prophets, and the Writings—that is, of the Old Testament (Matt 5:17–18; Rom 10:4). To be Christian, therefore, in any historic or orthodox sense, is to submit to the entire revelation of the Lord Jesus Christ in Scripture and to take every thought captive in obedience to Christ (2 Cor 10:5).

---

negative toward the possibility of God's presence in religious others. For a helpful summary, see Netland, *Dissonant Voices*, 10–14.

[19]Alister McGrath reminds us that "the identification of a fixed starting point—the history of Jesus as witnessed to in Scripture and the living experience of the Christian community—is of vital importance in anchoring Christian theology in the midst of a pluralist sea." A. E. McGrath, "The Christian Church's Response to Pluralism," *JETS* 35 (1992): 497.

My approach is identified with that stream of Christianity known as evangelicalism. The specific and deliberate use of the term *evangelical* dates back to at least 1846, when an association of Protestant leaders from different denominations gathered in London to consider an expression of the essential unity of Christians. The roots of evangelicalism, however, run much deeper. As Daniel Strange illuminates, evangelicalism adheres to all the major historic creeds (e.g., Apostles, Nicene, Athanasian, and Chalcedonian). It traces its roots through the Protestant Reformation, Puritanism, Pietism, and the revival movements of the seventeenth and eighteenth centuries in the West (associated with such notables as Jonathan Edwards, George Whitefield, and John and Charles Wesley).[20] Therefore, Strange is correct to summarize, "Evangelical Christianity is historic orthodox Christianity."[21] Evangelical distinctives include the following commitments: (1) worship of the one God who fully exists simultaneously and without division or confusion in three persons, the Father, the Son, and the Holy Spirit; (2) the authority of Scripture that is grounded in its inspiration by the Holy Spirit;[22] (3) the supremacy and centrality of Jesus Christ, demonstrated in his life, substitutionary death, resurrection, and ascension, as the hinge upon which all redemptive and human history turns; (4) the necessity of personal conversion and regeneration to enter the Kingdom of God;[23] (5) the lordship and guidance of the Holy Spirit; (6) the fellowship of the local church for worship, witness, and service; (7) the exercise of personal piety through spiritual disciplines; and (8) the priority of evangelism and mission manifest in the Spirit-

---

[20]Strange, *Possibility of Salvation Among the Unevangelised*, 5–6.

[21] Ibid.

[22]Evangelicals are committed to the Scripture principle that makes an identification between the Word of God and the 66 books of the Old and New Testaments. All Scripture, every word, is inspired by God. Inspiration is that concurrent work of a human author and the Holy Spirit whereby the Spirit so moved the author that the result was exactly what God wanted, down to the very word, without destroying the personality of the human author in the process (2 Tim 3:16–17; 2 Pet 1:20–21). The result is a text that is simultaneously divine and human where the human authors used their own distinctive styles to produce this divine-human text. The implications of the divine aspect of inspiration include the inerrancy of Scripture and its inherent authority. Wayne Grudem summarizes well when he writes that to disobey or disbelieve the words of Scripture is to disobey or disbelieve God. W. Grudem, *Systematic Theology* (Grand Rapids: Zondervan, 1994), 73. Because of the human aspect of inspiration (and God's commitment to communicate), evangelicals are convinced that the meaning of the text is discoverable by means of discerning the authorial intent through a canonical and historical-grammatical hermeneutic.

[23]The need for regeneration by the Holy Spirit assumes many other facets of Christian theology, including but not limited to the pervasive depravity of man and subsequent complete spiritual inability of fallen humanity; the just condemnation of humanity prior to regeneration; the need for conversion, including repentance and faith in the gospel; and election.

empowered proclamation of the gospel of Jesus Christ.[24] The name evangelical and its distinctives bear testimony to the centrality of the evangel, the gospel, in evangelicalism.

The Gospel of Christ

The apostle Paul summarized his gospel message in 1 Cor 15:1–8:

> Now brothers, I want to clarify for you the gospel I proclaimed to you; you received it and have taken your stand on it. You are also saved by it, if you hold to the message I proclaimed to you—unless you believed to no purpose. For I passed on to you as most important what I also received: that Christ died for our sins according to the Scriptures, that He was buried, that He was raised on the third day according to the Scriptures, and that He appeared to Cephas, then to the Twelve. Then He appeared to over 500 brothers at one time, most of whom remain to the present, but some have fallen asleep. Then He appeared to James, then to all the apostles. Last of all, as to one abnormally born, He also appeared to me.

This succinct summary of the gospel is packed with theological import and significance. Jesus Christ died "for" (*huper*) sins; that is, He died on behalf of, or in the place of, sinners. He was then raised from the dead for the justification of sinners (Rom 4:25). This message was preached by Paul and was believed for salvation by the Corinthians (1 Cor 15:11). This is also the message in the Gospel of John: "For God so loved the world, that he gave his only Son, that whoever believes in him should not perish but have eternal life" (John 3:16 ESV).

In reflecting on Paul's good news message, the Gospel Coalition, an interdenominational group of pastors and theologians dedicated to clear and uncompromised proclamation of the gospel by the Church, offers the following statement:

> We believe that the gospel is the good news of Jesus Christ—God's very wisdom. Utter folly to the world, even though it is

---

[24]This list of evangelical distinctives is similar to that of G. Marsden, *Understanding Fundamentalism and Evangelicalism* (Grand Rapids: Eerdmans, 1991), 4–5, and A. E. McGrath, *Evangelicalism and the Future of Christianity* (London: Hodder and Stoughton, 1994), 51. See also D. Wells, *Courage to Be Protestant: Truth-lovers, Marketers, and Emergents in the Postmodern World* (Grand Rapids: Eerdmans, 2008), 7.

the power of God to those who are being saved, this good news is christological, centering on the cross and resurrection: the gospel is not proclaimed if Christ is not proclaimed, and the authentic Christ has not been proclaimed if his death and resurrection are not central (the message is "Christ died for our sins . . . [and] was raised"). This good news is biblical (his death and resurrection are according to the Scriptures), theological and salvific (Christ died for our sins, to reconcile us to God), historical (if the saving events did not happen, our faith is worthless, we are still in our sins, and we are to be pitied more than all others), apostolic (the message was entrusted to and transmitted by the apostles, who were witnesses of these saving events), and intensely personal (where it is received, believed, and held firmly, individual persons are saved).[25]

The Gospel Coalition's statement helpfully unpacks the critical truths from 1 Corinthians 15 that were necessary aspects of Paul's proclamation because they are absolutely essential to the gospel. A right understanding of the gospel of Christ is critical in any formulation of a Christian theology of religions since apart from the biblical gospel there is no Christianity. A theology of religions that does not correctly comprehend and account for the biblical gospel is by definition not Christian.

Yet another aspect of the gospel that is crucial to a Christian theology of religions is the manner in which the gospel is normally disseminated, which follows from the fact that the Christian message is *news*. Scripture primarily uses two verbs, *kērussō* and *euangelizō*, which are usually both translated by the English verbs "preach" or "proclaim," to describe the act of gospel dissemination. The good news is heralded. According to Paul, it is "the gospel I proclaimed to you" (*to euangelion ho euēngelisamēn humin*; 1 Cor 15:1) and "the message I proclaimed to you" (*logō euēngelisamēn humin*; 1 Cor 15:2). The gospel message that Paul "passed on" to the Corinthians was precisely that which he himself had "received" (1 Cor 15:3). Christ

---

[25]"Confessional Statement," The Gospel Coalition, http://www.thegospelcoalition.org/about/foundation-documents/confessional (accessed 21 December 2008). D. A. Carson develops each of these points in a paper entitled, "The Gospel of Jesus Christ (1 Corinthians 15:1–19)," The Gospel Coalition, 7–10, http://www.thegospelcoalition.org/pdf-articles/Carson_The_Gospel_of_Jesus_Christ.pdf (accessed 24 December 2008).

was "preached [*kērussetai*] as raised from the dead" (1 Cor 15:12); and when that message was "preached" (*kērussomen*) by Paul and the other apostles, the result was that the Corinthians "believed" (1 Cor 15:11). Paul's teaching in 1 Corinthians that the gospel is disseminated through proclamation is consistent with the rest of the biblical testimony.[26] Throughout Scripture, the normal means of gospel conveyance is preaching and proclamation.[27] The gospel that saves has to be proclaimed through some medium, and the normal manner of doing so in the experience of the early church was through preaching.

Salvation Is of the Lord

In Acts 16:30, a distraught Philippian jailer asked Paul and Silas, "Sirs, what must I do to be saved?" Paul's response was uncompromising: "Believe on the Lord Jesus, and you will be saved" (Acts 16:31). Paul was not ashamed of the gospel, "because it is God's power for salvation to everyone who believes, first to the Jew, and also to the Greek" (Rom 1:16). The apostle to the Gentiles summarized the necessity of believing the gospel of Christ by stating, "This is the message of faith that we proclaim: if you confess with your mouth, 'Jesus is Lord,' and believe in your heart that God raised Him from the dead, you will be saved" (Rom 10:8b–9). The Christian understanding of salvation is particular and specific. It flows from the Bible's description of the nature of God, the human dilemma, and the specific promises of God that find their fulfillment in Jesus Christ. As will be demonstrated in chapter 4, it cannot be reduced to compatibility with the salvific conceptions of other religions without fundamentally distorting the Christian faith in general and Christian salvation in particular. The Christian

---

[26]The following is a list of occurrences where the gospel is tied to proclamation and preaching: Matt 4:23; 9:35; 11:5; 24:14; 26:13; Mark 1:14–15; 13:10; Luke 3:18; 4:18; 7:22; 9:6; 16:16; 20:1; Acts 8:25; 14:7,15; 16:10; Rom 1:15–16; 15:19–20; 1 Cor 1:17; 9:14,16; 15:1–2; 2 Cor 10:16; 11:4,7; Gal 1:11; 2:2; 3:8; 4:13; Col 1:23; 1 Thess 2:2; 1 Pet 1:12; 4:6; Rev 14:6.

[27]D. A. Carson writes, "Look up every instance of the word 'gospel' and discover how often, how overwhelmingly often, this news of Jesus Christ is made known through proclamation, through preaching. Earlier in this same letter Paul insists that in God's unfathomable wisdom 'God was pleased through the foolishness of what was preached to save those who believe' (1:21). The content was 'what was preached'; the mode of delivery was 'what was preached.' There are plenty of texts that talk about the importance of being salt and light, of course, or of doing good to all people, especially those of the household of God, or of seeking the good of the city. Yet when dissemination of the gospel is in view, overwhelmingly the Bible specifies proclamation. The good news must be announced, heralded, explained; God himself visits and revisits human beings through his word. This gospel is normally disseminated." Carson, "Gospel of Jesus Christ," 10–11.

conception of salvation is irreconcilable with the conceptions of all other religions in the world.

The concept of salvation in the ancient Near East and the Greco-Roman Empire had a wide range of applications. But the notion of Jesus Christ as the Savior is developed from the biblical idea of salvation. When the Bible calls Jesus the Savior, it is not meant in a generic or abstract sense. Jesus is the Savior in the exact manner described by the Bible. How each religion defines salvation is particular to that religion. Christianity is no different. The question is, does Christianity accurately describe the human condition, and does it offer salvation consistent with that dilemma? It is intellectually dishonest to ignore the Bible's presentation of the gospel of salvation and then claim that Christian salvation is no different from that of other religions.

In Scripture, salvation is "a comprehensive term denoting all the benefits, physical or spiritual, that are graciously bestowed on humans by God."[28] It expresses the idea of deliverance from danger into safety. The nature of salvation is best understood when we consider from what one is saved. In Scripture we can be saved from troubles (Ps 34:6), danger (Matt 8:25), illness (Mark 5:34), and oppression (Acts 7:25). But Scripture also speaks of salvation in a more particular way. It is God's work of rescuing His fallen and rebellious people (e.g., Rom 5:9–10; 1 Cor 1:18; Eph 2:5; 2 Tim 1:9; Titus 3:5). God is absolutely holy and perfect in His character and all His ways (Psalm 99; Isa 6:3). He is altogether righteous and cannot stand in the presence of sin, nor can He leave it unpunished (Prov 17:15; Rom 3:23–25; James 1:17). Adam's fall has rendered every human a sinner by position, nature, and action. Unless delivered by God, the sinner stands under the just wrath of God (Rom 1:18; Eph 2:1–3), is overpowered by sin (Rom 3:9), is condemned to die (Rom 5:21), and then will face judgment (Heb 9:27). The rebel is harassed and controlled by the world (Gal 4:3), the flesh (Rom 8:6–8), and the devil (Eph 2:2). He is a slave to fear (Rom 8:15; Heb 2:14–15), without hope and without God (Eph 2:12). From all this, Christ, "having been offered once to bear the sins of many, will appear a second time, not to bear sin, but to bring salvation to those who are waiting for Him" (Heb 9:28). According to Scripture, all humans stand justly condemned before God because of their sin, regardless of their access to the revelation of God (Rom 3:9). That is, a person is not condemned because

---

[28]M. J. Harris, "Salvation," *NDBT*, 762.

he has heard and rejected the gospel. The one who hears and rejects the gospel is "already condemned" (John 3:18) and the "wrath of God remains on him" (John 3:36). People are condemned because of their rebellion (Rom 1:18–32).

The good news is that God has stepped into time and space and has done for humanity what it could not do for itself (Matt 1:21–23). God sent His Son, Jesus Christ, to atone for human sin, satisfying His justice while demonstrating His love (Rom 5:6–11). A distinctive part of the Christian gospel is that humans cannot effect this salvation but must accept this precious gift of God's grace by faith (Eph 2:4–10). The Bible speaks of salvation as a past deliverance that has already taken place (Rom 8:24; Titus 3:5–8), based upon the life, death, and resurrection of Christ. Salvation is also a deliverance that is presently taking place (2 Cor 2:15; 1 Pet 1:9) because of the ongoing work of Jesus, the great high priest (Heb 7:25). Finally, salvation is a future event that has not yet taken place (1 Thess 5:8; Heb 1:14) because one day the believer will see Christ as He is and will be like Him (1 John 3:2). All salvation is tied to the life, death, resurrection, ascension, and return of Christ. It is inextricably tied to His story. As Christopher Wright explains:

> Other religions do not save *because they do not tell this story.* They may have Scriptures and cultures of great antiquity, wisdom and dignity, and we should rightly respect all of those things. What I am saying here is not in any way meant to deride or dismiss the great depths of human reflection, literature, wisdom, culture, ethics, music, art and aspiration to be found within religious traditions and texts all over the world. But we are not talking about the human richness of religious traditions; rather, we are talking about whether they can be means of salvation—in the same sense that the Bible speaks of salvation. And my argument is that they cannot because other religions do not tell *this* story—the story of our covenant God and his saving action in history. They cannot therefore connect people to that story and to the Savior who is the great Subject of the story. They have no gospel to tell to the nations; they have no good news, for they do not know this story which alone constitutes the good news.[29]

[29]C. J. H. Wright, *Salvation Belongs to Our God: Celebrating the Bible's Central Story* (Downers Grove, IL: InterVarsity, 2007), 108.

An essential part of Christian salvation is the truth that only God saves. "I, I am the LORD, and there is no other Savior but Me" (Isa 43:11; cf. Isa 45:21; Hos 13:4). Jonah recognized this truth after being delivered from drowning and prayed, while in the fish, "Salvation is from the LORD" (Jon 2:9). Throughout the Old Testament, only God or His Anointed One is a Savior. Jesus Christ was described by the Samaritan woman as "the Savior of the world" (John 4:42). The apostles preached that God had exalted Jesus "to His right hand as ruler and Savior, to grant repentance to Israel, and forgiveness of sins" (Acts 5:31). Paul declared Jesus to be "our great God and Savior" (Titus 2:13). Peter declared that believers in the gospel will be richly supplied "entry into the eternal kingdom of our Lord and Savior Jesus Christ" (2 Pet 1:11). The Greek term for Savior (*sōtēr*) is used in the New Testament eight times of God and 16 times of Jesus, but it is never used of anyone else. As Wright explains, "Nobody else deserves even the vocabulary of salvation, let alone the reality of it."[30]

CATEGORIES IN A CHRISTIAN THEOLOGY OF RELIGIONS

The typical taxonomy for discussing the relationships between salvation, the claims of Jesus Christ, and world religions employs the categories of exclusivism (often called particularism or restrictivism), inclusivism, pluralism, and universalism.[31] Exclusivism is the historic orthodox Christian position that will be explained and defended throughout this book. Exclusivists maintain that salvation is possible only through conscious faith in Jesus Christ. This conviction has motivated world missions from the earliest days of the church because apart from the message of Christ's life, death, resurrection, ascension, and return, there is no hope for humanity. This good news is a particular message that must be proclaimed and understood in order to be believed. The normal means of bringing the gospel to those who have

---

[30]Ibid., 43. Wright explains that the term *sōtēr* was common in the classical Greek world and was applied to all sorts of kings, heroes, and military deliverers, which makes the exclusive reference to God and Christ as saviors even more remarkable.

[31]This taxonomy is used by Okholm and Phillips, eds., *Four Views on Salvation in a Pluralistic Age*. Richard Plantinga suggests that there are six possible theological positions: nihilism, skepticism, exclusivism, inclusivism, pluralism, and universalism. But he quickly concludes that nihilism and skepticism are not theological options. R. Plantinga, "For God So Loved the World: Theological Reflections on Religious Plurality in the History of Christianity," in *Biblical Faith and Other Religions: An Evangelical Assessment,* ed. D. W. Baker (Grand Rapids: Kregel, 2004), 133. The categories of exclusivism, inclusivism, and pluralism were first used by Alan Race in his book, *Christians and Religious Pluralism.*

not yet heard is proclamation by human messengers (evangelists), but other means of bringing special revelation to others, such as dreams and visions, are certainly not precluded by exclusivism. However we hear the gospel, the important point is that we bow before Jesus Christ and embrace the gospel of life.

A number of evangelicals have begun to rethink the necessity of faith in the gospel for salvation, exchanging exclusivism for inclusivism. Though still firmly committed to the work of Christ as the basis for salvation, some inclusivists suggest that explicit faith in the death and resurrection of Christ is not necessary for salvation. This is typically summarized in terms of ontological and epistemic necessity. The work of Christ on the cross is ontologically necessary for salvation (Christ's death and resurrection had to happen in history), but it is not epistemically necessary (one does not need to believe in Christ's death and resurrection to be saved). Currently, many inclusivists are turning to the Holy Spirit to explain how salvation can be effected where the gospel is not preached and believed. They posit that the Holy Spirit is applying the salvific benefits of the work of Christ to certain individuals who have never heard and believed the gospel.

Some individuals outside the boundaries associated with evangelicalism have abandoned commitment to the necessity of Christ's atoning work on the cross altogether and have embraced religious pluralism. Religious pluralists reject the claims of Christian exclusivism and Christian inclusivism, believing that one can find salvation through various religious traditions, belief systems, and ethics. At the popular level, pluralism is best understood by the notion, "All roads lead to God." To the pluralist, Christ's life and death on the cross are powerful examples of a life committed to God, but there are no universal or ontological implications of Christ's life and ministry. Not all are "saved," but believers in the gospel do not enjoy a privileged position with regard to salvation over adherents to other religions.

A fourth category, universalism (or universal reconciliation), describes those who believe that in the end, all will be reconciled to God. Those having a "hope" for some sort of universal reconciliation that will eventually lead to hell being emptied and all being saved are growing in number. Universalism can be pluralistic (sharing many of the arguments of religious pluralism) or inclusivist (in the sense that all will eventually be saved through the work of Jesus Christ). Each of these positions will be explained in detail and critiqued in subsequent chapters.

The differences between the religions of the world are enormous. This four-category taxonomy is not designed to differentiate between world religions at all levels.[32] Those who use the taxonomy are not concerned, first and foremost, with evaluating the truth content or ethical practices of the different religions. Rather, the taxonomy is used by Christians when evaluating the religions of the world vis-à-vis the gospel, to answer the question: What hope is there, if any, for those who have never heard the story of the saving work of God in Christ? For that reason the taxonomy offers the most coherent means of categorizing and organizing thought on this essential issue. The burden of the Bible is salvation. The question, "What must I do to be saved?" is treated in the Bible not as an add-on to the quest for the better life ("What kind of car should I drive? What sort of man should I marry?"), nor is it merely an important question or even the most important question in a list of other important questions. Rather, "What must I do to be saved?" is a question of such supreme importance that it dictates the essence of the answers to all other questions, from the most simple to the most complex, from the most mundane to the most sublime. It dominates the biblical story line from Genesis to Revelation. Reconciliation of sinful humanity and the cosmos to God is the solution to the conflict that dominates redemptive history.[33]

A theology of religions attempts to provide perspectives on two different soteriological questions. The first question concerns the fate

---

[32]Richard Plantinga believes that the four-category paradigm is reductionistic. First, he claims that the taxonomy focuses too narrowly upon salvation, ignoring implications for the present world. Second, he is concerned that "more distinctions are needed in order to discuss the complex of theological matters involved in thinking about religions." Ibid., 134.

[33]Some have proposed that the exclusivist-inclusivist-pluralist-universalist paradigm does not account for significant differences that exist within each position. For example, there is a large difference between an inclusivist who believes in a postmortem opportunity to respond to the gospel of Christ and an inclusivist who believes that God may work savingly through other religions. In light of this, Christopher Morgan has proposed a ninefold scheme: (1) church exclusivism, (2) gospel exclusivism, (3) special revelation exclusivism, (4) agnosticism, (5) general revelation inclusivism, (6) world religions inclusivism, (7) postmortem evangelism, (8) universalism, and (9) pluralism. Morgan's taxonomy is more descriptive, but what is gained in description is lost in clarity, simplicity, and usefulness. Further, it makes divisions based on different criteria. It divides those who share essential agreement on the primary questions (e.g., Is conscious faith in Christ necessary for salvation?) on the basis of means (how is saving knowledge, such as it is, conveyed?). C. W. Morgan, "Inclusivisms and Exclusivisms," in *Faith Comes by Hearing: A Response to Inclusivism*, ed. C. W. Morgan and R. A. Peterson (Downers Grove, IL: InterVarsity, 2008), 26–36.

of the unevangelized. The second concerns the role of world religions in the redemptive purposes of God. These two questions are inextricably linked. The answers to one question will obviously impact the answers to the other.[34] For example, when exclusivists claim that conscious faith in the gospel is necessary for salvation, participants in religions where the biblical gospel is not proclaimed are by definition "unevangelized." Therefore, I will organize this book around the exclusivist-inclusivist-pluralist-universalist paradigm because I believe that the terms are robust enough to handle these questions without distortion.

A Note about Language

The term *exclusivism* is not popular today. Current cultural sensibilities call for that which "includes" over against that which "excludes." When it comes to the language of exclusivism, our society and culture are highly resistant to the label. Many are calling for different language to signify the position that conscious faith in the gospel is necessary for salvation. For example, after noting that the word *exclusive* is derived from the Latin *exclaudere*, meaning "to shut out, to exclude, even to expel," Bob Robinson comments, "It is surely unfortunate and unnecessary to describe the heart of the Good News in primarily negative and excluding categories."[35] T. R. Phillips believes that the word *exclusivism* "prejudicially connotes arrogance and close-mindedness." He is also concerned that many falsely restrict the term to describe those who deny God's universal salvific will.[36]

Despite these objections I am choosing to use the term *exclusivism*. It is a familiar term, and changing the vocabulary that has been used for the last 25 years cannot but confuse. Besides, there are some areas of life where we treasure exclusivity and particularity. Consider the exclusive devotion of a husband and wife toward each other or the desire to have particular promises kept. We really have no problem with exclusivism *per se*. It is only when we feel that we have been unfairly excluded that our hackles begin to rise. But the issue of fairness and justice is precisely the point being debated among

---

[34]So Strange, *Possibility of Salvation Among the Unevangelised*, 19.

[35]B. Robinson, "What Exactly Is Meant by the 'Exclusiveness of Christ'? An Examination of the Phrase and Other Suggested Alternatives in the Context of Religious Pluralism: Part II," *ERT* 26 (2002) 80.

[36]T. R. Phillips, "Christianity and Religions," in *EDT*, 231.

exclusivists, inclusivists, pluralists, and universalists. To argue that the term *exclusivism* is illegitimate because it is unfair that God would send those to hell who have never heard the gospel is to beg the question in dispute.

Most religions are exclusivistic. To deny this is simply naïve. As will be demonstrated in chapter 4, each of the major religions of the world makes truth claims about the nature of reality, God, salvation, and ethics that are incompatible with those truth claims of other religions. These claims are seen as distinctively true and therefore superior to all other options. As Harold Netland points out,

> In both Buddhism and Hinduism, liberation is linked to a correct understanding of the nature of reality, and each religion rejects what it regards as false views on the grounds that they impede liberation. Buddhism, for example, claims to tell the truth about how things are, and other accounts that are incompatible with Buddhist teachings are dismissed as mistaken, resulting in ignorance and further suffering. For Buddhists, only Buddhism leads to release from the ignorance giving rise to suffering.[37]

Specific examples could be multiplied with many of the world religions. Where there are irreconcilable convictions on the nature of reality, there will be irreconcilable or "exclusive" truth claims.

THE CASE FOR THE NECESSITY OF CONSCIOUS FAITH IN CHRIST FOR SALVATION

The case for salvation by grace through faith in the gospel of Jesus Christ is not difficult to make. The biblical testimony is consistent. The urgency with which the gospel was proclaimed in the New Testament is compelling. The first announcements of the imminence of the kingdom of God called for repentance and confession (Matt 3:1; 4:17). The first sermons preached after Pentecost called for repentance and faith in Jesus for forgiveness of sins (Acts 2:38–40; 3:15–21). The first defense of the apostles' fervent gospel proclamation was the simple statement that "there is salvation in no one else" (Acts 4:12; see below).

---

[37]H. A. Netland, "One Lord and Savior for All? Jesus Christ and Religious Diversity," 16, http://s4059.gridserver.com/pdf/netland.pdf (accessed 22 January 2009).

Most exclusivists hold to four nonnegotiables with respect to salvation and the gospel. First, Jesus Christ is the apex of revelation and the authoritative standard by which all other religious beliefs and claims are judged (Heb 1:1–4). Second, the death and resurrection of Jesus Christ are the only atoning acts by which sin and guilt are conquered (1 Cor 15:17). Third, consistent with Reformation convictions, exclusivists are convinced that proclamation of the death and resurrection of Christ as the decisive point in human history is central to the Christian faith (Acts 17:30–31; 1 Cor 15:1–4). Fourth, and the point of separation from inclusivists who are in general agreement with the first three nonnegotiables, exclusivists believe that salvation is available only through repentance and faith in Christ's cross work and that "no one can be saved without an explicit act of repentance and faith based on the knowledge of Christ" (Acts 4:12).[38]

The case for these nonnegotiables proceeds from exegesis and biblical-theological reflection. Explicit statements in Scripture declare the need for faith in the gospel in order to be saved. Those statements are part of a larger context, the biblical story line that portrays Jesus Christ as the only possible Savior from the human dilemma. Each of these lines of defense will be explained below.

Explicit Biblical Statements That Support Exclusivity

When the apostles were commissioned to take the good news of Jesus Christ from Jerusalem to the entire world, they did so with the conviction that apart from the proclamation of the gospel, there was no hope for humanity. In the economy of the early church, there was a direct correlation between the preaching of the gospel and salvation. When gospel proclamation was hindered, others could not be saved (1 Thess 2:16). Their commitment to the Great Commission was based on obedience to Jesus' explicit commands and the certainty borne of three years of walking with and being taught by Jesus.

Statements that affirm the necessity of belief in Christ pervade the Gospel of John. The right to become "children of God" is given

---

[38]These nonnegotiables of exclusivism are summarized in Tennent, *Christianity at the Religious Roundtable*, 17. Other summaries of exclusivism by those committed to the view are given in R. Douglas Geivett and W. Gary Phillips, "A Particularist View: An Evidentialist Approach," in *Four Views on Salvation in a Pluralistic World*, ed. Okholm and Phillips, 214; A. E. McGrath, "A Particularist View: A Post-Enlightenment Approach," in *Four Views on Salvation in a Pluralistic World*, ed. Okholm and Phillips, 163–66; Carson, *Gagging of God*, 278–80; Nash, *Is Jesus the Only Savior*; R. C. Sproul, *Reason to Believe* (Grand Rapids: Zondervan, 1982), 47–59.

to those who "receive" Christ (John 1:12). "Everyone who believes" in God's "One and Only Son . . . will not perish but have eternal life" (John 3:16). The passage goes on to teach that belief in Jesus is the only way to escape the condemnation that all rightfully deserve (John 3:18; cf. 5:24). It is the "will of My Father," Jesus said, "that everyone who sees the Son and believes in Him may have eternal life," and Jesus "will raise him up on the last day" (John 6:40). Jesus Christ, who is "the light of the world" (John 8:12), has come so that others "may have life" (John 10:10). Jesus described Himself as "the resurrection and the life" and promised, "The one who believes in Me, even if he dies, will live" (John 11:25). The life He promised is so Christ-centered that Jesus described eternal life as knowing Him and His Father, the only true God (John 17:3). Ultimately, the purpose of John's Gospel was that those who read it "may believe that Jesus is the Christ, the Son of God, and that by believing" they "may have life in his name" (John 20:31 ESV).

The apostles were commissioned with a message, in fulfillment of the Scriptures, to preach the death and resurrection of Jesus and the good news of "repentance for forgiveness of sins would be proclaimed in His name" (Luke 24:47; cf. Matt 28:18–20). From Peter to Paul, the apostles were faithful to preach the simple gospel message that Christ died for sins and rose again (2 Cor 15:1–4). The book of Acts records the apostles consistently calling upon others to believe in Jesus in order that they might be saved. In his sermon at Pentecost, Peter identified Jesus as the object of saving faith necessary for those who would call upon the Lord in order to be saved (Acts 2:21). At the conclusion of that sermon, Peter asked all who heard to repent and be baptized "in the name of Jesus Christ for the forgiveness of your sins, and you will receive the gift of the Holy Spirit" (Acts 2:38 ESV). Other clear statements that forgiveness of sins is made possible by Christ are found in Acts 3:19–20; 13:38; 16:30–31; 22:16; and 26:17–23.

Perhaps the strongest statement of the exclusivity of Christ in the entire Bible is found in Acts 4:12: "There is salvation in no one else, for there is no other name under heaven given to people by which we must be saved." Four aspects of this verse emphasize the teaching on exclusivity. First, in the Greek, the phrase "there is no one else" precedes the subject "salvation" (lit. "And there is not in another—no one—salvation"). This makes the point emphatically: "There is no one else at all other than Jesus who has the means to provide salvation, even for Jews who have access to God's revelation."[39] Second, the phrase "under heaven" demonstrates just how extensive Peter's exclusion of all other names actually is. No matter where one is, there is no other name available at all, anywhere. It is also instructive that Peter does not localize the statement with "no other name given to you" or "no other name given to Jews." Rather, there is no other name "given to people."[40] Third, the words "we must" (*dei*, "it is necessary") and "other" (*heteron*) speak to the total degree of exclusivity in view.[41] Any other name presented cannot save. Finally, the use of the word *name* points to far more than ontological source. Instead, the "authoritative fullness of the being and work of Jesus" is referenced.[42] Jesus is identified as the "name . . . given to people" (epistemological necessity) who is also the means by which they are saved (ontological necessity).[43]

Further evidence that the apostles found no basis for differentiating between ontological necessity and epistemological necessity is found in Acts 13. Paul delivered an evangelistic message in a Jewish synagogue in Antioch, where he argued from the Law and the Prophets that Jesus is the Christ and called on everyone to believe in Him for justification and forgiveness of sins (Acts 13:16–41). Coming back the next Sabbath, many Jews opposed and insulted Paul (Acts 13:45). Because they rejected the message of Christ, Paul rebuked the Jews and stated that he was turning to the Gentiles. Then he quoted Isa 49:6, a messianic prophecy, and applied it to himself. "I have appointed you as a light for the Gentiles, to bring salvation to the ends of the earth" (Acts 13:47). Those Gentiles who were "appointed to eternal life believed" (Acts 13:48). In context Paul's quotation was a prophecy of the servant of Israel, referring to Jesus and His work on the cross that provides salvation for all who would repent and believe in Him (ontological necessity), but Paul applies it to himself as the one who takes the message of salvation to the Gentiles (epistemological necessity).[44]

---

[39]D. Bock, *Acts*, ECNT (Grand Rapids: Baker, 2008), 194.

[40]Geivett and Phillips, "A Particularist View," 230. The word for "people" is the plural of *anthropos*, "man," which in the plural can refer to human beings in general" (BDAG, 81).

[41]Bock, *Acts*, 194.

[42]Geivett and Phillips, "A Particularist View," 231.

[43]See W. J. Larkin, "The Contribution of the Gospels and Acts to a Biblical Theology of Religions," in *Christianity and the Religions*, ed. Rommen and Netland, 80.

[44]See Bock, *Acts*, 464.

By Paul's way of thinking, the link between Christ's saving work and the proclamation of the gospel is so strong that he applies a messianic prophecy of hope to himself. Paul did not see any bifurcation between the ontological necessity and the epistemological necessity for which inclusivists argue.

Three more narratives in Acts bear directly on a Christian theology of religions. These are the stories of the conversion of Cornelius (Acts 9–10), the Jerusalem Council (Acts 15), and the Ephesian 12 (Acts 19:1–7). Cornelius is described as "a devout man" who "feared God" and "did many charitable deeds for the Jewish people and always prayed to God" (Acts 10:2).[45] Through angelic mediation, Peter was summoned to preach the gospel to Cornelius and his household. Peter summarized his gospel message of the death and resurrection of Christ by saying that Jesus "commanded us to preach to the people, and to solemnly testify that He is the One appointed by God to be the Judge of the living and the dead. All the prophets testify about Him that through His name everyone who believes in Him will receive forgiveness of sins" (Acts 10:42–43). Cornelius was a man who had responded to the revelation of God to Israel and had aligned himself with the covenant people of God (though remaining uncircumcised), attempting to worship the one true and living God. Evidence of this was found in his prayers to God and his acts of charity toward God's people. And yet Peter's message was that he had to believe in Jesus in order to be forgiven. Despite his religiosity Cornelius had to hear and believe the gospel before he could be saved. The proof of this is found in Acts 11:14 in Peter's retelling of the story to the church in Jerusalem. An angel went to Cornelius and told him that Peter "will speak words to you by which you and all your household will be saved." The Greek word, *sōthēsē*, translated "will be saved," is a future tense verb. The language is clear: Cornelius, despite his piety and charity, was not saved until he heard the proclamation of the gospel and believed.

Peter's speech at the Jerusalem Council is also decisive for the necessity of faith in Jesus for salvation. Peter recalled that he had been sent to the Gentiles so that they "would hear the gospel message and believe" (Acts 15:7). In response to the gospel, the Gentiles had been given the Holy Spirit, just as He had been given to the

---

[45] Inclusivists often refer to Cornelius as a "holy pagan" who is evidence that there are those outside the religion of Christianity who are saved. See, for example, Pinnock, *Wideness in God's Mercy*, 95–96. The concept of the holy pagan will be dealt with in chapters 2 and 6.

believing Jews (Acts 15:8). On this basis there ought to be no distinction between Jews and Gentiles because the Jews were saved "in the same way" that the Gentiles were (Acts 15:11). In other words, the hope of salvation for Gentiles was exactly that of the Jews in the Jerusalem church. How had Peter and his Jewish colleagues been saved? They were saved by grace through faith in Jesus. In Peter's reckoning, there was no second category for those who were saved by Jesus without believing in Him.

When Paul encountered a dozen of John the Baptist's disciples in Ephesus, he found that they had not received the Holy Spirit, nor had they even heard that the Holy Spirit had come (Acts 19:2).[46] They had followed John in his ministry of preparation for the Christ. They had been told to follow the One who would come after John, who was mightier than him and who would baptize with the Holy Spirit (Luke 3:16). But they were living in a transitional period in redemptive history and had only received John's baptism of repentance for the forgiveness of sins (Luke 3:3).[47] Their response to John and the redemptive purposes of God at the time was correct. They were anticipating the coming of the kingdom (Matt 3:2) and in preparation for the Christ had repented and were baptized (Matt 3:11). As far as they knew, they had done everything possible to follow the God of Israel. But the narrative is clear that the outpoured eschatological Spirit came only to those who believed in Jesus (Acts 19:4–6).

The New Testament writers continued the proclamation of salvation by grace alone through faith alone in Christ alone. In Rom 10:9–18, Paul taught that salvation comes through confession that Jesus is Lord and through belief that God raised Jesus from the dead (Rom 10:9–10). Jesus is the object of saving faith, the saving Lord of all, whether Jew or Gentile (Rom 10:12). "For everyone who calls on the name of the Lord," that is, the Lord Jesus, "will be saved" (Rom 10:13). Here Paul, quoting Joel 2:32, equates Jesus Christ with the Lord, the one God of Abraham, Isaac, and Jacob. This Lord is humanity's only Savior. But it is impossible to call upon the Lord in order to be saved if the gospel is not preached so that it can be believed (Rom 10:14–16).[48]

---

[46]So Bock, Acts, 599.

[47]See T. R. Schreiner, *New Testament Theology* (Grand Rapids: Baker, 2008), 456.

[48]Some inclusivists argue that this passage only teaches that those who believe the gospel will be saved, but it does not teach that if one does not believe the gospel one cannot be saved (see, e.g., Sanders, *No Other Name*, 67). D. A. Carson refutes this logic by pointing out that inclusivists are begging the question by wrongly assuming that there is a difference between

Faith comes through hearing the Word of Christ (Rom 10:17; cf. 1 Cor 1:18; Eph 2:8). It is holding to the message of the gospel that saves (1 Cor 15:1–4). Those who are "perishing," identified as those who do not believe the gospel, "cannot see the light of the gospel of the glory of Christ, who is the image of God" (2 Cor 4:3–4). Paul adamantly denied to the Galatians that there is any other gospel (Gal 1:6–10) and reminded them that it was only through "hearing with faith" that they received the Spirit, a demonstration that they were saved (Gal 3:2). The Ephesian Gentiles were "dead in . . . trespasses and sins" (Eph 2:1) until they had been brought near to God through the blood of Christ (Eph 3:13), and this salvation was appropriated "by grace . . . through faith" (Eph 2:8–9).

Jesus is the supreme revelation of God and is the "radiance" of the glory of God (Heb 1:1–4). The Lord Jesus and then the apostles declared the message of the "great salvation" (Heb 2:1–4). But the good news that is preached must be combined with faith if it is to be of any benefit (Heb 4:2). Those who would enter the sanctuary of God can do so only by the death of Jesus and through His high priestly work, in full assurance of faith (Heb 10:19–22). This faith, without which "it is impossible to please God" (Heb 11:6), is focused on Jesus who is "the source and perfecter of our faith" (Heb 12:2). The apostle Peter was likewise clear that it was "through the living and enduring word of God," which is "the word that was preached as the gospel," that his hearers were "born again" (1 Pet 1:22–25). The apostle John taught that listening to the apostolic witness was the prerequisite to fellowship with God. Those who repudiated the eyewitness message of the apostles did not listen to God (1 John 4:6).[49]

The Centrality of Christ in Scripture: A Biblical-theological Defense of Exclusivism

Jesus saw Himself as the fulfillment of redemptive history and the center of the biblical story. When Jesus inaugurated His public ministry in the synagogue in Nazareth, He read from Isaiah 61, a messianic prophecy, and announced, "Today as you listen, this Scripture

---

those who are saved and those who confess and believe in Christ. But Paul in fact presupposes a perfect coincidence between those who confess and believe in Jesus and those who are saved as the Romans 9 passage indicates. Carson, *Gagging of God,* 312–13. See also R. A. Peterson, "Inclusivism Versus Exclusivism on Key Biblical Texts," in *Faith Comes by Hearing*, ed. Morgan and Peterson, 194–97.

[49] So Schreiner, *New Testament Theology,* 709.

has been fulfilled" (Luke 4:21). He saw Himself as far more than the fulfillment of isolated prophecies. He was, in fact, that which all the Law, the Prophets, and the Writings (the entire Old Testament) anticipated and toward which they moved. Following His resurrection, while on the road to Emmaus, Jesus taught two of His disciples from "Moses and all the Prophets . . . the things concerning Himself in all the Scriptures" (Luke 24:27). Later, with a larger gathering of His disciples, Jesus claimed to be the focus of "the Law of Moses, the Prophets, and the Psalms." Then "He opened their minds to understand the Scriptures" (Luke 24:44–45). This illumination of the disciples was to enable them to see His proper and primary role in the Old Testament (John 1:44; Acts 3:18–24; 10:43; 17:2–3; 18:28; 26:22–23; 28:23; Rom 1:1–3; 16:25–27; 1 Pet 1:10–12).

For this reason Jesus rebuked the Jews for missing Him in the Scriptures. They would "pore over the Scriptures" because they rightfully thought that they contained eternal life (John 5:39), but they did not realize that those Scriptures testified to the One who stood before them. They claimed to believe Moses but would not believe Jesus, even though Moses wrote of Him (John 5:45–47). If they had come to Jesus, He would have given them the life they sought (John 5:40). Paul made much the same point in 2 Tim 3:15 when he wrote "the sacred Scriptures . . . are able to instruct you for salvation through faith in Christ Jesus." All the Old Testament promises of future salvation by the Lord are fulfilled in Jesus Christ (2 Cor 1:20).

So unique is the Lord Jesus Christ and so significant is His role in redemptive history that the apostle John summarized the ministry of Jesus as being the One who has "revealed" the God whom no one had ever seen (John 1:18). "He is the image of the invisible God" (Col 1:15) and the radiance of God's glory (Heb 1:3). Jesus is the Creator, the one by whom and for whom all things were made (Col 1:16). He is also the judge, the One before whom all people will one day stand (John 5:21–22; Rev 5:8–14). Jesus claimed, "I am the way, the truth, and the life. No one comes to the Father except through Me" (John 14:6). Those who had seen Jesus had seen the Father (John 14:9). In one of the clearest statements of exclusivity from the lips of Jesus, He said, "Anyone who does not honor the Son does not honor the Father who sent Him" (John 5:23). Regardless of how seemingly pious the attempt, it is impossible to honor God unless one honors Jesus Christ.

Jesus' role in Scripture is not merely as the One who fulfills prophecies of a future leader. He is portrayed as the only possible solution to a seemingly insoluble dilemma that dominates the biblical plotline. Positions on the fate of the unevangelized and religious others have to be grounded in a right understanding of the overall story of Scripture.[50] Attempts to posit a biblical justification for pluralism or even inclusivism may reference individual proof texts, but they fail at the canonical level. The story of the Bible is thoroughly Christocentric, and one cannot do justice to Jesus' focal role in redemptive history by claiming that some can be reconciled to God without bowing before the glorious Son of God.

BOOK SUMMARY

Defending the uniqueness of Christ and the necessity of gospel proclamation and belief in Christ does not allow for much creativity. Many excellent books have been devoted to the defense of exclusivism, arguing for the necessity of conscious faith in Christ for salvation.[51] This book is unique in that I am going to make my argument for the necessity of Christ-glorifying, Spirit-empowered faith in Christ based upon biblical-theological and Trinitarian foundations. In particular, I argue that the relationship between Jesus Christ and the Holy Spirit requires commitment to the necessity of conscious faith in Christ for salvation. This is significant because pluralists and inclusivists are turning to the Trinity, and the Holy Spirit in particular, to support their proposals. Christian pluralists are looking to the Spirit as the means by which the particularities of Christianity can give way to a genuine and charitable pluralism. Peter Hodgson believes that the Trinity is the starting point for religious diversity in the world. The diversity of God is reflected in the Trinity, and the nature of God is the reason "that a diversity of independent ways of salvation appears in the history of the world. . . . The mystery of the Trinity is for Christians the ultimate foundation for pluralism."[52] Paul Tillich, toward the end of his career, called for a rethinking of theology in light of the history of religions,

---

[50]This is precisely the point that D. A. Carson makes in his book, *The Gagging of God*, and it is why he spends more than 100 pages tracing the Bible's plotline (193–314).

[51]The most recent of which is Morgan and Peterson, eds., *Faith Comes by Hearing*.

[52]P. Hodgson, "The Spirit and Religious Pluralism," *Horizons* 31 (2004): 23.

focusing on the concreteness of the Spirit as a common starting point.[53] Karl Rahner, again late in his career, wrote that pneumatology is a better starting point for an inclusive view of religions than Christology.[54] As will be demonstrated in chapters 5 and 6, evangelical inclusivists have been willing to borrow from nonevangelical theologians at precisely this point. Clearly there is a need for a biblically faithful response that addresses the theology of the Son and Spirit as posited by pluralists and inclusivists. Far from creating space for inclusivism or pluralism, I am convinced that a study of the relationship between the Son and the Spirit as presented in Scripture demands exclusivism.

The purpose of this book is to develop a *Christian theology* of religions. It is not a science of religions, nor is it a comparative study of religions, as if it were possible to establish the essence of religion through historical study. Such efforts characterize pluralistic approaches to the religions and are largely reductionistic. The task of theology is to think God's thoughts after Him, to bring to bear upon all life's questions the powerful and expressive Word of God. The Word of God is found perfectly and supremely in Jesus Christ and in the Spirit-inspired Holy Scriptures that testify to Jesus (John 1:1–4; 5:39; 2 Tim 3:16). Therefore, the first task in thinking God's thoughts after Him with regard to religions is to search the Scriptures and listen to God's presentation of religions in the context of redemptive history. Chapter 2, working from Genesis to Revelation, summarizes the testimony of Scripture with regard to the religions, monotheism, the uniqueness of God, idolatry, revelation, and the missionary strategy of the early church. This chapter is the foundation for the defense of exclusivism, as well as the critiques of universalism, pluralism, and inclusivism.

Chapter 3 analyzes current suggestions that all will be saved. Focusing on theological revisions and responses to the doctrine of hell, I will summarize contemporary arguments for universalism, the

---

[53]Paul Tillich, "The Significance of the History of Religions for the Systematic Theologian," in *The Future of Religions,* ed. Jerald C. Brauer (New York: Harper & Row, 1966), 90–91.

[54]Karl Rahner, "Aspects of European Theology," in *Theological Investigations* 21, trans. Hugh M. Riley (New York: Crossroad, 1988), 97–98. Another striking formulation comes from the Christian-Hindu-Buddhist theologian Raimundo Panikkar. Using the image of rivers that meet not on earth but in the skies when their waters are vaporized in the form of clouds, he suggests that the religions of the world do not coalesce as organized religions. Rather they meet when they are "metamorphosized into Spirit, which then is poured down in innumerable tongues." R. Panikkar, "The Jordan, the Tiber, and the Ganges: Three Kairological Moments of Christic Self-Consciousness," in *The Myth of Christian Uniqueness: Toward a Pluralistic Theology of Religions,* ed. J. Hick and P. F. Knitter (Maryknoll, NY: Orbis, 1987), 92.

belief that all will be saved. Universalism is not an orthodox Christian option. Viewing the universalist arguments from Scripture, I will demonstrate that universalists distort the character of God as revealed in Scripture and misunderstand the gospel. Nevertheless, universalism is currently growing in popularity due to the deadly combination of teaching by some high-profile individuals who have professed Christ, a Church that is biblically illiterate, and a postmodern ethos where unanchored and incoherent sentimentalities trump the biblical presentation of God and His Christ.[55] A strong motivation behind universalism is an abhorrence of the notion of eternal punishment in hell for those who are not saved. Universalists deny that hell exists because all will be saved. Some Christians, though not universalists, share the belief that eternal hell is inconsistent with God's nature and is not taught in the Bible. They opt for a position known as annihilationism or conditional immortality. I will describe and critique this position and provide a defense of the doctrine of hell as eternal conscious punishment.

In chapter 4, I will summarize the work of pluralists: those who believe that many different viable paths lead to God, Christianity being only one of many alternatives. I will demonstrate that pluralism is not a valid Christian option. I will look at the social and epistemological underpinnings of pluralism and then summarize the primary arguments made by pluralists, the most significant of which are arguments of reduction and arguments of obfuscation. Many pluralists advocate that Christians turn from Christocentrism to theocentrism in order to

---

[55]Speculation abounds as to whether the most prominent leaders in the Emergent Church movement are universalists. The vagueness of their statements and refusal to divulge their doctrinal convictions has led to much of the confusion. Spencer Burke, founder of THEOOZE.com and coauthor with Barry Taylor of *A Heretic's Guide to Eternity* (San Francisco: Jossey-Bass, 2006), writes that he originally wanted to title his book *I'm a Universalist Who Believes in Hell* (196). On analysis he is not a universalist as defined in this book, but he really has some pluralist impulses. Doug Pagitt, pastor of Solomon's Porch in Minneapolis, has refused to answer direct questions regarding his convictions on the fate of the unevangelized or pious religious others, which has caused many to speculate that he is a universalist (see e.g., "Transcript of Todd Friel and Doug Pagitt on Way of the Master Radio," www.worldviewtimes.com/article.php// articleid-2713 [accessed 03 January 2009]). Brian McLaren's *The Last Word and the Word After That: A Tale of Faith, Doubt, and a New Kind of Christianity* (San Francisco: Jossey-Bass, 2005) raises serious questions about his theology regarding those who do not confess faith in Christ, but he explicitly denies "embracing a traditional universalist position." See "Brian McLaren's Inferno: the provocative church leader explains his view of hell," http://blog.christianitytoday. com/outofur/archives/2006/05/brian_mclarens.html (accessed 3 January 2009). Though there is significant reason to question the orthodoxy of their soteriology, it should be noted that in all three cases, none of the individuals is on record affirming universalism. The same could be said of Emergent leaders Tony Jones and Rob Bell.

see the commonality of the various religions. Interestingly, some pluralists suggest that the Spirit of God is that which brings commonality to all the different religions of the world. This shift to pneumatology is significant because inclusivists also recommend it. I will argue based on the revelation of God's character and His actions in redemptive history that pluralism is incoherent and cannot be embraced by any right-thinking Christian.

In chapters 5 and 6, I summarize and critique the position of inclusivists, those who believe that although reconciliation with God is possible only through the work of Jesus Christ on the cross, conscious faith in Christ is not necessary for salvation. Chapter 5 is committed to the work of nonevangelicals, including the teaching of the Roman Catholic Church, and individuals such as Karl Rahner and Georg Khodr. Particular emphasis is given to those proposals that advocate revisions in pneumatology and Christology giving priority to the Spirit over or against the Son. Chapter 5 is purely descriptive, as my desire there is to summarize nonevangelical proposals to demonstrate the continuity shared with the evangelical proposals.

Chapter 6 is committed to evangelical advocates of pneumatological inclusivism: those proposals that posit an independent work of the Holy Spirit in the lives of the unevangelized apart from any gospel proclamation or subsequent belief in Christ.[56] My conversation partners in the area of theology of religions are primarily the evangelicals Clark Pinnock and Amos Yong. Pinnock and Yong have published numerous works and are pioneering a pneumatological approach to Christian interaction with world religions.

Chapter 7 constitutes the first response to pneumatological inclusivism, concentrating on theological method. It centers on the question, "Is the reading of Scripture through a pneumatological lens allowed by the teaching of Scripture itself?" Granted the interrelationship between how one reads Scripture and how one develops a theological method,[57]

---

[56]The term *pneumatological inclusivism* is adapted from the nomenclature used by Clark Pinnock and expounded in D. Strange, "Presence, Prevenience, or Providence? Deciphering the Conundrum of Pinnock's Pneumatological Inclusivism," in *Reconstructing Theology: A Critical Assessment of the Theology of Clark Pinnock*, ed. T. Gray and C. Sinkinson (Carlisle, UK: Paternoster, 2000), 220–58.

[57]The notion of a hermeneutical spiral can be easily and rightly extrapolated to a methodological spiral. Theological method will heavily influence and alter the way that one reads Scripture, but theological method should also be heavily informed by Scripture. See G. R. Osborne, *The Hermeneutical Spiral: A Comprehensive Introduction to Biblical Interpretation* (Downers Grove, IL: InterVarsity, 1991), 6.

it is not question-begging to suggest that the way in which one reads Scripture should be determined by Scripture. I will demonstrate that beginning a theology of religions with pneumatology or viewing the mission of Jesus Christ as an aspect of the Spirit's mission can only proceed by distorting biblical theology and ignoring the Bible's own presentation of the Son and the Spirit.[58] I also provide a short proposal for how a theology of religions ought to be developed.

Chapter 8 is the culminating chapter of the book and constitutes my analysis of the relationship of the Son and the Spirit. My investigation into that relationship is built upon the foundation of a canonical biblical theology (proposed in chap. 7) that is consciously Christocentric. This analysis enjoys continuity with the theological structures of the past and addresses the needs of the day in our current postmodern and pluralistic context.

Chapter 9 draws the entire project together in terms of summary and answers some specific questions germane to a Christian theology of religions. It ends with a call to gospel proclamation and Christian mission.

---

[58]For a thorough critique of the inclusivism of Clark Pinnock, see Strange, *Possibility of Salvation Among the Unevangelised.*

Chapter Two

The Bible and Religions

INTRODUCTION

What does the Bible say about religions? This is a more difficult question to answer than one might think. The Bible does not come to us in encyclopedic form, nor is it a systematic theology with an index to which the investigator can turn to find a concise answer to any question. Rather, the Bible is the revelation of God's redemptive words and acts in history. There can be no questioning the Lord's wisdom in this mode of revelation, as the Bible has withstood the tests of time for thousands of years, transcending cultural and linguistic differences to speak directly to humanity. But when it comes to answering the question of the place of the religions in the redemptive purposes of God, the answers are not direct. The Old Testament is the revelation of God regarding His redemptive purposes through and for the nation of Israel and is not concerned with what the Lord may or may not have been doing with other nations and peoples.[1] The New Testament is the revelation of Jesus Christ and is therefore Christocentric by definition. A common criticism leveled by religious pluralists at those who defend the Christocentricity of soteriology is that because the Bible is a Christian book it will by necessity be Christocentric.[2]

---

[1]There are notable exceptions to this where the redemptive purposes of the Lord in and through Israel intersect with the Lord's governance of the nations (e.g., Isa 44:28; Obadiah; Hab 1:6), so the message of Scripture is clear that the God of Israel is the God of the nations.
[2]We will evaluate this criticism in chapter 7.

The challenge is exacerbated when one considers that religious pluralism is not directly addressed within the narrative, prophetic, or didactic portions of Scripture. But the presence of challenging worldviews is presupposed, and that presence provides the context for all of the biblical writings. Very little of the Old Testament was written in the context of a thriving and faithful theocracy. Rather, the Old Testament books were written to prepare the children of Israel to take possession of a land surrounded by people of different beliefs, to guide the children of Israel as they lived in that context, and to chastise and encourage the people, depending on the need, when their obedience to the Lord wavered. Likewise, the New Testament was not written in the context of a dominant Christian world empire but was written during a time when the Christian church was a persecuted minority and was actively involved in the beginning steps of spreading the good news of Jesus Christ to the nations. For this reason, the Bible, as in all things, provides the people of the Lord with the necessary revelation to live obediently and missionally in the world, especially in a pluralistic context.[3]

The purpose of this chapter is to investigate briefly a number of themes that are crucial to developing a Christian theology of religions. We will ask such questions as:

- What does the Bible say about other religions?
- What does the Bible say about the worship and religious practices of pagans and of God's people?
- What does the Bible say about idols and idolatry? Why does it condemn idolatry, and what implications does this have for the development of a Christian theology of religions?
- What roles, if any, does the demonic play in biblical narratives, idolatry, and other religions?
- How do the prophets and apostles interact with religious others?
- What is the Lord's disposition toward and plan for the nations?

In answering these questions, we will not be interested in the simple study of Israelite and Christian religious practices. There is

---

[3]See A. Köstenberger, "The Contribution of the General Epistles and Revelation to a Biblical Theology of Religions" in *Christianity and the Religions: A Biblical Theology of World Religions*, ed. E. Rommen and H. Netland (Pasadena, CA: William Carey Library, 1995), 114.

a significant difference between developing a theological response to questions (how things ought to be or were supposed to be) and describing Israelite practice (how things actually were).[4] For example, the archaeological evidence suggests that, prior to the Assyrian and Babylonian exiles, there was a diversity of religious practices in Israel (including acceptance of Asherah and Baal along with worship of the Lord).[5] This description from archaeology matches the description of Israelite religious practices found in the narratives where the Israelite kings and people were often idolatrous (e.g., 1 Kgs 16:31–33; 22:53; 2 Kgs 11:28), despite the continuous prophetic denouncement of that faithlessness. The fact that the description of Israelite behavior does not match that prescribed by the Lord through His prophets in no way renders the current study, rooted in the biblical text, irrelevant. We are to have our hearts and lives shaped by the Spirit-inspired prescriptive Word of God, regardless of the faithlessness of the people described in the biblical narrative. More importantly, it is precisely in the context of religious pluralism that we need to hear the Word of God. Scripture speaks specifically to and in that context.

Religions in the Old Testament

Creation

The best and only place to start, when seeking to understand the Bible, is the beginning. When the creation narrative is ignored, our ability to answer life's ultimate questions is severely diminished. The creation account is primarily valuable not because it offers a rich source for systematic inquiry (though it does) but because it provides the true and divinely inspired beginning to human and redemptive history. Everything that follows in the drama of redemptive history flows from the beginning—creation. The creation account must therefore be read in light of its place in the overall story including,

---

[4]See R. Hess, *Israelite Religions: An Archaeological and Biblical Survey* (Grand Rapids: Baker, 2007), 16.

[5]For a survey of the study of Israelite religion, see ibid., 43–80.

1. the fall of man,
2. the promises to the patriarchs,
3. the granting of the covenants,
4. the establishment of Israel,
5. the exile,
6. the promise and anticipation of the Messiah,
7. His life, death, resurrection, and ascension and the inauguration of His kingdom,
8. the creation of the church,
9. the promise and anticipation of the return of Christ,
10. the consummation of the kingdom, and re-creation.

To ignore the creation account guarantees that our understanding of these events will be diminished or confused, with the sure result that our biblical and systematic theology will suffer. This is especially true when developing a theology of religions.

Assuming Mosaic authorship, the Pentateuch was written to prepare the children of Israel to occupy the land, where they would be surrounded by pagan nations and religious others.[6] From the opening lines of Genesis, Moses' burden was to differentiate the Israelites from those surrounding peoples and their religious practices. In fact, there is much to suggest that Genesis 1 was written in part to refute pagan ideas of the creation of the universe and the perceptions of God that attended those ideas.[7] The tribes of Israel were instructed that their God, the Creator of all, enjoyed authoritative rights over His creation. The Lord who made a covenant with the children of Israel at Sinai was not only distinct from His creation but was supremely greater than the gods of the pagan nations that would surround Israel.

Creator-Creature Distinction   The first verse of the Bible establishes the Creator-creature distinction, perhaps the most critical and foundational tenet to the biblical worldview. Genesis begins with the statement that God created the heavens and the earth, that is, everything. No other god is mentioned. No other god contributes to or challenges the creation of the universe. Nothing exists, visible or invisible, that God did not make. God intentionally created the cosmos *ex nihilo* (out of nothing), by divine fiat alone without recourse to primeval matter.[8] This contrasts with pagan myth, where divine beings and powers

---

[6]J. Sailhamer, *The Pentateuch as Narrative: A Biblical-Theological Commentary* (Grand Rapids: Zondervan, 1992), 3–6.

[7]K. A. Mathews, *Genesis 1–11*, NAC (Nashville: B&H, 1996), 89.

[8]The intentional creation of the personal God of the Bible contrasts strongly with pagan myth, in which impersonal fate was unavoidable. W. VanGemeren, *The Progress of Redemption: The Story of Salvation from Creation to the New Jerusalem* (Grand Rapids: Baker, 1988), 55. Also see Mathews, *Genesis 1–11*, 129.

required a derivation (theogony), usually from the primordial realm.[9] For example, according to *Enuma Elish*, the Babylonian deities were shaped out of preexistent material.[10] The biblical creation account asserts that God made everything and that He preexisted all that He made. There was no divine "womb" from which God and other things or beings sprang. No rivals or antagonists to the Lord could ever be equal with Him.[11] Whatever demons, heavenly powers, principalities, and the heavenly host may be, they are qualitatively and quantitatively different from the Creator.

Image-Bearing and Relationship with God The differentiation between the Lord and pagan deities continued with the creation of humanity. Only mankind was created in the image and likeness of the one God, the Creator of heaven and earth (Gen 1:26–27). Every human person bears the image of the one God, regardless of whether that person is conscious of that fact. A fundamental dignity must be recognized in every person, not just in the orthodox worshipper. Further, as Creator of all, God has absolute rights over all that He has made, including the right and responsibility to judge. The Israelites were entering into a land where the inhabitants invoked and worshipped many deities. This did not change the fact that those people were accountable to their Creator. Israel was to know that every person owed allegiance to the one God who is Master over all.

The responsibility is given only to mankind to exercise dominion over "all the earth" and the creatures therein (Gen 1:26). Since God has Creator's rights over all that He made, He alone had the authority to delegate to mankind the responsibility to govern. With the delegated responsibility to exercise dominion came accountability before the one God on whose behalf people were ruling. As people spread throughout the earth, seeking to work the land and come to grips with their

---

[9]So P. House, *Old Testament Theology* (Downers Grove, IL: InterVarsity, 1998), 59; Y. Kaufmann, *The Religion of Israel: From Its Beginnings to the Babylonian Exile* (New York: Schocken, 1972), 68; W. Eichrodt, *Theology of the Old Testament*, vol. 2, trans. J. Baker (Philadelphia: Westminster, 1967), 98.

[10]See Eichrodt, *Theology of the Old Testament*, 2:113–17, for other critical differences between the Hebrew and Babylonian creation stories.

[11]Yehezkel Kaufmann explains, "The insubstantial role of the demonic in the Bible indicates that the absence of theogony is neither an accident nor the reflection of a primitive premythological religious level. Israelite religion conceived a radically new idea: It did not proclaim a new chief god, a god who ruled among or over his fellows. It conceived, for the first time, of a god independent of a primordial realm, who was the source of all, the demonic included." *Religion of Israel*, 66.

environs, they could not escape the creation mandate to rule, regardless of where or to whom their religious affections were directed.

Genesis 1:27 beautifully summarizes the creative strategy of the Lord in creating man and woman: "So God created man in His own image; He created him in the image of God; He created them male and female." Note the complex but intentional combination of singularity and plurality that is captured in the verse. Though the word for God (*'ĕlōhîm*) is plural, the possessive pronoun in the phrase "in his image" (*bĕṣelem*) and verb "create" (*bārā'*) are all singular, and God creates a singular man (*'ādām*). But God creates singular man in His image as a plural pair, male and female. Though this verse does not establish the Christian doctrine of the Trinity, it certainly allows for it. Christian theologians rightly see a complex interrelationality within God Himself that is the ground for the human need for relationship. As image-bearers of the relational God, humans need relationship with one another (cf. Gen 2:18). More importantly, image-bearers were created for relationship with their Creator (cf. Gen 3:8,22–23; 4:26).

The construction of the temple and tabernacle may indirectly demonstrate the singularity of God. G. K. Beale sees evidence in the creation of the cosmos that the Lord was creating a temple for Himself (Isaiah 65–66).[12] When the Israelites were directed to construct a tabernacle and then a temple (Exodus 25–26; 1 Kings 7; 1 Chronicles 28), it was according to the Lord's design and was meant to be a small model of the entire cosmos. Beale suggests that the outer court symbolized the visible earth and sea, the holy place symbolized the visible sky, and the holy of holies represented the invisible dimension where God dwelt. God alone was to be worshipped in His sanctuary; there was no provision for any other deity because there is no rival to the Lord in all of creation. In pagan religions idols and images were erected, and the pagan priests would serve their gods by feeding and taking care of each god's needs. But in the temple of the Lord, the priests were living images of God, and they were the "only images that were suitable for placement in the true temple."[13]

---

[12]G. K. Beale, *The Erosion of Inerrancy in Evangelicalism: Responding to New Challenges to Biblical Authority* (Wheaton: Crossway, 2008), 161–218; id., *The Temple and the Church's Mission: A Biblical Theology of the Dwelling Place of God* (Downers Grove, IL: InterVarsity, 2004).

[13]Beale, *Erosion of Inerrancy in Evangelicalism*, 183.

The Fall and the Promise   The need for a theology of religions is due to the entrance of sin into God's perfect creation. Before the fall of humanity, Adam and Eve enjoyed a sinless relationship with their God. The nature of that relationship is characterized by Gen 3:8 where the first man and his wife recognized "the sound of the LORD God walking in the garden at the time of the evening breeze" (Gen 3:8). I conclude that this was a familiar occurrence for Adam and Eve. But their disobedience radically disrupted their relationship with God, plunging the land they were to work into a cursed state and resulting in their expulsion from the garden their loving God had planted for them (Gen 3:17–24).

The fall also introduces us to a different supernatural being, the serpent. The rest of Scripture makes clear that the serpent is Satan (Rev 12:9), but his guise and strategy are instructive. The serpent is referred to as "the most cunning of all the wild animals" (Gen 3:1). The Lord God had delegated His authority over the animals to mankind, but Satan inhabits an animal and exercised dominion over the woman. Adam was to exercise loving leadership over his wife,[14] but his wife usurped the authority of the man, who in turn blamed the entire episode on the one to whom all things must submit, namely, God (Gen 3:12). Satan, a liar and murderer from the beginning, sought an exact reversal of the authority structure ordained and commissioned by God.[15] Satan's actions led to the hostility between him and the woman, but the Lord's curse makes it so (Gen 3:14–15). The result is destruction, physical pain, and separation from God, resulting not from the decree of demons but from the Lord. It was the sovereign God, not the demonic, who decreed increased pain in childbirth for the woman, who cursed the land bringing about struggle and toil for the man and who banished the man and the woman from His presence.[16] Demonic forces played a significant role in the narrative, but God, the Creator of heaven and earth, still exercised authority over all that He had made.[17]

---

[14]Some may disagree with the idea that Adam was originally intended to exercise authority over his wife, but the narrative leads me to that conclusion. See, for example, the six reasons given by Tom Schreiner in *Two Views of Women in Ministry*, ed. J. R. Beck and C. L. Blomberg (Grand Rapids: Zondervan, 2001), 201.

[15]J. Frame, *The Doctrine of the Christian Life* (Phillipsburg, NJ: P&R, 2008), 257.

[16]Kaufmann, *Religion of Israel*, 69. See also Eichrodt, *Theology of the Old Testament*, 2:226–27.

[17]Even the condemnation of the serpent to "eat dust" (Gen 3:14), a metaphor of submission to God, is evidence of the Lord's authority over Satan. VanGemeren, *Progress of Redemption*, 91.

In the midst of the devastating rebellion and subsequent curses, God established a trajectory that informs the rest of the biblical narrative. After condemning the serpent to move on his belly and eat dust all the days of his life, God brought hope to the human race when He promised that though the serpent would strike the heel of the woman's seed, the woman's seed would strike the head of the serpent (Gen 3:15). Theologians call this the *protoevangelium*, the first proclamation of the gospel, seeing in it the first announcement of the Messiah. The messianic promises are multiplied throughout the biblical narrative (e.g., Gen 12:1–3; 49:9–12; 2 Sam 7:11–16; Isa 11:1–5; 52:13–53:12), bringing a progressive development to the biblical anticipation of the One who would undo all the evil that humanity had wrought and bring reconciliation between the holy God and rebellious humanity. Redemptive history begins in Genesis 3, and according to Scripture, every living person on earth at the time heard the first announcement of the gospel promise and God's redemptive purposes. All subsequent redemptive activity is tied to the Gen 3:15 promise, and all human interaction with God, whether Jew or Gentile, must be seen in the light of God's announcement, immediately after the fall, to crush the serpent.

The promise of a Deliverer, however veiled, preceded the well-deserved curses on humanity. The order gives testimony that God's redemptive work is greater than the rebellion and condemnation of man. However rebellious humanity is portrayed through the rest of Scripture, the promise of a Savior dominates the biblical revelation. Whatever the peoples of the earth may do in their religious activities, we must remember that immediately after the fall, God promised a Savior through the seed of the first woman.

Multiplying and Theology of Religions   As image-bearers, humans are given the privilege of reproducing other image-bearers, including the One who would defeat the serpent. Even after sin had entered the world, the image of God in humanity was passed from one generation to the next through the act of procreation. Adam, who was created in the image and likeness of God, "fathered a child in his likeness, according to his image, and named him Seth" (Gen 5:3). The command, "Be fruitful, multiply, fill the earth, and subdue it" (Gen 1:28), was given to humanity by God and grants them the power to reproduce apart from the intervention or aid of any other deities.[18]

Throughout Scripture the Lord opens and closes wombs (e.g., Gen 29:31; 30:2,22; Deut 28:11,18; 1 Sam 1:5–6), even the wombs of those in places where there "is absolutely no fear of God" (Gen 20:11,18). He enables men and women to take part in the process, regardless of their faithfulness. More specifically, when Baal worshippers gave birth to a child, they had procreated one in whom resided not the image of Baal but the image of the one God, the Creator of heaven and earth.

Religions in Genesis 4–50

Following the exile of Cain in Genesis 4, we are told, "At that time people began to call on the name of the LORD" (Gen 4:26). The exact meaning of the expression "call on the name of the LORD" is disputed, but it is used of the patriarchs in 12:8; 13:4; 21:33; and 26:25. It appears to be a general phrase for worship, most likely including prayer and sacrifice. The latter verses of Genesis 4 describe the origins of nomadic herdsmen, music, and metalwork, so 4:26 most likely points to the beginning of organized and intentional public worship.[19]

Investigation of religions and religiosity in the Old Testament is immediately complicated by the vocabulary. The Hebrew words for God, *ʾel* and *ʾĕlōhîm*, are generic terms (much like *theos* in Greek) and are related to the Arabic *allah*. The terms *ʾĕlōhîm* and *ʾel* are nondescript and can refer to any supernatural power or deity, as well as to the Lord, the Creator of heaven and earth, depending on the context.[20] Genesis 12–50 often uses *ʾEl* in compound with other expressions such as *ʾEl ʿElyôn*, "God Most High" (Gen 14:18–22), and *ʾEl ʿôlām*, "God Eternal" (Gen 21:33).[21]

There is no Hebrew word for "religion," nor is there even a Hebrew word in the Bible for "faith" in the abstract sense.[22] Faith always requires an object, and though today it is popular to use such phrases as "my faith helped me through this or that difficulty," in the Bible (as

---

[18]Hess, *Israelite Religions*, 172.

[19]So G. Wenham, *Genesis 1–15*, WBC 1 (Waco: Word, 1987), 116. According to Wenham, though the covenant name of the Lord is used, this does not indicate that the people were beginning to call on the Lord in covenant relationship.

[20]G. Bray, "God," in *NDBT*, 513.

[21]J. Goldingay and C. Wright, "'Yahweh Our God Yahweh One': The Oneness of God in the Old Testament," in *One God, One Lord: Christianity in a World of Religious Pluralism*, ed. A. D. Clarke and B. W. Winter, 2nd ed. (Grand Rapids: Baker, 1992), 47.

[22]See Eichrodt, *Theology of the Old Testament*, 2:277–90.

in reality) it is the object of faith that makes all the difference. In the biblical economy, faith apart from an object is pointless, and faith in the wrong object is ridiculed and mocked. The only acceptable objects of ultimate belief are the person and promises of the Lord (e.g., 2 Chr 20:20, Ps 106:12; cf. 2 Kgs 17:14). In the Old Testament vocabulary, religious devotion is often concretized into specific expressions like "to call upon," "to bow down before" (e.g., Exod 20:5), "to walk before" (e.g., Gen 17:1), or to "serve" or "worship" (e.g., Gen 22:5).[23]

Many times these terms will have an ethical dimension. To "walk" before the Lord is to walk in the truth and to have a life that is characterized by faithfulness (1 Kgs 2:4). The most prominent phrase for virtuous and faithful living is "the fear of the LORD." Belief in God is often coupled with fearing the Lord in the Old Testament: "The people feared the LORD and believed in Him and in His servant Moses" (Exod 14:31). When trust in the Lord wanes, the result is that the object of the people's "fear" shifts to someone or something other than the Lord (Deut 1:29–32).[24] Scripture instructs us that "the fear of the LORD is the beginning of knowledge" (Prov 1:7) and of wisdom (Ps 111:10). In the book of Ecclesiastes, the Preacher summarizes what humans need to do: "fear God and keep His commands" (Eccl 12:13). Those who live rightly fear the Lord (Job 28:28). Conversely, where the fear of the Lord is not present, there may not be justice or safety. Abraham felt compelled to lie to Abimelech and the people of Gerar about his marriage to Sarah because, he said, "There is absolutely no fear of God in this place" (Gen 20:11).

Genesis 4–11   Until the call of Abraham, religious activity in the book of Genesis is given little description. Enoch was said to have "walked with God" (Gen 5:22) and was taken by God. Noah also "walked with God" (Gen 6:9), but this phrase is given ethical content: Noah was a "righteous" and "blameless" man, in stark contrast to the rest of the world, which is described as wicked and evil (Gen 6:5). Exercising His Creator's rights over His Creation, God destroyed every living thing on the earth except for Noah and his family. Immediately after his deliverance from the flood, Noah built an altar to the

---

[23]D. Block, "Other Religions in Old Testament Theology," in *Biblical Faith and Other Religions: An Evangelical Assessment*, ed. D. W. Baker (Grand Rapids: Kregel, 2004), 44.

[24]See W. C. Kaiser Jr., "Holy Pagans: Reality or Myth?" in *Faith Comes by Hearing: A Response to Inclusivism*, ed. C. W. Morgan and R. A. Peterson (Downers Grove, IL: InterVarsity, 2008), 126.

Lord and offered animal sacrifices. This act of worship was pleasing to the Lord (Gen 8:20–21), who made a covenant with Noah, promising never again to curse the land or to destroy every living thing (Gen 8:20–22). The sovereign Creator entered into an everlasting covenant relationship with Noah and all other living creatures, reaffirming the creation mandate to fill the earth and subdue it, and provided a sign of His commitment to the covenant by placing His bow in the sky (Gen 9:12–17). Following the impropriety of Ham, Noah praised the Lord and blessed Ham's brothers by the Lord. Following the Table of Nations in Genesis 10, where no description is given of worship or religious practices, the Lord executed judgment on the human race at Babel for their arrogance and pride by confusing their language and scattering the people (Gen 11). Throughout these narratives, there is no indication of demonic activity, and the Lord is responsible for judgment and cursing.

From the fall of humanity to the tower of Babel, Genesis chronicles the decline of humanity and the simultaneous judgment and mercy of God. We would expect that as image-bearers in an everlasting covenant relationship with the Lord (Gen 9:6–16), people would be engaging in religious activity, and this is reflected in the narratives. But we dare not conclude that these worship practices were beacons of bright and innocent spiritual activity in an otherwise dark world. Set in the context of the wickedness and failing of humanity, the religious activities have to be seen as falling short of the glory of God and in need of restoration. As Wright and Goldingay point out,

> The religions can thus be viewed both positively and negatively. They may provide a starting point and certain areas of common ground, but not a finishing point. All human religion is not only inevitably tainted by our fallen life in this earth, but can be the very means we use to keep at arm's length the God we choose not to obey. . . . Religion always has this duality or ambiguity—the simultaneous seeking after God our creator and fleeing from God our judge.[25]

The reason lies in the tension between the human as divine-image bearer, called into covenant relationship with the Creator, and the

---

[25]Goldingay and Wright, "Yahweh Our God," 46–47.

human as rebellious sinner, wanting to be like God, but not trusting the One who is God.

Genesis 12–50   With the call of Abraham[26] in Genesis 12, redemptive history took a dramatic turn and with it religious responses to God. For the first time since the *protoevangelium* in Gen 3:15, God gave details about His plan to redeem the world. Rather than focusing on the efforts of the peoples to "call upon the name of the LORD," God called a man to Himself (Gen 12:1–3). Whereas the people of Babel worked to "make a name" for themselves (Gen 11:4), God promised Abraham, "I will make your name great" (Gen 12:2). And whereas the efforts of Babel resulted in a divine curse with the nations being scattered, God promised that through Abraham "all peoples on earth will be blessed" (Gen 12:3).

Along with the active movement of God, there is a necessary narrowing in acceptable response to Him. The redemptive movement of God signals a shift in history from inclusiveness to exclusiveness. God promised Abraham that all the peoples of the earth would be blessed through him. But there is no evidence in Genesis (or the rest of the Bible) that the blessing is organically related to the efforts of the peoples. That is, the blessing is not the fulfillment of the people's religious activities. Rather, it must be seen as organically related to the original promise of God to crush the serpent. The narrative introduces men and women who are both part of the Abrahamic covenant (Abraham, Sarah, Isaac, Jacob, etc.), and those who are outside that covenant (Pharaoh, Abimelech, Esau, etc.). Interaction between these two groups is instructive for the development of a biblical theology of religions. As those who participate in the Abrahamic covenant encounter those who do not, the narrative does not allow us to conclude that the religious beliefs or activities of the Canaanites are valid alternatives to that of those participating in the covenant. In fact, the opposite conclusion is reached. The calling of Abraham signals the continuation of a process that will lead to God's self-revelation being housed first in Israel and then, ultimately, in Jesus Christ. Goldingay and Wright are correct when they conclude that, rather than uniting the religious practices of the world,

---

[26]Though Abram's name was changed to Abraham in Gen 17:5, I will refer to him as Abraham throughout this chapter for the sake of clarity and simplicity.

Once the fullness of Yahweh's self-revelation is earthed in Israel, the way is open to a critique of other gods and religions, and to the eschatological expectation that one day all peoples will acknowledge that truth and salvation are to be found in Yahweh alone and will join Israel in worshipping and obeying him, or face a destiny of judgment and destruction.[27]

By the time the children of Israel took possession of the promised land following the exodus from Egypt, Canaanite religious practices had grown so detestable to the Lord that He used Israel to exercise judgment on the other nations (Lev 18:24–28; Deut 18:9–12). As Creator of heaven and earth, the exercise of judgment is His exclusive right. In Genesis, God made distinctions between the behaviors of different people groups. For example, during Abraham's lifetime, the people of Sodom and Gomorrah were ready for judgment whereas the Amorites were not yet ready but soon would be (Gen 15:16; 19:1–29). Later, when the people of Israel were about to enter the promised land after their rescue from Egypt, Moses warned them:

> When you enter the land the LORD your God is giving you, do not imitate the detestable customs of those nations. No one among you is to make his son or daughter pass through the fire, practice divination, tell fortunes, interpret omens, practice sorcery, cast spells, consult a medium or a familiar spirit, or inquire of the dead. Everyone who does these things is detestable to the LORD, and the LORD your God is driving out the nations before you because of these detestable things (Deut 18:9–12).

This passage is instructive for two reasons. First, the Lord's evaluation of the Canaanite civilizations is based on their religious practices. God judged the people of Canaan because their religion was detestable to Him. No exemption was made for lack of special revelation. Apparently, general revelation and the traces of special revelation rooted in their common ancestry with Adam and Noah, remaining in the traditions of the people, however distorted by time and sin, were sufficient basis to condemn the cultic activities of the Canaanites. Second, God accomplished two things simultaneously when He led Israel into the promised land, namely, fulfillment of promises to bless and

---

[27]Goldingay and Wright, "'Yahweh Our God,'" 51.

judgment on sin. He made good on His promises to Abraham, Isaac, and Jacob by giving the land to their offspring. Their entrance into the land and displacement of other peoples there was also just because God simultaneously exercised judgment on the Canaanites for their sin and wickedness.

The special revelation of the Lord to Abraham and the subsequent move from inclusiveness to exclusiveness does not mean that there is no continuity between the religious practices of those within and those outside the Abrahamic covenant. Simultaneous continuity and discontinuity in the responses of God's covenant people and the responses of those outside the covenant mark the narratives. Truth about Abraham's God was available to His image-bearers, men and women whom Abraham encountered, including such things common to general revelation as creation, providence, and the divine attributes of eternal power, goodness, and mercy (cf. Rom 1:18–20; 2:1–16). God spoke to people in dreams and visions and was recognized as God (e.g., Abimelech in Genesis 20 and Pharaoh in Genesis 41). But the religious response of Abimelech was not equal to that of Abraham. Though Abimelech recognized the voice of God and was protected by God from committing greater sin, it was the recipient of the covenant, Abraham, who had to pray for the deliverance of Abimelech (Gen 20:7,17).

Following Abraham's rescue of Lot and the coalition of kings, Genesis introduces the reader to Melchizedek, the king of Salem and priest of ʾEl ʿElyôn, "God Most High" (Gen 14:18). Melchizedek, whom the book of Hebrews identifies as a type of Christ (Heb 5:6–10), knew that God is "Creator of heaven and earth," and he gives "praise to God Most High," recognizing the sovereignty of God to save and deliver (Gen 14:18–20). Melchizedek blessed Abraham, indicating Melchizedek's superior status (Gen 14:19), whereupon Abraham acknowledged the position of the priest by giving him a tenth of "everything" (Gen 14:20). Surely, if Melchizedek was the priest of a different god than that of Abraham, it would make no sense for Abraham to give to him a tithe, something normally set aside for the one living God. Therefore, it is clear that Melchizedek (and presumably others in Canaan who worshipped ʾEl) served the true God, though they did not know all there was to know about Him. For example, Melchizedek does not use the covenant name of the Lord but refers to him as "God Most High" and "Creator of heaven and earth" (Gen 14:19–20). Abraham does use the covenant name along with the same designations for God used by Melchizedek (Gen 14:22),[28] leaving no doubt to the reader that the God of Melchizedek and the God of Abraham are one and the same, rather than two separate deities.[29]

Where did Melchizedek learn of the one true God? This is a difficult question to answer because little information is provided in the narrative. Speculation abounds regarding the source of Melchizedek's faith. The inclusivist Clark Pinnock calls Melchizedek a "pagan saint" who provides biblical evidence that "God was at work in the religious sphere of Canaanite culture."[30] Don Richardson believes that Melchizedek is paradigmatic of those who learn of God from general revelation.[31] Both explanations strain the biblical evidence beyond what it can bear. Rather than deriving from general revelation or the insight of pagan religions, is it not more likely that Melchizedek's knowledge of God was passed down to him? Pinnock speculates that Melchizedek's use of the name ʾEl ʿElyôn is evidence of pagan origin for the name and that the patriarchs and Israel accommodated the name.[32] Is it not more likely (and more consistent with the biblical story) that Melchizedek's use of ʾEl ʿElyôn is evidence of residual knowledge of God that was gradually devolving due to human sinfulness and rebellion?[33] As Walter Kaiser explains, "All persons descended from Adam and that line, who at first knew God intimately and for some time, no doubt passed it on to their descendents."[34] Belief in the God Most High passed from Canaanite experience over time, resulting in their eventual judgment at the hands of the Israelites. It makes sense, then, that in later years Israel would conquer Melchizedek's city, Jerusalem, and locate the Lord's temple there.[35]

---

[28]See J. A. Motyer, *The Revelation of the Divine Name* (London: Tyndale, 1949), for an argument that the patriarchs knew God's covenant name (often rendered "Yahweh") before it was given to Moses. This would explain its use throughout the book of Genesis.

[29]See Kaiser, "Holy Pagans: Reality or Myth," 130.

[30]C. H. Pinnock, "An Inclusivist View," in *Four Views on Salvation in a Pluralistic World*, ed. D. L. Okholm and T. R. Phillips (Grand Rapids: Zondervan, 1995, 1996), 109; See also id., *A Wideness in God's Mercy: The Finality of Jesus Christ in a World of Religions* (Grand Rapids: Zondervan, 1992), 93–94.

[31]D. Richardson, *Eternity in Their Hearts* (Ventura, CA: Regal, 1981), 31.

[32]Pinnock, A *Wideness in God's Mercy*, 94.

[33]See G. Vos, *Biblical Theology* (Edinburgh: Banner of Truth, 1975), 63.

[34]Kaiser, "Holy Pagans: Reality or Myth," 132.

[35]Goldingay and Wright, "'Yahweh Our God,'" 48.

In summary, while there are areas of continuity between the Lord worshipped by the recipients of the Abrahamic covenant and the God (*'El*) worshipped by the Canaanites,[36] these points of continuity do not constitute identity or equality. It is surely instructive that as the patriarchs migrated throughout the promised land, they built their own altars and places of worship rather than worshipping with the Canaanites or using their shrines.[37] Genesis does not portray Canaanite and Israelite faith as equally legitimate forms of worship of the one true God, dependent on where one lived or what amount of revelation to which one was privy. As Wright and Goldingay conclude, "Canaanite religion had its insight and limited validity, but what God began to do with Abram was something of far-reaching significance, even for the Canaanites themselves."[38]

Old Testament Monotheism

When the children of Israel were camped on the eastern shore of the Jordan River, poised to enter the land for which their parents refused to trust the Lord, Moses delivered to them the law of the Lord. After rehearsing the history of the Israelite wanderings since the exodus from Egypt, he exhorted them:

> For ask now of the days that are past, which were before you, since the day that God created man on the earth, and ask from one end of heaven to the other, whether such a great thing as this has ever happened or was ever heard of. Did any people ever hear the voice of a god speaking out of the midst of the fire, as you have heard, and still live? Or has any god ever attempted to go and take a nation for himself from the midst of another nation, by trials, by signs, by wonders, and by war, by a mighty hand and an outstretched arm, and by great deeds of terror, all of which the LORD your God did for you in Egypt before your eyes? To you it was shown, that you might know that the LORD is God; there is no other besides him (Deut 4:32–35 ESV).

---

[36]Richard Hess has a helpful summary of religious practice in Genesis; see *Israelite Religions*, 149–50.

[37]G. Wenham, "The Religion of the Patriarchs," in *Essays in the Patriarchal Narratives*, ed. A. R. Millard and D. J. Wiseman (Leicester, UK: Inter-Varsity, 1980), 184.

[38]Goldingay and Wright, "'Yahweh Our God,'" 48–49.

The questions are rhetorical. There is no other god who had done what the Lord had done for Israel. But do these questions acknowledge the existence of other deities? Was Moses' statement that "the Lord is God; there is no other besides him" only a call for the loyalty and worship of Israel to be exclusively devoted to the Lord? Or was it also an ontological statement denying the existence of other divine beings?

Monotheism is the belief that only one god exists, while henotheism is the commitment to worship only one god regardless of whether that deity is the only one in existence. Unquestionably, Israel was set apart from its Canaanite neighbors by its laws concerning the worship of the Lord alone, the prohibition of idolatry, and the observance of the Sabbath.[39] The faithfulness of the Israelites may have varied and lapsed, their witness may have been inconsistent, but they were to be characterized by their worship of only one God.[40]

The first command of the Decalogue forbids the worship of any god other than the Lord who had delivered them "out of the land of Egypt, out of the place of slavery" (Exod 20:2). He had demonstrated His commitment to the children of Israel and His sovereignty over the nation and gods of Egypt. Therefore, the Israelites were forbidden from having "other gods besides" the Lord (Exod 20:3). This was a categorical command that proscribed worship of the gods of the pagan nations that Israel drove out and the deities of the nations with whom Israel lived in peace. Richard Hess argues, "This implies an allegiance to the nation of Israel and to its covenant, as opposed to an alliance with any other nation and its god(s). Yahweh is not just first but alone worthy of devotion."[41]

The question of whether the Israelites believed that their covenant Lord was the only deity in existence (monotheism) or whether they were to worship only their Lord while granting some sort of existence to the gods of the other nations (henotheism) is the subject of some debate.[42] Some argue that monotheism is a modern category that is

---

[39]Hess, *Israelite Religions*, 163. Walther Eichrodt suggests that parallels to Israel's unequivocal commitment to the Lord's oneness throughout their existence cannot be found anywhere else in the history of civilized people: *Theology of the Old Testament*, vol. 1, trans. J. Baker (Philadelphia: Westminster, 1961), 222.

[40]The consistent call throughout the Old Testament to exclusive worship of the Lord is so pervasive that Paul House believes monotheism could be an appropriate centering theme for Old Testament theology: see *Old Testament Theology*, 539.

[41]Hess, *Israelite Religions*, 163.

[42]J. F. A. Sawyer suggests that there are three groups of texts in the OT: (1) texts that are monotheistic; (2) texts that are not necessarily monotheistic but are interpreted that way; and

imported into rather than read off the pages of Scripture and that the Old Testament affirms the existence of other gods.[43] But these arguments are flawed. Regardless of whether the Israelites consciously ascribed any kind of ontological existence to the Canaanite deities, the practical effect of the command to worship the Lord alone was the practice of a *de facto* monotheism by the Israelite people.[44] Bauckham is surely correct when he contends, "If all that matters is that Israel is not to worship them, we seem to be back with the idea that (the Lord's) uniqueness really is nothing more than his election of Israel."[45] The consistent call to exclusive worship of the living God is grounded in claims of uniqueness and incomparability that render the deistic claims of all others empty and unpersuasive.[46]

The Shema   Ranking alongside the first commandment of the Decalogue, the strongest call to exclusive worship of the Lord is the *Shema*: "Hear, O Israel: The LORD our God, the LORD is one. You shall love the LORD your God with all your heart and with all your soul and with all your might" (Deut 6:4–5 ESV).[47] Repeated twice daily by orthodox Jews even to this day, the *Shema* was to remind the Israelites that they were to be radically committed to their covenant Lord with the totality of their being. But is it a statement of monotheism? Daniel Block argues that the Shema ought to be interpreted as "Hear O Israel, our God is Yahweh, Yahweh alone."[48] But this interpretation unnecessarily narrows the implications of the Shema, and makes it a bare call to exclusive devotion, void of ontological implications. The statement, "The LORD is one" means that God alone is constant and He alone is truly real, "an inner unity, both love and power, both creator and

---

(3) texts that are definitely polytheistic. See "Biblical Alternatives to Monotheism," *Theology* 87 (1984): 172–80.

[43]For example, see N. MacDonald, *Deuteronomy and the Meaning of 'Monotheism'* (FAT 2/1; Tübingen: Mohr Siebeck, 2003). Richard Bauckham provides an excellent summary and critique of MacDonald's work in "Biblical Theology and the Problems of Monotheism," in *Out of Egypt: Biblical Theology and Biblical Interpretation*, ed. C. Bartholomew and A. C. Thiselton (Grand Rapids: Zondervan, 2004), 190–91.

[44]Bray, "God," 512.

[45]Bauckham, "Biblical Theology and the Problems of Monotheism," 193.

[46]Christopher Wright argues that the affirmations of the Lord's uniqueness and universality so permeated all of the genres of the Hebrew Scriptures that "there was a radically monotheistic core to Israel's faith from a very early period, however much it was obscured and compromised in popular religious practice." C. J. H. Wright, *The Mission of God* (Downers Grove, IL: InterVarsity, 2006), 73.

[47]Though not as poetic or familiar, the HCSB translation, "Listen, Israel: The LORD our God, the LORD is One," captures well the force of the imperative to pay attention.

[48]Block, "Other Religions in Old Testament Theology," 63.

redeemer.""[49] Other biblical allusions to the Shema reinforce this fact. Zechariah 14:9 teaches that in the final days, the Lord will "be king over all the earth. On that day the LORD will be one and his name one" (ESV).[50] On the day of the Lord, He alone will be recognized as God and the nations will be unified under the reign of that God alone. Paul picks up the same theme in Romans by asserting that both Jews and Gentiles are justified by faith because God is the God of both Jews and Gentiles, "since God is one" (Rom 3:30 ESV). Clearly, the Shema mandates an exclusive devotion to the Lord and that is grounded in the unique, undivided nature and purpose of God.[51]

The Uniqueness of God: Who Is like the Lord? Israel was to worship only the Lord, the Creator of heaven and earth, because He alone is worthy of devotion. There were two primary categories of argumentation used by the Old Testament writers in their calls for singular devotion. First, the Israelites were to worship the Lord alone because He is absolutely and transcendentally unique. Second, the Israelites were to be solely devoted to the Lord because there is no other being on heaven or on earth that compares to Him. These two categories sound much the same, but they function in two different ways.[52] The uniqueness of God affirms that God is in a class all by Himself. His incomparability is demonstrated by several points of contrast between Him and other so-called gods.

The point of many Old Testament passages is that the Lord is in a class all by Himself. Comparisons are impossible because the Creator Lord is wholly other than all His creation. Fundamental to Old Testament monotheism is not merely the explicit denial of other "gods," though such denials are there and, as we have seen, such a denial is implicit in the calls to worship the Lord alone. Rather, the Israelite people were to worship the Lord God who is essentially and categorically different from any other being, whether real or imagined, natural or supernatural, who was worshipped as "god" by the surrounding

---

[49] J. Goldingay, *Old Testament Theology: Israel's Faith,* vol. 2 (Downers Grove, IL: InterVarsity, 2006), 38.

[50] Bauckham, "Biblical Theology and the Problems of Monotheism," 220.

[51] "To confess that 'Yahweh is one' was to claim that he was faithful and consistent in purpose and being, undivided in heart and mind and will." E. Mathews, "Yahweh and the Gods: A Theology of World Religions from the Pentateuch," in *Christianity and the Religions*, ed. Rommen and Netland, 32.

[52] Ibid., 31–32.

peoples.[53] The name given to Moses at the burning bush, "I AM WHO I AM" (Exod 3:14), speaks to His self-existence and self-sufficiency. It also introduces the people of God to the covenant name of the Lord, indicating that all that the Lord was, He was *for* Israel (Exod 6:2–3). "I am the LORD. I appeared to Abraham, to Isaac, and to Jacob, as God Almighty, but by my name the LORD I did not make myself known to them" (ESV).[54] The patriarchs were the focal point for God's redemptive plan to bless all the peoples of the earth, but not even they were the recipients of the totality of God's revelation or redemptive actions. The progress of revelation and of redemptive history does not leave people in equal places or with equal responsibilities.

Often affirmations of the Lord's uniqueness are framed as rhetorical questions. The psalmist writes, "Your righteousness reaches heaven, God, You who have done great things; God, who is like You?" (Ps 71:19). Here the uniqueness of the Lord is grounded in His character and how He alone governs (see also Pss 35:10; 113:5–8). Micah asks the rhetorical question while contemplating the forgiveness and patience of the Lord (Mic 7:18). Sometimes the questions point out a specific attribute: "LORD God of Hosts, who is strong like You, LORD?" (Ps 89:8). At other times the Lord Himself asks the question: "For who is like Me? Who will summon Me? Who is the shepherd who can stand against Me?" (Jer 49:19; cf. 50:44). Sometimes, the rhetorical questions are framed as comparisons to other so-called gods: "Or has a god ever attempted to go and take a nation as his own out of another nation, by trials, signs, wonders, and war, by a strong hand and an outstretched arm, by great terrors, as the LORD your God did for you in Egypt before your eyes?" (Deut 4:34; see also 3:24). The point of the contrast is that there is no comparison. Significantly, the question is asked in the context of the Lord's election and redemption of Israel. No one can do the things that the Lord has done and can do, and He has uniquely revealed Himself through mighty acts for Israel.

---

[53] I follow Bauckham at this point, who refers to the Lord's uniqueness as "transcendent uniqueness," a uniqueness that refers not to being the best within a group, but a uniqueness that puts the Lord in a class of His own: "Biblical Theology and the Problems of Monotheism," 210–11.

[54] Richard Hess believes that the name of God revealed to Moses in Exodus 6 is unique and marks a transition from the inclusiveness of Genesis where the generic name, *Elohim*, was used. In part this is because the covenant name of the LORD (Yahweh) was not revealed until that time: *Israelite Religions*, 173–74.

At times the biblical writers made simple affirmations of the Lord's uniqueness. Moses told the Israelites, "The LORD is God; there is no other besides Him" (Deut 4:35). Moses also used such declarations to remind the Israelites of the awesome privilege of being elected and protected by their Sovereign: "There is none like the God of Jeshurun, who rides the heavens to your aid on the clouds in His majesty" (Deut 33:26; cf. Joel 2:27). Hannah uses the unparalleled holiness of the Lord as an opportunity for praise: "There is no one holy like the LORD. There is no one besides You! And there is no rock like our God" (1 Sam 2:2). Nehemiah appeals to the Creator-creature distinction to affirm the unique identity of the Lord: "You alone are the LORD. You created the heavens, the highest heavens with all their host, the earth and all that is on it, the seas and all that is in them. You give life to all of them, and the heavenly host worships You" (Neh 9:6). By attributing to the Lord the creation of all that is, Nehemiah put the Lord in a class that is far above all others.[55] As the one and only God, there is only one Savior for the nations, and it is incumbent upon the Lord's people to bear witness to this fact (Isa 43:9–12). Because there is "no one like" the Lord "among the gods" falsely imagined by the nations, the psalmist could only conclude that the end result will be that "all the nations You have made will come and bow down before You, Lord, and will honor your name" (Ps 86:8–9).

The Incomparability of the Lord   Throughout the Old Testament, Jewish monotheism was based upon the superiority of the Lord over all the so-called gods of the surrounding nations. The Lord's superiority was demonstrated by both predicating something of the Lord that was claimed of pagan deities and by achieving a victory over a rival nation or the gods themselves. If the uniqueness of the Lord denies that comparisons to the living God can be made, the incomparability of the Lord demonstrates the folly of trying to compare anything or anyone to the living God. More prominent in Scripture, these passages refer to contrasts made between the Lord and those things or beings that are worshipped as gods. These contrasts are not necessarily affirming the existence of other gods. Whether or not Baal existed was irrelevant; what was important is that only the Lord could deliver what was

---

[55]Bauckham, "Biblical Theology and the Problems of Monotheism," 211.

predicated of the other gods. To say that no one is like the Lord (e.g., Exod 8:10; 9:14) is to say that there is no God but the Lord.[56]

Many Old Testament passages describe the Lord and His works in terms commonly employed by pagan worshippers of their deities. By alluding to pagan deities and then attributing their titles and accomplishments to the Lord, His superiority is established over the false gods.[57] For example, Daniel Block notes that Moses exploits Canaanite myths throughout the giving of the Law in Deuteronomy. Moses establishes the sovereignty of the Lord over all areas of life upon which people are most dependent for security (e.g., fertility) and for which the Canaanites sought the aid of local deities like El and Baal (Deut 7:9–10,13–14; 33:26–28).[58] Robert Chisholm finds many allusions to Baal in the declarations of Moses concerning the Lord. Rather than Baal, the Lord controls the storm (Exod 9:22–26) and rides through the heavens (Deut 33:26). In the victory song of Moses celebrating the exodus from Egypt (Exod 15:8–12), the Lord establishes His authority over the sea and death, opponents of Baal in Canaanite myth.[59] These "Baal-like exploits" are proof of the Lord's superiority over Baal and of His incomparability and "validated His right to demand Israel's exclusive loyalty and worship."[60] The use of Canaanite imagery in Scripture (see also Job 15:7–8; Pss 7:12–14; 18:13–15; 29:10; 89:9–10; 93:3–4; 104:3–9; Isa 14:12–15; 51:9–16; Ezek 28:12–19; Hab 3:3–15) does not serve to endorse pagan myths. Rather, the allusions turn pagan worship on its head by inferring that everything claimed for pagan deities can only be rightfully ascribed to the Lord who alone rules all things in heaven and on earth.

There are instances in Scripture where there is a direct confrontation between the Lord and the gods of the nations. It was common custom in the ancient Near East to attribute the victory of one nation over another to the superiority of the victor's god over the god of the conquered (e.g., 1 Sam 5:1–2; Isa 36:18–20). Though there are no explicit references to Egyptian deities in the plague narratives, many

---

[56]Goldingay, *Old Testament Theology*, 38.

[57]Block, "Other Religions in Old Testament Theology," 60.

[58]Ibid., 50.

[59]R. Chisholm, "To Whom Shall You Compare Me? Yahweh's Polemic Against Baal and the Babylonian Idol-Gods in Prophetic Literature," in *Christianity and the Religions*, ed. Rommen and Netland, 59.

[60]Ibid., 61. C. J. H. Wright points out that the language of 15:18, in context, gives the sense that Yahweh "has now demonstrated that He is the king, He is now reigning, and He will go on reigning forever." *Mission of God*, 78.

scholars find the 10 plagues the Lord brought upon Egypt as a direct demonstration of the Lord's power over the elements supposedly controlled by Egyptian deities.[61]

On occasion the Lord engaged in a direct assault against the pagan deities worshiped by those who surrounded the Israelites. The most dramatic confrontation is described in 1 Kings 18 where the Lord won a mighty victory over Baal, and Elijah first mocked the prophets of Baal and afterward destroyed them. In Isa 44:24–25, Isaiah prophesied that the Lord would overthrow the entire divination system that was so fundamental to the warp and woof of life in the pagan nations.

The greatest difference between the Lord and other so-called gods is that only the Lord can save, while the gods are powerless to do so. In the Song of Moses, he taught the Israelites,

> For the LORD will vindicate his people and have compassion on his servants, when he sees that their power is gone and there is none remaining, bond or free. Then he will say, "Where are their gods, the rock in which they took refuge, who ate the fat of their sacrifices and drank the wine of their drink offerings? Let them rise up and help you; let them be your protection! See now that I, even I, am he, and there is no god beside me; I kill and I make alive; I wound and I heal; and there is none that can deliver out of my hand" (Deut 32:36–39 ESV).

This passage emphasizes the incomparable power of the Lord in contrast to that of the other gods, and because of this unparalleled power, wielded on Israel's behalf, Israel was supposed to recognize the Lord as God. Wright summarizes well:

> But the contrast between Yahweh and all other gods is especially clear. They are simply impotent in this key department of deity.

---

[61] In particular, turning the Nile to blood challenged the deification of the Nile as Hapi, the Egyptian lifegiver (Exod 7:15–25). The plague of frogs challenged Heqat who symbolized abundance and prosperity (Exod 8:1–14). The plague of gnats and flies challenged Kheprer, the flying beetle and god of resurrection (Exod 8:16–24). The plague on the animals challenged the cult of Apis and the deities of Re and Ptah who were personified as bulls (Exod 9:1–7). The plague of boils challenged the Egyptian healer deities Sekhmet or Amon-Re (Exod 9:8–12). The plague of hail challenged the sky deities Nut, Shu, and Tefnut (Exod 9:13–35). The plague of locusts challenged Senehem, divine protector against pests (Exod 10:1–20). The plague of darkness was a direct challenge to the chief deity of Egypt, Amon-Re, and the personification of the sun (Exod 10:21–29). The plague on the firstborn was a direct challenge to Pharaoh, who was considered the god of Egypt (Exod 11–12). Hess, *Israelite Religions*, 153–54.

False gods are as much identifiable by their proven inability to save as the living God is identifiable by his proven power to do so. This is the essential contrast between false gods and the one true living God.[62]

The other gods cannot save, rendering them something less than divine. Only the Lord can deliver, therefore only the Lord is God.[63]

The absolute supremacy of the Lord is expressed through the term "God of gods" (Deut 10:17; Ps 136:2; Dan 2:47; 11:36). This reality was to sustain the Israelites when they entered the promised land and fought those who worshipped lesser gods. "For the LORD your God is the God of gods and the Lord of lords, the great, mighty, and awesome God, showing no partiality and taking no bribe" (Deut 10:17). Testimony of the unparalleled power of the Lord eventually spread to the Canaanite nations, causing Rahab of Jericho to confess, "When we heard this, we lost heart, and everyone's courage failed because of you, for the LORD your God is God in heaven above and on earth below" (Josh 2:11).

As God of gods, the Lord has the exclusive right and ability to exercise judgment over the nations. The Israelite conquest of Canaan was not to be interpreted as a statement that the Lord of Israel was able to win a territorial battle because He was stronger than the gods of the Canaanite nations. Rather, entrance into the land marked a period when the Lord of Israel was judging the other nations for their disobedience and rebellion against Him. After warning the Israelites not to follow the nations in their detestable worship practices, Moses said, "For the men who were in the land prior to you have committed all these abominations, and the land has become defiled. If you defile the land, it will vomit you out as it has vomited out the nations that were before you" (Lev 18:27–28). The religious rituals of the pagan nations were an abomination to the Lord, regardless of the fervency of their devotion to their gods. The Lord gave to Israel the responsibility of purging the land of false religion (Deuteronomy 13). Even when Israel went into exile, it was not to be interpreted as meaning that the gods of the Assyrians and Babylonians were stronger than the Lord. The

---

[62]C. J. H. Wright, *Salvation Belongs to Our God: Celebrating the Bible's Central Story* (Downers Grove, IL: InterVarsity, 2007), 51.

[63]Bauckham uses this same logic to argue persuasively for monotheism over against henotheism: "Biblical Theology and the Problems of Monotheism," 194.

arrogant Assyrian monarch Sennacherib, who taunted and challenged the people of Judah and the Lord (Isa 36:18–20), was a mere tool in the hand of God to exercise judgment upon His own people, Israel and Judah (Isa 37:26–29). Israelite claims about the sovereignty of their God may appear ridiculous when the immediate context is considered. Israel and Judah were about to be swept away and sent into exile. But the prophets were adamant that while other gods cowered (Isa 46:1–2), the Lord declared, "I am God, and there is no other; I am God, and no one is like Me. I declare the end from the beginning, and from long ago what is not yet done, saying: My plan will take place, and I will do all My will" (Isa 46:9–10). Commenting on this text, Wright notes,

> Yet the prophetic texts that spoke into the captivity of the Judean exiles dared to call the other nations and their gods into court, to challenge them to a grand contest to see which of their gods really was in control of history—and which one could therefore legitimately claim to be the true God."[64]

The Lord does not just control the events of His covenant people; He is Master and Judge over all that transpires throughout the world.

Syncretism in the Context of Monotheism Monotheism was prescribed throughout the Old Testament, but the description of Israelite religion reveals both faithfulness and faithlessness. The account of Aaron and the golden calf in Exodus 32 is a prominent example. While Moses was receiving the law of the Lord on Mount Sinai, Aaron was leading the children of Israel into idolatry.[65] Hosea condemns the Israelites for attributing to Baal what ought to have been attributed to the Lord (Hos 2:8). Shockingly, the children of Israel had even taken to calling the Lord "My Baal" (Hos 2:16). The most blatant case of syncretism occurred when the Assyrians repopulated the Northern Kingdom with people from other conquered nations: "So they feared the LORD but also served their own gods, after the manner of the nations from among whom they had been carried away" (2 Kgs 17:33 ESV). Archaeological evidence also suggests that it is impossible to sustain a

---

[64]Wright, *Mission of God*, 84.

[65]Hess writes, "In light of the discovery of a calf at Ashkelon and of Janzen's identification of Exodus with military ritual, it seems appropriate to understand the condemned ritual at Mount Sinai as an attempt by Aaron to portray or invoke a deity, perhaps Yahweh, as coming forth from a southern mountain or mountainous land such as Sinai, Kadesh or Teman in order to lead his people on to military victory." *Israelite Religions*, 157–58.

simple division between those who worshipped the Lord faithfully and those who worshipped Baal or another god. Instead, "the majority of scholars find more inviting and inherently more probable the presence of multiple religions existing side by side in ancient Israel."[66]

Rather than a simple and faithful monotheism, the practice described in the Bible is not uniform. Richard Hess describes three levels of monotheism found in the Old Testament.[67] First, the prophets advocated a stubborn monotheism by their steadfast denunciation of the worship and cult of Baal and Asherah. Overall the prophetic stance toward worship of other gods was one of condemnation and rebuke. The people were exhorted to turn away from other gods, in both worship and recognition. Second, many of Israel's kings and queens tolerated and even instituted the pagan cult practices of the neighboring nations (1 Kgs 11:1–11; 12:25–33; 16:28–33; 21:25–26; 2 Kgs 1:2–3; 21:3–7). Third, most of the people acknowledged the Lord as the state deity but lived outside the political circle and found it easy to ignore the state deity. Instead the people sought the aid of local and family deities. Often this "expressed itself in Canaanite customs or rituals associated with reverence and perhaps worship of dead ancestors. The prophets, such as Hosea, Amos, and Isaiah, attacked these attitudes."[68]

The prophets unequivocally called the people of God to exclusive devotion to the Lord. The biblical narratives teach that the unfaithfulness recorded in the stories was met with denunciation and judgment. There is not even a hint that anything other than exclusive worship of the Lord, on His terms, is acceptable. A common mistake of religious pluralists is to equate what the Bible describes or recounts with what it condones (or even prescribes).[69] The Scriptures describe the work of the Lord to redeem a fallen world. It should come as no surprise that sinful activity, such as idolatry, is recorded. The description of idolatry

---

[66]Ibid., 14. Hess points to inscriptions mentioning "Yahweh and his Asherah" found at the Northern Sinai site of Kuntillet Ajrud as evidence. Ibid., 13.

[67]R. Hess, "Yahweh and His Asherah? Religious Pluralism in the Old Testament World," in *One God, One Lord*, ed. Clarke and Winter, 15–16.

[68]Ibid., 16. See also H. Ringgren, *Israelite Religion*, trans. D. Green (Philadelphia: Fortress, 1966), 96.

[69]Such argumentation is not limited to the theology of religions arena. In a public debate on the acceptability of homosexual marriage, my opponent argued that the fact that the Bible records the reality of homosexual and adulterous activity means that the Bible implicitly affirms such activity.

and its subsequent condemnation in the narratives and prophetic literature is evidence of the Lord's exclusive claims.

Ancient Near Eastern thought equated a nation's superiority with that of the nation's gods. To be conquered by a rival nation was a demonstration that your god was inferior to that of the conquering nation (1 Sam 5:1–2; 1 Kgs 20:23; 2 Kgs 18:33–35). Israel was unique among the nations in that her defeat and subsequent exile were proof of the Lord's glory and His sovereignty over all the nations (Amos 1–2).[70] When Israel was faithful, the Lord delivered Israel from her enemies (Isa 37:29–35). When Israel was unfaithful, the Lord raised up a nation and delivered Israel into the hands of that nation (Deut 28:36–37,49–52; Ezek 5:8). The Assyrian and Babylonian exiles were not victories over the God of Israel but were actually victories of the Lord over His unfaithful people. The task of many of the prophets was to remind the exiles that the sovereign Lord may have temporarily chastised them for their sins, but He still held their destinies in His hands. He could and would deliver them. No person or "god" could thwart His plans (Isa 44:24–45:7).[71]

Do Other Gods Exist?

If the Lord is named in Scripture "the God of gods," then does this not give a *de facto* affirmation to the existence of other gods? The biblical writers referred to the Moabites as the "people of Chemosh" (Num 21:29) and the Ammonites as belonging to Milcom (Jer 49:1). Biblical passages such as these seem to admit that other gods exist, while some Scriptures indicate that there is no God but the Lord. Many scholars see a movement across the Old Testament from polytheism to henotheism to a true ontological monotheism,[72] but is the message across the canon that inconsistent? Do other gods exist or not? The answers to these questions are critical for a theology of religions because the Law was written for a people (Israel), who were surrounded by nations claiming that Baal and Chemosh were great gods. The Bible, in fact, speaks unequivocally that there is no God but the Lord and that He is unique, above all His created order. But Scripture

---

[70]Wright explains, "The name (reputation) of YHWH among the nations was at stake in what God did *against* his own people, just as it was involved in all that he did *for* them." Wright, *Mission of God*, 88.

[71]Chisholm, "To Whom Shall You Compare Me?" 64.

[72]For a summary, see Wright, *Mission of God*, 137–38.

does indicate that the gods of the other nations have a subjective existence in the lives and cultures of those who worship them, and there is often a supernatural but created power, not equal to the Lord but powerful nonetheless, behind the gods of religious others.[73]

Only the Lord Is God   Deuteronomy 4:32–39 provides one of the strongest statements of biblical monotheism in the entire Bible. There is a comparison made to other gods in 4:34. "Has a god ever attempted to go and take a nation as his own out of another nation, by trials, signs, wonders, and war, by a strong hand and an outstretched arm, by great terrors, as the LORD your God did for you in Egypt before your eyes?" The question is rhetorical and the point is that the other nations of the world had never been privileged to experience what Israel had experienced and thus to possess this unique knowledge of a true God. This point is emphasized in the following verse: "You were shown these things so that you would know that the LORD is God; there is no other besides Him" (v. 35, cf. v. 39). No other nation had ever heard their god speak or been delivered through miraculous means by their god precisely because only the Lord is God and the gods of the nations are actually not gods at all.[74]

Knowledge that the Lord alone is God was not to be limited to Israel but was to be universal. At the dedication of the temple, Solomon asked the Lord to uphold Israel, "so that all the peoples of the earth may know that the LORD is God" (1 Kgs 8:60; see also 1 Sam 2:2; 2 Sam 7:22; Joel 2:27). Solomon's request cannot mean that he desired the world to know that the Lord is the only god for Israel but that the Lord alone is God over all the earth.[75] The pagan Naaman understood the absolute reign of the Lord when, following his miraculous healing, he declared, "Behold, I know there is no God in all the earth but in Israel" (2 Kgs 5:15 ESV).

Other Gods Do Exist   Having affirmed the absolute exclusivity and incomparability of the Lord, there are many biblical passages that point to some sort of existence for other gods. The Old Testament use

---

[73]So ibid., 81; Goldingay, *Old Testament Theology*, 43.

[74]There is division of scholarly opinion on whether these texts are monotheistic or henotheistic. Helpfully Wright asks, "But suppose an Israelite truly wanted to make the ontological claim that YHWH was indeed the sole universal deity, what more could he or she say than Deuteronomy 4:39?" *Mission of God*, 81.

[75]So Bauckham, "Biblical Theology and the Problems of Monotheism," 195.

of the word "god" (*ĕlōhîm*) is not limited to referring only to the Lord or even to major deities but, like other Middle Eastern languages, can connote cosmic enemies, demons, living and dead kings, idols, or anything that is not seen as "regular humanity."[76]

The word *ĕlōhîm* refers directly to an idol, as when Jacob told his family, "Get rid of the foreign gods that are among you" (Gen 35:2; see also Gen 31:32; Exod 20:23; 32:31; Lev 19:4). *Elōhîm* is also used to compare the Lord to rival beings or things, real or imagined. Moses said, "LORD, who is like You among the gods?" (Exod 15:11; see also Pss 95:3; 97:7–9). Here, Moses refers to other supernatural deities, but the point is to highlight the vast superiority of the Lord.[77]

Elōhîm can refer to a deity worshipped by others without committing to whether the god actually exists. In bargaining with the king of the Amorites, Jephthah said, "Will you not possess what Chemosh your god gives you to possess? And all that the LORD our God has dispossessed before us, we will possess" (Judg 11:24 ESV; see also Num 25:2; Josh 23:16; Ruth 1:15; 1 Sam 26:19). Joshua said to the Israelites, "But if it doesn't please you to worship the Lord, choose for yourselves today the one you will worship: the gods your father worshipped beyond the Euphrates River, or the gods of the Amorites in whose land you are living" (Josh 24:15; see also Exod 23:32; 2 Kgs 5:17). At times *ĕlōhîm* is used to describe that which may not be divine but is something beyond human. Psalm 29:1 says, "Ascribe to the LORD, sons of gods, ascribe to the LORD glory and strength" (my translation). Some suggest that Deut 4:19, which states that the Lord has "provided" the sun and moon "for all people everywhere under heaven," is evidence that the Lord has providentially granted the sun and the moon for some nations to worship.[78] But this interpretation ignores the immediate and canonical context of the passage. In the immediate context, Deut 4:35 and 4:39 clearly state that there is no God but the Lord. At the canonical context level, the Scriptures speak with an otherwise unequivocal voice against idolatry. Furthermore, the reason given in Gen 1:14–18 for the existence of the sun and moon is anthropocentric, to "serve as signs for festivals and for

---

[76] Goldingay, *Old Testament Theology*, 36.

[77] So Ibid., 37.

[78] So P. C. Craigie, *The Book of Deuteronomy*, NICOT (Grand Rapids: Eerdmans, 1976), 137; S. R. Driver, *A Critical and Exegetical Commentary on Deuteronomy*, ICC (Edinburgh: T&T Clark, 1902), 70. See E. H. Merrill, *Deuteronomy*, NAC (Nashville: B & H, 1994), 123, for an excellent criticism of this interpretation.

days and for years" (Gen 1:14).[79] Job 31:24–28 is clear that worship of heavenly bodies is illegitimate. Therefore to claim that the Lord not only allowed but also ordained the worship of other gods is to misinterpret the passage.[80]

Summary Scripture is clear that there is no God but the Lord and that He has no rivals. Nothing can be compared to the God of Israel because only the Lord possesses the attributes of deity and only the Lord is able to save and deliver. There might be others that people worship as gods, but they do not deserve the title of god because they are categorically inferior to the Lord and are unable to deliver. The use of the Hebrew word *ʾĕlōhîm* is not definitive because many things were called *ʾĕlōhîm*, and ultimately the decisive issue is how these so-called gods compare to the Lord.[81] Zephaniah 2:11 is definitive: "The LORD will be terrifying to them [the nations] when He starves all the gods of the earth. Then all the distant coastlands of the nations will bow in worship to Him, each in its own place."

Nevertheless, even though these so-called gods are nothing in comparison to the Lord, they are something in the hearts and minds of those who worship them. Scripture may deny the reality of other gods, but they were absolutely real in the subjective experience of the pagans. So if the gods are not truly god in any sense that rivals the Lord but are undeniably real to those who worship them, then what are they? Christopher Wright suggests that if the gods are something but are not God, then they have to be part of the created realm. If the gods are part of the created realm, then they must either be part of the physical realm (created by God or created or formed by a created being) or the invisible world of nonhuman spirits that were created by God. Therefore, the gods must be either objects within the physical creation, demons, or the creation of human hands.[82]

Worship of Other Gods and the Worship of Demons

When compared to the New Testament, the Old Testament contains

---

[79] J. Sailhamer argues that the difference in syntax between Gen 1:6 and 1:15 indicates that on the fourth day of the creation week the sun and moon are given a purpose. The burden of Gen 1:14–18 is to "emphasize that God alone created the lights of the heavens and thus no one else is to be given the glory and honor due only to him." *The Pentateuch as Narrative*, 93.

[80] So Block, "Other Religions in Old Testament Theology," 67. See also Goldingay, *Old Testament Theology*, 46.

[81] Bauckham, "Biblical Theology and the Problems of Monotheism," 211–12.

[82] Wright, *Mission of God*, 142.

relatively few references to the demonic.[83] Demons are rarely invoked as causal agents for evil.[84] Keeping with the incomparability and exclusivity claims of Jewish monotheism, the Lord is sovereign over all aspects of life, from death to life, from harming to healing, and from calamity to blessing (Deut 32:39; 1 Sam 2:6–8; Isa 45:5–7). The chief demonic character is not an ancient god but is the rebel Satan who seeks to enlist others in his sin. The serpent in Eden was not a rival of God but a being that took the guise of a "beast of the field" and seduced and enticed human rebellion rather than engaging in direct confrontation with the Lord. Evil, therefore, is moral rebellion against the holy Lord, not a metaphysical reality that shares equal but opposite polarity with God. Destructive agents in the Old Testament, satanic or demonic, do not constitute an equal domain opposing the Lord but, like the angels, are His messengers (1 Kgs 22:19–23).[85] Satan presents himself before the divine court to accuse and is rebuked (Zech 3:1–2) or has sharp boundaries placed upon his behavior (Job 1–2). Not one of the gods after whom Israel strayed prior to and during the First Temple period left his or her name to the demons of the Second Temple period.[86] Demons are not prominent in Old Testament theology because the conviction that good and bad are both controlled by the holy hand of the living God renders demonic activity superfluous.[87] Sacrifice to demons, divination, sorcery, and fortune-telling were not forbidden merely because they represented a fracture in the exclusive loyalty that was due the Lord (Deut 18:9–14). Entanglement with the demonic at any level was fundamentally nonsensical in light of the character and sovereignty of the one God.

There are a few Old Testament texts that connect the worship of other gods with the worship of demons. Deuteronomy 32:16–21 specifically ties sacrificing to foreign and unknown gods (*ʾĕlōhîm*) with sacrificing to demons (*šēd*): "They provoked His jealousy with foreign gods; they enraged Him with detestable practices. They sacrificed to demons, not God, to gods they had not known, new gods that had just

---

[83]The Hebrew term *šēd* occurs twice in the Old Testament (Deut 32:17 and Ps 106:37), referring to evil spiritual forces who stand in opposition to God yet receive sacrifice as false gods.

[84]See House, *Old Testament Theology*, 128.

[85]See also Kaufmann, *Religion of Israel*, 64. Kaufmann makes the point that Israelite religion is remarkable in that "it failed to transmute either its ancient pantheon or the gods of the nations into demons" (63).

[86]Ibid., 65.

[87]Ringgren, *Israelite Religion*, 103.

arrived, which your fathers did not fear" (Deut 32:17). Leviticus 17:7 called for a cessation of the offering of sacrifices to "goat demons" (*śĕʿîrîm*) "after whom they whore" (ESV; cf. Isa 34:14). Despite the relatively small role that the demonic plays in Old Testament theology, the paucity of biblical texts relating the worship of other gods with worship of demons should not lead us to overlook the fact that the connection was made (a connection that is amplified in the New Testament). Worship of other gods was tied to the worship of demons. But the reasons for the prohibition on worshipping demons were identical to the reasons for worshipping the Lord alone. The demons were no more equals to God than the gods of the pagan nations were equals to God. Worship of other gods, whether demonically inspired or not, provoked the jealousy of the Lord because it was worship directed at something or someone other than the only One to whom worship is rightfully due.

Idolatry in the Old Testament

Idolatry can refer to either the worship of images and things or the worship of foreign gods.[88] Whereas the first commandment of the Decalogue prohibits the worship of foreign gods, the second commandment declares:

> You shall not make for yourself a carved image, or any likeness of anything that is in heaven above, or that is in the earth beneath, or that is in the water under the earth. You shall not bow down to them or serve them, for I the LORD your God am a jealous God, visiting the iniquity of the fathers on the children to the third and the fourth generation of those who hate me, but showing steadfast love to thousands of those who love me and keep my commandments (Exod 20:4–6 ESV).

The command includes a prohibition of every kind of idolatry and an explanation of how seriously the Lord takes idolatry because of its ability to corrupt through the generations.[89] Initially, it would appear that the command prohibits the making of any image (*pesel*) or likeness (*tĕmûnâ*), but references to images required in the tabernacle and temple (Exod 25:18–20; 1 Kgs 6:23–28) render this interpretation invalid.

---

[88]B. Rosner, "Idolatry," *NDBT*, 571.
[89]D. Stuart, *Exodus*, NAC (Nashville: B&H, 2006), 449.

Exodus 20:5 makes clear that the commandment prohibits the making of images for the purpose of worshipping them, thus the HCSB and NIV translate the Hebrew word as "idol." Leviticus 26:1 commands, "Do not make idols [*'ĕlîlîm*] for yourselves, set up a carved image [*pesel*] or sacred pillar [*maṣṣēbâ*] for yourselves, or place a sculpted stone in your land to bow down to it, for I am the LORD your God." The erecting of "sacred pillars" can have a positive use in Scripture (e.g., Gen 28:18), so it is clear that the prohibition on making carved images is tied to idolatry, the making of an image for the purpose of bowing down and worshipping it.

Acts of submission or reverence directed toward objects that represent or replace the living God are absolutely forbidden, so much so that the prohibition is built into the first two commandments of the Decalogue.[90] The prohibition is amplified in Deut 4:15–31. Moses warned the Israelites that idolatry is the first sign of forgetting the covenant (4:23) and then spelled out the deathly consequences of worshipping images (4:24–27). If the Israelites chose to behave like the Canaanites by acting corruptly and making idols, then the Israelites would share the same judgment as the Canaanites: they would be removed from the land.[91]

Most of the commands against idolatry are found in the books of Exodus through Judges, which recount the Lord preparing Israel to drive out the pagan nations and take the promised land. The relationship between a pagan god and its idol was more than representative. Yet pagans did not believe that when they made an idol, they were creating a deity. Rather, the essence of the god attached itself to the idol to such a degree that, in the mind of the worshipper, to be in the presence of the idol was to be in the presence of the deity.[92] For this reason the biblical writers often did not distinguish between the pagan gods and their idols because, to the prophets and psalmists, there was simply no distinction in reality. The alleged gods had no real power or existence of their own, and they were just as much a product of human creation as the idols purported to represent them.[93] Joshua's command

---

[90]Block, "Other Religions in Old Testament Theology," 62.

[91]Ibid., 64.

[92]So Stuart, *Exodus*, 450. Goldingay points out, "The fact that [asherah] is both the name of a god and a term for a column representing the god is a symbol of the fact that Israelites involved in worship of Asherah would have made little distinction between the two meanings; they would have identified the cult symbol and the deity." *Old Testament Theology*, 42.

[93]Wright, *The Mission of God*, 152.

to the Israelites to "get rid of the gods your ancestors worshiped" (Josh 24:14) is not so much an ontological statement about the existence of other gods but a simple command to give undivided and unadulterated worship to the Lord alone. In contrast to the pagan identification of the gods with their idols, the Lord of Israel was not to be identified with anything, including the ark of the covenant. Even though the Lord had commissioned and designed it, the narrative of the capture of the ark in 1 Sam 4:1–11 makes clear that control of the ark is irrelevant to the work and power of the living God. The prohibition of idolatry also includes strong condemnation of any attempt to make an image of the one true God, the Covenant Lord of Israel. Worship of an image, even if the image is meant to be the Lord, is exactly equivalent to worshipping another god because a god who can be imaged by human hands cannot be the Lord.[94]

The Old Testament is unequivocal in its condemnation of idolatry. The prohibition against idol worship is repeated throughout the Pentateuch (Lev 19:4; 26:1; Deut 4:25–26; 5:8). The psalmist hated those who were "devoted to worthless idols" (Ps 31:6). Ultimately, the Lord sent His people into exile because they had "returned to the sins of their ancestors" and "followed other gods to worship them" (Jer 11:10). Further, the children of Israel were to be literally iconoclastic. When the Israelites entered the land, they were not to enter into any treaty alliance with the nations that the Lord would drive out before them, for that would inevitably lead to spiritual adultery. Rather, the Israelites were to "tear down their altars, smash their sacred pillars, and chop down their Asherah poles" (Exod 34:13; see also Exod 23:24; Deut 7:25; 12:2–3).

Idols and Demons   Idolatry is an abomination because in some texts the worship of idols is explicitly tied to the worship of demons. Deuteronomy 32:16–21 draws a clear link between "foreign gods" (32:16), sacrificing to "demons" (32:17), and the worship of "worthless idols" (32:21). The connection is explicitly present in Psalm 106: "They sacrificed their sons and daughters to demons. They shed innocent blood—the blood of their sons and daughters whom they sacrificed to the idols of Canaan; so the land became polluted with blood" (vv. 37–38). These

---

[94]Goldingay, *Old Testament Theology*, 43. He writes, "Talking in the same breath about Yhwh and an image or about Yhwh and a god who can be represented by an image involves a travesty of the facts" (29).

passages make clear that in the Old Testament economy, sacrificing to idols and foreign gods is sacrificing to demons.

Idols Are the Work of Human Hands Idolatry is an abomination because the worship of idols is the worship of things made by human hands. The polemic response to idolatry in the Old Testament is instructive. The most prominent strategy used by the biblical writers was to contrast the incomparable Lord with the gods/idols of the other nations. This strategy often led to satirical ridicule.[95] Whereas the gods/idols were the works of human hands, the Lord is the Creator of both humanity and the materials used to fashion the idol. In Isa 41:21–23, the Lord challenged the "gods" to do that which only God can do, namely, tell the future.[96] Of course, they could not, and the Lord's conclusion was, "Behold, you are nothing, and your work is less than nothing; an abomination is he who chooses you" (Isa 41:24 ESV). Robert Chisholm summarizes from the book of Isaiah the contrast between the Lord and idols:

> Human craftspeople make the idol-gods (40:19–20; 41:7), but Yahweh created the craftspeople (54:16). In other words, Yahweh created the creator of the idol-god! A craftsperson makes an idol from wood (40:22), but Yahweh created the trees which supply the wood (41:19) and receives their worship (44:23). All of Lebanon's great trees could not fuel an adequate sacrificial fire for Yahweh (40:16), but an idol is made from the same wood people use to cook their food and warm their hands (44:15). Craftspeople exhaust their strength to form their idols (44:12), but Yahweh can give his weary people supernatural strength (40:29–31). Idol worshipers use the refining process (40:19; 41:7; 46:6) to shape their metallic gods (44:9–10), but Yahweh refines (48:10) and forms (44:2) his people. . . . In these passages Yahweh is the active king of the world; humanity is the product of his creation and the recipient of his help. By contrast the pagan idol-gods are inactive products of frail human creative efforts and cannot help their worshipers.[97]

---

[95] So Rosner, "Idolatry," 570.

[96] Open theists, who deny that even God knows the future fully, seem to have forgotten this very fact. B. Ware, *God's Lesser Glory: The Diminished God of Open Theism* (Wheaton, IL: Crossway, 2003), 103–7.

[97] Chisholm, "To Whom Shall You Compare Me," 64–65.

The polemic against idolatry as the senseless worship of that which human hands have created is found in the Pentateuch (Deut 4:28), the Prophets (Jer 2:27–28; 10:1–16; 14:22; Hos 8:4–6; 13:2; Hab 2:18–19), and the Writings (Pss 115:2–8; 135:15–18).

The mocking of idolatry extends even into the historical narratives. Genesis 31:30–35 records the comical account of Laban searching for his gods who were hidden under a menstruating woman. When Gideon tore down the altar of Baal, his father defended his son against the angry mob by asking, "Would you plead Baal's case for him? Would you save him? . . . If he is a god, let him plead his own case, because someone tore down his altar" (Judg 6:31). The account of Micah suggests that the gods and their idols were little more than talismans for hire (Judges 17–18). When the ark of the covenant was captured in battle by the Philistines and taken to the temple of the Philistine god Dagon, the Philistine god, much to the dismay of his worshippers, fell, prostrate and broken, before the ark of God (1 Sam 5:1–4).

Occasionally there was direct confrontation between the Lord and the idols/gods of the nations. Elijah faced the prophets of Baal on Mount Carmel, and he too used the strategy of deriding Baal with taunts that exposed the sheer stupidity of idol worship (1 Kgs 18:20–29). Elijah ridiculed the prophets of Baal, imploring them to speak louder so as to capture the attention of their god. The result of the affair is poignant and decisive: "All afternoon, they kept on raving until the offering of the evening sacrifice, but there was no sound, no one answered, no one paid attention" (v. 29). The Lord won a mighty victory on that day when the prophets of Baal were first mocked and then destroyed (v. 40). When Jerusalem was surrounded by the formidable forces of the Assyrian monarch Sennacherib, his deputy, the Rabshakeh, attempted to liken the Lord of Judah to the impotent gods of the other nations. This prompted the Judean King Hezekiah to pray:

> LORD God of Israel who is enthroned above the cherubim, You are God—You alone—of all the kingdoms of the earth. You made the heavens and the earth. Listen closely, LORD, and hear; open Your eyes, LORD, and see; hear the words that Sennacherib has sent to mock the living God. LORD, it is true that the kings of Assyria have devastated the nations and their lands. They have thrown their gods into the fire, for they were not gods but made

by human hands—wood and stone. So they have destroyed them. Now, LORD our God, please save us from his hand so that all the kingdoms of the earth may know that You are the LORD God—You alone (2 Kgs 19:15–19).

Hezekiah rightly understood that because human hands made the "gods" of the other nations, they were not able to see or hear, nor were they able to save even themselves from the fire. In contrast the Lord is the Creator of all (including human hands and the wood and stone used to fashion the "gods"), able to see and hear ("I have heard your prayer to Me," v. 20), and able to save ("I will defend this city and rescue it for My sake and for the sake of My servant David," v. 34). False gods and their idols "never fail to fail. The trouble is, we never fail to forget this fact."[98]

Idolatry Evokes the Lord's Jealousy   The prohibition of idolatry differentiated Israel from all of its pagan neighbors. Whereas the pagan nations needed idols in their worship, Israelite worship of the Lord was aniconic, exemplified by the invisible enthronement of the Lord upon the ark of the covenant between the cherubim (Exod 25:22; Num 7:89).[99] Therefore, the Israelites were to detest and abhor the gods of their pagan nations lest they become ensnared by idolatry (Deut 7:25–26; Ps 106:36; Isa 45:16).

The theological ground for the unequivocal denunciation of idolatry is the jealousy of God: "You shall worship no other god, for the LORD, whose name is Jealous, is a jealous God" (Exod 34:14 ESV).[100] The reason for the Lord's jealousy lies in His incomparability (Isa 40:18–20) and unique ability to care for His people.[101] Any attempt to fashion an image of Him for the purpose of worship will inevitably reduce the Lord to something far less than He is. This was precisely the reason Moses gave to the Israelites. "Be extremely careful for your own good—because you did not see any form on the day the LORD

---

[98]Wright, *Salvation Belongs to Our God*, 54.

[99]Hess, *Israelite Religions*, 160.

[100]All of the pentateuchal references to the jealousy of the Lord have to do with idolatry. Rosner, "Idolatry," 570. See also id., "No Other Gods: The Jealousy of God and Religious Pluralism," in *One God, One Lord*, ed. Clarke and Winter, 149.

[101]C. Scobie notes, "This jealousy is not an irrational emotion; it is the valid response of the one God who yearns to protect his people from the dire consequences of failing to acknowledge him only." C. Scobie, *The Ways of Our God: An Approach to Biblical Theology* (Grand Rapids: Eerdmans, 2003), 113.

spoke to you at Horeb out of the fire—not to act corruptly and make an idol for yourselves in the shape of any figure" (Deut 4:15–16). The Lord chose to use words without forms to reveal Himself at Horeb and expressly forbade the deification of anything in the created order. Deuteronomy 4:17–19 lists potential objects of false worship from the creation (from humans to the heavenly bodies) in the opposite order of their creation in Genesis 1. Engaging in idolatry, thereby denying the Creator-creature distinction in their worship, "produces disorder in all our fundamental relationships."[102]

Idolatry robs God of the glory of which He alone is worthy. The Lord demanded exclusive worship, and He was not tolerant of any rivals (Isa 42:8; Ps 97:7–9). Other gods were incapable of performing the most basic Godlike acts, and they certainly could not save people (Deut 32:37–39). They were only gods in the sense that pagans believed the promises attributed to them. Compared to the Lord, the gods were impotent and completely unworthy of devotion. To divert devotion, praise, and glory to a so-called "god" for actions that only the Lord can perform is a heartbreaking abomination. "Has a nation ever changed its gods? (Yet they are not gods at all.) But my people have exchanged their Glory for worthless idols" (Jer 2:11 NIV).

For this reason the biblical authors likened idolatry and the worship of other gods to adultery and prostitution (Lev 17:7; Hos 2:13).[103] Just as there are exclusive claims by a husband on his wife's love and affection, so the Lord, who is able to protect and provide for His subjects, has every right to make exclusive claims on their exclusive trust and obedience.[104] To reject the Lord for an idol or another god is not only fundamentally stupid given the incomparability of the Lord; it is also adulterous and evokes the jealousy of God (Ezek 8:3). The punishment for idolatry was severe. The children of Israel would "perish" (Deut 8:19–20), the Lord's anger would burn, and He would bring every curse against them (Deut 29:26–28), and He would "hurl them" from the land (Jer 16:11–13). Perhaps the most severe punishment for idolatry is that of being given over to the futility of extended idolatry. "So I will hurl you from this land into a land that you and your fathers

---

[102]Wright, *Mission of God*, 143.

[103]See R. Ortlund Jr., *God's Unfaithful Wife: A Biblical Theology of Spiritual Adultery* (Downers Grove, IL: IVP, 2003), for an excellent summary of adultery as a metaphor for unfaithfulness to God traced through the Bible.

[104]See Rosner, "Idolatry," 573.

are not familiar with. There you will worship other gods both day and night, for I will not grant you grace" (Jer 16:13–14). As Brian Rosner comments, "Idolatry called for the strictest punishment, elicited the most disdainful polemic, prompted the most extreme measures of avoidance, and was regarded as the chief identifying characteristic of those who were the very antithesis of the people of God, namely, the Gentiles."[105] Restoration will occur when the Lord eliminates idolatry and takes vengeance on the nations that have disobeyed Him (Mic 5:12–15).

Idolatry Is Failing to Worship the Lord According to His Commands   Another implication of the Lord's jealousy is His absolute requirement that people approach Him on His terms. Worship was acceptable to the Lord only if it was based on true knowledge of the Lord and according to His will.[106] The requirements of the Old Testament for worship, sacrifice, and the construction of the tabernacle and temple are detailed and explicit. The penalties for ignoring the Lord's requirements were devastating and immediate. From the earliest stages of the biblical narrative, the Lord differentiated between the worship practices of the people. For reasons not specifically given in Scripture, the Lord "did not have regard for Cain and his offering" (Gen 4:5). Exodus 25–31 provides critical instructions for the construction of the tabernacle, including the creation of a "sanctuary," a holy place (Exod 25:8). It is ironic that the account of the golden calf (Exodus 32) is set immediately after the Lord sets apart His own Spirit-inspired craftsmen to make His tabernacle according to His prescriptions (Exod 31:1–11). From the outer court to the holy of holies, the tabernacle was designed to reflect God's holiness. Coupled with the sacrificial system and Day of Atonement, the entire system "expressed the truth that human beings could not come into [God's] presence on their own terms."[107] The cultic-prescribed practices included sacrifices, offerings, Sabbath observance, festivals, dress, and diet, and were designed to keep a sinful people in relationship with their covenant Lord.

Throughout the Old Testament there are severe penalties for ignoring the Lord's prescriptions in approaching Him. Almost immediately after the inauguration of the Levitical priesthood, Nadab and

---

[105]Ibid., 570.
[106]See Peterson, "Worship," in *NDBT*, 857.
[107]Ibid.

Abihu were put to death for presenting unauthorized fire before the Lord. No explanation is given concerning their exact offense, but the Lord's words were repeated, "I will show My holiness to those who are near Me, and I will reveal My glory before all the people" (Lev 10:3). Saul was rejected as the king of Israel for offering improper sacrifice (1 Sam 13:8–14). Even King Uzziah, described in Scripture as one who "did what was right in the LORD's sight" (2 Chr 26:4), was severely punished with an unclean skin disease for illegitimately offering incense (2 Chr 26:16–23).

When David attempted to move the ark of God, the Lord put Uzzah to death "on the spot for his irreverence" when he reached out to steady the ark when the oxen transporting it had stumbled (2 Sam 6:6–7). David and his men had dishonored the Lord when they did not "inquire of Him about the proper procedures" (1 Chr 15:13). They failed to obey the Lord's specific command through Moses that the Levites carry the ark on poles (vv. 14–15). Not only were David and the Levites to obey the Lord in approaching Him, but they also required His enabling to do so. It was "because God helped the Levites who were carrying the ark of the covenant of the LORD" that the procession and sacrifices were acceptable to God (v. 26).

RELIGION IN THE NEW TESTAMENT

The ultimate context for any passage in the New Testament is the entire canon of Scripture. The New Testament writers saw their mission as the direct result of the mission of God established in the opening pages of Genesis. Their witness to Jesus of Nazareth as the Christ was the fulfillment of the redemptive hope first expressed at the fall of Adam and Eve and repeated throughout the Prophets and the Writings. Because the God of Abraham, Isaac, and Jacob is the God and Father of the Lord Jesus Christ, what is true of God in the Old Testament— His character, essence, and purposes—is also true of God following the incarnation, death, resurrection, and ascension of Jesus. Many of the topics covered in the previous section, such as monotheism, creation, *imago Dei,* and idolatry are assumed in the New Testament on the basis of the Old Testament.[108] Therefore, I shall not retrace ground already covered.

---

[108] See House, *Old Testament Theology,* 547.

The New Testament was written in the context of religious pluralism, so its value to a theology of religions is immeasurable. It is invalid and disingenuous to argue that because the Bible is the Christian's book its authority and insight is limited to the Christian community.[109] Jesus and the apostles routinely encountered religious others. The polytheistic Greco-Roman world may not have had postmodern philosophers like Derrida and Foucault, but it cherished religious pluralism as much as our postmodern world.[110] In the Greco-Roman mind-set, as today, religious pluralism was not just a description of how things were but of how things ought to be. Jesus' claims to be the only way to the Father (John 14:6) and the only way to honor God (John 5:23) were condemned by His audience. Jesus' apostles discovered that proclamation of the work and words of Jesus was equally offensive to Gentiles and Jews (e.g., Acts 16:16–24; 17:16–34; 19:21–41).

The New Testament and Religious Others

The New Testament's consistent response to its pluralistic context is gospel proclamation. The world (*kosmos*) hates Christ (John 7:7), is judged along with its ruler (John 12:31), and is unable to receive the Spirit because it "neither sees him nor knows him" (John 14:17 ESV). Though the world and its people are the focus of God's love (John 3:16; 4:42), it is made up of rebellious people who have established a system, an "alternative focus of trust and commitment" that stands against God's kingdom and God Himself (1 John 2:15–16).[111] Religions that do not exalt Jesus are a part of that system and are consistently critiqued throughout the Gospels. Gentiles or "the nations" (*ethnoi*) are in the dark and in need of light and revelation (Matt 4:15–16; Luke 2:32; John 1:9–10). Such darkness and the need for revelation indicate an unacceptable ignorance or rebellion in religious practices. The nations (*ethnikoi*) are known for the vain repetition of their prayers, a practice common to paganism (Matt 6:7). "All the nations of the world" (*panta ta ethnēē tou kosmou*) do not know or

---

[109]E.g., Stanley Samartha argues that because the Bible is the Christian's book, it is not a sufficient source for establishing criteria for discerning the work of the Holy Spirit in religious others. S. J. Samartha, *Courage for Dialogue: Ecumenical Issues in Inter-Religious Relationships* (Geneva: World Council of Churches, 1981), 72.

[110]I often tell my hermeneutics students that biblical interpretation gets easier day by day because the Pacific Northwest culture continually grows in its resemblance to first-century Greco-Roman culture.

[111]T. Renz, "World," *NDBT*, 854

trust the Lord, so they are preoccupied with seeking after the basic provisions of life (Luke 12:30 ESV; cf. Matt 6:32). Jesus does not merely condemn particular religions; rather, He condemns "all the nations of the world," a general term that includes and encompasses every religion of the world for their lack of trust in God. Far from being sympathetic to the religions of the world, Jesus was critical of religious practices not motivated by a heart reconciled to God. His criticism usually fell not on irreligious people but religious ones.[112] Jesus' confrontations with the Pharisees and Sadducees pervade the Gospels. In the Sermon on the Mount, Jesus condemned people who engaged in religious practices like prayer and giving to the poor (Matt 6:1–8) but who did so from a faulty theological basis and for reasons other than those prescribed in Scripture.[113]

Biblical accounts of encounters with religious others contain no softening of the message of reconciliation only through Jesus. This is particularly true of Jesus Himself. His pattern of interaction was not dialogue in which He was seeking knowledge or understanding. Jesus always was the Master who knew all the answers. He asked questions to drive the listeners to the truth He was proclaiming.[114] On meeting the Samaritan woman, Jesus told her that her people were in error in their efforts to worship the God of Jacob (John 4:22), but a day was coming when Jews and Gentiles would "worship the Father in spirit and truth" (v. 23). He pointed her to Himself, telling her that He was the Christ, the one for whom she and her people had been waiting (vv. 25–26). The Syrophoenician woman was clearly in great need, and Jesus helped her only after stating the singular purpose of His mission (Mark 7:24–30). The Samaritan leper was praised for having more faith and giving more glory to God through gratitude to Jesus than the Jews who were also healed (Luke 17:11–19). The Roman centurion's faith that so amazed Jesus was focused specifically on the person and ability of Jesus (Matt 8:5–13).

---

[112]See T. Keller, *The Reason for God: Belief in an Age of Skepticism* (New York: Dutton, 2008), 58.

[113]Religion, even Christianity, is too often used to oppress people and ignore the marginalized of the world. Jesus, the prophets, and the apostles led the way in condemning this abuse of religion. Tim Keller concludes, "The typical criticisms by secular people about the oppressiveness and injustices of the Christian church actually come from Christianity's own resources for critique of itself." Ibid., 61.

[114]W. J. Larkin, "The Contribution of the Gospels and Acts to a Biblical Theology of Religions," in *Christianity and the Religions*, ed. Rommen and Netland, 77.

Simultaneous with Jesus' confrontation with religious others was a demonstration of His heart for the nations. As the Jewish Messiah, Jesus' primary focus was on reaching the people of Israel (Matt 15:24; John 1:11). Yet in the Old Testament prophetic anticipation, the kingdom of God, which the Messiah would inaugurate and bring to consummation, always included the nations (e.g., Isa 42:1–4; cf. Matt 12:17–21; 51:4–5; 55:5; 60:2–3; 66:18–23). Simeon understood this, for upon finally seeing the desired Messiah, he declared Jesus would be "a light for revelation to the Gentiles and glory to Your people Israel" (Luke 2:32). As was demonstrated above, during Jesus' first advent ministry, He preached and ministered to Gentiles. Some Gentiles repented and put their faith in Jesus, whereas most of the Jews, and their leaders in particular, refused to heed the invitation to the long-awaited kingdom. The parable of the large banquet testifies to this very fact (Luke 14:15–24). The nation of Israel was invited to the kingdom feast but rejected the offer, so Gentiles were invited to the banquet. The coming of Gentiles to seek out Jesus provided the impetus for Jesus to proclaim that the hour of His glorification, that is, His substitutionary death and resurrection, was at hand (John 12:20–22).

Jesus' parting charge to His disciples after His resurrection was for them to carry the message of His redemptive kingdom to all nations. In Matthew, Jesus told His disciples to make disciples of "all nations" (*panta ta ethnē*), thereby bringing them under His universal authority (Matt 28:18–19). Luke ends with Jesus' summarizing the Scriptures as a mandate that "repentance for forgiveness of sins would be proclaimed" in the name of the Messiah "to all the nations" (Luke 24:47). Just before His ascension to the Father, Jesus told His disciples that He would send the Holy Spirit to empowerer them to witness to Him "in Jerusalem, in all Judea and Samaria, and to the ends of the earth" (Acts 1:8). The book of Acts chronicles the fulfillment of Jesus' directive. Clearly the nations figure into the redemptive purposes of God, but their inclusion in the kingdom requires they respond in faith to the proclamation of the particular life and work of the Jewish Messiah.

Commitment to sensitive confrontation and gospel proclamation is demonstrated throughout the book of Acts. Charged with making disciples of all nations, the first Christians found that the nations were already "extremely religious in every respect" (Acts 17:22). Far from sitting idly by, waiting for someone to bring them religion, the nations of the world even had state religions, thus making Christian gospel proclamation not just unpopular but potentially a criminal endeavor. Nevertheless, Christian missionaries in Acts, notably Paul, the apostle to the Gentiles, did not hesitate to proclaim the gospel of Christ to the world. N. T. Wright describes the heart of Paul's message and strategy to the Gentiles:

> At the heart of his polemical engagement with paganism was a radical and deep-rooted affirmation of the goodness of the created world, and, with that, of the possibility that pagans, and their ideas and beliefs, could be redeemed by the Christ through whom the world was made in the first place. Hence, good news for the pagans; not the sort of good news that told them they were more or less all right as they were, but the sort of good news which told them that, though they were at present going about things in a totally wrong way, the God who made them loved them and longed to remake them.[115]

Paul described the condition of non-Christians as being "ignorant" (Gal 4:8; 1 Thess 4:5) and "separated from Christ, alienated from the commonwealth of Israel and strangers to the covenants of promise, having no hope and without God in the world" (Eph 2:12 ESV). This condition does not imply that non-Christians are as bad as they can possibly be, nor does it mean there is no vestige of truth in the theology and practice of religious others. There is true knowledge of God through general revelation (Rom 1:19–21). The problem is that the darkened thinking of non-Christians reflects an absence of the gospel and saving grace.[116] Humanity's rejection of the one true God has resulted in their hearts becoming dark and their thinking becoming futile. That is, the very center of human personhood, the seat of human reasoning, thought, and will, "has become devoid of life and truth."[117] What knowledge they do have from creation and conscience is suppressed and distorted (Rom 1:18). For this reason Paul could affirm

---

[115]N. T. Wright, *What Saint Paul Really Said: Was Paul of Tarsus the Real Founder of Christianity?* (Grand Rapids: Eerdmans, 1997), 81.

[116]B. Demarest, "General and Special Revelation: Epistemological Foundations of Religious Pluralism," in *One God, One Lord*, ed. Clarke and Winter, 206.

[117]E. J. Schnabel, "Other Religions: Saving or Secular," in *Faith Comes by Hearing: A Response to Inclusivism*, ed. Morgan and Peterson, 104.

true knowledge of God by pagans in some texts and still refer to them as ignorant, without hope and without God.

Paul's typical practice upon entering a new city was to preach to Jews and God fearers in the local synagogue, but that did not mean he was unconcerned to make a gospel appeal to Gentiles. Paul's message to the Gentiles in Lystra was to turn from idols to the living God (Acts 14:15). His encounter with the demonic in Philippi resulted in his imprisonment, which gave him the opportunity to tell the Philippian jailer, "Believe on the Lord Jesus, and you will be saved" (Acts 16:31). Paul confronted Epicureanism and Stoicism while in Athens, a city "full of idols," and proclaimed the resurrection of Jesus with such determination that he was brought before the Areopagus, accused of being a "preacher of foreign deities" (Acts 17:16–18). Christ's victory over the demonic in Ephesus was so compelling that many Ephesian pagans feared that their worship (and related profits) was at risk. Meanwhile, the name of the Lord Jesus was magnified among the Ephesians (Acts 19:11–34).

Paul's strategy for engaging the Jews and pagans could be described as dialogical, but like Jesus, Paul did not dialogue to learn but to create opportunities for his apostolic witness. We must be clear that the content of Paul's theology and gospel message was not informed by dialogue with religious others. According to Paul, while all people have knowledge of the one true God through general revelation, the religious practices of religious others were the result of suppression of the truth, a refusal to honor God or to be thankful, and the exchange of God's glory for images of created things (Rom 1:19–23). Some may argue that Paul's quotation of prominent Greek poets, Epimenides and Aratus, in his Areopagus address is evidence that his understanding of God was enhanced by his interaction with religious others (Acts 17:28).[118] But it is far more likely that Paul's quotations were an *ad hoc* attempt to create a point of contact with his audience rather than to give credit to pagan poets for completing his theology. The points Paul raised in his citation of the poets are basic to his Jewish background, involving humanity's relationship with their Creator and subsequent dependence upon God for life and all things. These are lessons more clearly explicated in the Law, the Prophets, and the Writings and were

---

[118]See, for example, Pinnock, *A Wideness in God's Mercy*, 139; G. R. McDermott, *Can Evangelicals Learn from World Religions? Jesus, Revelation & Religious Traditions* (Downers Grove, IL: InterVarsity, 2000), 80–81.

part of the lifeblood of Paul's Jewish and then Christian worldview. Any learning on Paul's part that arose from dialogue contributed to his ability to contextualize the gospel and to be "all things to all people" (1 Cor 9:22).

New Testament Monotheism

As discussed earlier, the primary distinctives of Old Testament theology were monotheism and the Creator-creature distinction. The New Testament proclamation of Christ maintained both these distinctives, including a strident dedication to monotheism. Given the complexities of the Trinity, the early church might more easily have affirmed some sort of bi-theism or tri-theism, but commitment to the truth of monotheism would not allow for that. Judaism was seen in the Greco-Roman world as being intolerant of the Greek and Roman pantheon of gods, which provoked the charge of atheism against the Jews and early Christians for their refusal to accept the reality of other gods.[119]

Jewish monotheism was one of the primary presuppositions of Paul's thoughts about God, and it guided his polemic against the inappropriate ways the Lord was conceived of and worshipped.[120] Monotheism, among other things, motivated Paul's missionary activity. Because there is only one God, then He must necessarily be the God of the Gentiles also (Rom 3:28–30). The Lord cannot be the one God if He is only the God of Israel.[121] Paul took the words of the Septuagint version of the Shema (*kurios ho theos hēmōn kurios heis estin*) and inserted Jesus into the middle of it. Deuteronomy 6:4 reads, "The LORD our God, the LORD is one." In the context of teaching the Corinthians how to live faithfully in a pagan society, Paul taught that "for us there is one God" (1 Cor 8:6), repeating the typical Jewish monotheistic formula. But he glossed *theos* with "the Father, from whom are all things, and we for Him," and then glossed *kurios heis estin* with "one Lord, Jesus Christ, through whom are all things, and we through Him."[122] In this passage the only way to maintain monotheism is to affirm that Jesus Christ is the Lord, that is, Jesus is all that is affirmed of the Lord in the Shema.[123]

---

[119]Josephus, *Ap.* 2.148.
[120]J. Dunn, *The Theology of Paul the Apostle* (Grand Rapids: Eerdmans, 2006), 33.
[121]Bauckham, "Biblical Theology and the Problems of Monotheism," 219.
[122]So N. T. Wright, *Paul: In Fresh Perspective* (Minneapolis: Fortress, 2005), 94.
[123]Bauckham, "Biblical Theology and the Problems of Monotheism," 224–26.

Supremacy of Jesus   The gospel hinges on the deity of Jesus Christ. For this reason the New Testament authors insisted that Jesus was in fact the one unique God. The Gospel of John begins with the affirmation that Jesus, the Word, was with God and was God (John 1:1) and that He is "the only God, who is at the Father's side" and makes the Father known (John 1:18 ESV). The Son of God was credited with creation of the universe, an act for which only God can be credited (John 1:3; Col 1:16). Jesus was accused of blasphemy for forgiving sins (Mark 2:7) and "calling God His own Father, making Himself equal with God" (John 5:18). Jesus claimed that if you had seen Him, you had seen the Father (John 14:9). Jesus was called "God" (John 20:28). Perhaps most convincingly, Jesus, a strong Jewish monotheist who knew that worship was to go to the Lord God alone (Deut. 6:13; cf. Matt. 4:10), accepted worship (Matt 14:33; 28:9,17; Luke 24:52; John 9:38).[124]

Arguments for the deity of Christ are essential in a Christian theology of religions because if Christ is uniquely and fully God, then He is the God before whom all the peoples of the world are accountable. His claims to be the only way to reconciliation with the Father take on a finality that is formidable. The arguments cannot be sustained in the face of the deity of Christ.[125] The book of Hebrews asserts that Jesus is the supreme and final revelation of God (Heb 1:1–4). This speaks decisively against all later prophets, be they Muhammad or Joseph Smith, who claim to have further revelation from God that sets aside or contradicts the revelation of God in Christ. Andreas Köstenberger rightly asks, "How can anyone, in the light of the assertions made in Hebrews 1:1–2, claim to provide divine revelation beyond Christ without being subject to the charge of blasphemy?"[126]

The New Testament and Other Gods   Given the New Testament commitment to monotheism, what of the existence of other gods? The questions surrounding the Old Testament regarding monotheism or henotheism do not exist in the New Testament. Though some may assert that ontological monotheism is an Enlightenment category, the teaching of the New Testament is clear. There is only one God and

---

[124] See R. M. Bowman Jr. and J. E. Komoszewski, *Putting Jesus in His Place: The Case for the Deity of Christ* (Grand Rapids: Kregel, 2007) for a strong defense of the deity of Christ.

[125] So Köstenberger, "Contribution of the General Epistles and Revelation to a Biblical Theology of Religions," 126.

[126] Ibid., 118.

claims to deity by any others are necessarily and categorically false. Paul reminded the Christians in Galatia that before being saved by Christ, they "did not know God," and they were "enslaved to those that by nature are not gods" (Gal 4:8 ESV). Anyone other than the Lord that is worshipped is referred to by Paul as a "so-called god," including the man of lawlessness (2 Thess 2:4; cf. Rev 14:9–11; 16:1–2). Paul's reference to "so-called gods" in 1 Cor 8:5 is even more emphatic: "There is no God but one" (1 Cor 8:4).

As in the Old Testament, though the conclusion of the New Testament is that there is no one like the Lord, other gods do "exist" in the subjective experience of pagan thought. This explains Paul's use of the term "so-called." The inhabitants of Lystra clearly believed in at least the possibility of other gods because they were quick to attribute deity to Paul and Barnabus—even naming them Hermes and Zeus respectively (Acts 14:8–13). Non-Christians in Corinth apparently attributed deity to things or beings "in heaven and on earth," but this attribution, though popular in the pagan worldview, was erroneous.[127] Paul's phrase, "yet for us there is one God" (1 Cor 8:6) makes clear that the Christian community was to remain faithful and steadfast, even in their pluralistic context, and never ascribe deity to anything or anyone other than the one God, known in the Father and the Son.

Idolatry in the New Testament

Since there are no other gods, except in the subjective experience of pagan worshippers, then there is no divine reality behind the idols that they are meant to represent. The prohibition against idolatry in the New Testament is unchanged from that of the Old Testament: idolatry is expressly forbidden. Idol worship is condemned throughout the book of Acts in both the narratives (14:8–20; 19:23–41) and the sermons (7:41–43; 17:29–31). Idolatry is derided as foolish (1 Cor 12:2) and condemned as being characteristic of the pagans (1 Pet 4:3–5). It is included in lists of grievous sins (1 Cor 5:10–13; Gal 5:19–21) and will earn the wrath of God (Rom 1:18–32). Idolaters will not enter the kingdom of God (1 Cor 6:9; Eph 5:5–6; Rev 22:15) but instead will be thrown into the lake of fire (Rev 21:8). Christians are warned to flee from and to guard themselves against idolatry (1 Cor 10:14–22;

---

[127]B. Winter, "In Public and in Private: Early Christians and Religious Pluralism," in *One God, One Lord*, ed. Clarke and Winter, 144.

1 John 5:21). The same polemic used by the Old Testament prophets is taken up by John in the book of Revelation. Idols are not able to see, hear, or walk because they are the work of human hands (Rev 9:20). Further, the idolatry of Israel's past was used to warn the Corinthians against sexual immorality (1 Cor 10:6–12).

The New Testament does not simply rehearse the warnings of the Old Testament. Rather, the condemnation against idolatry is expanded and explained. Paul traced idolatry back to the refusal to glorify God. All people have true knowledge of God through creation and innate knowledge of God through reason and conscience, but that knowledge is suppressed and distorted (Rom 1:18–20). Once humanity's knowledge was severed from God's lordship, "their thinking became nonsense, and their senseless minds were darkened" (Rom 1:21). Seeking to create substitutes for the true God, they engage in the great exchange: the glory of God for idolatry (Rom 1:23).[128] So fundamental is idolatry to rebellion against God that Paul is able to state that all things worldly, including "sexual immorality, impurity, lust, evil desire, and greed," are ultimately idolatry (Col 3:5–6). Idolatry is not just one sin but is the "defining feature of the heathen" whose way of life is characterized by distortion, ignorance, and sin.[129] Further, just like the Old Testament, the New Testament makes explicit the connection between the worship of idols and the worship of demons.

Satan and Demons   The New Testament, coinciding with the advent of Jesus Christ, sees a dramatic rise in the activity of Satan, the demonic, and unclean spirits. Whereas the Hebrew term *śāṭān* for "adversary" is used 17 times in the Old Testament when referring to Satan (14 times in Job 1–2, twice in Zech 3:1–2, and in 1 Chr 21:1),[130] in the New Testament the Greek term *diabolos*, "slanderer," occurs 36 times and *satanas*, "Satan," also 36 times. Satan is also referred to descriptively with such terms as "the evil one" (e.g., Eph 6:16; 1 John 5:18–19), "the prince of the power of the air" (Eph 2:2 ESV),

---

[128]G. Bray, "God," 511. See also T. Schreiner, *Paul, Apostle of God's Glory in Christ: A Pauline Theology* (Downers Grove, IL: InterVarsity, 2001), 105.

[129]Rosner, "Idolatry," 570.

[130]The Hebrew word *śāṭān* is not a name but a common noun, preceded by the article "the," except in 1 Chr 21:1. Goldingay notes, "'The adversary' is not a supernatural being with power over against Yhwh. His authority is strictly circumscribed. He can accuse, but he cannot judge (Zechariah 3). He can tempt, but he cannot overwhelm; he requires human cooperation (1 Chronicles 21). He can test but only within boundaries that God allows (Job 1–2)." *Old Testament Theology*, 55.

a "murderer" (John 8:44), "the accuser of our brothers" (Rev 12:10), and "the god of this age" (2 Cor 4:4). Whereas Satan is described sparingly in the Old Testament, the description of Satan and his activities is significantly developed in the New Testament. Satan is the ruler of the present evil world system (Matt 4:8–10; Acts 26:18; 2 Cor 4:4; 1 John 5:19) and the demonic forces (Matt 12:24; Rev 12:7–9). He desires to thwart the gospel (Matt 13:19,38–39; 2 Cor 4:4; 1 Thess 2:18) and to tempt God's people to sin (Luke 4:1–13; 1 Cor 7:5; 2 Cor 2:11; Eph 4:26–27; 6:10–20; 1 Tim 3:7). Satan has the ability to bring about sickness (Luke 13:10–17), oppression (Mark 5:1–20; 1 Cor 5:5), and death (Heb 2:14). He can also enter and possess individuals (Luke 22:3–4; cf. John 13:2,27; Acts 5:3). He is the accuser of God's people (Rev 12:10), a murderer (John 8:44), and a liar (Matt 24:24; 2 Cor 11:3; Rev 12:9). The devil is an enemy of the gospel and attempted to derail the redemptive purposes of God by turning Jesus, the Lord's Messiah, to idolatry in the desert (Matt 4:1–11). Satan played a role in Peter's attempt to discourage Jesus from traveling the path of the cross (Mark 8:32–33), sought to "sift" the Lord's disciples (Luke 22:31), and "entered" Judas before the betrayal of Jesus (John 13:27).

The Gospels portray Satan as an enemy of Christ, but the narratives do not allow us to conclude that Satan is in any way equal to the Lord. As in the book of Job, Satan's activities are circumscribed by the sovereign permission of God (Luke 22:31–32). Jesus withstood every temptation of the devil (Luke 4:13), and He "watched Satan fall from heaven like a lightning flash" (Luke 10:18). Jesus has authority over Satan (Matt 4:10) and is able to give that authority to His disciples (Luke 10:19). The result is that God "will soon crush Satan under" the feet of those who follow the Lord (Rom 16:20).

Although the term *angel* (literally, "messenger") is sometimes used of evil spiritual beings (Matt 25:41; Rev 12:9), the more common designation for these evil powers is *demon* or *unclean spirit*.[131] Demons are spiritual beings (Matt 25:41; Eph 6:12; Rev 12:9) with intelligence (Matt 8:28–29; Mark 1:24,34), emotion (Matt 8:28–29; James 2:19), and will (Matt 8:31; 2 Pet 2:4). But they are morally evil beings (Matt 10:1; Luke 7:21) that are doctrinally corrupt and deceitful (1 Tim 4:1–3; James 3:15), cruel and hurtful (Matt 17:14–18;

---

[131] The Greek term *daimonion* appears 60 times in the New Testament, all but eight of these in the Gospels, and *daimon* appears five times, three of these in the Gospels.

Mark 5:1–5), and powerful (Mark 5:1–5; Acts 19:14–16). Their primary activity is to advance the purposes of Satan (Matt 12:24; 25:41; Rev 12:7–9). This is accomplished through the promotion of idolatry and the worship of demons (1 Cor 10:20; Rev 9:20), the promotion of false teaching (1 Tim 4:1–3; 1 John 4:1–4), and the performance of false signs and wonders (2 Thess 2:8–10; Rev 13:12–15).

Jesus secured the defeat of Satan and his demons at the cross (John 12:31; Col 2:15; 1 John 3:8), and though the full manifestation of that defeat remains future, it is certain (Rom 16:20; Rev 12:7–17; 20:7–10). Satan and his demons will never be offered salvation (Heb 2:16) but will be judged by redeemed humans (1 Cor 6:3). Their destiny during the millennial reign of Christ is the abyss (Rev 20:1–3; cf. Luke 8:31), and their final destiny is the "eternal fire" (Matt 25:41), the "lake of fire" where "they will be tormented day and night forever and ever" (Rev 20:10).

The Gospels record numerous encounters between Jesus and demons. During the ministry of Jesus, demons oppressed people (Matt 4:24; 8:28–33; Mark 1:32; 7:25–26; Luke 4:31–37), causing such physical maladies as dumbness (Matt 9:32), blindness (Matt 12:22), deformity (Luke 13:11), and seizures (Matt 17:14–21). Demonic activity was so common that people explained the incredible phenomena surrounding John (Matt 11:18) and Jesus (Matt 9:34; John 8:48–52; 10:20–21) by accusing them of having demons. Those who were demonized may have possessed superhuman strength (Luke 8:26–29). Many times the demonized attempted to reveal the true identity of Jesus, displaying supernatural knowledge (Luke 4:34; 8:28). Jesus, the Son of God and Spirit-anointed One, apparently not wanting the testimony of unclean spirits, silenced the demons with a word and delivered those who were possessed with a command.

The authority of Jesus Christ over the demonic has continued into the church age as demonstrated in the book of Acts. The strategy of the demonic during the formative years of the church was directed against the gospel. At times the attack was indirect. Simon Magus and the sons of Sceva attempted to co-opt the power of the gospel (Acts 8:9–24; 19:13–16). While Paul and Silas were in Philippi, a slave girl who had a "spirit of prediction" followed them, desiring to discredit the gospel (Acts 16:16–18). At other times the demonic attack against the gospel was more direct, as when Elymas attempted to "turn the proconsul away from the faith" (Acts 13:8).[132]

The response of the apostles to the demonic is instructive for a biblical theology of religions. In the book of Acts, there were numerous power encounters between the apostles and the demonic (Acts 8:7–13; 13:6–12; 16:16–18; 19:13–16). Nevertheless, in his narratives Luke makes only oblique references relating the activity of demons to human religious practices. The general call in the book of Acts is to "turn from darkness to light and from the power of Satan to God" (Acts 26:18). Paul makes connections between the demonic and human religiosity that are far more explicit. He clearly believed that Satan and his demons had an ontological reality and were intensely active to capture people's minds and hearts and to keep them from the gospel of Christ and devotion to Him (2 Cor 4:4; 11:3,13–15; Eph 2:2; 6:12–17; 1 Thess 3:5; 1 Tim 3:7; 5:15). The activity of Satan could be found in temple banquets (1 Cor 10:19–21), magic (Gal 5:20), human philosophy (Col 2:4,8) and false doctrine (1 Tim 4:1–3).[133] Bent on evil, destruction, and hostility toward God, Satan is still under the sovereign control of God; and his actions ultimately serve the redemptive purposes of the Lord (1 Cor 5:5; 1 Tim 1:20).

Demons and Idols   The Old Testament is clear that worship of idols is actually the worship of demons. The New Testament expands on the tie between idolatry and the demonic. Gentiles, who are characterized by idolatry (Rom 1:22–25), must have their eyes opened so they may turn from the "power of Satan to God" (Acts 26:18). Clearly referring to Deut 32:16–21, Paul warned the Corinthian church to flee from idolatry because to offer sacrifices at a pagan altar is to offer sacrifices to a demon (1 Cor 10:14–22). Though what idol worshippers believe the idol represents, a god, does not exist; demons exploit their fantastic but culpable ignorance so that what they are actually worshipping is a demon.[134] The only reference in the New Testament to the Lord's jealousy is explicitly tied to idolatry (1 Cor 10:22). As repeated over and over in the Old Testament, idolatry provokes the Lord's jealousy. Paul had to warn the Corinthians of the dread seriousness of their

---

[132]Larkin, "Contribution of the Gospels," 84.

[133]D. Howell, "The Apostle Paul and First Century Religious Pluralism," in *Christianity and the Religions,* ed. Rommen and Netland, 104–5.

[134]See Bauckham, "Biblical Theology and the Problems of Monotheism," 221. See also Dunn, *The Theology of Paul the Apostle,* 37.

idolatrous actions. You cannot provoke God's jealousy with impunity. Brazen worship of demons through idolatry is characteristic of the last days and will bring about the certain white-hot wrath of the Lord (Rev 9:20).

Confrontation with Idolatry Paul's interaction with idolatry was necessarily set in a pluralistic environment. What we find in the narratives of Acts and the teaching in Paul's letters is a consistent message of the condemnation of idolatry and a plea for his listeners to turn from idolatry to the living God. As demonstrated earlier, idolatry spawns wickedness and is the defining feature of the heathen. Idolaters will be judged with wrath and eternal torment. However, the tone of his evangelistic encounters differs dramatically from that of his letters to the churches.

In Lystra, Paul was horrified that he should be worshipped as a god and beseeched the inhabitants to turn from "worthless things to the living God, who made the heaven, the earth, the sea, and everything in them" (Acts 14:15). He offered the gospel to the people of Lystra, reminding them of the merciful provision and revelation of God (Acts 14:16–17). While in Athens, Paul's spirit was "troubled" when he saw the city "full of idols" (Acts 17:16). His response was to reason in the synagogue and marketplaces, "telling the good news about Jesus and the resurrection" (v. 18). The tenor of his Areopagus address is one of explanation, not condemnation, though he does speak of a judgment to come and calls the Athenians to repent (vv. 30–31). Paul's stand in Ephesus against idolatry was clear. Idolatry is absurd because "gods made by hand are not gods" (Acts 19:26). In these encounters with idolatry, Paul presented the gospel and undercut the notion of idolatry without denigrating the idolaters or disparaging the particulars of their religious activity.[135] Whereas Paul's letters to established believers treat idolatry as rebellion, his evangelistic efforts treat idolatry as ignorant and foolish.[136]

Paul's counsel to the Corinthians regarding meat sacrificed to idols in 1 Corinthians 8 and 10 is particularly helpful. In these passages Paul advised the Corinthians how to live in a manner that honors Christ in the context of religious pluralism and idolatry. Most of the meat sold

---

[135]Larkin, "The Contribution of the Gospels," 76.

[136]Wright summarizes, "Paul could excoriate idolatry as 'a lie' before his Christian readers, but did not blaspheme Artemis before her pagan worshipers." Wright, *Mission of God*, 182.

in the marketplaces of Corinth had first been offered on pagan altars as sacrifices to some "so-called gods" (8:5). Temples therefore served as the focal points for religious, social, and even economic life. This situation presented an enormous dilemma for the Corinthian Christian because the lines that separated idolatry and the most basic social functions were virtually indistinguishable.[137]

Paul first addressed participation in pagan feasts (1 Cor 8:1–13; 10:1–22) and then turned his attention to meat sold in the marketplace (1 Cor 10:23–30).[138] He began by stating that the deities represented by the idols have no real ontological existence (1 Cor 8:4; cf. 12:2). To the extent that gods and idols do exist, they exist solely in the subjective experience of the pagan who gives allegiance and worships them. These gods and idols do not have the divine existence of the biblical God (1 Cor 8:5–6). The problem is that the phenomenological existence of idols is so powerful in the "weak" Christian that his conscience can be injured by eating meat at the pagan feasts (1 Cor 8:7–10). Ultimately the weak Christian can be "ruined" by the actions of those who know that idols are nothing (1 Cor 8:11).

The same issues are raised in the context of eating food sold in the marketplace. The Christian is free to eat because the Lord, the one God, owns everything, including the meat set before the Christian, regardless of whether it had been offered to an idol (1 Cor 10:25–26). The issues are ethical, and Paul's concern was for the weaker brother, but his counsel for living as a Christian in the context of idolatry was completely consistent with the biblical testimony concerning idols. There is only one God, the Lord, the Creator of heaven and earth. There is no divine reality behind the idol, but there is a subjective reality in the mind and heart of the one who ascribes reality to the so-called god. The Christian ought to flee idolatry because to participate in pagan sacrifices is ultimately to participate in the worship of demons.

Paul's Interaction with Religious Others

To this point, we have looked at what the Bible says on issues that are significant to the development of a Christian theology of religions, including religious others, monotheism, and idolatry. The Christian Scriptures were written in the context of religious pluralism, so it is

---

[137] So Howell, "The Apostle Paul and First Century Religious Pluralism," 100–1.

[138] So G. D. Fee, *The First Epistle to the Corinthians*, NICNT (Grand Rapids: Eerdmans, 1987), 475–76.

instructive to see the theology of the apostles worked out in their evangelistic encounters in the book of Acts.[139] Paul's theology regarding the position and plight of the Gentiles apart from Christ is not hopeful. Gentiles are "dead in trespasses and sins," are "by nature children of wrath," and live under the thrall of the world, the flesh, and the devil (Eph 2:1–3 NKJV). They serve idols, rather than the living God (1 Thess 1:9), and are blinded by Satan (2 Cor 4:1–4). Gentiles are "separated from Christ, alienated from the commonwealth of Israel and strangers to the covenants of promise, having no hope and without God in the world" (Eph 2:12 ESV).

Although Gentiles do not have the Law, the special revelation of God, they are guilty before God because they have ignored general revelation. In the first two chapters of Romans, Paul spelled out his convictions on the epistemological, ethical, and eschatological state of the Gentiles, and these convictions guided Paul in his evangelistic encounters with the Gentiles. All people everywhere have true knowledge of God (Rom 1:18–19,21; 2:14). They know that God exists; they know of His "eternal power and divine nature" (1:20). Gentiles also know that they ought to behave in a certain way in light of those truths. They ought to glorify God, be thankful, and give God their obedience (1:20–21). Instead, sinful hearts continually suppress the knowledge of God (1:18). They know that they are accountable to this God and that their disobedient actions warrant death (1:32; 2:15). When that judgment does not come, it is because God is kind and patient and is providing time for repentance (2:4). One must remember that these were Paul's convictions that drove his gospel proclamation in the book of Acts.

Paul's evangelistic encounters with pagans were marked by respectful confrontation.[140] His typical missionary practice upon entering a

---

[139]For example, D. Howell writes, "Paul's dismay at Athens as a city 'full of idols' (Acts 17:16) and his perception of the Athenian philosophers as 'in every way very religious' (Acts 17:22) could apply equally to many of the major cities and their inhabitants to whom he introduced the Christian gospel—Tarsus, Syrian Antioch, Pisidian Antioch, Philippi, Thessalonica, Corinth and Ephesus. In the multi-cultural city of Corinth, for example, worshippers streamed to the temples of Apollo, Tyche, goddess of good fortune, Aphrodite, goddess of love and fertility, Poseidon, the sea god, and to the sanctuaries of Asclepius, the god of healing, the Greek mystery cult of Demeter and Kore, and the Egyptian mystery cults of Isis and of Sarapis." Howell, "The Apostle Paul and First Century Religious Pluralism," 92–93.

[140]N. T. Wright suggests that Paul confronted his pagan audience at six levels: (1) Paul offered the reality of the true God who created everything. (2) Paul offered a challenge at the level of cultic and religious practice. (3) Paul offered a challenge to paganism at the level of power and empire. (4) Paul set out a way of being truly human. (5) Paul provided a true metanarrative that

new city was to go to the synagogue and reason from the Scriptures that Jesus is the Christ (Acts 17:2–3). In both Acts 14 and Acts 17, Paul addressed Gentile audiences that were ignorant of the Hebrew Scriptures and redemptive history. But he did not appeal to some sort of common ground or proclaim a gospel different from that which he proclaimed to the Jews and God fearers in the synagogues. Paul did appeal to general revelation, but that does not mean he abandoned the biblical-theological categories of the gospel.[141] To do so would drain the gospel not only of its context but also of its meaning. Instead, Paul had to appeal to general revelation to bring his audience up to speed quickly. He had to present to his listeners the biblical categories necessary for the gospel to make sense. In particular, Paul taught that God is the Creator; God is the independent and self-sufficient sustainer of all life; God is sovereign over the nations; God is self-disclosing; and humanity is sinful and rebellious. Without these fundamental truths that challenged the pagan peoples at the core of their worldview, the gospel message of the life, death, resurrection, ascension, and return of Christ does not make any sense. With these truths, the gospel not only makes sense; it is absolutely necessary.

Paul and Barnabas at Lystra   After healing a man in Lystra who had been lame from birth, Paul and Barnabas were hailed as the gods Hermes and Zeus, prompting the priest of Zeus to begin preparations to offer sacrifices to the two horrified missionaries (Acts 14:8–13). Significantly, Paul and Barnabas did not appeal to the Lystrans as fellow seekers after God but as fellow humans who had to repent. The two Christians protested that they were mere mortals and urged the people of Lystra to turn from idolatry to the living God (Acts 14:15). Presenting a clear challenge to the pagan worldview, Paul and Barnabas identified the living God as the Creator of all things, an implicit argument for monotheism in the Old Testament tradition. This God demonstrated His sovereignty over the nations in that He had "allowed" them to "walk in their own ways" (Acts 14:16 ESV). The Lystrans had not sought after the true God. Rather, it was God who had sought the people of Lystra by leaving Himself a "witness," specifically, His

---

undercut pagan mythology. (6) Paul offered a challenge to the pagan philosophies of the world. *What Saint Paul Really Said,* 86–92.

[141] See D. A. Carson, *The Gagging of God: Christianity Confronts Pluralism* (Grand Rapids: Zondervan, 1996), 496–501.

providential care and benevolent blessing toward the Lystrans.[142] On this basis Paul and Barnabas urged the people of Lystra to repent and turn to the living God. To turn from the "worthless things" to the one sovereign Creator meant that the Lystrans would have to reject the pluralistic ideology of many gods and the practice of idolatry.[143] This message and call to repentance Paul summed up as being "good news" (Acts 14:15).

Paul at Athens   The narrative of Paul's evangelistic efforts in Athens provides the best example of a gospel encounter in a pluralistic context in the Bible, so it should be the object of careful study by those seeking to minister in post-Christian, postmodern, and pluralistic contexts. The Athenian world was pluralistic; the Athenians were well-versed in philosophy and the latest trends, but they were biblically illiterate. Paul was not able to assume any knowledge from Scripture on the part of his audience, so he had to develop the necessary biblical categories, usually from general revelation, for the gospel to make sense.[144]

Paul arrived in Athens after being chased out of Thessalonica, and he waited there for Silas and Timothy. Athens was one of the primary intellectual centers in the Greco-Roman world, leading the way in architecture, literature, science, and philosophy. But as Paul surveyed the city, "his spirit was provoked within him" because the city was "full of idols" (Acts 17:16 ESV). The city contained about 30,000 idols by reasonable estimates.[145] Far from regarding the idols as merely beautiful works of art and culture (as some might wrongly be inclined), Paul was outraged at the thought of so many held captive by idolatry and was thus compelled to reason in the synagogue and in the marketplace "every day with those who happened to be there" (v. 17). In doing so, he entered into a dispute with two significant worldviews of the day: Epicureanism and Stoicism.

Epicureans were naturalistic in their thinking, believing that all of life was dependent on the random interaction of atoms, just molecules in motion. Therefore, humans should pursue pleasure (hedonism),

---

[142]B. Winter notes, "There is a silent witness of God in his good works. That goodness is reflected in his activity aimed at satisfying men's needs. He did this in order to bring joy to their hearts." "In Public and in Private," 130.

[143]Ibid., 142.

[144]G. Beale notes the strong continuity between Paul's speech in Athens and Isaiah 42. See "Other Religions in New Testament Theology," in *Biblical Faith and Other Religions: An Evangelical Assessment*, ed. Baker, 84ff.

[145]Demarest, "General and Special Revelation," 192–93.

particularly if it was constituted by detachment from pain, passion, and fear. The "gods," if they existed, were remote and uninterested in interfering in the affairs of men. Stoics were panentheistic, believing that "God" was an all-pervasive world soul. Stoics were also fatalistic. History was caught in an eternal cycle of existing, being destroyed through conflagration, then beginning again, only to repeat the same pattern again down to the smallest details of human life. Because people were caught in a cycle that could not be changed, they had to resign themselves to trying to live in harmony with nature and reason. People could not control the circumstances of their lives, but what they could control was their reaction to their circumstances and fate by pursuing their duty.

The Athenians' reaction to the gospel was mixed. Some accused him of being a "babbler" (literally, "seed-picker"), a derogatory term reserved for those who ignorantly peddled ideas they collected from various places (v. 18a ESV).[146] Others accused him of preaching "foreign gods," a most serious charge given that it was the grounds for the condemnation of Socrates. The basis for this charge was Paul's proclamation of Jesus and the resurrection (v. 18b). Some were curious, wanting to hear more of the "new teaching" (vv. 19–20). Luke describes the Athenians as spending their time "in nothing except telling or hearing something new" (v. 21 ESV). Clearly they were a "tolerant" and "open-minded" people! So Paul was brought before the Areopagus, the old court in Athens with jurisdiction over all things moral, religious, and civil.

Paul's Areopagus address is a model for respectful confrontation with pagan cultures. He was simultaneously courteous and bold.[147] Paul established a point of contact with them through his earlier observation of an altar on which was inscribed "To an unknown God" (v. 23). But his mention of the altar was not an appeal to common ground between the two of them. The point of contact is human ignorance. The Athenians were "extremely religious in every respect" (v. 22), but Paul's purpose was to oppose their worldview and confront their ignorance and superstition by proclaiming the one true God. The irony of

---

[146] See BDAG on *spermologō*.

[147] Ajith Fernando describes it as a twofold attitude. "On the one hand there is firm belief in the wrongness of life apart from Christ. On the other hand there is a respect for all individuals because they are intelligent human beings endowed by God with the privilege and responsibility of choosing to accept or reject the gospel. This caused Paul to reason with them about the truth of God." *The Christian's Attitude Toward World Religions* (Wheaton: Tyndale House, 1987), 26.

the narrative is rich. Paul was brought before a group of learned men to be examined, but Paul began by emphasizing their ignorance.

Paul's proclamation of God began with a transition from neuter pronouns—"What [*ho*] you worship in ignorance, this [*touto*] I proclaim to you"—to masculine pronouns—"He [*houtos*] is Lord of heaven and earth" (vv. 23–24). This demonstrates that Paul was not going to proclaim to them simply the identity of one whom they worshipped in ignorance. There is no basis for contending that religious others, who are seeking God but do not know His name, are in a saving relationship with God. Rather, Paul argued from that which the Athenian god represents, namely, human ignorance, to that which the gospel makes known, specifically the God and Father of Jesus Christ.[148] Paul described the God of whom the Athenians were ignorant by laying a theological foundation he derived from the pages of Genesis. He began by establishing the Creator-creature distinction. God is the Creator; He made the world and everything in it. Contrary to Epicurean thought the universe is not the result of blind chance, and matter is not eternal. Nor is God part of the world, the evolution of the world Spirit, as the Stoics taught. Rather, the universe was created by a personal and sovereign God. Paul began by confronting and denying the most basic aspect of the Epicurean and Stoic worldviews by positing the essential truth that God is God and all that He created is not. The Creator-creature distinction entails that God is transcendent and enjoys Creator's rights over all that He made. He has the right to be obeyed, and His creation is obligated to honor Him. This was an entirely different worldview because the Greeks did not believe they were ethically responsible to the gods.

Paul then taught that God is utterly independent because He is completely self-sufficient. He has no needs that have to be met by humans. Rather, God gives to His creation "life and breath and all things" (Acts 17:25). God does not need humanity and cannot be bribed because He needs nothing. The Greeks viewed the gods as being dependent upon humanity to meet their needs. The gods had to be satisfied in order to evoke a blessing from them. But this was not true of the God Paul proclaimed. The God who is the independent Creator is sovereign over the nations (v. 26). Paul's language was strong and confrontational.

---

[148] So Larkin, "Contribution of the Gospels," 82–83.

God "determined" and "appointed" the times and boundaries whereby every nation lives.

The sovereign God is also a self-disclosing God (vv. 27–28). The purpose of His control over the affairs of human history is "so that" people might seek Him. Paul's expression of God's purpose, "in the hope that they might feel their way toward him and find him" (v. 27 ESV), indicates blind groping. The point is that sin's intervention has rendered humanity blind in their search for God.[149] The problem is not God's revelation. The problem is human sin, for which humanity alone is responsible and culpable. God is self-revealing, and humanity cannot escape knowledge of Him. Even the pagan poets, Epimenides and Aratus, with all their bogus ideologies and false ideas and despite their active suppression of truth, could not rid themselves of God's powerful and meaningful revelation. God will not be shut out of His world! Paul's message was confrontational at this point. The problem for the Athenians was not that their "unknown" God was silent or hiding. Rather, God had revealed Himself, and the Athenians had suppressed that revelation. The Athenians may have been ignorant, but it was a culpable ignorance. Ultimately God may have been unknown to the Athenians but not because He is silent or hard to find. The problem was that the Athenians did not want to know God. And for that they were guilty.

Only after teaching the Athenians on the nature and actions of God did Paul turn to the implications for humanity. His understanding of humanity in his gospel proclamation is theocentric rather than cultural, sociological, or anthropological. Given who God is, who humanity is, and what humanity has done in response to God's governance and revelation, why does He allow humanity to live in idolatry and open defiance without bringing swift judgment against them? Paul's response includes four critical aspects. (1) God overlooked ignorance in the past; (2) now people everywhere are commanded to repent; (3) the call to repentance is urgent because a day of judgment is coming; and (4) God has validated Jesus as judge by raising Him from the dead.[150] Each aspect of Paul's response is crucial for constructing a theology of religions.

The first phrase of v. 30 ("Therefore, having overlooked the times of ignorance") is a difficult passage to interpret, and theologians and

---

[149]Ibid.
[150]A. Fernando, *Acts,* NIVAC (Grand Rapids: Zondervan, 1998), 476.

biblical exegetes differ on its meaning. Paul began his Aeropagus address by underscoring the ignorance of the Athenians. He ends his address by returning to the same theme. Previously, the Athenians had lived in "times of ignorance" which God had overlooked. The verb *huperoraō* means "overlook," "ignore," or, negatively, "scorn."[151] In context, it probably means that God had not judged the Athenians' idolatry as severely as He might have (cf. Acts 14:16; Rom 1:18–23; 3:25).[152] Paul's statement is definitive. The "times of ignorance" in the past are contrasted with "now" (*nun*). God may have overlooked the times of ignorance in the past but no longer. Ignorance is no longer a valid excuse for failing to respond to God because "now" God gives a comprehensive command that "all" (*pantas*) people "everywhere" (*pantachou*) should repent.[153] There is no chronological or geographical limitation placed upon the call for repentance. Consistent with the experience of Cornelius, redemptive history and the particularities of people's required response to God had changed for all people in all places with the advent of Jesus.[154] As F. F. Bruce explains, "The coming of Christ marks a fresh start in God's dealings with the human race."[155]

The very sovereign God who created the world, made every nation of people, and determined their boundaries has vowed that judgment will come. Though the timing is not specified, the coming judgment is certain and will be performed justly, or "in righteousness." It will be exercised through or by means of a Man of divine appointment. The resurrection serves as God's validation of Jesus to "everyone" and is therefore a "universal demonstration and proof of God's call to Jesus

---

[151]D. L. Bock, *Acts,* ECNT (Grand Rapids: Baker, 2007), 569.

[152]Ibid.

[153]Ibid. The need for the command (*parangellein*) points to the inadequacy of general revelation "without correction and supplement." L. T. Johnson, *The Acts of the Apostles,* Sacra Pagina (Collegeville: The Liturgical Press, 1992), 317.

[154]Chapter 6 will demonstrate that many inclusivists posit that those today who have never heard the gospel can be saved in a way that is analogous to those in the Old Testament who were saved because they trusted God but who did not have access to the gospel because the life, death, and resurrection of Jesus had not yet occurred. That is, the particularities of the gospel were chronologically inaccessible to them so they were not responsible for understanding or believing them. Likewise, those who live chronologically after Christ's first advent but have no access to the gospel are said to be in the same position epistemically as those who lived before Christ. They live after Christ but are "epistemically before Christ." See M. J. Erickson, *Christian Theology,* 2nd ed. (Grand Rapids: Baker, 1998), 197, for an example of this logic. However, I would argue that Paul's address to the Athenians and Peter's encounter with Cornelius (see chap. 1) militates against such logic.

[155]F. F. Bruce, *The Book of the Acts,* NICNT (Grand Rapids: Eerdmans, 1988), 340.

to be judge."[156] That Luke does not mention the name of Jesus in his account of Paul's Areopagus speech is not significant. Paul had been proclaiming "the good news about Jesus and the resurrection" earlier (v. 18). Further, we are told that at the end of Paul's presentation, "some men joined him and believed" (v. 34). Luke's use of the word "believed" (*episteusan*) is definitive in Acts. It refers to saving faith in Jesus Christ. According to Paul, Christ's qualifications were validated by the resurrection. Given everything that Paul had said about God, His governance, His revelation, and humanity's need for repentance, everything depends upon Jesus Christ. He is not merely one among many for the task. He is the only One qualified for the task because He comes at the initiative of the sovereign God. It is hardly surprising that some Athenians were offended by the talk of the resurrection because Paul had just portrayed Jesus as the Lord, Savior, and Judge of humanity. Then as now people are offended by such a portrayal of Jesus.

---

[156] Bock, *Acts,* 570.

Chapter Three

Universalism, Hell, and Conditional Immortality

INTRODUCTION

On July 8, 1741, Jonathan Edwards preached to the congregation of Enfield, Connecticut, from the text of Deut 32:35, choosing
to expound the statement, "In due time their foot will slip." Deliv-
ering his sermon in his characteristic style of vocal intensity with
little physical movement, Edwards warned his hearers of imminent
destruction. Each listener stood poised to receive just judgment, and
it was only the Lord's benevolence that kept them from entering into
damnation. God was able to cast them into hell. They deserved to
be cast into hell. They were already under the sentence of hell. And
even as they listened, they were already objects of that same anger
and wrath of God. In what is now the most familiar paragraph of
what became America's most famous sermon, "Sinners in the Hands
of an Angry God," Edwards warned the congregation of impending
judgment:

> The God that holds you over the pit of hell, much as one holds
> a spider, or some loathsome insect over the fire, abhors you, and
> is dreadfully provoked: his wrath towards you burns like fire; he
> looks upon you as worthy of nothing else, but to be cast into the
> fire; he is of purer eyes than to bear to have you in his sight; you

are ten thousand times more abominable in his eyes, than the most hateful venomous serpent is in ours. You have offended him infinitely more than ever a stubborn rebel did his prince; and yet it is nothing but his hand that holds you from falling into the fire every moment. It is to be ascribed to nothing else, that you did not go to hell the last night; that you were suffered to awake again in this world, after you closed your eyes to sleep. And there is no other reason to be given, why you have not dropped into hell since you arose in the morning, but that God's hand has held you up. There is no other reason to be given why you have not gone to hell, since you have sat here in the house of God, provoking his pure eyes by your sinful wicked manner of attending his solemn worship. Yea, there is nothing else that is to be given as a reason why you do not this very moment drop down into hell.[1]

The impact on those listening was so dramatic that Edwards was not able to complete the sermon. According to those who were there, the shrieks and cries of desperation that filled the room were piercing and amazing. Edwards had demonstrated from Scripture that the sins of those in the room were dragging them toward the fires of hell and they were justly under the wrath of the most holy God, who was demonstrating remarkable mercy by forestalling judgment. The clergy of Enfield wandered among the people ministering the gospel to the individuals who were brought under conviction, resulting in the salvation of several that day.[2]

Such a sermon would not be welcome in most Western churches today. Rather than considering their position before the long-suffering God portrayed by Edwards, many in attendance would question the character of such a God who would condemn so many to hell. Consider the following examples, Charles Duthie questions, "Which of us finds it possible to be at ease with a God who creates human beings in such a manner that the abuse of their freedom, however terrible, is visited with unending penalty?"[3] Emergent church visionary Brian McLaren believes that the "conventional doctrine of hell has too often engendered a view of a deity who suffers from borderline personality

---

[1] J. Edwards, *Sinners in the Hands of an Angry God*, 1741.
[2] See G. Marsden, *Jonathan Edwards: A Life* (New Haven, CT: Yale University Press, 2003), 220–21.
[3] C. S. Duthie, "Ultimate Triumph," *SJT* 14 (1961): 169.

disorder or some worse sociopathic diagnosis."[4] Clark Pinnock goes so far as to characterize any god who would condemn individuals to an eternity in hellfire as being on a lower moral plain than Adolf Hitler.[5]

Although universalism is a minority position in the United States, it is growing in popularity. According to Pew Research Data released in 2008, 59 percent of Americans surveyed believe that hell awaits the evil person,[6] down from 71 percent belief in the existence of hell found in a 2001 Gallop survey.[7] Despite the growing number of dissenters, the majority belief in hell demonstrates that universalism still runs counterintuitive to the majority mind-set.[8] The reason for this is not that heaven and hell are cultural or religious constructs but are essential to people's idea of final justice. The concept of recompense for righteous and unrighteous actions is written on the human conscience and is consistent with the way the world works. People expect that there will be punishment and reward in the afterlife to balance the scales of rights and wrongs during this lifetime. Though most do not believe they are as righteous as someone like Mother Teresa, they cannot fathom sharing the eternal destiny of one like Hitler. But universalism does have its proponents, and it is a growing number. By the late twentieth century, there was perhaps no traditional doctrine that had been so widely abandoned as that of eternal conscious torment in hell.[9]

The current impulse against the idea of hell extends beyond the simple denial of eternal conscious torment in hell. In many cases those

---

[4]B. D. McLaren, *The Last Word and the Word After That: A Tale of Faith, Doubt, and a New Kind of Christianity* (San Francisco: Jossey-Bass, 2005), xii. Emergent leader Doug Pagitt also denies the existence of hell, preferring to see judgment as the re-creation of the heavens and the earth.

[5]C. H. Pinnock, "Response to John F. Walvoord," in *Four Views on Hell*, ed. W. Crockett (Grand Rapids: Zondervan, 1996), 38.

[6]"U. S. Religious Landscape Survey, Religious Affiliation: Diverse and Dynamic," The Pew Forum on Religion & Public Life, Washington, DC (2008): 168–69.

[7]"Americans Describe Their Views About Life After Death," *The Barna Update* (21 October 2003) [online]; accessed 19 December 2003; available from http://www.barna.org/FlexPage.asp x?Page=BarnaUpdate&BarnaUpdateID=150; Internet.

[8]For an excellent history of the erosion of the doctrine of hell as eternal conscious torment, see R. A. Mohler Jr., "Modern Theology: The Disappearance of Hell," in *Hell Under Fire: Modern Scholarship Reinvents Eternal Punishment*, ed. C. W. Morgan and R. A. Peterson (Grand Rapids: Zondervan, 2004), 15–41. For a contrary view, see E. Fudge, *The Fire That Consumes: A Biblical and Historical Study of the Doctrine of Final Punishment* (Lincoln: iUniverse.com, 1982, 2000).

[9]R. Bauckham, "Universalism: A Historical Survey," *Themelios* 4/2 (1979): 48.

who are uncomfortable with the idea of hell, those who see eternal conscious punishment as running contrary to the character and nature of God have found a home in universalism, the belief that all will ultimately be saved. The hope and conviction that all will eventually enter into the loving presence of God is not a new phenomenon, but the pluralist mind-set characteristic of postmodernity has brought about a resurgence of universalism in various forms. For the sake of this study, it is fitting to break universalism into two categories: Christian and pluralistic. Christian universalism, sometimes called universal reconciliation, is the doctrine that the final holiness and happiness of all humans will be brought about by the grace of God through the life and work of Jesus Christ. The work of Christ is decisive and necessary to bring about the consummated end for all. Salvation is defined in solely Christian terms, and heaven is understood as described in the Christian Scriptures. Christian universalists see Christianity as the fulfillment of all the world religions.

Pluralistic universalism, on the other hand, does not attach any priority whatsoever to the doctrines, Scripture, or experience of Christianity (or any other religion for that matter). This independence from particular doctrinal commitments may satisfy the postmodern impulse that resists assigning supremacy or priority to one view over another, but it makes discourse about the commitments of pluralistic universalism difficult. As will be demonstrated in chapter 4, the religions of the world have different, even contradictory, notions of God, the human dilemma, the eternal state, and salvation. It is difficult, if not impossible, to discuss universal salvation when the participants cannot agree on either the nature of God or the nature of salvation. Because pluralistic universalism flows from the religious and philosophical pluralistic mind-set, many of the arguments for pluralistic universalism are common to the arguments for pluralism. In fact, many of the proponents of pluralistic universalism are also the most prolific proponents of pluralism in general,[10] so the reader is directed to chapter 4 for a discussion and critique of the pluralist position. The focus of this chapter is limited to the history, arguments, and criticism of Christian universalism (hereafter referred to simply as "universalism").

---

[10]See for example, J. Hick, *Death and Eternal Life* (London: Collins, 1976).

History and Description

Universalism has been prominent in theological thought for millennia beginning with Origen in the third century.[11] Origen's views arose in his attempt to counter the radical dualism of Valentinian Gnosticism.[12] When God restores all things, Origen reasoned, then evil will be entirely eliminated.[13] Under his doctrine of *apokatastasis*, or restoration, Origen taught that the punishment meted out by God is always remedial and temporary, for the purpose of purifying the individual. The Greek word *apokatastasis*, which became the title of Origen's universalist doctrine, is found in the New Testament in Acts 3:21, referring to the restoration of all things.[14] Origen's theory was strongly influenced by Platonism, which saw all the world and life as a great cycle of emanation from God that would ultimately return to God.[15] To Origen, life and hell are stages in the journey back to God. A strong proponent of free will, Origen believed that the option to exercise the human will extended past this life and into the next. Therefore, the remedial punishment of hell might last for a long time. But in the end the goodness of God will prevail, and all hell will be emptied. This aspect of Origen's teachings was condemned as heretical at an ecumenical Council at Constantinople in 553. The condemnation at Constantinople and Augustine's open refutation of universalism and other views on the extent of salvation that were more generous than his were sufficient to discredit universalism throughout the Middle Ages, largely until the Enlightenment period.[16]

With a few notable exceptions (such as Gregory of Nyssa in the fourth century and John Scotus Erigena in the ninth century),[17] few Christian theologians embraced the doctrine of *apokatastasis* until the nineteenth century. In the sixteenth through eighteenth centuries,

---

[11]R. Bauckham notes that Origen's universalism was partly anticipated by Clement of Alexandria in "Universalism: A Historical Survey," 49.

[12]Origen, *First Principles* 1.6.1–3.

[13]Henri Crouzel has raised questions regarding Origen's commitment to universal reconciliation. Many of Origen's writings on *apokatastasis* were in the context of "research theology" and ought not to be "hardened into a categorical statement." *Origen*, trans. A. S. Worrall (Edinburgh: T&T Clark, 1989), 263. J. R. Root cautions that Origen's universalism was more speculative than dogmatic. "Universalism," in *EDT*, ed. W. A. Elwell, 2nd ed. (Grand Rapids: Baker, 2001), 1233. This does not change the fact that *apokatastasis* originated with Origen.

[14]Variant forms of the verb *apokathistanō* are found eight times in Scripture (Matt 12:13; 17:11; Mark 3:5; 8:25; 9:12; Luke 6:10; Acts 1:6; Heb 13:19).

[15]Bauckham, "Universalism: A Historical Survey," 49.

[16]Augustine, *The City of God* 21:17–27.

[17]B. Demarest, "Apokatastasis," in *EDT*, 81.

one of the stronger arguments employed against universalism was that the threat of eternal torment was a necessary deterrent against immoral living. The Enlightenment period saw a resurgence of interest in universalism. F. D. E. Schleiermacher was the first significant modern theologian to teach universalism. Coinciding with the rise of nineteenth-century Christian liberalism, Schleiermacher taught that all people were elected to salvation in Christ and none of God's redemptive purposes could fail. Schleiermacher's argument that the enjoyment of eternal heaven by the redeemed will be marred by the ongoing torment of the unredeemed in hell still has strong appeal.[18]

The universalist movement enjoyed perhaps its most widespread acceptance during the nineteenth century, eventually giving birth to a denomination that bore the name "Universalist."[19] Universalists rested their doctrine on the following five central tenets: (1) the universal fatherhood of God, (2) the spiritual authority and leadership of His Son Jesus Christ, (3) the trustworthiness of the Bible as containing a revelation from God, (4) the certainty of just retribution for sin, and (5) the final harmony of all souls with God.[20] A common conviction of universalism is that death is not the final determiner; after death there is still opportunity for moral progress and repentance. The Christian Scottish pastor and novelist George MacDonald taught much the same thing. He believed that all would eventually come to God after a period of purgation. The popular Christian novelist Madeleine L'Engle shared the same convictions.[21]

Modern universalists break into two camps in their defense of universal reconciliation. The first group attempts to defend their doctrine through exegesis of the pertinent biblical texts. This is a difficult task because of the sheer number of Scriptures that support the doctrines of heaven and hell and the eternal separation of the saved and the lost. Nevertheless, especially at the popular level (books and Web sites), biblical defense of universalism is still attempted.[22] The second

---

[18]F. Schleiermacher, *The Christian Faith*, ed. H. R. MacKintosh and J. S. Stewart (Edinburgh: T&T Clark, 1999), 720–22.

[19]The Universalist denomination eventually merged with the Unitarians in 1961.

[20]These are the five essential principles of the Universalist faith commended at the General Convention of Universalists in 1899. K. Allen, "What is meant by the term Christian Universalism?" Available from http://www.auburn.edu/~allenkc/chr-univ.html; Internet; accessed 8 October 2008.

[21]M. L'Engle, *The Irrational Season* (New York: Seabury, 1979), 97.

[22]See M. T. Chamberlain, *Every Knee Shall Bow* (Longwood, FL: Xulon, 2004); G. MacDonald, *The Evangelical Universalist* (Eugene, OR: Cascade Books, 2006); T. Talbott, *The*

approach is to treat the Bible passages that speak of an eternal division of the saved and the lost as though they are threats rather than true predictions.[23] More radically, some universalist apologists simply disagree with the biblical authors, thereby compromising the authority of the Bible. In so doing, modern universalists are not bound to the explicit teaching of the Bible but can base their doctrine of universalism on their perceptions of the love of God.[24]

The most persuasive representative of the latter group is John A. T. Robinson, bishop of the Church of England. His clearest defense of universal restoration is presented in his book *In the End God*.[25] Robinson saw two incompatible "myths" in the NT: universal restoration and eternal punishment. For Robinson the justice of God is a "quality" of divine love.[26] Therefore, eternal punishment and eternal love would be a contradiction. The omnipotent, omniscient, and eternal God is patient and will not dominate humanity, but He will work with humans until all eventually accept His salvation. Robinson reasoned that if God is omnipotent, then not even human freedom is able to overcome His love. That is, if people are able to hold out in rebellion until the end, then God is not truly all-powerful.[27] Robinson believed that because all people are elect in Christ, hell is an ultimate impossibility because "already there is not one outside Christ."[28] Robinson was aware that Jesus warned His audiences about the horrors of hell and admitted, "It is futile to attempt to prove that Christ taught no belief in hell or eternal punishment."[29] Therefore, the choice between heaven and hell is real. Robinson reasoned that the two myths uphold "the eternal seriousness of the choice before man."[30] The eternal punishment myth was important to Robinson because it did not allow people to weaken the

---

Inescapable Love of God (Boca Raton, FL: Universal Publishers, 1999); id., "Universal Reconciliation and the Inclusive Nature of Election," in *Perspective on Election*, ed. C. O. Brand (Nashville: B&H, 2006), 206–61; D. L. Watson, *God Does Not Foreclose: The Universal Promise of Salvation* (Nashville: Abingdon, 1990); K. R. Vincent, *The Golden Thread: God's Promise of Universal Salvation* (Bloomington, IN: iUniverse Inc., 2005).

[23] David Edwards dismisses as hyperbolic Jesus' references to hell in D. L. Edwards and J. Stott, *Evangelical Essentials: A Liberal–Evangelical Dialogue* (Downers Grove, IL: InterVarsity, 1988), 301.

[24] Bauckham, "Universalism: A Historical Survey," 52.

[25] J. A. T. Robinson, *In the End God* (New York: Harper & Row, 1968); originally published in 1950.

[26] Ibid., 115; id., "Universalism—Is it Heretical?" *SJT* 2 (1949): 143.

[27] Robinson, *In the End God*, 118.

[28] Ibid., 130.

[29] Robinson, "Universalism—Is it Heretical?," 154.

[30] Robinson, *In the End God*, 131.

seriousness of that choice. Not to choose Christ is an infinitely hellish choice. But that does not mean it is an eternal choice.

CHRISTIAN UNIVERSALIST ARGUMENTS

Universalists give the loving character of God priority in the interpretation of biblical texts. The result is that the theological presuppositions of universalists dominate and distort their exegesis of Scripture. There is no such thing as bias-free or presuppositionless biblical interpretation. But when one studies the exegesis of universalists, it is clear that they are overlaying the text with their theology, reading their theological desires into the text with little consideration for the context of the passages. For this reason it is more legitimate and helpful to summarize the theological commitments of the universalists before we look at their efforts to justify their doctrine of universal salvation from specific biblical texts.

Common Theological Arguments for Universal Restoration

The primary emphasis of universalist argumentation is the character of God. Universalists are convinced that eternal conscious torment in hell would have catastrophic implications for such divine attributes as the love and mercy of God. For some universalists the doctrine of God is at stake.[31] God has revealed Himself in history, and the end of history will vindicate His redemptive purposes and His claims to be just, loving, patient, merciful, and compassionate.

The Sovereign Love of God　Preeminent in the theological reckoning of universalism is the love of God. Reflecting on 1 John 4:8, Thomas Talbott writes, "The point, then, hardly seems to be that God just happens to love us, as if it were a happy accident that he does; the point seems to be that it is his nature to love us."[32] In fact, most universalists believe that only commitment to universal salvation will do justice to the love of God. If any persist eternally in rebellion or under punishment, then God could be judged to be less than loving. Further, God is also sovereign over human affairs and history. The result of the sovereignty of God coupled with His driving love is that all will be saved. It is unthinkable and illogical to the universalist that all will not be saved in a universe sovereignly governed by an all-loving God. If all are not

---

[31]See Robinson, "Universalism—Is It Heretical?," 139.
[32]Talbott, "Universal Reconciliation," 208.

saved, then that necessarily means that God is either not loving (He created a universe where He desires the eternal damnation of some) or that God is not sovereign (He is unable to carry out his universal salvific will). But God is both loving and sovereign, and therefore all must necessarily be saved.[33]

Because the love of God is preeminent, the justice of God flows from and serves the love of God. That is, the justice of God is a quality of God's love. Therefore, it is illegitimate to the universalist to posit a situation where God has loving, salvific desires for all of humanity but is constrained by His justice to condemn some to hell. Love and justice are not two opposing poles. Justice is the "characterization of [love's] working."[34] In the end God's justice will be satisfied but not at the expense of His love because eternal suffering is completely incompatible with divine love. Universalists, therefore, believe God will govern eternity in a manner that allows His love to be fully expressed through the salvation of all. Universalists are not certain how the final victory will be achieved. They are certain that God's loving sovereign will must be fulfilled.

The Omnipotence, Patience, and Eternality of God   Universalists also focus on other attributes of God, including His eternality, patience, and omnipotence. Because God is eternal, He is not limited by time. If the destinies of people are fixed at death, then the capacity of God to work out His loving desires is limited by time. God is also infinitely patient. He has all eternity to woo people to Himself. It is a wooing because love will not allow God to overwhelm the freedom of humanity as they ultimately accept His salvation.[35] Duthie describes the persistent effort of God as "the outgoing, world-embracing, utterly faithful, endlessly self-spending grace of God towards mankind."[36] The sovereign God is also omnipotent, so He has the resources to accomplish all His desires, including the salvation of all humanity. David L. Edwards explains his hope in the omnipotence of a completely loving God:

> If [God] is all-powerful, will he not exert his infinite power to the utmost to save all the perishing? If he is all-loving, will he not save any soul with a glimmer of a belief that the rejection of Christ

---

[33]N. Ferré, *Evil and the Christian Faith* (New York: Harper & Brothers, 1947), 118.
[34]Robinson, "Universalism—Is It Heretical?," 143.
[35]Ibid., 141.
[36]Duthie, "Ultimate Triumph," 168.

would deserve blame? I would rather be an atheist than believe in a God who accepts it as inevitable that hell (however conceived) is the inescapable destiny of many, or of any of his children, even when they are prepared to accept "all the blame."[37]

The Nature and Experience of Heaven and Hell   Finally, universalists focus on the nature of heaven and hell. As already explained, the universalist understanding of hell, if it exists at all, is remedial and purifying, not punitive. They question both the legitimacy and coherence of the doctrine of eternal conscious suffering in hell. If hell is eternal, then there would exist an inconsistent dualism for all eternity: a loving God and unconquered evil. Curiously, for many universalists, hell should be preached because it is real, but its purpose is to prepare people for heaven, purifying the unrighteous so that they can enter into eternal glory.[38] The teaching on hell in the Bible is used to warn people to repent. It does not mean that it is actually the plan of God to create hell and then populate it with some of His image-bearers. Universalist Nels Ferré wrote, "To preach to sinners that all will be saved will not reach them on their level of fear and hate of God. It will only secure them in their sin and self-sufficiency. Therefore, headed as they are away from God, they must be told: Repent or perish!"[39]

For many universalists, hell is not eternal but finite in duration, lasting only long enough to prepare all of fallen humanity for heaven. Further, perfected souls in heaven could never rejoice while others are suffering in hell. Ferré reasoned that heaven and hell are such polar opposites that heaven can only be heaven if all of hell is eventually emptied. Finally, from the universalist perspective, the suffering in the world today only makes sense if it ends for all eventually.

Commonly Used Biblical Proof Texts
for Universal Restoration

Though there is a remarkable amount of teaching in the New Testament regarding the eternal division of the saved and the lost, some universalists attempt to ground their salvific commitments in Scripture.[40]

---

[37]Edwards, *Evangelical Essentials*, 291.
[38]N. Ferré, *The Christian Understanding of God* (New York: Harper, 1951), 234.
[39]N. Ferré, "Universalism: Pro and Con," *Christianity Today* 7 (1 March 1963): 24.
[40]John Sanders uses much the same taxonomy in his evaluation of universalism. See *No*

Cosmic Restoration Texts   The first and most important set of biblical texts focuses on the eschatological promises of cosmic restoration. At that time all things will be restored. All people will be reconciled to God. In Acts 3:21, Peter teaches that in the future consummation there will be a "restoration of all things." In 1 Cor 15:22–29, Paul explains that the resurrection of Christ guarantees that "all will be made alive" and that in the end "everything" will be subjected to God, then "the Son Himself will also be subject to Him . . . so that God may be all in all." The logic employed by universalists is that the nature of the subjection of "everything" is described as the same as the subjection of the Son to the Father. The hymn of Phil 2:6–11 teaches that in the end "every knee should bow—of those who are in heaven and on earth and under the earth—and every tongue should confess that Jesus Christ is Lord." This universal confession of the lordship of Christ is evidence to the universalist that in the end all will recognize the glory and lordship of Christ and be saved (following the Rom 10:9 formula). Colossians 1:19–20 speaks of the universal implications of the atonement. God has reconciled "everything to Himself by making peace through the blood of His cross—whether things on earth or things in heaven." Universalists suggest that cosmic peace implies the salvation of all.

Universal Salvific Desire Texts   The second set of biblical texts focuses on God's desire that all be saved. Romans 11:32 states that God's desire is to have "mercy on all."[41] First Timothy 2:4 teaches that God "wants everyone to be saved and to come to the knowledge of the truth." The apostle Peter says much the same thing in 2 Pet 3:9 when he explains that God is patient with people, "not wanting any to perish, but all to come to repentance." The universalist reasons that if God, who is omnipotent and omniscient, has this desire, then there is nothing that can prevail against His will. In the end God's will shall be done, and all shall be saved.

Unlimited Extent of the Atonement Texts   The third category of texts speaks to the extent of the atoning work of Christ on the cross. To the universalist, when the desire that all be saved is coupled with the clear statements that the work of Christ on the cross extends across the cosmos, the result is that all will be reconciled in the end. Unlimited

---

Other Name: An Investigation into the Destiny of the Unevangelized (Grand Rapids: Eerdmans, 1992), 83–85.

  [41]So Edwards, *Evangelical Essentials*, 297.

atonement entails universal salvation. For example, in John 12:32 Jesus said that when He was lifted up (a clear reference to His crucifixion), "I will draw all people to Myself." Hebrews 2:9 instructs that Christ tasted "death for everyone." First John 2:2 makes clear that Jesus' sacrifice was sufficient to propitiate the wrath of God for the sins "of the whole world."

Results of the Atonement Texts   The final set of texts discusses the result of the atoning work of Christ. Universalists find here evidence that the universal desire that all be saved, coupled with an atonement that was directed toward the sins of all, results in an actual salvation for all. Perhaps most significant among these texts is Rom 5:12–21. Here Paul contrasts the first Adam and the second Adam. According to universalists, just as Adam's sin resulted in death for all people (universal in scope), in the same way Christ's obedience on the cross ushers in salvation for the same scope, specifically, all people. Through Christ's sacrifice "there is life-giving justification for everyone" (Rom 5:18).[42] Other texts include 2 Cor 5:19, which teaches that God reconciled "the world to Himself." Paul told Timothy that he labored for Jesus Christ, "who is the Savior of everyone" (1 Tim 4:10), while in Titus 2:11, Paul wrote that "the grace of God has appeared, with salvation for all people."

Some universalists find in 1 Pet 3:18–22 evidence of a postmortem opportunity to respond to the gospel of Christ. Because Christ "suffered for sins once for all," it is right that the offer of salvation based on that suffering be offered to all. Universalist interpreters claim that this text goes on to describe Christ's journey to Hades to offer the benefits of His work on the cross to "the spirits in prison who in the past were disobedient." This text describes the kind of opportunity that is available to all who have either not heard the gospel or have not responded to it during their lifetimes.

RESPONSE

I will look at the arguments from Scripture first before turning to the theological arguments. I will end with a short excursus on the biblical doctrine of hell, critiquing the universalist doctrine and the doctrine of conditional immortality that is generating increasing interest in evangelical circles.

---

[42] Ibid.

Analysis of Christian Universalist Exegetical Arguments

Universal Restoration Texts   The universalist doctrine of *apokatasta-sis* hinges on texts that speak of a future restoration. Scripture does use language of restoration and consummation. Indeed, the great hope for God's people has always been the consummation of God's redemptive purposes and the future reign of Messiah. The question is whether the promises of restoration, reconciliation, and consummation in the biblical texts entail the salvation of every human. In Acts 3:19–21, a text often referenced by universalists to support their doctrine of res-toration, Peter called on his Jewish hearers to repent for forgiveness of sins. If they did, then the Lord would send "seasons of refreshing" and "Jesus, who has been appointed Messiah." The promise of Acts 3:21 is that Jesus would not return until "the times of the restoration of all things." What does "restoration of all things" represent? The answer must be found in its biblical, theological context. Jesus had already come, so the seasons of refreshing promised probably refer to the eschatological gift of the Spirit.[43] The coming of Jesus represents the culmination of God's redemptive purposes, the beginning of which was inaugurated with the gift of the Spirit. In this context "restora-tion of all things" refers to the consummation of an eschatological plan inaugurated with the first advent of Christ and His sending of the Spirit at Pentecost.[44] There is no basis in the text for understanding "restoration of all things" to mean "salvation of all people" unless it can be demonstrated elsewhere that the consummation of God's prom-ises will result in universal salvation. However, the biblical writers did not express any discomfort with the simultaneous existence of the new heavens, new earth, and hell.

Paul speaks in Col 1:19–20 of the working of Christ at the cross, whereby God reconciled "everything to Himself." The scope of the reconciliation is clear from the text: it is "whether things on earth or things in heaven." This is a merism that hearkens back to Gen 1:1 and speaks of all things in the created order. The nature of the reconcilia-tion is demonstrated by the phrase, "making peace through the blood of His cross." Universalists gloss "reconcile everything to Himself" with "bringing salvation to every human," but such a reading does

---

[43]J. B. Polhill, *Acts*, NAC (Nashville: B&H, 1992), 134–35.
[44]So T. Schreiner, *New Testament Theology: Magnifying God in Christ* (Grand Rapids: Baker, 2008), 806.

not follow. The peace that Christ brought must be understood in light of Col 2:15, where Paul explains that Christ "disarmed the rulers and authorities and disgraced them publicly; He triumphed over them by Him." The peace of Christ can be either freely accepted or coercively imposed; the latter is clearly in view in Col 2:15. These "rulers and authorities" are not joyfully submitting to the person of Christ but have been subjugated by a dominant power. They have been pacified and are unable to rise up in rebellion or mount any threat against God, but they have not been done away with or annihilated.[45] Indeed, it seems from the context that their ongoing subjugated existence is an occasion for the accrual of greater glory to Christ (cf. Rev 19:1–3). So there is no reason to understand the reconciliation of all things as a universal salvation for all humans. The context of Colossians points in an entirely different direction. In the same way the universalist interpretation of Paul's line "every knee should bow—of those who are in heaven and on earth and under the earth—and every tongue should confess that Jesus Christ is Lord" (Phil 2:10–11) is equally reductionistic. The passage teaches that one day there will be cosmic subjection to Christ and recognition that Christ is Lord. The disrupted order of the universe will be set right. There is no reason that this could not be accomplished through the punishment of rebellion. Besides, in Phil 3:19, Paul speaks of some whose "end is destruction." J. I. Packer was surely correct when he observed that universalist exegesis is so poor in their determination to disregard the immediate context, that they are effectively accusing the New Testament writers of "intellectual schizophrenia."[46]

The universalist reading of 1 Cor 15:22–29 also denies both the immediate and biblical theological contexts. Paul makes a comparison between the repercussions of Adam's sin and Christ's obedience in 15:22, stating, "For just as in Adam all die, so also in Christ all will be made alive." Universalists argue that the scope of both instances of "all" in 15:22 is the same. All humanity has died in Adam; likewise, all humanity will be made alive in Christ. This argument would be persuasive if Paul did not restrict the meaning of "all" who are saved to

---

[45]So P. T. O'Brien, *Colossians, Philemon,* WBC 44 (Waco, TX: Word, 1982), 56; F. F. Bruce, *Commentary on the Epistles to the Ephesians and the Colossians,* NICNT (Grand Rapids: Eerdmans, 1957), 210.

[46]J. I. Packer, "The Way of Salvation: Part III, The Problems of Universalism," *BSac* 130 (January 1973): 7.

"those in Christ." The benefits of Christ's death are granted to all who are in Christ, just as the penalty of Adam's sin is exercised on all who are in Adam. Further, the triumphant eschatology of 1 Corinthians 15 is not compatible with universalism, which does not account for the biblical theology of judgment developed in the passage.[47]

Divine Desire for Universal Salvation Texts   First Timothy 2:4 states that God "desires all people to be saved and to come to the knowledge of the truth" (ESV). Universalists suggest that the divine desires of an omnipotent God cannot be thwarted, and eventually all will be saved. However, a desire that all be saved does not entail that all will be saved, even when that desire comes from the sovereign Lord of human history. Consider that Paul's statement comes in the context of a call for Christians to pray for "kings and all those who are in authority" to the end that Christians might "lead a tranquil and quiet life in all godliness and dignity" (1 Tim 2:2). God's desire that Christians pray for leaders does not entail that God will respond in anticipated ways by causing the leaders to govern in such a way that makes it possible for Christians to lead tranquil and quiet lives. After all, the Roman emperor at the time of Paul's writing was Nero, the notorious persecutor of the Church. Surely no one would question that God desires such prayers to be made or that He is capable of moving the heart of even the most hardened tyrant to care for His loved ones. It must be possible, therefore, that God, in the complexities of His mind and sovereign governance, can genuinely value many states of affairs that are not compatible with His particular plan for each individual or for the cosmos in general. Further, the broader context of 1 Timothy militates against universalist conclusions. Paul warns that there will be some who depart from the faith into gross sin and misconduct (1 Tim 1:6–11) and listen to "deceitful spirits and the teachings of demons, through the hypocrisy of liars whose consciences are seared" (1 Tim 4:1–2). The result of sins, both hidden and apparent is "judgment" (1 Tim 5:24), "ruin and destruction" and "many pains" (1 Tim 6:9–10). The larger context of 1 Timothy teaches an impending and devastating judgment that is incompatible with universalism.[48]

Likewise, Peter's teaching in 2 Pet 3:9 that the Lord is patient, "not wanting any to perish, but all to come to repentance" does not

---

[47]N. T. Wright, "Towards a Biblical View of Universalism," *Themelios* 4/2 (1979): 56.
[48]So ibid., 57.

entail that all will in fact repent. Scripture abounds with examples where the Lord's patience, though incomparable to that of humans, does in fact run out. It is not infinite (e.g., Gen 6:5–6; Exod 32:7–10). The affirmation of divine desire that none should perish in 2 Pet 3:9 must be read within the context of the entire letter where language of judgment abounds. Peter assures his readers that although false teachers will come, their "condemnation" was pronounced long ago and their "destruction" is certain (2 Pet 2:3). In fact, the stories of God's judgment from the past (the flood, Sodom and Gomorrah, etc.) demonstrate that the Lord knows how to "rescue the godly from trials" and "keep the unrighteous under punishment until the day of judgment" (2 Pet 2:9–10). Those who blaspheme the Lord without fear "will be destroyed, suffering harm as the payment for unrighteousness" (2 Pet 2:12–13). The "gloom of darkness has been reserved" for those who abandon "the straight path" (2 Pet 2:15–17). Just as the world was destroyed by the Lord in the time of Noah, so the "present heavens and earth are held in store for fire, being kept until the day of judgment and destruction of ungodly men" (2 Pet 3:7). Peter's statement that the Lord does not desire that any should perish comes in the context of a plea for repentance. So certain is the coming judgment that sinners ought to repent immediately. Destruction of the unrepentant has been promised by God, but the Lord, in His patience, is forestalling that judgment so that people will have time to repent (see Joel 2:12–13; Rom 2:4). That not all will repent is made clear by the previous verses, but the Lord's patience is motivated by a genuine desire that all turn to Him.[49]

Universal Atonement Texts　The so-called "universal atonement" texts—such as John 12:32; Heb 2:9; and 1 John 2:2—have occasioned significant interpretive discussions across the Christian spectrum. These texts are crucial to those who argue for an unlimited extent to the atonement, and there is disagreement between inclusivists and exclusivists (and within the exclusivist camp) on the extent of the atonement and of God's saving desires. However, disagreement over the correct interpretation of a text does not legitimate all interpretive

---

[49] How is it that the Lord can desire that all be saved and still ordain the judgment and destruction of many? Attempts abound to reconcile these two biblical truths without denying the Lord's sovereignty, omnipotence, love, or His commitment to judge. I will address this issue in my analysis of Universalist Precommitments under "The Omnipotence, Patience, and Eternality of God."

proposals or the conclusions from which they flow. Even where disagreement exists on the correct interpretation of these passages, the universalist interpretations can be demonstrated to be fallacious.

Just prior to the Last Supper and upper room discourse, Jesus stated, "If I am lifted up from the earth I will draw all people to Myself" (John 12:32). Jesus' announcement came on the heels of some Gentiles requesting to see Him while in Jerusalem for the Feast of the Passover (John 12:20–21). Jesus knew that this event signaled the moment of His glorification, His crucifixion, which would atone for the sins of the world. In the prologue to John's Gospel, John explained that Jesus "came to His own, and His own people did not receive Him. But to all who did receive Him, He gave them the right to be children to God, to those who believe in His name" (John 1:11–12). It is evident from the overall context that only those who "believe in His name" are saved. This criterion is repeated throughout the Gospel of John (3:16; 5:24; 8:24; 10:25–26; 11:26; 20:31). To believe that John taught universalism based on 12:32 is to ignore the rest of his Gospel that requires faith for salvation. Besides, Jesus had already told His disciples that at the sound of His voice, "those who have done wicked things" will come out "to the resurrection of judgment" (John 5:29). Therefore, the best way to understand 12:32 is that the coming of the Gentiles indicated that the moment of Jesus' cross work was at hand. His own, the Jewish people, had rejected Him (though not all), and the way of salvation was now open for all who would believe, both Jews and Gentiles. All, without distinction, who have faith in Jesus will be saved. No one, without exception, who refuses God's plan of salvation in Jesus, will be saved.

Universalist understandings of 1 John 2:2 likewise ignore the context of John's writings. In addition to the thorough commitment to salvation through faith in John's Gospel outlined above, John repeats the theme in his first epistle. Only those who believe the apostolic teaching on the Son can have eternal life, fellowship with the Father, and their sins forgiven (1 John 1:1–3,7). Only those who believe the Son have the testimony of eternal life and assurance of it, while those who deny the Son of God have made Him a liar (1 John 5:10–13). So the affirmation that Jesus is the propitiation for the sins of the whole world must be read in the larger context of John's writings. Given John's commitment to faith as the precondition to eternal life, the best understanding of 1 John 2:2 is that the cross has cosmic and universal implications, such as defeating the principalities and powers (Col 1:19–20; 2:14–15), enabling the restoration of creation in the new heavens and earth (Rom 8:20–23), and making possible the *bona fide* offer of the gospel to all people (Matt 28:18–20; Luke 24:46–47; 1 Tim 4:10). But these implications do not entail that all people are necessarily saved. Hebrews 2:9 would have a similar meaning. Universalist theology would require that even fallen angels be saved, but in the immediate context, the author of Hebrews explicitly states that God's help in the work of Christ does not extend to angels (Heb 2:16). Besides, the book of Hebrews is replete with warnings of impending judgment for those who do not repent (e.g., Heb 2:2–3; 6:4–6; 10:26–31). It is true that Jesus tasted death for all people; that is, Christ died, and a *bona fide* gospel offer is open to all. But that does not mean that all will believe and be saved.

Universalists make the same mistake in their interpretation of Rom 11:32. By ignoring the context, they are able to assert that the statement "so that He may have mercy on all" is evidence of the salvation of all people. However, in Romans 9–11, Paul has labored to demonstrate that God would be faithful to His promises to Israel, despite the fact that all appearances pointed to God's having abandoned the Jews and embraced a Gentile church. Paul explained that both Jews and Gentiles had, at different times, disobeyed, so that the Jews and Gentiles, at different times, could receive mercy. But in Rom 11:23 Paul is explicit about the precondition for God's mercy, namely, "if they do not remain in unbelief." Universalists wish to read the "all" of Rom 11:32 as "all people everywhere, regardless of faith." In context, the "all" of Rom 11:32 must be read as "Jews and Gentiles alike."[50]

Universal Results of the Atonement Texts   As in all biblical interpretation, the biblical texts that testify to the results of Christ's atoning work on the cross must be understood in context. Romans 5:18 affirms that through the "righteous act" of Jesus in redemption, "there is life-giving justification for everyone." Universalists wish to affirm that the scope of those who will be justified is the same as those who have been condemned in Adam, namely, everybody. But Paul describes the scope of those who will be justified in the prior verse, and it is narrower than

---

[50]Ibid., 56.

that of those who are in Adam. "Since by the one man's trespass, death reigned through that one man, how much more will those who receive the overflow of grace and the gift of righteousness reign in life through the one man, Jesus Christ" (Rom 5:17). Only those who "receive the overflow of grace" will be justified. The immediate context does not allow a universalist reading of Rom 5:12–21, nor does the larger context, as was demonstrated in the discussion of Rom 11:32.

Second Corinthians 5:19 states that "in Christ, God was reconciling the world to Himself." Universalists see in this text a declaration that all people have been brought into a life-giving relationship with the Lord. Again, this only demonstrates that the cross effects God's reconciliation with the world, but it does not specify exactly what kind of reconciliation that is (see the prior discussion of Col 1:19–20). It hardly entails that all will be saved. In 2 Cor 5, Paul differentiates between the world and those who have been saved. The Christian is one who has been reconciled to God, who is an ambassador to the world, and to whom the ministry of reconciliation has been given (2 Cor 5:18, 20). The phrase, "in Christ, God was reconciling the world to Himself," is best understood to convey the salvific idea that God was reconciling the world in or through the agency of Christ (cf. 2 Cor 5:18).[51] However, reconciliation is two-sided: there is something in God and something in humanity that must be taken care of before there can be peace. To be sure, God's work to effect reconciliation is immeasurably greater than humanity's responsibility. In fact, humanity's responsibility cannot rightfully be called a work at all (Eph 2:8–9). But that does not negate the fact that "God's act of reconciliation requires a human response."[52] Otherwise, why would Paul's ambassadorial appeal be, "We plead on Christ's behalf, 'Be reconciled to God'" (2 Cor 5:20)? Despite the work of God in Christ, there will be those who persist in rebellion and will not be reconciled to God.

First Timothy 4:10 asserts that Jesus is the "Savior of everyone, especially of those who believe." We have already seen that 1 Timothy differentiates between those who are saved and those who are judged. In this instance Paul makes a strong claim that Jesus is the only Savior. There is no other. But Paul distinguishes between those who believe and those who do not. Jesus is the Savior in fact of those who believe,

---

[51] So R. P. Martin, *2 Corinthians,* WBC 40 (Waco: Word Books, 1986), 153–54; D. E. Garland, *2 Corinthians,* NAC 29 (Nashville: B&H, 1999), 293.

[52] Garland, *2 Corinthians,* 154.

while those who do not believe have turned their back on the only One who can save them. Paul uses the same logic in Titus 2:11 where he writes, "For the grace of God has appeared, with salvation for all people." Again this is a strong statement of the uniqueness of Christ and of the salvation that He brings. There is no other Savior. He is the Savior of all people in the sense that if "all people" are to be saved, it will only be through Jesus. This is clear from the subsequent verses. Those who have been saved by God have been regenerated and renewed by the Holy Spirit (Titus 3:5) and are justified by His grace and "heirs with the hope of eternal life" (Titus 3:7). The Spirit is poured out on those who are saved by Jesus (Titus 3:6). Paul identifies the recipients of this great salvation as "us" and "we" (3:5–7). In the context of the letter, it is those who share in the common faith (Titus 1:4), those who have been purified for God as His own possession (Titus 2:14), and those who have "believed in God" (Titus 3:8). Neither Paul's theology nor the context of the letter will allow for a universalist understanding of Titus 2:11.

Finally, some universalists find in 1 Pet 3:18–22 grounds for hope that all will eventually come to saving faith in the gospel. Jesus' "proclamation to the spirits in prison" is understood to be paradigmatic of the kind of opportunity that is available to all who do not respond to the gospel in their lifetimes. This line of reasoning fails to persuade because, as most commentators agree, Peter meant that Jesus proclaimed His victory to evil spirits and that their power was broken.[53] Further, 1 Pet 4:17–18 makes clear that those who "disobey the gospel of God" will face judgment.

Analysis of Universalist Theological Precommitments

The theological precommitments of universalists dominate and distort their exegesis of the biblical texts. A brief look at the context of each passage is sufficient to reject the universalist interpretation of their selected proof texts. However, universalist writings, pamphlets, and Web sites are not concerned to develop their position from strong exegetical or biblical-theological bases. Rather, their material

---

[53]So J. R. Michaels, *1 Peter*, WBC 49 (Waco: Word Books, 1988), 206–11; P. H. Davids, *The First Epistle of Peter*, NICNT (Grand Rapids: Eerdmans, 1990), 139–40; K. H. Jobes, *1 Peter*, ECNT (Grand Rapids: Baker, 2005), 242–45; T. R. Schreiner, *1, 2 Peter, Jude*, NAC 37 (Nashville: B&H, 2003), 189. The easiest way to understand the verse is to see the "spirits" of 3:18 as another term for the "angels, authorities, and powers" in 3:22.

is typically dominated by emotional appeals to the love of God and the injustice of hell. But a naked appeal to the love of God, void of biblical-theological context, does not make the case for universalism.

The Sovereign Love of God   That God is love is undeniable (1 John 4:8). Further, that God is simultaneously sovereign and all-powerful is indisputable (1 Chr 29:11–12; Acts 4:24). God cannot be thwarted, and He is able to accomplish all that He desires. But universalists are guilty of reducing the love of God into a one-size-fits-all sort of affair that does not account for the complexity of God's love represented in the biblical narrative. Instead, the love of God in the biblical texts is effectively flattened, read as though it is uniform toward all people and all things, not allowing for any variation or particularity.

D. A. Carson has written a decisive rebuttal to those who make the mistake of ignoring the variance in the Bible's presentation of the love of God. In his book *The Difficult Doctrine of the Love of God*, Carson finds five distinct ways that the love of God is taught in Scripture.[54] First, the Bible speaks of the unique intra-Trinitarian love of the Father for the Son and the Son for the Father (John 3:35; 5:20). Second, God is the providential Lover over all His creation. He cares for and knows the world as its Creator. This care is evident in such things as the clothing of the sparrow and the sending of rain on both the righteous and unrighteous (Matt 5:45; 10:29). Third, God has a loving salvific stance toward the fallen world (Ezek 33:11; John 3:16). The logic of John 3:16 is that it was God's love for the world that motivated Him to send His Son. Carson comments, "However much God stands in judgment over the world, he also presents himself as the God who invites and commands all human beings to repent. He orders his people to carry the Gospel to the farthest corner of the world, proclaiming it to men and women everywhere."[55] Fourth, God has a particular, effective, selecting love toward His elect people. The Lord kept his promises to Israel and demonstrated mercy to her because He loved her more than the other nations. There was nothing in Israel that warranted that love, but it was given nonetheless. In the same way, the Lord has set His love upon His elect in Christ who gave His life for the Church (Deut 7:7–8; 10:14–15; Isa 43:1–5; Mal 1:2–3; Eph 1:4–5; 5:25; 1 John 4:8–10).

---

[54]D. A. Carson, *The Difficult Doctrine of the Love of God* (Wheaton: Crossway, 2000), 16–21.

[55]Ibid., 17–28.

Fifth and finally, God has a provisional love that is conditioned on the obedience of His chosen people. Though there is a committed and unconditional love that God has for His people, His disposition toward them changes depending on their faithfulness (Exod 20:6; Ps 103:9–11; John 15:9–10; Jude 21). Carson then reminds the reader of the potential errors that occur when God's love is reduced to one and the same thing in all contexts. Universalists are guilty of this error by flattening the variation in God's love, conflating His electing love with His loving salvific stance toward the world. Qualitatively and quantitatively, they are two different loves and effect two different outcomes in the lives of those upon whom His love rests. The electing nature of God's love is revealed and demonstrated in Jesus Christ. He "loved the church and gave Himself for her" (Eph 5:25). Further, while in the garden of Gethsemane, Jesus prayed for those who would believe in Him but specifically not for the world ("I do not pray for the world," John 17:8–9 NKJV). Clearly, there is a particularity to God's love. Universalists may deny this, but they do so in the face of insurmountable biblical evidence.

Beyond the diversity in the love of God, it is not clear from the biblical presentation of God that love enjoys pride of place among His attributes. Is it legitimate to suggest that the justice of God (or any other divine attribute for that matter) is an aspect of His love? Universalists may wish it to be so, but the faithful Christian must pay attention to God's self-revelation and allow Him final determination of who He is and how He is to be understood. Universalists appeal to 1 John 4:8 which clearly states that "God is love." But many other verses speak just as strongly of God's holiness (Lev 11:44), jealousy (Exod 20:5), and faithfulness (Deut 7:9). One could just as easily privilege one of those attributes as any other. By this logic the love of God could be seen as an attribute of His holiness. The key to the discussion has to be context and the Bible's presentation of God and His attributes. Each passage of Scripture has to be read in the context of the entire Bible, as God's revelation of Himself comes as a whole, progressively developed through redemptive history. When the attributes of God are understood as presented throughout the entire canon, the result is a remarkably integrated balance.

One passage that is emblematic of this balance is Exod 34:6–7. Here God granted Moses' request to see God's glory. The result was the Lord passing before Moses and proclaiming His name (Exod 34:5). As God passed before Moses, He proclaimed: "The LORD, the LORD, a God merciful and gracious, slow to anger, and abounding in steadfast love and faithfulness, keeping steadfast love for thousands, forgiving iniquity and transgression and sin, but who will by no means clear the guilty, visiting the iniquity of the fathers on the children and the children's children, to the third and the fourth generation" (Exod 34:6–7 ESV). God proclaimed His name by reciting for Moses who He is. God told Moses that love (*ḥesed*, a loyal love informed by His particular covenant promises), faithfulness, and mercy characterize Him. But in this same passage, the Lord explained that He also punishes transgressions and "will by no means clear the guilty."

However the love of God is to be understood, His holiness and commitment to punish the guilty must be taken into consideration. To focus on any one attribute of God to the exclusion of others not only distorts the character of God, but ironically it does not bring one to proper understanding of the attribute in focus. Universalists who elevate the love of God and redefine holiness and justice as an aspect of His love ultimately distort and misunderstand both the divine attribute of love and God in His complex totality.

The Omnipotence, Patience, and Eternality of God Universalists argue that God's omnipotence and sovereignty require that He save all. A truly omnipotent sovereign would not allow any to escape His saving designs, especially if that sovereign "wants all men to be saved and to come to a knowledge of the truth" (1 Tim 2:4). Universalists reason that the only conclusion possible from the two premises (God's omnipotence and His desire that all be saved) is that all in fact will ultimately be saved. This is not a valid conclusion. Scripture is clear that God desires all to be saved and that He does not take any pleasure in the death of the wicked (Ezek 18:23). Further, God is the sovereign Creator who is able to do all that He desires (Pss 89:8; 115:3; Rom 4:21; Eph 1:11,19–21; 6:10; Rev 1:6; 4:11). The faithful Christian ought not to deny or explain away these affirmations. They speak to the loving and compassionate, unchanging character and ability of God. But is it not possible for God genuinely to value many possible states of affairs that are not compatible with His particular plan for the cosmos and humanity?[56] That is, in God's mysterious but glorious plan it may be that many will be justly judged without denying the validity of the affirmation that He does not delight (in some sense) in that judgment. And this can be so without contradiction.

In a similar argument some universalists suggest that the omnipotence of God necessarily entails that God will save all without exception. If God does not save all, then it is because He is not able to save all. The omnipotent sovereignty of God entails universal salvation. The assumption is that the outworking of God's sovereignty has to be that He saves all without exception. But this is an untenable assumption. Why can the Lord not omnipotently exercise His sovereignty by sending some to hell?[57] By the same logic, but with a different premise, if God was not able to send some to perdition, then would that not also deny God's sovereignty and omnipotence?[58]

Appeals to God's eternality and patience are no more helpful to the Christian universalist. First, there are no passages in Scripture that affirm that God has infinite patience. God is eternal; His patience is not. God is patient and forbearing (Rom 2:4). He even endures "with much patience objects of wrath ready for destruction" (Rom 9:22), rather than destroying them immediately. First Timothy 1:16 describes the patience or long-suffering (*makrothusian*) of the Lord as *hapasan* ("utmost," HCSB, or "perfect," ESV, NASB). But the patience that is in view is directed toward Paul in particular, not the world in general.[59] But perfect or utmost patience is not necessarily eternal or unending patience.[60] We must allow God to describe Himself as He is, not as we

---

[56]See S. J. Wellum, "Saving Faith: Implicit or Explicit?" in *Faith Comes by Hearing: A Response to Inclusivism*, ed. C. W. Morgan and R. A. Peterson (Downers Grove, IL: InterVarsity, 2008), 146–47. I have found John Piper's investigation into the two wills of God to be especially helpful in coherently balancing the affirmation that God genuinely desires the repentance of all with the affirmation that God unconditionally elects some to salvation. J. Piper, "Are There Two Wills in God?" in *Still Sovereign: Contemporary Perspectives on Election, Foreknowledge, and Grace*. ed. T. R. Schreiner and B. A. Ware (Grand Rapids: Baker, 2000), 107–31.

[57]H. Lindsell writes: "God is sovereign; He is infinite. But God has sovereignly ordained that those who refuse His grace shall perish. We may not like it; we may seek for ways to circumvent this teaching; we may rearrange, reinterpret, allegorize, overlook, neglect, pervert, misuse, or rule out what the Scriptures say. But none of these things will alter God's truth." "Universalism Today: Part Two," *BSac* 122 (January 1965): 39.

[58]So ibid., 32.

[59]So W. D. Mounce, *Pastoral Epistles*, WBC 46 (Nashville: Nelson, 2000), 58. Mounce prefers the translation "complete." Fee prefers the phrase "full extent of his forbearance." G. D. Fee, *1 and 2 Timothy, Titus*, NIBC (Peabody: Hendrickson, 1984, 1988), 54. Given the object of God's patience being Paul in particular, the NIV translation "limitless" is not helpful.

[60]First Timothy 1:16 uses the word *aiōnion* to describe the life that is available for those who believe in Jesus Christ, not to describe the patience of Christ.

wish Him to be. The Lord is patient, far more so than any human, but the patience of the Lord does run out. It is not limitless. The biblical narratives back this up. The Lord demonstrated patience toward the different Canaanite nations for years, but eventually their sin "reached its full measure" (Gen 15:16), and they were judged. For centuries, the Lord endured sin and rebellion by His own people Israel with "perfect" and "utmost" long-suffering, before executing horrific judgment upon them. Eschatological judgment does not present the Bible reader with a new category for evaluating the long-suffering of the Lord; rather, judgment is completely consistent with God's activities in human history. The burden of proof lies with universalists to demonstrate that the Lord's patience is eternal, but they will not find any support in the Bible.[61]

The theme of judgment in both the Old and New Testaments cannot be dismissed or explained away. The psalmist was comforted by the thought that "the eyes of the LORD are on the righteous" but "the face of the LORD is set against those who do what is evil" (Ps 34:15–16). Many prophets anticipated the great and terrible "day of the Lord" that would result in the vindication of the righteous and judgment of the wicked (Isa 13:6,9; Jer 46:10; Ezek 30:2–3; Joel 1:15; 2:1,11,31; Amos 5:18,20; Obadiah 15; Zeph 1:14–16; Zech 14:1; Mal 4:5).[62]

Jesus picked up on that strong prophetic anticipation in His teaching. According to Jesus, God can destroy both body and soul in hell (Matt 10:28). Those who will be judged guilty and cast into the fires of hell include those who cannot conquer lust or anger (Matt 5:27–30; Mark 9:43–47), scribes and Pharisees who lead someone astray (Matt 23:15), the offspring of the evil one (Matt 23:33), and the unrighteous whose lives are not characterized by acts of righteousness and mercy (Matt 25:41–46). Jesus Himself is designated as the judge of the living and the dead (John 5:27; Acts 10:42).

The rest of the New Testament concurs with Jesus' teaching. Paul preached a judgment to come (Acts 24:25), and it permeated his writings. He depicted God's judgment as the outpouring of His wrath (*orgē*) and describes it not in remedial language but as destruction

---

[61] See T. K. Beougher, "Are All Doomed to Be Saved? The Rise of Modern Universalism," in *Who Will Be Saved? Defending the Biblical Understanding of God, Salvation, & Evangelism*, ed. P. R. House and G. A. Thornbury (Wheaton: Crossway, 2000), 95.

[62] J. A. Motyer, "Judgment" in *NDBT*, 615.

and death.[63] Such punishment is executed on the disobedient (Eph 5:6; Col 3:6), both in this age (Rom 1:18; Eph 2:3) and in the final judgment (Rom 2:5). All will stand before God and be judged (2 Cor 5:10; 11:15), and that judgment will be impartial and just (Rom 2:6–16). Eternal destruction awaits the unrighteous (2 Thess 1:9), and it will be certain (Phil 1:28), swift, and terrible (1 Thess 5:3). The writer of Hebrews described the judgment to come in terms of vengeance and recompense (Heb 10:29–30), while James taught that those who did not show mercy would be judged without mercy (Jas 2:13). Peter reasoned that if judgment begins at the household of God, then that which awaits those who disobey the gospel is much worse (1 Pet 4:17–19). Of course, the book of Revelation is replete with testimony to a coming judgment that will be horrific in its scope, content, and duration (Rev 8:2–9:21; 15:5–16:21; 19:1–20:15). Contrary to universalist thinking, the judgment of God does not create questions and problems regarding His justice and righteousness; rather, the judgments of God are the biblical solution to questions of fairness, justice, and righteousness.

Though universalism is a minority view in the church, it is necessary for Christians to understand the utter theological and exegetical bankruptcy of the view. Universalist appeals to the fairness and justice of God strike a chord with postmodern sensibilities. Coupled with the legitimate *imago Dei* desire that all be saved, many Christians are perplexed when confronted with universalist reasoning. Therefore, it is all the more important that the faithful Christian ground his understanding of the nature, purposes, and actions of God in the Lord's revelation of Himself. Much like the first questioning of God's good plan in Genesis 3, universalist appeals ultimately reduce to the satanic lie, "No! You will not die." Christians ought to learn from the disastrous results of the first human sin and flee to the trustworthy Word of God.

HELL AND CONDITIONAL IMMORTALITY

The prospect of eternal hell is a horrifying thing to contemplate. It is a punishment given to one who has persisted in sin and rebellion even unto death. That person denied the One in whose image he was created, rejected the gospel of grace, or continually suppressed the testimony of God in creation and conscience. In spite of the biblical testimony that punishment in hell is eternal, conscious, and terrifying,

---

[63]Schreiner, *New Testament Theology*, 836–38.

universalists categorically reject the doctrine of hell. In universalist understanding, if hell exists at all, it will be remedial and purifying, not punitive, and temporal in duration, not eternal.

Rejection of the doctrine of hell as eternal conscious punitive torment is not limited to universalists but is currently gaining traction in other evangelical circles. Some, such as Clark Pinnock and John Stott, have advocated a position called conditional immortality, conditionalism, or annihilationism.[64] Only those who believe in Christ are granted eternal life. Those who do not believe, perhaps after a finite period of just punishment, are annihilated and cease to exist. A person's eternality is conditioned on their belief in Christ. Christian interest in "rethinking" hell is not limited to the academy but includes popular writers as well. Emergent Church leader Brian McLaren has written an entire volume, the third and final installment of his New Kind of Christian Trilogy, *The Last Word and the Word After That,* attempting to "deconstruct our conventional concepts of hell in the sincere hope that a better vision of the gospel of Jesus Christ will appear."[65] Many of the arguments against hell are common to both universalism and conditionalism, and this in spite of the seemingly significant differences between the two concepts. For many evangelicals the idea of conditional immortality is tied to discussions of the doctrines of God, eschatology, and Scripture. Evangelical theologians who embrace conditional immortality do not share the same convictions on these crucial Christian doctrines as those who opt for universalism. Nevertheless, there is significant overlap in the theological and exegetical arguments used by conditionalists and Christian universalists who question the doctrine of hell as eternal conscious torment, so it is fitting to discuss and critique the arguments for conditional immortality in this chapter. As the challenge to the doctrine of hell has increased, evangelicals have attempted to defend the doctrine at the exegetical and theological level.[66] Arguments for the existence of hell will provide the strongest argument against universalism and also address the concerns of those who posit conditional immortality.

---

[64]Other prominent evangelical advocates of conditional immortality have included F. F. Bruce, Dale Moody, and John Wenham.

[65]McLaren, *The Last Word and the Word After That,* xvii; see especially 95–121.

[66]Morgan and Peterson, eds., *Hell Under Fire*; Crockett, ed., *Four Views on Hell*; D. A. Carson, *The Gagging of God: Christianity Confronts Pluralism* (Grand Rapids: Zondervan, 1996), 515–36; K. D. Boa and R. M. Bowman Jr., *Sense and Nonsense About Heaven and Hell* (Grand Rapids: Zondervan, 2007).

The Biblical Teaching on Hell

There is little debate, even among those who deny the doctrine of hell, as to the biblical figure most responsible for the doctrine's origin: Jesus.[67] Christ taught extensively on hell. Consider the following examples. In the Sermon on the Mount, Jesus taught that anger and the cursing of an image-bearer is worthy of punishment in hell. "But I say to you that everyone who is angry with his brother will be liable to judgment; whoever insults his brother will be liable to the council; and whoever says, 'You fool!' will be liable to the hell of fire (Matt 5:22 ESV). In the same context Jesus taught that one should take draconian measures to avoid sin because of the threat of hell.

> If your right eye causes you to sin, tear it out and throw it away. For it is better that you lose one of your members than that your whole body be thrown into hell. And if your right hand causes you to sin, cut it off and throw it away. For it is better that you lose one of your members than that your whole body go into hell (Matt 5:28–29 ESV).

Jesus taught His disciples not to worry or fear man but to fear God because God could punish them in hell. "And do not fear those who kill the body but cannot kill the soul. Rather fear him who can destroy both soul and body in hell" (Matt 10:28 ESV). Even in His parables, Jesus spoke of hell to describe the judgment that is to come. In the parable of the talents, Jesus concluded, "And cast the worthless servant into the outer darkness. In that place there will be weeping and gnashing of teeth" (Matt 25:30 ESV).

Sheol, Hades, and Gehenna   The Old Testament teaching on hell is not nearly as developed as what we find in the teaching of Jesus or the rest of the New Testament. *Sheol* is identified throughout the Old Testament as the place of the dead, particularly the ungodly.[68] Old Testament descriptions of *Sheol* are "sparse," but what does occur suggests

---

[67]For a summary of Jesus' teaching on hell, see R. W. Yarbrough, "Jesus on Hell," in *Hell Under Fire*, ed. Morgan and Peterson, 67–90.

[68]See P. S. Johnston, *Shades of Sheol: Death and Afterlife in the Old Testament* (Downers Grove, IL: InterVarsity, 2002), 69–85. Johnston's argument that Sheol is in fact the place of punishment for the wicked is a departure from traditional scholarship that sees Sheol as the grave, the indiscriminating abode of the righteous dead and the unrighteous dead. See, for example, B. Milne, *The Message of Heaven and Hell* (Downers Grove, IL: InterVarsity, 2002), 15. Johnston's scholarship to the contrary is persuasive.

"a somnolent, gloomy existence without meaningful activity or social distinction."[69] The arm of the Lord reaches into *Sheol*, and it provides no refuge from those who would hide from Him (e.g., Job 26:5; Ps 139:8). In most Old Testament references, *Sheol* describes the fate of the wicked.[70] It is a fitting destiny for the ungodly (Num 16:30; 1 Kgs 2:6; Pss 9:17; 49:14; Prov 5:5; Isa 14:11), while the righteous dread it and hope for deliverance (Pss 16:10; 18:5; 30:3; 86:13; Prov 15:24; Hos 13:14).[71] When the godly speak of entering *Sheol*, it is often under extreme duress or in times of despair (Gen 37:35; 42:38; 44:29; Job 14:13).[72]

In the New Testament two words are typically translated as hell: *Hades* and *Gehenna*. *Hades* is the Greek word used to translate the Hebrew *Sheol* in the LXX and is used 10 times in the New Testament (Matt 11:23; 16:18; Luke 10:15; 16:23; Acts 2:27,31; Rev 1:18; 6:8; 20:13,14). New Testament reference to *Hades* is consistent with the Old Testament concept of Sheol, but the theology of *Hades* is further developed. Beginning in the Gospels, *Hades* is the location of the unrighteous dead, while the righteous go to "paradise" or "Abraham's side" (Luke 16:23). Further, *Hades* is explicitly a place of conscious torment for the unrighteous (Luke 16:23; Matt 11:23). *Gehenna* comes from the "Hinnom Valley" (*gê [ben] hinnōm* in Hebrew), a valley near Jerusalem infamous for its defilement by idolatry, child sacrifice, and the disposal of dead bodies (2 Kgs 16:3; 21:6; cf. 23:10). The prophets warned that the sins committed in the valley would be judged (Jer 7:32; 19:6), and the valley, because of its association with fire, judgment, and death, became a symbol of eternal judgment thereafter.[73] The word *Gehenna* is used 12 times in the New Testament, 11 of which come from Jesus (Matt 5:22,29,30; 10:28; 18:9; 23:15,33; Mark 9:43,45,47; Luke 12:5; James 3:6).

---

[69] Johnston, *Shades of Sheol,* 85.

[70] Johnston summarizes, "Sheol cannot be identified simply as the Hebrew term for the underworld which awaits all. It is almost exclusively reserved for those under divine judgment, whether the wicked, the afflicted righteous, or all sinners. It seldom occurs of all humanity, and only in contexts which portray human sinfulness and life's absurdity. Thus Sheol is not used indiscriminately to describe human destiny at death." Ibid., 83.

[71] K. D. Boa and R. M. Bowman Jr., *Sense and Nonsense about Heaven and Hell* (Grand Rapids: Zondervan, 2007), 34.

[72] Daniel I. Block traces the Old Testament background to the New Testament doctrine of hell and believes that the doctrine of eschatological resurrection, judgment and reward is a natural corollary to Israelite anthropology. "The Old Testament on Hell," in *Hell Under Fire*, ed. Morgan and Peterson, 43–65.

[73] R. P. Lightner, "Hell," in *EDT*, 548; P. S. Johnston, "Hell," in *NDBT*, 543.

Descriptive Phrases   The biblical testimony to hell is not limited to the words *Hades* and *Gehenna*. The biblical authors used descriptive and figurative phrases to describe the place of eschatological judgment. In Scripture hell is described as "the eternal fire" (*to pur to aiōnion*). Jesus taught, "It is better for you to enter life maimed or lame, than to have two hands or two feet and be thrown into the eternal fire" (Matt 18:8). Jude used the same phrase when he wrote that Sodom and Gomorrah "serve as an example by undergoing a punishment of eternal fire" (Jude 7 ESV). In a critical verse on the doctrine of eternal hell, Jesus taught in the parable of the sheep and the goats, "And they go away into eternal punishment (*kolasin aiōnion*), but the righteous into eternal life (*zōēn aiōnion*)" (Matt 25:46). This passage contrasts eternal punishment with eternal life. The same adjective of duration, *aiōnion*, describes both the punishment of the wicked and the life of the righteous. Whatever the length of eternal life, eternal punishment lasts just as long.

The apostle Paul described hell as "eternal destruction" (*olethron aiōnion*). God will inflict vengeance "on those who do not know God and on those who do not obey the gospel of our Lord Jesus. They will suffer the punishment of eternal destruction, away from the presence of the Lord and from the glory of his might" (2 Thess 1:8–9 ESV). Although those who will be punished are guilty of afflicting the Thessalonian saints (2 Thess 1:6–7), that affliction is the acting out of those characterized by a more decisive test. They do not know God. They do not obey the gospel of Christ. The author of Hebrews describes hell as an "eternal judgment" (*krimatos aiōnion*, Heb 6:2), which indicates that the judgment is not temporal in nature. Finally, Jesus taught that whoever blasphemes the Holy Spirit is "guilty of an eternal sin" (*aiōnion hamartēmatos*, Mark 3:29).

Figurative Expressions   The term "figurative" is not meant to detract from the reality of hell but is intended to convey that the imagery used stretches and even transcends the human imagination. Too often individuals who disagree with certain biblical teachings dismiss the words of Scripture with an appeal to figurative language, as though there is no reality to which the metaphors refer.[74] Figures of speech always

---

[74]For example, Clark Pinnock argues that the fire imagery employed in New Testament descriptions of hell is "metaphorical," referring to "the pain of loss but not the pain of sense." "The Conditional View," in *Four Views on Hell*, ed. Crockett, 141.

have a referent, and that referent is not always abstract. For example, Jesus and John describe hell in terms of fire (Matt 5:22; Rev 20:15), while Peter and Jude use the term "darkness" (2 Pet 2:17; Jude 6). Two competing metaphors are used to describe the punishment reserved for the wicked.[75] So the question must be asked, "Of what are they figurative?" The truth communicated in these passages is that the punishment that awaits the wicked is horrifying.

An appeal to figurative language is not a legitimate denial of truth content. Rather, in the following verses, the language used is powerful precisely because of the imagery it conveys. John the Baptist described the judgment work of Christ by saying, "His winnowing fork is in his hand, and he will clear his threshing floor and gather his wheat into the barn, but the chaff he will burn with unquenchable fire" (Matt 3:12 ESV). Jesus used the same term to describe hell in Mark 9:43. The language conveys the idea of a punitive fire that can never be put out. There is no relief from the torment. Jesus borrowed from the prophet Isaiah (Isa 66:24) to describe hell as the place "where their worm does not die, and the fire is not quenched" (Mark 9:48). Here the two figures are combined to convey in a multiplicative sense the same idea. The torment will not be abated, and there is no hope of a respite because the fire cannot be put out and the worm never dies. Coupled with Jesus' teaching from the parable of the talents where the wicked are cast into "outer darkness" where there "will be weeping and gnashing of teeth" (Matt 25:30), the inevitable conclusion regarding the torment is that it is conscious. The wicked are offered no respite from the fire and worm, and their contemplation of their destiny results in despair and anger manifest in weeping and gnashing of teeth.

The book of Revelation contains strong images and profound teaching on the subject of hell. In Rev 14:9–11, the apostle John writes that those who worship the beast and its image will "drink the wine of God's wrath, which is mixed full strength in the cup of His anger." The result is that those with whom the Lord is wrathful will be "tormented with fire and sulfur" and that the "smoke of their torment will go up forever and ever." The passage continues that while suffering under fire, "there is no rest day or night for those who worship the beast and his image." The same phrase in Rev 19:3 expresses the joy of heaven

---

[75]William V. Crockett provides many examples in his essay, "The Metaphorical View," in *Four Views on Hell*, ed. Crockett, 43–81.

in the victory over Babylon. God's judgments on the wicked will be total and final. The smoke is an ever-present and eternal reminder of God's righteousness and justice that has been vindicated in His victory. For this reason the multitudes in heaven praise the Lord. It is not due to a perverse desire to see the suffering of others but because justice has at last been enacted, the persecuted righteous have been vindicated, and all rebellion against the most holy God has been put down. Finally, John tells us that in the end the destiny of the Devil, the beast, and the false prophet is the "lake of fire and sulfur" and "they will be tormented day and night forever and ever" (Rev 20:10).

In summary, the biblical teaching on hell is persuasive. Jesus and the apostolic writers portray hell as the just recompense for rebellion against God. Its duration is eternal and its experience is conscious. Unfortunately, a growing number of evangelicals are questioning this teaching.

Conditional Immortality Explained

Conditional immortality, commonly known as conditionalism or annihilationism, is the belief that God has created all human beings only potentially immortal. Whether they will actually be granted immortality depends on their response to the revelation of God. The unbeliever never receives the capacity to live forever and, perhaps after a finite period of punishment for wrongs done during his lifetime, will be punished forever by being annihilated. Conditionalism argues that outside of Christ there is no capacity for immortality, and the unbeliever will eventually be reduced to nonexistence. The view is called conditional immortality because every person's capacity for immortality is contingent on his or her response to the gospel of Christ. Evangelical proponents of conditional immortality include Clark Pinnock, Edward Fudge, and John Stott.[76]

A strong appeal of conditional immortality is emotional. The thought of humans suffering eternal torment in hell is horrifying. John Stott writes, "Well, emotionally I find the concept intolerable and do not understand how people can live with it without either cauterizing their feelings or cracking under the strain."[77] Clark Pinnock provides a

---

[76]See Pinnock, "The Conditional View," 135–66; Fudge, *Fire That Consumes*; E. W. Fudge and R. A. Peterson, *Two Views on Hell: A Biblical & Theological Dialogue* (Downers Grove, IL: InterVarsity, 2000); and Edwards and Stott, *Evangelical Essentials*.

[77]J. Stott, "John Stott's Response to Chapter 6," in Edwards and Stott, *Evangelical Essentials*, 314.

rather extreme testimony to those who find eternal conscious torment conceptually troubling. Responding to the orthodox view penned by John F. Walvoord, Pinnock writes:

> He actually asks us to believe that the God who wills the salvation of the world plans to torture people endlessly in physical fire if they decline his offer of salvation. Questions leap to mind. Who would want to accept salvation from a God like that? Has Walvoord visited the burn unit in his local hospital recently? Is he not conscious of the sadism he is attributing to God's actions? I am baffled, knowing that John is a kindly man, how he can accept a view of God that makes him out to be morally worse than Hitler.[78]

Pinnock's statement is shocking, and it is clear that he misunderstands the just nature of eschatological punishment. After all, if Pinnock is wrong, he has just placed Hitler, and his perverse and demonic attempted extermination of the Jews, on a higher moral plain than God and His just punishment of the wicked. Though thoroughly misguided, Pinnock does provide a striking example of the emotion that motivates conditionalists.

Conditional Immortality Arguments and Responses

Language of Destruction Implies Cessation of Existence　Many biblical references to hell use language of "destruction," translated from the *apōleia* and *olethros* word groups. To the conditionalist, biblical references to the destruction of the wicked imply that they will be destroyed and thus cease to exist.[79] For example, Paul wrote of the enemies of the cross of Christ, "Their end is destruction; their god is their stomach; their glory is in their shame" (Phil 3:19). The same language of destruction is found in 1 Thess 5:3; 2 Thess 1:9; and 2 Pet 3:7. Conditionalists often focus their attention on the Greek word for fire (*pur*) and argue that the word denotes exactly that which we would expect. It is rightly translated "fire," and fire by its very nature is destructive.[80] The imagery of fire connotes that which devours, consumes, and utterly destroys.[81] If an object has been destroyed by

---

[78]Pinnock, "Response to John F. Walvoord," 38.
[79]Stott, "John Stott's Response to Chapter 6," 315–16.
[80]E. Fudge, "The Final End of the Wicked," *JETS* 27 (1984): 328–29.
[81]Stott, "John Stott's Response to Chapter 6," 316.

an unquenchable fire, in what sense could that object still exist other than in remnant form or ashes, which does not constitute existence of the original object? It has been thoroughly and utterly ruined, that is, destroyed.

In response, to gloss "destruction" with "cease to exist" is to fall into the fallacy of limited semantic range, a gross error of translation and interpretation, equivalent to reading every occurrence of the word *green* in a text to mean "surface on which golfers putt," even when the word in context is referring to one who is envious. Words have a semantic range of meanings, and the meaning of any particular usage of a word must be determined by both the immediate and larger contexts. Cessation of existence may well be part of the semantic range of the *apōleia* and *olethros* word groups, but whether it has that meaning in any particular text has to be determined from the context. A survey of the occurrences of the word groups in question demonstrates that cessation of existence is rarely the meaning. The *apōleia* and *olethros* word groups signify "functional ruination" (comparable to the totaling of a car) rather than "ontological abolition" (the removal of an object from existence).[82] For example, in Matt 9:17, Jesus uses the word *apolluntai* to refer to the "destruction" of old wineskins. In Matt 26:8, the disciples are indignant that a jar of perfume was used on Jesus, protesting, "Why this waste" (*apōleia*)? In neither case does the object in question cease to exist. The old wineskin is ruined and useless. The perfume still exists on the body of Jesus, but it was "destroyed" or "wasted" in the sense that it was used and could no longer be sold for profit. Another example is 1 Cor 5:5 where the man under discipline was to be delivered to Satan for the "destruction" (*olethron*) of his flesh. In the course of church discipline, his flesh did not cease to exist, though he may have suffered in the body. In either case the argument that the *apōleia* and *olethros* word groups necessarily imply the cessation of existence is categorically false. Of course, the case for eternal conscience torment is not made by pointing this out because passages such as Phil 3:19 and 1 Thess 5:3 still *could* teach a cessation of existence, but that case must be made by appeal to the statements in their context, not merely the definition of the word.

---

[82] J. I. Packer, "Universalism: Will Everyone Ultimately Be Saved?" in *Hell Under Fire*, ed. Morgan and Peterson, 185.

Conditionalist appeals to "fire" language are likewise unpersuasive. Fire can eventually consume that which it burns. But this is why it is important to recognize that the language used to describe the experience of hell is strongly figurative. Jesus' use of the term "flame" (*phlogi*) in the parable of the rich man and Lazarus is clearly meant to convey the ongoing torment of pain rather than a flame that consumes (Luke 16:24). The point of the "fire and sulphur" imagery is to conjure up images of God's complete judgment on Sodom and Gomorrah. The fire imagery does not necessarily imply a fire that burns things into nonexistence. After all, in Rev 14:10–11, the "smoke of their torment goes up forever and ever." As long as there is smoke, something is burning. The image implies ongoing punishment and torment. The fire metaphor conveys the harsh reality that God's judgment is devastating and horrific, from which there is no relief or appeal. The descriptions of hell must be taken as a whole, and when this is done, it is difficult to conclude that punishment in hell is anything other than eternal and conscious.

Questions Regarding the Word Translated "Eternal"   A second argument by conditionalists focuses on the meaning of the Greek word *aiōn*, commonly translated "eternal." Some conditionalists suggest that *aiōn* does not necessarily mean "forever" but should be translated as "age," connoting the "age to come."[83] Other conditionalists recognize that the adjective *aiōnios* does denote everlasting time but argue that the adjective modifies the result of the action modified, not the action itself. Edward Fudge writes that when the adjective *aiōnios*, which carries both a temporal aspect and a qualitative aspect, modifies words which name acts or processes in the Bible, it not only connotes "the other age quality," but *aiōnios* "usually describes the issue or result of the action rather than the action itself."[84] Therefore, when the Bible describes something as an eternal punishment, it is the eschatological result of the punishment that is in view, not the actual punishing action itself. If the wicked suffer conscious torment for a finite period of time

---

[83]"This does not primarily indicate unending quantity of life or death, but ultimate quality. It means life of the age to come or ruin for the age to come." M. Green, *Evangelism through the Local Church* (Nashville: Thomas Nelson, 1992), 73. This argument is prevalent at the "pew" level among both conditionalists and universalists.

[84]Fudge, *Fire that Consumes*, 49. Fudge argues that this is the meaning of "eternal judgment" in Heb 6:2; "eternal redemption" in Heb 9:12; "eternal salvation" in Heb 5:9; "eternal sin" in Mark 3:29; "eternal destruction" in 2 Thess 1:9; and "eternal punishment" in Matt 25:46. Ibid., 44–48.

commensurate with their crimes and rebellion while alive and then are annihilated without hope of restoration, then their punishment could still be said to be "eternal."[85]

In response to the argument that *aiōn* refers to the "age to come," the same hermeneutical arguments must be made. The Greek word *aiōn* may or may not refer to an eternal age. Context is everything, and Jesus' teaching in Matt 25:46 is decisive. The unrighteous "will go away into eternal punishment [*eis kilasin aiōnion*], but the righteous into eternal life [*eis zōēn aiōnion*]." The same preposition and adjective are used to describe the entrance into punishment that is used to describe the entrance into life. In each case the duration is the same, *aiōnion*. The conditionalist is on the horns of a dilemma with this verse. Either *aiōnion* carries the meaning of eternal, in which case the punishment described is eternal, or *aiōnion* means an age of limited duration, in which case the reward of heaven is not eternal. Neither option is suitable for the conditionalist. Since the biblical testimony is clear that the life granted by faith in Christ is eternal, the only possible interpretation of Matt 25:46 is that the punishment of the wicked is likewise eternal.[86]

The argument that *aiōnios* modifies the result of the action named, rather than the action itself, is also unconvincing. It may be true that *aiōnios* modifies the result of an action rather than the action itself in some cases, but it is reductionistic to claim that the adjective behaves in such a way in all cases. For example, the reference to blasphemy of the Holy Spirit as an "eternal sin" in Mark 3:29 most likely refers to an act that occurred during Jesus' first advent ministry with eternal results. But can the same be said of the use of *aiōnios* in Heb 5:9 where the author writes of Jesus being "perfected" and becoming "the source of eternal salvation to all who obey Him." Fudge argues that "God has in mind the result He will accomplish rather than the act He will perform. . . . Once the saving has taken place, the salvation remains. And that 'eternal' outcome of God's finished action will never pass away."[87] It is true that the results of Jesus' saving act are eternal, but to claim that salvation is only a past event with eternal results is to fly in the face of the biblical doctrine of salvation. The Bible does

[85] See Fudge, "The Final End of the Wicked," 333; id., *Fire That Consumes*, 37–50; P. E. Hughes, *The True Image: The Origin and Destiny of Man in Christ* (Grand Rapids: Eerdmans, 1989), 405.

[86] See Carson, *Gagging of God*, 523, for an excellent summary of the interpretive options for Matt 25:46.

[87] Fudge, *Fire that Consumes*, 46.

describe salvation in Christ as a past act (e.g., Rom 8:24) but also as a present act (e.g., 2 Cor 2:15) and a future act (e.g., 1 Thess 5:8). If "eternal salvation" could connote an ongoing saving action, then it is in keeping with the biblical use of *aiōnios* to ask whether "eternal punishment" could refer to an ongoing punitive action.[88] The case against this conditionalist understanding of *aiōnios* is further developed when one considers the biblical references to eternal punishment that require ongoing existence, such as 2 Thess 1:5–10 ("These will pay the penalty of everlasting destruction, away from the Lord's presence and from His glorious strength") and Rev 14:10–11("the smoke of their torment will go up forever and ever").[89]

Eternal Suffering Is Incompatible with God's Love   Conditionalists argue that an eternal hell full of conscious pain and suffering is inconsistent with the love and justice of God, especially when the pain and suffering are an infinite punishment for finite crimes.[90] There is an inequitable disproportion between sins committed in finite time-space reality and a punishment that is eternal. There are two aspects to this argument. The first aspect is that to the conditionalist endless punishment for finite crimes seems to serve no purpose. God seems cruel and vindictive. The second aspect is one of fairness. In what sense is an eternal punishment commensurate with finite crimes and sins?

In response we must assert that judgment is retributive. When conditionalists make the argument that eternal conscious punishment is pointless, they are assuming punishment must always be remedial or redemptive. Christians are disciplined by God, and that discipline is loving, purifying, and remedial (Deut 8:5; Heb 12:6). But to infer that punishment in hell is the same is to make a category mistake because hell is where God's wrath (*orgē*) is poured out (Rev 14:10–11). Scripture is clear that while judgment and discipline are part of the church's experience (1 Pet 4:17), God's wrath is not ever to be experienced by the church. Jesus has rescued the church "from the wrath (*orgēs*) to come" (1 Thess 1:10 ESV) with the result that "God did not appoint us to wrath (*orgēn*) but to obtain salvation through our Lord Jesus Christ" (1 Thess 5:9).

---

[88] So Carson, *The Gagging of God,* 523.

[89] So C. W. Morgan, "Annihilationism: Will the Unsaved be Punished Forever?" in *Hell Under Fire,* ed. Morgan and Peterson, 203.

[90] See Stott, "John Stott's Response to Chapter 6," 318–19.

Furthermore, God's punishment and justice do not create problems; they solve them.[91] According to Scripture, the question that troubles the human experience is not, How can a just God punish someone forever? The critical question is, How can a holy God forgive the sin of any, given that "acquitting the guilty and condemning the just—both are detestable to the LORD" (Prov 17:15)? How can God be both just and the justifier of the unrighteous (Rom 3:26)? The faithful cry for justice, wondering why God's righteous justice does not come sooner. Why do the wicked prosper (Ps 94:3; Jer 12:1)? Why are they not judged immediately (Rev 6:10)? Indeed, eschatological judgment is portrayed in the Bible in terms of relief and vindication, not that which troubles the conscience (Prov 11:10; Rev 19:1–4). Furthermore, the justice of God in Scripture is always seen as right and glorious. The reason is the depth of human sin. The biblical promise is that when God exposes every hidden motive and thought of the human heart, "unbelievers will finally realize the incredible depth of their sin and believers will better appreciate the infinite price of Christ's death (Rom 2:16; 1 Cor 4:5; 2 Thess 1:6; Heb 4:12–13)."[92]

The punishment of hell must be seen in light of the person against whom we have sinned, that is, the glorious God of Scripture. Sin is fundamentally rebellion against the Lord who is perfect in all of His attributes. Hell is eternal because we have sinned against God. Sin against the infinite God is likewise infinite in its quality, and the relationship between the offender and the offended is decisive. We recognize this intuitively, and it is built into our justice system. Christopher Morgan provides a helpful illustration at this point. He notes that if a gunman broke into somebody's house, he would receive a far greater punishment for killing a human than if he killed the family cat.[93] God is not only different from human beings in degree; he is different in kind and being. Because sin is against this qualitatively different God, who is infinitely worthy of obedience, sin merits an infinite punishment.

I wonder if conditionalists underestimate the sinfulness of human sin and rebellion. Do we see sin from God's perspective or from our own? Do we evaluate the human condition from our perspective or

---

[91]J. I. Packer writes, "The thought of eternal judgment is the reverse of embarrassing to the Bible writers; on the contrary, it is fundamental to their theodicy, their gospel, and their knowledge of God." "Way of Salvation," 6.

[92]Morgan, "Annihilationism," 208.

[93]Ibid., 210.

from God's? I suspect that conditionalists are guilty of minimizing sin because they are viewing sin from their own perspective. Since the fall of Adam, sin has been the universal human experience for all, with Jesus as the only exception. We can hardly expect to evaluate rightly the perniciousness of (our) human sin. This lack of perspective is precisely why we must rely on God's revelation to understand the depth of human sin. We must not question His righteous judgments or His fair and equitable punishments. We simply do not have the capacity or perspective to do so rightly.

One insight we do get into the weight of sin is the cross of Jesus Christ. The horror of human rebellion must be evaluated in light of the crucifixion. When we consider what was necessary to save us, the death of the perfectly righteous incarnate Son of God, is it really hard to believe in eternal punishment? Remarkably, a stronger case could be made for the minimization of human sin if sinners are annihilated. In what sense is this a punishment since there would be no consciousness of pain? Again this hardly accounts for the horror of the cross. Consider also Jesus' warning for the one who betrayed Him. "It would have been better for that man if he had not been born" (Matt 26:24). By Jesus reckoning, nonexistence would be preferable to the punishment that awaited Judas. But of course Judas was born, and his punishment was eternal damnation. Some conditionalists argue that the unsaved will suffer torment for a finite period of time, then finally be annihilated. But such a proposal flies in the face of the logic that flows from the redemptive story. Does the finite time of punishment envisaged by the conditionalist actually atone for the unbeliever's sin and satisfy God's holy justice? If it does (and again, this hypothetical situation hardly accounts for the death of the Son of God), then how is it just that the unbeliever then be annihilated? Why should he not be let into heaven since he paid for his sin? Ironically then, finite punishment followed by annihilation is the scenario that actually calls into question the justice of God.

Eternal Hell Is Incompatible with the New Heavens and New Earth Conditionalists consider an eternal place of torment inconsistent with the new heavens and new earth. The biblical description of the eternal state is one of absolute joy, without sadness or regret. Will not the reality and specter of creatures suffering in hell mar the perfection of heaven? This objection shares much in common with the arguments for universalism that hold that the final victory of God is incommensurate with sinners existing in hell where external rebellion is only ended through coercive punishment rather than the conversion of rebels to God.[94]

But will the existence of hell mar the glories of the new heavens and new earth? John, in his Revelation, had no problem asserting the new heavens and the new earth in simultaneous existence with the lake of fire. In fact, John portrays the ongoing punishment of the wicked as an eternal emblem of the vindication of God's righteousness (Rev 19:1–6; 20:10). The punishment of sin is the solution to the problem of rebellion. When sin goes unpunished, the glory and righteousness of God are called into question. In John's vision of the last days, the judgment of God is an occasion for praise. This judgment is tied inextricably to the salvation offered by our gracious king. For when the Lord judges, the saints of God cry out, "Hallelujah! Salvation, glory, and power belong to our God, because His judgments are true and righteous. . . . Hallelujah! Her smoke ascends forever and ever" (Rev 19:1–3). Therefore, the simultaneous existence of both heaven and hell will serve to remind the redeemed and glorified saints of the riches of God's righteousness and grace demonstrated toward them, who but for that grace of God would be sharing the fate of the unredeemed.

Conclusion

The biblical teaching on heaven and hell is clear. Packer, upon reflecting on the clarity of the biblical passages that speak to the eternal punishment of the impenitent, is right to ask, "How could our Lord and his apostles have made this belief any clearer?"[95] For those who would deny the Bible's teaching on hell, Lindsell's words are still appropriate:

> The universalist must change the Apocalypse of John into a love feast, the threats of the lake of fire into the sea of glass, and the fire of judgment into the waters of the river of life. Brimstone must become the attar of roses, and blessing must be held out to those who are said to have no part in the first resurrection. The judgment of the great white throne, which witnesses to the opening of the book of life in which are to be found the names of men and

---

[94]Stott, "John Stott's Response to Chapter 6," 319.
[95]Packer, "Universalism: Will Everyone Ultimately Be Saved?," 184.

'whosoever was not found written in the book of life was cast into the lake of fire,' becomes poetic imagery designed to frighten men into coming into the kingdom of God earlier, although their failure to come now will not keep them out later. And heaven, despite John's contrary testimony, will be populated by liars, murderers, sorcerers, idolaters, the unbelieving and the abominable. The lake of fire is imaginary for it will be emptied of its occupants who will flood the corridors of heaven and mingle with the holy, the pure, the righteous and the sanctified.[96]

In John's majestic vision of heaven recorded in Revelation 4–5, John is ushered into the throne room of heaven where he witnesses the worship of God by magnificent creatures. All things are as they should be. God is on His throne being worshipped by beings created to worship, crying out, "Our Lord and God, You are worthy to receive glory and honor and power, because You have created all things, and because of Your will they exist and were created" (Rev 4:11). But when a scroll is brought forward, the harmony of heaven is broken. We find that the scroll represents the initiation of final judgment (Rev 6–8), and there is no one anywhere "in heaven or on earth or under the earth" (Rev 5:3) who is able to open the scrolls. And John despairs. He wails. John is in the presence of God where all is supposed to be right and he "cried and cried" (Rev 5:4). The problem is not that judgment is going to come. The problem is that judgment ought to come, but no one is worthy to open the scrolls and initiate that judgment. But Jesus Christ, "the Lion . . . of Judah . . . one like a slaughtered lamb" (Rev 5:5–6), steps forward and is found worthy to open the scrolls. He is worthy because He suffered and died to redeem for God a people "from every tribe and language and people and nation" (Rev 5:6,9). This majestic chapter in John's Revelation links Jesus' sacrifice to His worthiness to judge. "You are worthy to take the scroll and to open its seals; because You were slaughtered" (Rev 5:9). Jesus' atoning sacrifice is tied inextricably to His right and responsibility to judge. In heaven God is praised for being Creator and Savior and Judge (Rev 4:8–11; 5:9–14; 7:10–17; 11:15–18; 12:10–12; 15:3–4; 16:5–7; 18:2–20; 19:1–8). In light of this clear teaching, is it possible to affirm the glory of God and the joy of salvation while simultaneously denying the Lord's righteous

---

[96]Lindsell, "Universalism Today: Part Two," 39.

judgments? Is it possible to preach the biblical gospel while simultaneously rejecting the future reality of hell? The biblical writers were convinced that it is not. We would do well to hear them speak and model our praise, eschatological hope, and understanding of the gospel on their words.

Chapter Four

Pluralism

Pluralism Introduced and Defined

More than 4,000 people gathered in the Hall of Columbus in Chicago to participate in the opening ceremonies of the inaugural World's Parliament of Religions. At ten o'clock a dozen representatives of the different world religions marched into the hall, hand in hand, accompanied by the striking of the Columbian Liberty Bell, which tolled 10 times in honor of Buddhism, Christianity, Confucianism, Hinduism, Islam, Jainism, Judaism, Shintoism, Taoism, and Zoroastrianism, the 10 great religions of the world. The purpose of the parliament was to facilitate dialogue between the leaders of these religions and to reveal the large number of important religious truths that they held in common.[1] Such a gathering would hardly raise eyebrows in today's pluralistic world, but the date of the first World's Parliament of Religions was September 11, 1893. Even though 41 religious groups were represented at the 1893 meeting, the event was planned and run predominately by Christians. The opening ceremonies included the singing of the Christian (and explicitly trinitarian) "Doxology." Over three-quarters of the nearly 200 papers delivered at the Parliament were written by Christians. Christian missionaries figured prominently in the program, Christian hymns were sung,

---

[1] *The World's Parliament of Religions: An Illustrated and Popular Story of the World's First Parliament of Religions, Held in Chicago in Connection with the Columbian Exposition of 1893,* ed. J. H. Barrows (Chicago: The Parliament Publishing Company, 1893), 1:18.

and the Parliament closed with the singing of Handel's "Hallelujah Chorus."[2]

By contrast, over 6,000 individuals representing 125 different religious groups attended the 1993 World's Parliament of Religions, also in Chicago. Though some Christians in 1893 had spoken out for the uniqueness of Jesus Christ, this was not the case in 1993. The 1993 Parliament was "predominantly an other-than-Christian assembly, with the Christians who were present maintaining a modest profile and assiduously avoiding Christian claims of uniqueness or superiority."[3] The dramatic shift illustrated by the two World's Parliament of Religions is thoroughly manifest in the post-Christian West.

The United States is not just a country where many different world religions are represented, where religious diversity is merely an empirical fact. In the hearts and minds of many Americans, religious diversity is a value to cherish. The American pluralistic ethos is seeping into the Christian church as well, and the results are troubling. In a recent Pew Forum & Public Life Forum Report, based on a 2008 survey, 52 percent of Christians surveyed think that at least some non-Christian faiths can lead to eternal life. Of those who responded affirmatively to the statement, "Many religions can lead to eternal life," 80 percent named at least one non-Christian religion (choosing between Judaism, Islam, Buddhism, or atheism/nonreligion) that can lead to salvation.[4] Only 45 percent of white evangelicals surveyed believe that one must be born again through faith in Jesus to gain eternal life (compared to 26 percent of black Protestants, 9 percent of white mainline church members, and 3 percent of white Catholics). The problem is a startling lack of understanding of the gospel. As Alan Wolfe, professor of political science at Boston University explains, many people who claim to be religious "have no command of theology, doctrine or history, so it's an empty

---

[2]A. Neely, "The Parliaments of the World's Religions: 1893 and 1993," *International Bulletin of Missionary Research* 18.2 (1994): 62. Not every Christian was convinced the Parliament was a good idea. D. L. Moody held prayer and evangelism meetings across the street from the Parliament while it was in session. Other Christian leaders, such as A. T. Pierson, were outspoken in their condemnation of the event.

[3]Ibid.

[4]"Many Americans Say Other Faiths Can Lead to Eternal Life," The Pew Forum on Religion & Public Life: Surveys (a study released 18 December 18), [online]; accessed 5 January 2009; available from http://pewforum.org/docs/?DocID=380; Internet.

religiosity."[5] At least in America, ignorance is the soil that cultivates religious pluralism.

Religious pluralism represents the idea that many religions are salvific; it often marches under the banner of multiple paths to God. Such religious convictions do not grow in a philosophical vacuum, however. They are the products of the times, and the rise of religious pluralism is tied to rise of philosophical pluralism.[6] Often labeled the philosophy of postmodernity, philosophical pluralism is easier to identify by what it denies than by what it affirms. It is characterized by a gnawing epistemological skepticism and a rabid suspicion of any truth claim that pits one party over against another. Philosophical pluralism is attended by a commitment to the culturally situated nature of truth and a radical perspectivalism. Reality cannot be known as it actually is but only how it appears to the knower. Because of this, objective knowledge is impossible. The result is that if absolute truth exists at all, it cannot be known with certainty. Therefore, any suggestion that a particular ideology or religious truth claim is superior to another is necessarily false. Religious truth claims are usually dismissed because, according to the philosophical pluralists, a "God's-eye" view of the world from which absolute statements about God and the world can be made does not exist. Even if such a perspective existed, how is humanity to verify the reality of that perspective? When such truth claims are made, it is the job of the "deconstructionist" to expose the ulterior motive (usually a coercive demonstration of power) of the speaker.

The thesis of this book is that there is one supreme God, the Creator, who is sovereign over all. He has revealed Himself as triune and has uniquely revealed Himself in Jesus Christ, the incarnate Son of God, the second person of the Trinity. Humanity, due to its rebellion against God, stood condemned before God, utterly without hope. God, in His rich mercy and love, reached out to us in Jesus Christ, paving not just a way but the only way for relationship with Him through conscious and intentional repentance and faith in Christ. In short, there is one way to the Supreme Creator God, and that is through His Son, Jesus Christ.

---

[5] C. L. Grossman, "Believers OK with Many Paths," *USA Today*, 24 June 2008, D2. Grossman was commenting on the results of an earlier Pew Forum Research study that prompted the survey referenced above.

[6] See D. A. Carson, *The Gagging of God: Christianity Confronts Pluralism* (Grand Rapids: Zondervan, 1996), 13–54, 142–50, for a discussion of the relationship between philosophical and religious pluralism.

In our current context this is an unpopular thesis to defend. Twenty-first-century America is post-Christian and thoroughly pluralistic. We live in a world with many religions and competing truth claims. Religious others are no longer located only overseas; they live next door, teach in elementary schools, own stores, wait on tables, run department stores, manage banks, and play sports. Whatever lifestyles and activities characterize the West, religious others are active participants. We live and learn with Hindus, Muslims, Buddhists, Pagans, Scientologists, and others (including television "gurus"). With the different religions come a variety of ideas and recommended cures for all that ails us. The individual has a seemingly endless array of choices, an ideological smorgasbord, where one can sample and choose religious entrees according to taste and preference without fear of cultural reprisal.[7]

The simultaneous existence of many philosophies, ideologies, and religions has been the case for millennia, but through advanced technology the world is now interconnected as never before. The philosopher John D. Caputo describes our current world as irreducibly pluralistic. He writes, "We live in a world of instant global communication, linked by satellite communication systems to the most remote corners of the world, which exposes us at every turn to a plurality of voices and choices, races and places, cultures and religions, to the multiplicity of lifestyles and ways to be."[8] But religious and philosophical pluralism are not just descriptive of the current situation. They also describe the ethos that attends our world. The public perception about religious and philosophical pluralism has changed in the last century. In the West, because of factors such as the rise of the global village and the relativistic mind-set of postmodernity, where tolerance has been redefined and elevated to the status of the preeminent virtue, what was once a simple reality is now "cherished" in the Western value system. In our postmodern context, where any attempt to establish the certainty of a truth claim is met with skepticism and suspicion, the easiest path to take is often that of epistemological nonresistance. If one makes no truth claims, then one will not offend anybody. Such a

---

[7]This is not to say that American pluralism is not without its tensions. Robert Wuthnow chronicles the struggles that attend one trying to live out his or her religious commitments in a society trying to cling to its Christian roots in *American and the Challenges of Religious Diversity* (Princeton: Princeton University Press, 2005).

[8]J. D. Caputo, *What Would Jesus Deconstruct? The Good News of Postmodernism for the Church* (Grand Rapids: Baker, 2007), 42.

climate provides fertile ground for the cultivation of pluralism. The world has almost always been pluralistic, and people understood this even if they did not like it. Today, in our postmodern ethos, pluralism is embraced and cherished. Pluralism is not merely the way of things; it is thought to be the way things ought to be.

PLURALIST ARGUMENTS

In post-Christian America, the exclusive truth claims of Christianity are met with incredulity and hostility. As Harold Netland describes, pluralists "repudiate the suggestion that there is anything unique, normative, or superior about Jesus Christ or the Christian faith."[9] Attacks from unbelievers are to be expected. The alarming trend is that many attempts to argue against the uniqueness of Christ are originating within Christianity itself. Religious pluralists, at both the popular and academic level, write prolifically. Writers such as John Hick, Paul Knitter, Raimundo Panikkar, and Stanley Samartha present influential arguments for religious pluralism at the academic level, and writers such as Eckhart Tolle exercise popular influence through both fiction and nonfiction works.[10]

Most of the arguments employed by the pluralist in answering the question, "Are there many paths to one God?" fall into two basic categories that I will label *reductionism* and *obfuscation*. Reductionism occurs when the claim is made that the major religions are essentially the same and ultimately teach the same things. Obfuscation occurs when the assertion is made that because God is complex and mysterious, any claims to particularity are finally impossible. Perhaps each religion contributes something of the truth but never the whole. Both categories of arguments attempt to do the same thing, namely, to make the case that there are many equally valid paths to God. Reductionism attempts to reduce the essence of each religion

---

[9]H. A. Netland, *Dissonant Voices: Religious Pluralism and the Question of Truth* (Grand Rapids: Eerdmans, 1991), 26.

[10]Eckhart Tolle exerts considerable influence due to Oprah Winfrey's zealous advocacy and promotion. In 2008, Winfrey and Tolle hosted 10 Web seminars that were viewed by more than 27 million people. Tolle's religious convictions are an eclectic blend of Christianity, Hinduism, Buddhism, and mysticism. His books, which include *A New Earth: Awakening to Your Life's Purpose* (New York: Dutton, 2005) and *The Power of Now: A Guide to Spiritual Enlightenment* (Vancouver: Namaste Publishing, 1999), are sprinkled liberally with quotes from Jesus, but his worldview is thoroughly pluralistic, denying the deity and personhood of Christ, the human self (*a la* Hinduism), and the essential difference between God and creation (*a la* Buddhism). See J. A. Beverley, "Nothing New," *CT* 52/8 (August 2008): 50.

down to a lowest common denominator. Obfuscation is more specific to Christianity, attempting to demonstrate that the specific doctrines that lead toward differentiation and supremacy are actually incoherent and untrustworthy.

Though Christian faithfulness demands that each pluralist writer be answered, space constrains me to interact generally with the work of pluralists who claim to be Christian.[11] My reason is twofold. First, the church is typically affected most deeply from within (e.g., Acts 20:29–30). Much ink has been spilled in the attempt to reconcile pluralistic tendencies with orthodox Christian faith.[12] The attacks of religious pluralism that assail the thinking of the church would have far less effect if those who professed to be Christian were not mouthing the same words of those who do not claim to know or love Christ. Second, the language and categories of Christian pluralists are typically Christian and trinitarian. Even when they do not embrace the pluralist position, Christians are often moved by the arguments. As we will find, many pluralist arguments have found their way into the thinking of Christian inclusivists.

The summary of arguments for religious pluralism that follows is drawn from many authors, the most significant of whom is John Hick. Hick has been the most provocative voice of Christian religious pluralism for the past four decades, and he is especially compelling to many due to his background.[13] While in his late teens, Hick embraced Christianity but gradually moved through Christian inclusivism to pluralism. In his book *God and the Universe of Faiths*, Hick describes a shift in his thinking (which he describes as "Copernican") from believing that Christianity was at the center of theology to the realization that God is at the center, "and that all religions of mankind, including our

---

[11]See especially *The Myth of Christian Uniqueness: Toward a Pluralistic Theology of Religions*, ed. J. Hick and P. Knitter (Maryknoll, NY: Orbis, 1997).

[12]For example, Terrence W. Tilley attempts to demonstrate through a proof similar to the freewill defense of evil that a modest pluralism such as that described above can be logically coherent with orthodox Christian faith. "Christian Orthodoxy and Religious Pluralism," *Modern Theology* 22/1 (January 2006): 51–63.

[13]Hick often gives his "testimony" when speaking to Christian audiences. See, for example, J. Hick, "A Pluralist View," in *Four Views on Salvation in a Pluralistic World*, ed. D. L. Okholm and T. R. Phillips (Grand Rapids: Zondervan, 1995, 1996), 38. J. Hick chronicles his spiritual journey from orthodox Christian to religious pluralist in J. Hick, *Disputed Questions in Theology and Philosophy of Religion* (New Haven, CT: Yale University Press, 1993), 139–45. See also H. Netland, *Encountering Religious Pluralism* (Downers Grove, IL: InterVarsity, 2001), 158–77.

own, serve and revolve around him."[14] Since that time Hick's model of religious pluralism has undergone significant development. Whereas he used to think of God in Christian terms, Hick has since arrived at a pluralism in which particular truth claims of the divine are impossible. The result is that Hick can no longer bring himself to refer to the object of his worship by personal names, such as "God," for doing so would infer personhood in the divine. Instead, Hick refers to God as "the Real."[15]

Arguments of Reduction

Reductionism occurs when pluralists downplay the differences in the world religions and then claim that there is no essential difference between them. The methodology appeals to the transcendence of God, often asserting a Kant-like bifurcation between who God is in Himself (the noumenal) and human perceptions of Him (the phenomenal). No one human conception of God can be privileged over another and, when cultural conditioning is taken into account, each of the major religions ultimately accomplishes the same thing.

The Transcendence of God Leading to Different, Often Divergent, Human Conceptions of Him   In his understanding of the Real's transcendence, Hick does not hold that we are uncertain as to which categories apply to God, nor is he proposing to understand God through the negation of human concepts (*via negativa*). Rather, he asserts that no substantial concepts apply to God either positively or negatively.[16] Consistent with his testimony, Hick takes the reality of religious others as an ontological necessity and constructs his understanding of God from that point:

> The hypothesis is that in order to account for the existence of the different religio-cultural totalities . . . as apparently more or less equally effective contexts of salvation/liberation, we have to postulate an ultimate transcendent reality, the source and ground of

---

[14]J. Hick, *God and the Universe of Faiths: Essays in the Philosophy of Religion* (New York: St. Martin's, 1973), 131.

[15]See, for example, Hick, "Pluralist View."

[16]Hick writes, "To be agnostic, e.g., about whether the divine Essence is personal or impersonal would be to assume that it is one or the other, but that one does [not] profess to know which. However what I have proposed is that all such dualities as 'either personal or impersonal,' do not apply to it." "Response to Dr Recber," *Islam and Christian-Muslim Relations* 16/1 (2005): 12.

everything, that is in itself beyond the scope of human conceptuality but is variously conceived, therefore variously experienced, and therefore variously responded to in life, from within these different religious totalities.[17]

How is it possible to worship the Real if it is beyond all human characterization and its incomprehensible and ineffable nature leads to divergent human concepts of the Real? The answer to Hick is simple. We cannot worship the Real in itself; rather, we worship particular manifestations of itself to humanity (e.g., the heavenly "parent" of Jesus' teaching, the Qur'anic Allah, or the Adonai of Judaism).[18]

The World Religions as Different Receptions of and Reactions to the Same Ineffable God Many pluralists appeal to the now-familiar parable, popularized by John Godfrey Saxe in his poem *Blind Men and the Elephant*, of multiple blind men trying to describe an elephant. The entire elephant is inaccessible to the men, and they blindly grope at particular parts. Although each blind man touches the same elephant, the parts of the elephant that each one encounters are so different that each describes the one elephant in completely different terms. The man who feels the massive sides of the elephant believes that he is touching a wall; the next blind man touches the elephant's tusk and believes he is holding a spear; another grabs the elephant's trunk and is convinced he is grasping a snake, and so forth. So it is with human descriptions of God. Our finiteness and perspective limits our understanding to some particularity that may very well be different from that of another attempting to describe the same god. Because of both the transcendence and infinitude of God, coupled with the finitude of humanity, human attempts to describe God are necessarily perspectival and reductionistic. People, in addition to being finite, are conditioned by their culture and upbringing. Objectivity when attempting to describe the infinite God is impossible. Raimundo Panikkar takes the argument a step further by arguing that the ineffability of God has far more to do with the pluralistic nature of God than it does with human

---

[17] Hick, "Pluralist View," 50.

[18] Ibid., 50. The Jewish Enlightenment philosopher and pluralist Moses Mendelssohn argued that although metaphysical truths can be known, they cannot be adequately signified into language. M. Gottlieb, "Mendelssohn's Metaphysical Defense of Religious Pluralism," *JR* (2006): 207.

epistemological limitations.[19] For this reason Panikkar actually resists the reductionistic attempts of pluralists, arguing that no one religion can be universalized. Each is a valid perspective of a radically complex God.

Human capacity to respond to any stimuli is conditioned by culture, circumstance, background, education, tradition, and a host of other factors. If there is a complete bifurcation between the Real in itself and the Real as humanly perceived (which Hick takes to be axiomatic), then it follows that the great religions of the world are "culturally conditioned human responses to the one ultimate reality."[20] For Hick, Christianity and all other world faiths are human responses to the divine. God as known to Christians, Jews, Muslims, Buddhists, Hindus, and others represents different manifestations of the Real to humanity.[21] The differences in the world religions lie in the fact that each sees the Real through a different conceptual lens.[22] This is not to say that there are different and incompatible revelations of the Real but that there can be different and contradictory responses to the revelation of the Real.[23] This phenomenon also accounts for diversity in religious experience. Different religious practices, themselves culturally conditioned, will necessarily result in different experiences of the Real.[24]

Because the Real has an ontology of its own and is not itself conditioned by human perception, Hick expects that there will be varying degrees of continuity between the different human perceptions of the Real. On this basis Hick is able to make the spectacular claim that when the cultural veneer (language, concepts, liturgical actions, ethos) of each religion is stripped away the differences shrink in significance. Hick writes of the religions,

---

[19]R. Panikkar, "The Jordan, the Tiber, and the Ganges: Three Kairological Moments of Christic Self-Consciousness," in *Myth of Christian Uniqueness*, ed. Hick and Knitter, 89–116.

[20]Hick, "Response to Dr Recber," 12.

[21]Hick refers to these different manifestations of God in religious experience as "different 'faces' or 'masks' or *personae* of God, the Ultimate Reality." "Pluralist View," 39.

[22]This is precisely the point made by Gordon D. Kaufman and Wilfred Cantwell Smith in their pluralistic approach to world religions. They argue that when particularities in any one religion become absolutized, the result is idolatry. See G. D. Kaufman, "Religious Diversity, Historical Consciousness, and Christian Theology," in *Myth of Christian Uniqueness*, ed. Hick and Knitter, 5; W. C. Smith, "Idolatry: In Comparative Perspective," in ibid., 53–68.

[23]Hick, "Response to Dr Recber," 12.

[24]Hick, "Pluralist View," 44–45.

From a religious point of view basically the same thing is going on in all of them, namely, human beings coming together within the framework of an ancient and highly developed tradition to open their hearts and minds to God, whom they believe makes a total claim on their lives and demands of them, in the words of one of the prophets, "to do justice, and to love kindness, and to walk humbly with your God" (Mic. 6:8).[25]

This is not to say that every religion is exactly the same or that each is equivalent at every point. Apprehension of the divine, religious practices, and ethics will vary qualitatively and quantitatively. Still, Hick is convinced that the plurality of religious traditions will constitute different, but "more or less equally salvific, human responses to the Ultimate."[26]

Salvation Is Redefined   In order to render the claim workable that the major religions are essentially equal salvific responses to the Real, salvation itself must be redefined. To define salvation in Christian terms is unfair and unacceptable to pluralists like Hick. That is, it is begging the question to define salvation as being forgiven and reconciled to God based on the death and resurrection of Jesus and then conclude that Christianity alone is able to offer the way of salvation. Therefore, Hick prefers to redefine salvation using more general concepts that are not bound to the particularity of any one religion. For Hick, salvation is the gradual transformation from self-centeredness (with all the resultant human evils) to reality-centeredness (manifest in what Christians call fruit of the Spirit but that other religions name differently).[27] If salvation is so designated, then it is apparent to Hick that the same thing takes place in all the major religions. The different concepts and experiences of the world religions in the pursuit of what Hick calls "salvation/liberation" are "all forms of the same fundamental human transformation from self-centeredness to a recentering in the ultimately Real."[28] Jacques Dupuis does much the same thing when he argues for a "*de jure*" religious pluralism. He finds that religious traditions other than Christianity have a "positive salvific significance" for

---

[25]Ibid., 38.
[26]Ibid., 47.
[27]Ibid., 43.
[28]Ibid., 44.

their followers that fits into the eternal plan of God for humanity.[29] He does not explain how the different religious conceptions of salvation fit into the plan of God. It is enough to posit the possibility.

Little Ethical Difference in the Participants of Various Religions According to pluralists, there is not only little difference in the ultimate goal of each religion, but there is little ethical difference in the participants of each religion. In their estimation the virtues and vices seem to be distributed evenly and without distinction. Ultimately, they conclude that it is impossible to establish the moral superiority of the adherents of one religion over another. Hick writes,

> But when we look, as I believe we must today, beyond the borders of our own inherited tradition we see that all the major world religions produce, so far as we can tell, a more or less equal mixture of saints and sinners, a more or less equal degree of transformation within their devout followers from natural self-concern to an acceptance of others as equally . . . children of God.[30]

If the fruit of the Christian faith is neither better nor worse than the fruit of other faiths, then why should Christianity be privileged over any other religion? For those who are familiar with the piety and goodness of religious others based on their experience, religious pluralism offers an explanation and an invitation to consider other paths to God.

Arguments of Obfuscation

The goal of obfuscation is to demonstrate that theological doctrines that would privilege one religion over another are ultimately incoherent and unsustainable. The orthodox and historical Christian expression of doctrines such as the inspiration of Scripture, the deity of Christ, and the hypostatic union, are inherently nonpluralistic. That is, if these doctrines are true, then there is little room for discussion

---

[29]J. Dupuis, "Inclusivist Pluralism as a Paradigm for the Theology of Religions," an unpublished paper presented to the conference, "Religious Experience and Contemporary Theological Epistemology: Leuven Encounters in Systematic Theology IV" (Katholicke Universiteit Leuven, 7 November 2003), 6. Dupuis's formulations of religious pluralism are typically Christocentric, so I will discuss his work at length in chapter 5 under nonevangelical Christian approaches to inclusivism.

[30]Hick, "Response to Dr Recber," 12–13. See also id., "The Non-Absoluteness of Christianity," in *The Myth of Christian Uniqueness*, ed. Hick and Knitter, 23–30.

about multiple paths to God. The goal of pluralists is to undercut non-pluralist claims by denying the coherence of these doctrines.

Pluralists and the Authority of the Bible   If the Christian doctrines of revelation and inspiration are correct, then the claims of the Bible are true by definition. The Christian Scriptures claim that the Bible is a concurrent work of the holy God and the human author whereby the Holy Spirit so moved the human author that God speaks exactly as He desires without compromising the personality of the human author (2 Tim 3:16; 2 Pet 1:20–21). The doctrine of inspiration, so formulated, entails that the words of the Bible are true and accurate because the Lord who is perfect and cannot lie inspired them. Pluralist claims cannot be sustained if God has spoken truly in and through Jesus Christ and in the Christian Bible. Simply, if the claims of Jesus are true as revealed in the Bible, the contrary claims of all other religious figures are false. Therefore, the pluralist must define inspiration to be something other than what the Christian doctrine affirms. If the Christian doctrine of inspiration is denied, then the reliability and authority of the Bible can be called into question. Again, Hick's attack on the Scriptures is representative of pluralist attempts to deny the reliability of the Bible. Hick claims that the reliability of the Bible should be questioned because it was written over a thousand years ago by a variety of authors in a variety of genres. The authors lived during an era when scientific understanding was low and disease was attributed to supernatural causes.[31] Hick questions the reliability of the gospel accounts, making a distinction between the Jesus of history and the Christ of faith. He claims that the gospels are documents of faith written long after Jesus' death by people who were not eyewitnesses to the events they describe.[32]

Hick and other pluralists explicitly deny that God reveals propositional truth to people through human language.[33] Pluralist understandings of revelation and inspiration are rooted in religious experience. Revelation occurs when humans who are open to the divine have a vivid awareness of God.[34] Further, the words God inspires are open to interpretation. Pluralist arguments regarding the obscurity of language

---

[31]Hick, "Pluralist View," 33.

[32]Ibid., 34–35.

[33]Hick writes, "Theology is a human creation. I do not believe that God reveals propositions to us, whether in Hebrew, Greek, English, or any other language." Ibid., 36.

[34]Ibid., 34.

have found a welcome place in postmodern hermeneutics, where claims of the recoverability of authorial intention are met with skepticism. If authors do not control meaning, then there is no reason to privilege one interpretation over another.

Pluralists and the Deity of Christ   When the reliability of the Gospels is called into question, then the claims to deity contained therein are also suspect. Following the lead of liberal scholars and the Jesus Seminar, pluralists are quick to deny that the Bible accurately records the words of the historical Jesus.[35] Of Jesus' own claims to deity, Hick explains,

> Among mainline New Testament scholars, both conservative and liberal, Catholic and Protestant, there is today a general consensus that these are not pronouncements of the historical Jesus but words put into his mouth some sixty or seventy years later by a Christian writer expressing the theology that had developed in his part of the expanding church.[36]

When the Gospel accounts are rejected as unreliable and the rest of the New Testament is dismissed as the biased theologizing of a self-interested church, then the doctrines of the church regarding the person of Christ have no real meaning in history. In particular, the hypostatic union of Christ, the union of His true human nature and true divine nature in one person, is rejected. Pluralists do not deny that Jesus was remarkable, but the hypostatic union is nonsensical to them.[37] For example, Alan Race, in his book *Christians and Religious Pluralism*, one of the earliest studies in developing a Christian theology of religions, outlines the exclusivist, inclusivist, and pluralist views on salvation, then dedicates an entire chapter to the incarnation of Christ. He ultimately argues that the incarnation is a myth, preferring to see Christ as a human in which God was inordinately active. "Jesus' divinity is more a quality of his role in opening up access to God the Father's love and grace, than . . . of his personal nature."[38] Viewing Jesus in this way has the benefits of avoiding "the problems of incoherence in the

---

[35] See J. Hick, ed., *The Myth of God Incarnate* (Philadelphia: Westminster Press, 1976).

[36] Hick, "Pluralist View," 53. See also id. "Non-Absoluteness of Christianity," 23–30.

[37] Hick, "Pluralist View," 57.

[38] A. Race, *Christians and Religious Pluralism: Patterns in the Christian Theology of Religions* (Maryknoll, NY: Orbis, 1982), 128.

language of pre-existence,"[39] "rescues Christianity from embarrassment in an age of radical historical consciousness . . . (and) releases him to make his impact afresh in the dialogue, at the important level of religious experience."[40] Hick argues much the same way, viewing Jesus as embodying divine moral qualities as well as any human in history and being particularly open to the Spirit of God.[41]

Arguments for a Turn to Theocentrism (Via Pneumatology) over Christocentrism

A prevailing strategy of religious pluralists is to call the church to move to a more general theocentric set of criteria for evaluating religions rather than Christocentric criteria.[42] The logic is that if God, without the particularity of Jesus Christ, could become the basis for comparison between the religions, then the similarities necessary for pluralism would be found. Of course, the transition from Christocentrism to theocentrism cannot be performed without doctrinal remainder and revision. In order to posit a robust pluralist theology of religions, one has to revise the historic doctrines of the Christian faith, including, but not limited to, the doctrine of God and Christology. Many pluralists are turning to pneumatology, citing the universal presence of the Holy Spirit as the way forward in moving to theocentric pluralism. Peter Hodgson, Paul Knitter, and Stanley Samartha offer representative examples of this turn to pneumatology.

Peter Hodgson   A recent proposal by Peter Hodgson for a pluralist theology of religions built upon pneumatology demonstrates the revisionism of biblical doctrines that is taking place in the rush to embrace the pluralist mind-set.[43] Hodgson believes that "Spirit" is "a more universally available religious symbol" than "Christ" and should be embraced by Christians as the starting point for a theology of religions.[44] In order for this to be workable, however, Hodgson must revise

---

[39] Ibid., 129.

[40] Ibid., 137.

[41] Hick, "Pluralist View," 58.

[42] In a sense all pluralistic approaches are theocentric. For this reason Veli-Matti Kärkkäinen categorizes pluralistic approaches to theology of religions as "theocentric" compared to christocentric or ecclesiocentric. V. Kärkkäinen, *An Introduction to the Theology of Religions* (Downers Grove, IL: InterVarsity, 2003), 169.

[43] Peter Hodgson is Charles G. Finney Professor of Theology, Emeritus, in the Divinity School of Vanderbilt University, where he taught from 1965 to 2003.

[44] P. Hodgson, "The Spirit and Religious Pluralism," *Horizons* 31/1 (2004): 22.

the Christian doctrines of God, Christ, and the Holy Spirit. Sharing much in common with process theology, Hodgson posits God as a process. The relationship between God and the world generates the Trinitarian figures. God is a perfect yet abstract being differentiated from the world. "Christ is a determinate, limited, self-critical manifestation of divine creative-redemptive power. For Christians, he is the definitive clue to the whole process but not the whole itself. Of necessity he points beyond himself to other creative-redemptive figures and practices, and demands of us openness toward them."[45] The Spirit is the "consummation of the world in God by which a more inclusive whole is generated."[46]

With specific regard to the Holy Spirit, Hodgson denies the eternal personhood of the Spirit (and the Son for that matter). All that exists is God and the potential for relationships in the world that are actualized when God creates the world. "Spirit is simply the creative and redemptive power of God at work in the world. It is the power by which God calls into being and dwells within all that is. It is the power of being by which beings are."[47] As such, the Spirit has not only the form of the Holy Spirit of Christian theology but also that of human spirit, world spirit, and natural spirits.[48]

Hodgson rightly recognizes that the presence of the Spirit was manifested in Jesus Christ and through Him Christians recognize the Holy Spirit. The anointing of the Spirit upon Jesus made Him the Christ. The character and power demonstrated by Jesus defines the Spirit and provides the Christian with a basis for distinguishing between divine power and demonic power. But Hodgson is adamant that the Spirit transcends Christ and appears in many different religions and their leading figures. Therefore, the Spirit cannot be limited to the historical and concrete particularity of Jesus.[49] Further, because the Spirit emerges from the interaction of God with the world, the Spirit proceeds not just from the Father and the Son but also from God and the world. Therefore, there can be no subordination of the Spirit to Christ.[50] Hodgson cautions Christians to be careful not to establish Christological criteria by which to identify the work of the Spirit. He

---

[45] Ibid., 24.
[46] Ibid.
[47] Ibid., 27.
[48] Ibid.
[49] Ibid., 29.
[50] Ibid., 29–30.

reasons that it is possible to be other than Christ without being against Christ. It is self-evident to Hodgson that today there are "a plurality of saving shapes of divine presence, and we should be able to affirm that the Spirit proceeds from this plurality, not from Christ alone."[51] The criterion for discerning the work of the Spirit is a spiritual principle, not Christological. Therefore, it is naïve to think that Christ establishes the criterion for discernment of the Spirit's presence in the world. In fact, because the relationship between Christ and the Spirit is so complex, Hodgson believes that we are helped to interpret the Christ-Spirit interplay through "concretions of the Spirit in other religions."[52]

For Hodgson, a theology of religions serves a twofold purpose. First, a theology of religions should expose and eliminate the evil that is present in the religions of the world. Second, a theology of religions should draw the world religions into mutually enriching dialogue and practices.[53] Because of the universal presence of the Spirit, pneumatology offers the most promising foundation for a pluralistic theology of religions. The work of the Holy Spirit in the world provides the lens for the Christian to view and to appreciate the plurality of world religions. "A theology of the Spirit is a Christian way of construing this diversity and plurality, relating it to the purposes, activity, and being of God. It is only one such construal, and it must accept that other religions interpret the diversity differently. It has no monopoly on the truth."[54] For this reason Hodgson asserts that the right-thinking Christian should be open to truth wherever the Spirit chooses to manifest it. The Christian should be open to dialogue and willing to learn from others.

Paul Knitter   Paul Knitter has played a significant role in moving many Christians (particularly fellow Catholics) who are dissatisfied with the narrowness of inclusivism to embrace a kind of pluralism that leaves room for the uniqueness of Jesus Christ. Paul Knitter, former Divine Word missionary and professor emeritus of theology at Xavier University, where he began teaching in 1975, is perhaps the most influential Catholic voice in America on the topic of interreligious

---

[51] Ibid., 30.

[52] Ibid.

[53] Ibid., 32. His example of eliminating evil is the critique that the feminist movement brought to the patriarchal structures that institutionalized the oppression of women. His example of enrichment is David Kreiger's attempt to articulate a global theology based on a synthesis of Wittgenstein and Gandhi.

[54] Ibid.

dialogue.[55] Dissatisfied with the "inclusive uniqueness" of Christ found in the teaching of the Catholic Church and Karl Rahner whereby Jesus Christ has an anonymous cosmic presence in world religions or is seen as their final fulfillment,[56] Knitter advocates a "theocentric Christology."[57] Jesus has a relational uniqueness; that is, as He relates to other religious figures, His standing is based entirely on God the Father. He exercises no exclusive or normative claims personally. If Jesus stands out among other religious figures to any degree, it is not because of who He is in Himself. Rather, Jesus is theocentric, "a universally relevant manifestation (sacrament, incarnation) of divine revelation and salvation."[58] While Jesus is considered authoritative revelation from God, He is not necessarily definitive or normative revelation. There may be other savior figures among other religions.[59]

Knitter has recently begun to investigate the cosmic role of the Holy Spirit as a point of common ground for interreligious dialogue.[60] This comes to full fruition in his response to criticism of his five theses for advancing a distinctly Christian pluralism.[61] In response to criticisms from theologians, including evangelical inclusivists Clark Pinnock and John Sanders,[62] that his theses ignore the centrality of Christ in salvation, Knitter appeals to a pneumatological Christology:

---

[55]A former student of the inclusivist Karl Rahner, the spiritual pilgrimage of Paul Knitter in many ways follows the pattern of that of the pluralist John Hick. Knitter approached his missionary service in the 1950s from an exclusivist perspective but was heavily influenced by Vatican II and the teaching of Karl Rahner to advocate an inclusivist position. His exposure to pious people of other religious traditions caused him to rethink his inclusivist commitment, moving him toward a theocentric pluralism. Knitter writes of how his friendship with a devout Muslim from Pakistan caused him to abandon the inclusivism inspired by Rahner. P. Knitter, *Jesus and Other Names: Christian Mission and Global Responsibility* (Maryknoll, NY: Orbis, 1996), 8. The movement of Knitter's theology of religions is well summarized in A. Yong, *Discerning the Spirit(s): A Pentecostal-Charismatic Contribution to Christian Theology of Religions* (Sheffield, UK: Sheffield Academic, 2000), 46–50.

[56]The teaching of the Roman Catholic Church and Karl Rahner will be summarized in chapter 5.

[57]P. Knitter, *No Other Name? A Critical Survey of Christian Attitudes Toward the World Religions* (Maryknoll, NY: Orbis, 1985), 171–204.

[58]Ibid., 172.

[59]Knitter, *No Other Name*, 205.

[60]P. Knitter, "A New Pentecost? A Pneumatological Theology of Religions," *CD* 19 (1991): 38. This article also demonstrates the profound effect that Georg Khodr (discussed in chap. 5) has had on pneumatological approaches to theology of religions.

[61]P. F. Knitter, "Five Theses on the Uniqueness of Jesus," in *The Uniqueness of Jesus: A Dialogue with Paul F. Knitter*, ed. L. Swidler and P. Mozjes (Maryknoll, NY: Orbis, 1997), 4–14.

[62]Pinnock and Sanders are concerned that the pluralistic Christianity of Knitter will lead to a "rather lackluster Christian witness." P. F. Knitter, "Can Our 'One and Only' also be a 'One Among Many'? A Response to Responses," in *Uniqueness of Jesus*, ed. Swidler and Mozjes, 175.

"Christology in general, and a theology of religions in particular, must be consistent with trinitarian theology; this means it must be more formed by a theology of the Holy Spirit."[63] According to Knitter, a balance between Christology and pneumatology must be achieved that does not subordinate the Holy Spirit to the Son or reduce the economy of the Holy Spirit to that of the Son:

> While the Spirit can never be understood and experienced without reference to the Word, neither can the Spirit, explicitly or implicitly, be reduced to the Word, subordinated to the Word, or understood as merely a different "mode" of the Word. There is a "hypostatic independence," that is, real, effective difference. . . . And yet, such independence is qualified, for both the economy of the Word and that of the Spirit are essentially bonded to each other in a relationship that is complete with the Deity (*ad intra*) but still in process of realizing itself and being discovered by humans in the history of creation (*ad extra*).[64]

Knitter believes that when the relationship between the incarnate Word and the Holy Spirit is understood in a theocentric sense, it will bring "clarification that would enable a more resolute openness to what the Spirit might be doing in other religious traditions."[65] The relation between Christ and the Holy Spirit is not found in a Christocentric purpose of the Holy Spirit but in the theocentric natures of the missions of the Son and Spirit. The continuity in those missions is found not in Christ but God. This allows for significant discontinuity in the economies of the Son and the Spirit while still affirming continuity as each relates to God:

> Recognizing this activity of the Spirit as genuinely different from but essentially related to what has been revealed in the incarnate Word, we would not be able to continue our insistence that Jesus brings us the "final" or the "definitive" or the "unsurpassable" truth about God and world, for such claims would subordinate the Spirit to the Word. But we could announce that whatever is found with the realm of the Spirit and other religions has to be brought

---

[63]Ibid., 179.
[64]Ibid., 181.
[65]Ibid., 182.

into a sometimes confirmatory and sometimes critical relationship with the universality, decisiveness, and indispensability of what the Word of God has spoken in Jesus of Nazareth. Because of their real differences, the Spirit or the Word will sometimes reveal truths that are "greater" than what is contained in the other; but because of their relatedness, the truth of each will not contradict the other. What this means concretely, how to discern what is truly of the Word or of the Spirit of God, can be known only in the dialogue itself.[66]

Knitter is convinced that a pneumatological approach to a theology of religions will allow theologians to recognize the work of the Holy Spirit in the traditions of religious others. This work may be different and distinct from that of the Son, particularly concerning the redemptive work of Jesus Christ. For Knitter this presents a way forward for pluralists because it leaves room "to view the possible truth of other religions as really different from Christian revelation."[67] The freedom of the Spirit to speak truth different from that of the Christian tradition is important, and Knitter cautions that one must not move too quickly from the work of the Spirit in other religious traditions to the work of Jesus Christ.[68]

Because the economies of the Son and Spirit are united in the overall work of God, there is an interrelatedness between the Spirit and the Son that Knitter believes will satisfy the concerns of Christian inclusivists:

> Because the pneumatological approach insists that the activity of the Spirit in other faiths is essentially related to the Word spoken in Jesus Christ, it is not content simply to marvel at the "newness" and the differences of other religions; what is new and different must be brought into relation with the "grace and truth" that have appeared in the man Jesus (John 1:17).[69]

Ultimately, Knitter is agnostic as to what this relationship will look like. It is easy to assert a redemptive work of the Spirit in world religions but less easy to identify this work with any certainty. But

---

[66] Knitter, "Can our 'One and Only,'" 182.
[67] Knitter, "A New Pentecost," 38.
[68] Ibid.
[69] Ibid.

Knitter remains hopeful that ultimate complementarity between the economies of the Spirit and Son will be found. How that complementarity will express itself will be answered only in dialogue.[70]

Stanley Samartha   Stanley Samartha (1920–2001), an ordained Indian Methodist for over 50 years, was convinced that Christians in India should be active participants in the growth of the nation and its culture.[71] Such involvement would necessarily include partnering with religious others in India, particularly Hindu leaders. Effective partnerships demand common ground that can only be found through honest and earnest dialogue.

From this experience Samartha developed a theology of dialogue based upon the following three concepts. First, dialogue is modeled by God in Jesus Christ in the incarnation. Second, the gospel offer of reconciliation between peoples inevitably leads to dialogue. Third, Jesus Christ promised that the Holy Spirit would lead His people into all truth. Samartha understands truth not in the propositional sense but in a relational sense. Truth "is to be sought not in the isolation of lonely meditation but in living, personal confrontation between God and man, and people and people."[72] The relational nature of truth is supported by the reality of the plurality of religions and cultures. This does not relativize truth, but it does relativize different responses to truth. Therefore, no one particular response to truth can claim absolute status.[73] It is the foundational role that the Holy Spirit plays in dialogue and interpretation that is of fundamental interest to this project.

Samartha believed that because all people share common struggles, there is an interdependence which opens all people to the activity of the Holy Spirit. Because of the freedom and creativity that is essential to the activity of the Spirit, the Holy Spirit cannot be limited to a specific time, place, or people.[74] For this reason Samartha saw study of

---

[70]Ibid., 38–39.

[71]Ordained in the Church of South India and professor at the United Theological College in Bangalore, Samartha initiated and served as director of the WCC Sub-Unit on Dialogue with People of Living Faiths and Ideologies from 1970 to 1981. Samartha summarizes his commitment to dialogue and his work with the WCC in "The World Council of Churches and Men of Other Faiths and Ideologies," *ER* 22 (1970): 190–98.

[72]S. J. Samartha, *Courage for Dialogue: Ecumenical Issues in Inter-Religious Relationships* (Geneva: World Council of Churches, 1981), 11.

[73]S. J. Samartha, "The Holy Spirit and People of Other Faiths," *Ecumenical Review* 42 (1990): 253.

[74]S. J. Samartha, *One Christ—Many Religions: Toward a Revised Christology* (Maryknoll, NY: Orbis, 1991), 97.

the Holy Spirit as having enormous implications for interreligious dialogue.[75] His goal was not merely to "extend the work of the Holy Spirit outside the hedges of the church" but to formulate "a more inclusive doctrine of God himself."[76] By recognizing the work of the Holy Spirit outside the Christian church and Christian faith, Samartha believed that the saving activity of God could be better evaluated as wider than previously formulated. This would ultimately lead to a shift in Protestant theology from its Christomonistic tendency to a more theocentric approach to religions. A Christian theology of religions is possible if it is recognized that the word *religions* does not refer to established institutions which are defined by boundaries and separation from others. Rather, Samartha preferred to speak of "the spiritual resources within religions, the inner experiences of the Spirit, their visions of reality, their responses to the Mystery of Truth, the liberative streams within religions that break through human limitations to reach out to neighbors in the global community."[77]

A theocentric approach to religions demands that Christology be reevaluated theocentrically. Developing a theocentric Christology that shared much in common with Paul Knitter, Samartha did not believe that the uniqueness or distinctiveness of Jesus should be understood in terms of his divinity. Doing so would reduce Jesus to the mere tribal God of Christians in contrast to the tribal gods of other peoples. A theocentric approach to Christ, which emphasizes His consciousness of God and the kingdom, is "more helpful in establishing new relationships with neighbors of other faiths."[78] Furthermore, Samartha advocated rejection of the *filioque* clause, preferring the Orthodox understanding of the procession of the Holy Spirit solely from God the Father. Rejecting a flow of the Holy Spirit restricted to a "Christomonistic channel" creates theological space "for the Spirit proceeding from the Father to breathe freely through the whole *oikoumene* that includes neighbors of other faiths as well."[79]

---

[75]Over 20 years into his work on interreligious dialogue, Samartha would declare, "The work of the Holy Spirit in creation and in the lives of our neighbors of other faiths and secular convictions has scarcely entered into the debate so far." Samartha, *One Christ—Many Religions*, 11.

[76]Samartha, *Courage for Dialogue*, 64.

[77]Samartha, *One Christ—Many Religions*, 37.

[78]Ibid., 76–77. It should be recognized that Samartha's theocentric Christology is driven by its utility to dialogue, not by biblical attestation.

[79]Samartha, "The Holy Spirit and People of Other Faiths," 255.

Recognizing the activity of the Holy Spirit as evidence of God's saving commitment to people of other religions is consistent with the activity of the Holy Spirit as revealed in Scripture, particularly in the creation account. Though Samartha's exegetical work was minimal, he did question the commitment of exclusivists to reserve the use of the term *Holy Spirit* to describe God's activity in Christ and the church. Samartha saw evidence of the work of the Holy Spirit in a much broader context:

> Is it the same Spirit that brooded upon the waters over all creation, spoke through the prophets of the Old Testament, was present with Jesus at the critical points of his life and ministry, and manifested itself in "outpouring" in Acts, which also activated Yajnavalkya, the Buddha, the Prophet Muhammad and (why not) Mahatma Gandhi, Karl Marx, and Mao Tse Tung?[80]

Samartha acknowledged that an affirmative answer to this question requires a paradigm change: a commitment to seeing the Holy Spirit at work in religious others. Though the New Testament presents a Holy Spirit that is exclusively focused on Jesus Christ and the church, this is not problematic. According to Samartha, the Christocentric focus of the Holy Spirit in Scripture is easily explainable: "How then can any criteria for discussing the work of the Holy Spirit in relation to people of other religions be derived from the New Testament when its writers were concerned exclusively with the work of the Spirit within the community of the faithful?"[81] At this point Samartha could easily be accused of begging the question of the Spirit's work outside the church, but his experience told him that when two individuals of different religious commitments meet, struggling and searching for meaning, the work of the Holy Spirit cannot be limited to the Christian participant. Furthermore, looking back over Indian history, Samartha believed that Christian denial of the activity of the Holy Spirit in religious others has "marked Christians with an arrogance which is at variance with Christlike humility and has confused Christian communities wherever they have sought to be responsibly involved with their neighbors in tackling common concerns in society."[82]

---

[80]Samartha, *Courage for Dialogue*, 65.

[81]Ibid., 66.

[82]Ibid., 70. Samartha was critical of those who even questioned the inclusion of people of other faiths in the preparatory discussions on the theme of the WCC Assembly (1991) "Come

In reading the works of Stanley Samartha, one does not find a commitment to the authority of Scripture. He clearly departs from orthodoxy with regards to the sufficiency of Scripture and biblical interpretation. Interpretation of sacred writings (not just Scripture) does not lie in determining authorial intent or developing methods of textual analysis; these are only a minor part of hermeneutics. The major part of hermeneutics is being open to the Spirit. The religious community plays an important role in listening to the Spirit. Because of the Spirit's universal role, the larger human community must also be taken into consideration. Even small Christian communities are part of larger multireligious and multicultural communities. Listening to what the Spirit is saying in these larger diverse communities is necessary in order to understand what the Spirit is saying to the Christian church.[83]

Samartha taught that the Holy Spirit also continually breathes life into the sacred writings of different religions. Because of the pilgrim nature of religious life, Scriptures should not be seen as "petrified texts written once for all," nor should one trap oneself in "a continual hermeneutical exercise seeking to interpret texts handed over from the past."[84] To do so would be tantamount to muting the voice of the Spirit, "ignoring the leading of the Spirit into new realms of truth and blocking the possibilities of new insights being recognized to sustain life on the way."[85]

Due to lack of data, Samartha was hesitant to develop a robust theology of the Spirit in other religions, but he was convinced of the following points: First, the Bible does not speak to the question of the relationship between the Holy Spirit and people of other faiths. This led Samartha to question the sufficiency of Scripture for interreligious dialogue: "Therefore, one may at least raise the question whether it is helpful to claim the authority of the Scriptures alone for an exclusive or an inclusive attitude towards the work of the Spirit in relation to people of other faiths."[86]

Holy Spirit—Renew the Whole Creation." "How a theme like the Holy Spirit, whose very character is freedom (wind and fire), and who is called upon by the Assembly to renew the whole creation, can be discussed only by Christians, ignoring the rest of humanity created by God . . . is beyond the comprehension of ordinary mortals like this writer." *One Christ—Many Religions*, 97.

[83] Ibid., 71. Samartha's emphasis on listening to the Spirit in community has similarities to that of evangelical Stanley Grenz (see discussion in chap. 6).

[84] Ibid., 74.

[85] Ibid., 74–75.

[86] Samartha, *Courage for Dialogue*, 72.

Second, the divergent opinions and doctrines within the Protestant, Orthodox, and Catholic heritages entails that it is possible for Christians to hold different positions on the work of the Holy Spirit in world religions. Therefore, no one position is the norm by which to judge another. If disputes between those who share the same Bible cannot be resolved, how can Christians hope to speak with any authority over those who have different sacred writings? This uncertainty should lead Christians to ask not how to come to closure on the issue but how to "relate themselves now to their fellow human beings under God."[87]

Third, Spirit-led dialogue should ensue between people of different religious traditions, regardless of the seeming inconsistencies between the religions. Samartha also believed that the role of the Holy Spirit in world history should be investigated. If God can empower the pagan Cyrus by the Spirit, why can He not do the same with Gandhi, Castro, or Mao Tse-Tung?

Fourth, Samartha believed that establishing a set of criteria for discerning the work of the Holy Spirit in religious others was extremely problematic because any set of criteria will limit the activity of the Spirit and negate His freedom. A commitment to the freedom of the Spirit does not mean doctrinal considerations are unimportant, but that they must be "subordinated to the discernment of the actual working of the Spirit in the lives of people."[88] Samartha did suggest the following set of broad criteria for discussion: The Spirit brings life, not death. The Spirit brings order, not chaos.[89] The Spirit brings new relationships and new communities, not separation.[90] Any other attempts at criteria will be broken up by the "boundless freedom of that very Spirit who refuses to be organized and smothered by human limitations."[91] Samartha also suggested that a profound mark of the Spirit is "inwardness, interiority, the power to root people's lives in the depths of God's being."[92] This is a departure from an ethical criterion, but Samartha felt it was necessary because ethics flows from theology, which in turn

---

[87]Ibid. Samartha makes the mistake of concluding that because there are divergent opinions on the work of the Holy Spirit in world religions, there is therefore no resolution to the problem and the Christian response should be to opt for a wider work of the Holy Spirit. There is a crucial difference between confusion caused by people being in error (epistemological uncertainty) and ontological uncertainty.

[88]Samartha, "The Holy Spirit and People of Other Faiths," 257.

[89]Samartha, *Courage for Dialogue*, 74.

[90]Samartha, "The Holy Spirit and People of Other Faiths," 258.

[91]Samartha, *Courage for Dialogue*, 74.

[92]Samartha, "The Holy Spirit and People of Other Faiths," 261.

flows from the inner life. This opens up the possibilities for discernment of the Spirit because "in all religious traditions the quality of inwardness, the marks of a life rooted in the depths of God, are self-authenticating and regarded as needing no proof."[93]

Finally, the uncertainty in establishing a set of criteria for discerning the work of the Holy Spirit demands that there be a shift from conceptual or dogmatic criteria to existential criteria.[94] Though Samartha did not believe that theological distinctives should be eliminated, "when the existential involvement of Christians with people of living faiths and ideologies is taken seriously, older methods of theological approach will inevitably be affected."[95] In Samartha's economy, life takes precedence over logic, love takes precedence over truth, and "the neighbor as a person may become more important than his or her belief."[96] Samartha had little patience with theological formulations that refused to operate according to this existential hierarchy, declaring that conceptual and dogmatic criteria lead to "ponderous theological deliberations."[97] He lamented the lack of treatment of the work of the Holy Spirit in the lives of religious others.[98]

RESPONSE TO PLURALISM

The arguments of religious pluralists are hardly groundbreaking to the biblical writers. The Bible is not surprised by the reality of religious others or pluralism. Scripture was written by and for people who were surrounded by religious others. The response of the Old Testament prophets to the religious others that surrounded Israel was proclamation of the one living God. The response of Jesus Christ and the apostles to the religious pluralism of their day was univocal:

---

[93] Ibid.

[94] The evangelical pneumatological inclusivist Amos Yong is critical of returning too quickly to Christology in his theology of religions, but he does believe that an existential criterion to discern the activity of the Holy Spirit in world religions would be helpful. A. Yong, *Beyond the Impasse: Toward a Pneumatological Theology of Religions* (Grand Rapids: Baker Academic, 2003), 96–98.

[95] Samartha, *Courage for Dialogue*, 74.

[96] Ibid.

[97] Ibid., 76.

[98] In a critical turn, Samartha called for further reflection on the work of the Holy Spirit by reevaluating the traditional doctrine of the Trinity: "And the question of the Holy Spirit must inevitably lead to the doctrine of God himself and of the Trinity in far more inclusive ways than Christian theology has done before. It must take into account the unknowability, the incomprehensibleness, and the mystery of God and the work of his Spirit among others no less than his revelation in Christianity through the Holy Spirit." Ibid., 76–77.

Proclamation of the good news of the one living God in the person and work of Jesus Christ. There is no hint of theological compromise or revisionism in the response of those called to witness to the living God and His saving ways. The biblical response to the question, What about religious others? is, Proclaim to them the good news of Jesus Christ! In the remainder of this chapter, I will provide a Christian response to the arguments of pluralists summarized above. My response to the turn to pneumatology by both pluralists and inclusivists is the subject of chapters 7 and 8.

Many Paths to Many Gods

In its most basic form, the assertion of pluralism is that there are many paths to God. According to the Christian Scriptures, the response to that pluralist assertion is twofold: there are many paths to many gods but only one path to the living God. As demonstrated in chapter 2, there are many paths to many gods. This is true of the Old Testament and the New Testament. Both Israel in the ancient Near East and the early church in the Greco-Roman Empire were surrounded by those who believed and worshipped differently. Israel and the Church were surrounded by those who worshipped other gods. Further, the gods of these nations clearly did have an existence in the life, culture, and history of those who treated them as their gods. Old Testament Israel interacted with those who worshipped Baal, Molech, and Asherah, among others. The Christians of the early church faced those who worshipped Zeus and Artemis, among others. Although these gods are nothing in relation to the God of Abraham or Jesus, they are something in relation to their worshippers.

The Lord's response to those who worship other gods is critical for the present discussion on pluralism. He forbids the worship of other gods. Scripture is explicit. "Do not make an idol for yourself, whether . . . in the heavens above or on the earth below or in the waters under the earth. You must not bow down to them or worship them; for I the LORD your God, am a jealous God" (Exod 20:4). Idolatry of any kind is forbidden because human attempts to create an image of the true and living God are illegitimate. Interestingly, the theological ground for the prohibition on idolatry is the jealousy of God. In forbidding idolatry in the Ten Commandments, the Lord describes Himself as jealous. Worship not directed toward the One who is most worthy is unacceptable and intolerable. Jewish monotheism did not deny the reality of religious others, nor did it deny that there were powers that the other nations worshipped (e.g., Lev 17:7; Deut 32:17; Josh 24:15). Rather, Jewish monotheism was a clarion call to the nation of Israel to worship the LORD, and to do so in the manner prescribed by the Lord. The essence of Jewish monotheism lies in what it affirms about the Lord, not primarily in what it denies about other gods or powers. Of course, what is affirmed about the Lord has enormous significance for what is claimed about other gods. Only the God of Israel is the Creator (Gen 1:1; 14:19; Isa 40:28; 45:18). Only the God of Israel is sovereign (Dan 4:34–37). Only the God of Israel can save (Isa 44:17; 45:21–22). Only the God of Israel hears (1 Kgs 18:26,29; Isa 38:5). Only the God of Israel is "God of gods" (Deut 10:17; Ps 136:2) and executes mastery over the gods of the nations (Zeph 2:11). Only the God of Israel holds life and death, judgment and reward, in His hands (Deut 32:39; Isa 45:5–7).

New Testament Christian monotheism is no different. The same claims are made of God with Jesus Christ thrust into the monotheistic equation. Jesus Christ is the Creator (John 1:1–3; Heb 1:3,10). Jesus Christ is sovereign (1 Tim 6:15). Only Jesus Christ can save (Acts 4:12; Titus 2:13; 1 John 4:14). Only Jesus Christ is the faithful high priest who always hears (Acts 7:59–60; Heb 4:14). Jesus Christ is "Lord of lords" (Phil 2:10–11; Rev 19:16), and He executes mastery over the nations (Rev 19:11–21). Jesus Christ holds life and death, judgment and reward, in His hands (John 5:21–22; 10:28–30; Rev 1:17–20; 22:12).

Only One Path to the Sovereign Creator

The Bible is also clear that although there are many paths to many gods, but there is only one path to the supreme God. No attempt is made, in either the Old or New Testament, to accommodate the worship practices of the Lord to that of religious others. Syncretism of any kind is strictly forbidden. Many of the Mosaic laws that seem so strange to modern ears (e.g., Exod 34:26; Lev 19:26) are prohibitions on the intermingling of pagan worship practices with worship of the Lord.[99] The Mosaic law mandated the separation of Israel from the

---

[99] See D. K. Stuart, *Exodus*, NAC (Nashville: B&H, 2006), 733.

nations that surrounded her. Israel was not to intermarry with the other nations (Deut 7:3), dress like the other nations (Lev 19:19), eat like the other nations (Lev 11:1–23), and or worship like the other nations (Exod 23:13; Lev 18:21). Granted, the Israelites' record of obedience is marked by failure, and the Israelite worship practices described in the Old Testament show a breathtaking proclivity to intermingle worship of the Lord with worship of Baal and other false gods (e.g., 1 Kgs 11:1–11; 2 Kgs 21:3–7). However, the Bible's record of Israelites engaged in the worship practices of religious others is not affirmation of those activities. A common pluralist mistake is to confuse description of real events with prescription of what ought to be. Simply put, "is" is not equivalent to "ought." Pagan worship practices, though described, are unequivocally condemned throughout Scripture. Nor is worship of another god or power ever excused due to ignorance. Worship of the Lord is to be done on His terms as specifically prescribed by the Lord, without exception.

When the Jewish Davidic heir, Jesus Christ, arrived in fulfillment of prophecy, He claimed to reveal God in unique and unparalleled ways. Witness the claims of Jesus in the Gospel of John alone. Jesus taught that those who believe in Him would escape condemnation and receive eternal life (John 3:16–18; 6:40; 10:28). Jesus has life in Himself and the exclusive right to judge (5:21–22,26). The one who does not honor the Son does not honor the Father (5:23). Jesus came down from heaven to do the will of the Father (6:38). He is the bread of life that gives life (6:48–51). Jesus offers living water, and He is the One who gives the Holy Spirit based on belief in Him (4:10,13; 7:37–39; 15:26; 16:7). He offers true freedom from sin (8:36). He is the light of the world (8:12; 9:5). Jesus is the Good Shepherd who offers the only access to God (10:1–2,9–10). He is the resurrection and the life (11:25). He offers exclusive access to the Father, and apart from Him no one can see God (1:18; 14:6–11). The list of biblical affirmations to the uniqueness of the Son of God could be multiplied from John and the other Gospels. The apostle Peter summarized the testimony of Jesus in this way: "There is salvation in no one else, for there is no other name under heaven given to people by which we must be saved" (Acts 4:12).

Although the Bible admits to the existence of religious others and even the zeal with which they worship, it does not countenance compromise or allow for pious efforts made in good conscience. Jesus' response to the Samaritan woman when confronted with her confusion over places of worship bears testimony to the exclusive demands of God the Father. She expressed offense that the Jews would question the legitimacy of her place of worship, a place where her fathers worshipped (John 4:19–20). Contemporary sensibilities would affirm her commitment to worship and downplay her errors, but Jesus' answer is dramatically different. Far from affirming the woman's efforts, He corrected the woman's error: "You Samaritans worship what you do not know. We worship what we do know, because salvation is from the Jews" (4:22). Her problem was morally culpable ignorance, and it had to be corrected because the Father is seeking "true worshipers" who will "worship in spirit and truth" (4:23). True worship is grounded in the work of the Holy Spirit and in truth. Because Jesus is the truth (14:6), genuine Spirit-empowered worship will honor the Son.[100] When confronted with her error, her response was absolutely correct: "When [the Messiah] comes, He will explain everything to us" (4:25). The Samaritans did not have any hope within their own tradition or people.[101] They were absolutely dependent on the particularity of the Jewish Messiah to lead them to right worship of God. The expression of her need for a Prophet-Messiah is undoubtedly why Jesus chose to reveal Himself to her as the One for whom she had been waiting.[102]

Addressing Reductionism: Affirming the Uniqueness and Personhood of God

In a truly pluralistic system, Christianity (along with Islam, Buddhism, and Hinduism, among others) must be seen as one of the great religious faiths, a stream of religious life that leads invariably to some sort of ultimate reality that Christians choose to call "God the Father." In order to fit Christianity into the pluralist agenda, to enable Christianity and the other religions of the world to coexist intellectually, pluralists are forced to deny the very essence of Christianity (and that

---

[100]So T. R. Schreiner, *New Testament Theology* (Grand Rapids: Baker, 2008), 461.

[101]There are messianic prophecies in the Pentateuch of which the Samaritans would have been aware. The Samaritans were waiting for the *Taheb*, "the Restorer" to come, but it seems that this was a perverted vestige of the Jewish messianic hope. The statement still stands that their tradition would not provide for them what only the Jewish Messiah could give. See L. Morris, *The Gospel According to John*, rev. ed., NICNT (Grand Rapids: Eerdmans, 1995), 241; D. A. Carson, *The Gospel According to John*, PNTC (Grand Rapids: Eerdmans, 1991), 226; C. S. Keener, *The Gospel of John: A Commentary*, vol. 1 (Peabody: Hendrickson Publishers, 2003), 619–20.

[102]So J. R. Michaels, *John*, NIBC (Peabody: Hendrickson Publishers, 1984, 1989), 73.

of every other religion). That is, they intentionally discard or reconceive every distinctive Christian doctrine that preserves the identity of Christianity. These pluralists "repudiate the suggestion that there is anything unique, normative, or superior about Jesus Christ or the Christian faith."[103] When one engages in this Procrustean reduction, all that is left are some ethical teachings that may or may not be attributed to Jesus (depending on the influence of "scholars" from such groups as the Jesus Seminar)[104] but little else resembling orthodox historical Christianity. The Christian who believes that Buddhism, for example, is a legitimate path to the God he worships, either has not thought clearly or does not understand Christianity.

The most famous proponent of pluralist reductionism, John Hick, has reduced the religions down to their lowest common denominator—something that looks like a watered-down version of Buddhism (i.e., a Buddhism with which most Buddhists would not be satisfied). Recall that as Hick trimmed off more and more of the religious understandings of God, he came to the point where he could no longer refer to God as God (indicating a personal name); rather, Hick now refers to God as "The Real." What does Hick's conception of the "Real" have to do with the God and Father of Jesus Christ? The concepts of God in the different religions are not just differences in name or perspective but essential differences in being. In the pluralist zeal to find commonality between the religions, it is not Christianity (or any other religion for that matter) that is related to the other world faiths but little more than a parody, a caricature of the living faith, that is based more on the presuppositions of twenty-first century non-Christian Westerners than on any historical reality. Christians must remember that the identity of Christianity is inextricably linked to the uniqueness of Jesus Christ: all that He taught, all that He claimed, and all that He did. The implications are enormous, for the Christian's idea of God is not rooted in his personal experience but in the revelation of God in the historical person of Jesus Christ. When the Christian's testimony of God in Christ is

---

[103]Netland, *Dissonant Voices*, 26. Geivett and Phillips rightly assert, "Traditional Christian theology is not compatible with religious pluralism." R. D. Geivett and W. G. Phillips, "Response to John Hick," in *Four Views on Salvation in a Pluralistic World*, ed. Okholm and Phillips, 79.

[104]See, for example, R. W. Funk, *The Gospel of Jesus: According to the Jesus Seminar* (Santa Rosa, CA: Polebridge, 1999); id., *The Five Gospels: What Did Jesus Really Say? The Search for the Authentic Words of Jesus* (Santa Rosa, CA: Polebridge, 1993); *The Lost Gospel Q: The Original Sayings of Jesus*, ed. M. Powelson and R. Riegert; M. Borg, consulting ed. (Berkeley: Ulysses, 1996).

either denied or relativized, then the discussion has turned away from the God of Christianity. N. T. Wright correctly notes, "Any suggestion that there is more than one way of salvation is not merely an attack on the uniqueness of Jesus Christ . . . but also contains the implication that there is more than one God."[105]

It is ironic that in this postmodern age of tolerance, religious pluralists have ignored their own criticisms of the "intolerant" faiths and established themselves as the evaluators of the truth claims of other religions.[106] What is their vantage point that privileges their judgments? On the basis of this model, it is not the individual religions that have access to the truth; ultimately it is the Western religious pluralist, who insists that each religion be seen in the context of the others before it can be evaluated. This means that the Western doctrine of religious pluralism is defined as the only valid standpoint for evaluating individual religions. But why should Christians accept that definition?[107]

The simple reality is that the different major religions of the world have different conceptions of God. Often those conceptions are contradictory and utterly incompatible. Christians believe that God is personal and relational. Theravadin Buddhists (who are atheists for all practical purposes) reject this most basic assertion.[108] Christianity (and Judaism and Islam) are committed to an unmoving monotheism, while Hindus and Mahayana Buddhists would never affirm such a thing. Though Christianity, Judaism, and Islam are committed to monotheism, Judaism and Islam deny the Christian doctrine of the Trinity. The Christian doctrine of sin and salvation shares little in common with Karma. These are not peripheral issues, nor can they be ignored. Let us make it simpler: some religions affirm the existence of God (e.g., Christianity, Judaism, Islam), while other religions are decidedly nontheistic (e.g., Theravadin Buddhism). Is it not absurd for a religion that says there is a God to be compatible with a religion that

---

[105]N. T. Wright, "Towards a Biblical View of Universalism," *Themelios* 4/2 (1979): 57–58.

[106]J. A. DiNoia is rightly critical of pluralistic claims that flatten essential religious differences: "Pluralist Theology of Religions: Pluralistic or Non-Pluralistic?" in *Christian Uniqueness Reconsidered: The Myth of Pluralistic Theology of Religions*, ed. G. D'Costa (Maryknoll, NY: Orbis, 1996), 119–34.

[107]A. McGrath, "The Challenge of Pluralism for the Contemporary Christian Church," *JETS* 35/3 (September 1992): 371.

[108]Langdon Gilkey attempts to reconcile God as a personal being and God as a nonpersonal being by appealing to what he calls "relative absoluteness." See L. Gilkey, "Plurality and Its Theological Implications," in *Myth of Christian Uniqueness: Toward a Pluralistic Theology of Religions*, ed. Hick and Knitter, 47–50.

denies the existence of God? Netland is right to observe, "It is difficult indeed to escape the conclusion that some of the central affirmations of Christianity, Hinduism, Buddhism, Islam, and Shinto are opposed; so long as the meanings of the doctrines within the respective religious communities are preserved, they cannot be jointly accepted without absurdity."[109] Pluralists are wrong to affirm the essential equality of all the religions, while ignoring such questions.[110]

Hick accuses Christians of a tautology by defining salvation according to Jesus and then claiming that Jesus is the only way. Of course, Hick would have a valid point if Jesus and His claims were the creations of Christians. But Christians do not claim to be the creators of Jesus or His claims. Rather, they are witnesses to the real person and historical words of Jesus Himself (John 16:12–13; Acts 1:8). Christian doctrine is based on eyewitness testimony to the authoritative person and teachings of Christ; that is, Christianity claims to be built upon the revelation of God. Of course, pluralists have the right to question that claim, and it is the responsibility of Christians to demonstrate its validity. But intellectual integrity demands that pluralists address Christianity where it starts, with its own truth claims. As it turns out, the ones who are actually guilty of tautological reasoning are religious pluralists themselves. For example, Hick has defined salvation as the transformation from self-centeredness to reality-centeredness. He evaluates each of the world religions according to his criterion, trimming away particular doctrines that exceed his definition (many of which are essential to that particular religion), then he claims he has found the basis of unity among the religions in their pursuit of "salvation." Obviously, his conclusion is assumed in the creation of his own dubious premise. Christians are right to cry foul when pluralists engage in such question begging.

Recently some scholars have been questioning the coherence of pluralism and inclusivism as typically formulated. S. Mark Heim and Joseph DiNoia argue rightly that all religions, on inspection, are particular and exclusive.[111] That is, each religion has different ultimate

---

[109] Netland, *Dissonant Voices*, 110–11.

[110] See John Meyer's critique of Hick's theology of religions where he analyzes the epistemological reductionism of Hick, in J. R. Meyer, "John Hick's Theology of Religions and Inter-Religious Dialogue: A Critique," *Religion and Theology* 8/3–4 (2001): 274–97. See also A. E. McGrath, "The Christian Church's Response to Pluralism," *JETS* 35/4 (1992): 487–501.

[111] J. DiNoia, "The Universality of Salvation and the Diversity of Religious Aims," *World Mission* (Winter, 1981–82): 4–15; S. M. Heim, *Salvations: Truth and Difference in Religion*

goals, different ideas of "salvation," and different paths to get there (whatever "there" is uniquely construed to be). Further, each religion claims to offer a unique path to its unique ultimate goal. Pluralist attempts to find commonality among the major religions of the world are reductionistic and effectively deny any pluralism of real consequence.[112] In place of reductionism, Heim offers a pluralistic theology of religions that attempts to take seriously the essential differences between the religions. The different religions may have different notions of salvation and different, even contradictory, goals. Contrary to the reductionistic models of many pluralists, however, Heim believes the differences in the religions ought to be respected and affirmed.[113] Borrowing from the "orientational pluralism" of Nicholas Rescher,[114] Heim suggests that the different religions are different perspectives on the same God and are therefore real and legitimate.[115] Each religion has a different understanding of salvation because there may in fact be different salvations that God has providentially provided. In other words, the salvation offered through Christ is different from the nirvana of Buddhism or the Paradise of Islam, but each is a genuine offer by God to that particular people group.

Heim is right to argue that the concepts of salvation understood by each religion are distinct and impossible to unify without fundamentally altering the essence of each religion. But where is the biblical evidence to affirm that each is a legitimate offering by the one God? Christianity is coherent and compelling because its doctrine of salvation flows consistently from its doctrine of God and doctrine of man. The Christian cannot accept the Buddhist teaching on nirvana without sacrificing the biblical teaching on the character and nature of God, sin, and the human dilemma. The suggestion of Heim and DiNonia pretends to respect the vast differences between the world religions' understandings of salvation but does so by asking each religious participant to sacrifice their most fundamental doctrines.

Pluralists are fond of observing that virtues and vices are spread evenly throughout the adherents of each world religion. Besides questioning the legitimacy of that observation (it seems that the fruit of the

---

(Maryknoll, NY: Orbis, 1995).

[112]G. R. McDermott, *Can Evangelicals Learn from World Religions? Jesus, Revelation & Religious Traditions* (Downers Grove, IL: InterVarsity, 2000), 43.

[113]Heim, *Salvations*, 6–7.

[114]N. Rescher, *The Strife of Systems* (Pittsburgh: Pittsburgh University Press, 1985).

[115]Heim, *Salvations*, 133–34.

Christian gospel is far more powerful and transformative to cultures than pluralists are willing to credit), is the conclusion justified? Is ethical behavior a valid justification for belief? Pluralists seem to imply that it does not matter what one believes as long as one behaves in a certain way, but the bifurcation between belief and behavior can only be made if one ignores the central tenets of the Christian faith. Christian behavior change is based on recognition of the sinful human condition, the need for the forgiveness of the one holy God whose wrath was satisfied at the cross of Christ, the regeneration of the believer in Jesus Christ and His gospel, and the work of the Holy Spirit to transform the believer into the image of Christ. These doctrinal assertions, based on the Christian gospel, are vehemently denied by religious others. However, to eliminate any one of them is to undercut the Christian doctrine of sanctification. As Geivett and Phillips point out, "The unique moral superiority of Christianity is not founded on the moral character of fallible Christians but is attested by Jesus' own sinless life as the incarnate God-man whose righteousness is imputed to those who believe in him."[116] When pluralists sever Christian sanctification from the gospel, they reduce behavior change to humans attempting to pull themselves up by their own moral bootstraps. Pluralists may be fine with this, but they have distorted Christianity beyond recognition in their attempt to find common ground.

Even if one accepts the pluralist observation that Christian behavior is neither better nor worse than that of religious others, there are important considerations to be made. First, Christians are, by definition, those who know they need a savior. It stands to reason that the church will be filled with people who are not always the most morally upright. Tim Keller explains:

> It is often the case that people whose lives have been harder and who are "lower on the character scale" are more likely to recognize their need for God and turn to Christianity. So we should expect that many Christians' lives would not compare well to those of the nonreligious (just as the health of people in the hospital is comparatively worse than people visiting museums).[117]

---

[116]Geivett and Phillips, "Response to John Hick," 78.
[117]T. Keller, *The Reason for God: Belief in an Age of Skepticism* (New York: Dutton, 2008), 54.

Second, the failure of self-proclaiming Christians to be ethically distinct is an intolerable condition and speaks more to the failure of the Western church to preach boldly the whole counsel of God and to discipline its members than it speaks to the inefficacy of the Christian gospel. In contrast to the pop-theology that passes for Christian doctrine in many circles, it is not true that Christians are merely a group of sinners, different only in that they are forgiven. Believers in Jesus Christ have been set free from the bondage of sin (Rom 6:22) and transferred from the domain of darkness into the kingdom of Christ (Col 1:13). Believers, who constitute the body of Christ, are called to holiness (1 Pet 1:16) and are "being built into a spiritual house for a holy priesthood to offer spiritual sacrifices acceptable to God through Jesus Christ" (1 Pet 2:5). The Lord calls Christians to a higher ethical standard, and their failure is a matter of disobedience.

Finally, ethical behavior, as a criterion for evaluating religions, is difficult to quantify and is notoriously subjective. Further, one's experience will inevitably influence one's ability to evaluate the evidence. As Keller points out, if one has met wonderful and faithful Christians, then the ethical case for Christianity will be more plausible. If, on the other hand, one has only met nominal Christians or self-righteous hypocrites (neither of whom are obeying the Lord they claim to follow), then the ethical case for Christianity over against pluralism will be more difficult.[118]

Addressing Obfuscation: Affirming the Uniqueness of Jesus Christ

The best response to religious pluralism is to proclaim steadfastly the uniqueness of Christ. Christianity stands and falls upon the Christian claims that Jesus is the Son of God and the resurrected Savior of the world. The claims of Jesus, rooted in history, should exercise a controlling influence over the Christian's approach to religious others. For the Christian, Jesus is qualitatively different from the leaders of other religions.[119] If Jesus is who He says He is, and the church is also correct in its testimony about Him, then pluralism cannot be sustained.

---

[118]Ibid., 52.

[119]See A. McGrath, "Response to John Hick," in *Four Views on Salvation in a Pluralistic World*, ed. Okholm and Phillips, 67.

Pluralists recognize this fact and attempt to call into question the basis of the Christian's confidence in Christ's uniqueness.

Pluralists often question the viability of making any truth claims about God. After all, is not God ineffable and unknowable? Of course, such a claim is ultimately self-refuting because if God is truly unknowable and truth claims about Him cannot be made, we cannot know that He is unknowable. If we know that God is unknowable, then He really is not unknowable anymore (we know at least one fact about Him), which is impossible if He is unknowable. The pluralist who wants to go the route of obfuscation puts himself on the horns of a dilemma. If God is unknowable, then we cannot actually know that He is, and the pluralist assertion is impossible. But if we can know something about God (such as, that He is unknowable) then He is knowable, at least to a degree, and the pluralist assertion is false. Besides, if God was unknowable, how would we know that?[120] Appealing to religious experience will not help. If God is unknowable, why ought we to trust our senses and experiences? The pluralist must speculate that God is unknowable or that the unknowable God has revealed to humans that He is unknowable. Either option leads nowhere quickly.

Pluralists such as Hick claim that it is impossible to worship the Real in itself and that the different religions of the world are always some manifestation of the Real to humanity. But where is the evidence for such an assertion? Why not just say that the religions are different and that we ought to respect them as such? If there is no true access to God (the Real), then it is impossible to know what any of His properties are. But if this is the case, then how can God manifest Himself through experience?[121] For the Christian, Jesus Christ was a real person who walked the earth in real time-space history. The church has looked to Jesus as the center of reality. In contrast Hick offers "the Real" which the individual cannot know apart from his own construction. He is forced to create a god that puts himself at the center of reality. Lesslie Newbigin rightly comments, "The Hickian revolution is exactly the opposite of the Copernican. It is a move from a view

---

[120]See L. Newbigin, "Religion for the Marketplace," in *Christian Uniqueness Reconsidered*, ed. D'Costa, 141–42.

[121]Geivett and Phillips, "Response to John Hick," 78.

centered in the objective reality of Jesus Christ, to a view centered in my own subjective conception of ultimate reality."[122]

As we saw earlier, pluralists often attack the Christian doctrine of revelation. If God is ineffable, as many pluralists claim, then He cannot reveal Himself through human agency as distinctly as evangelicals claim. Recall that Hick suggests that revelation is rooted in religious experience, being exceptionally open to the divine presence.[123] This is not what the Bible says revelation is, and it is not fair to define revelation as one thing and then dismiss other proposals because it does not match your own definition. When analyzing the claims of different religions, intellectual integrity demands that we pay attention to how each sacred text presents itself. The Bible's own presentation of itself has to be the starting point of any discussion on its veracity. The Bible is a book composed of many genres written over hundreds of years by multiple authors. This fact does not in itself present any challenge to the faithfulness or accuracy of the Bible, given its own doctrine of inspiration, which celebrates both human and divine participation. The Bible was written during a time prior to our own scientific revolution, but this does not mean the biblical writers were naïve or foolish. The miracles in the Bible are presented not as the normal course of things but as extraordinary events accomplished through divine agency (e.g., Mary did not have to live through the twentieth-century Western sexual revolution to know that women do not normally conceive and yet maintain their virginity). To dismiss the supernatural elements in the Bible on the basis of scientific naiveté is to engage in chronological snobbery.[124]

Obfuscationists also attack the doctrine of Christ directly, particularly the deity of Christ. Did Jesus really claim to be God? Is the doctrine of the incarnation a creation formulated by the church after Christ died? Questions such as these seek to erode Christian confidence in the supremacy of Christ. But is it true that Jesus did not teach the incarnation? Pluralists can line up biblical critics that deny the accuracy of the

---

[122]Newbigin, "Religion for the Marketplace," 142. McGrath comments, "Professor Hick offers us an unknowable 'Real' as a postulated universal and generic entity behind the phenomena of the 'religions.' This is highly convenient for his evidentially-deficient hypothesis. But for more critical observers, it confirms that the pluralist hypothesis is simply one among many explanations of the diversity and divergence of the world's religions." McGrath, "Response to John Hick," 70.

[123]Hick, "Pluralist View," 34.

[124]See C. S. Lewis, *Miracles: A Preliminary Study* (New York: The Macmillan Co, 1947), 46–55.

Gospels, but their scholarship is not persuasive.[125] Geivett and Phillips make the point that for pluralists to deny that Jesus ever claimed to be God, while maintaining a high regard for Jesus, they must do the following: (1) identify the core of Jesus' sayings, (2) rebut scholars who claim that there is a high Christology in the Gospels, and (3) demonstrate that substantial knowledge of Jesus is still possible when the Gospels are disregarded.[126]

A tactic employed by pluralists to cast doubt upon the uniqueness of Jesus Christ is to argue against the intelligibility of the hypostatic union. Clearly if Jesus is simultaneously fully human and fully divine, then His claims to uniqueness stand, so pluralists are quick to question its coherence.[127] Ironically, those who argue that God is ineffable are the same ones seeking to deny Christ's uniqueness based on their capacity to understand the incarnation. Leaving aside the inconsistency of pluralists on this point, why should Christians accept that the mystery of the incarnation must be made intelligible to pluralists before it can be believed? Since when did exhaustive knowledge of divine mysteries become the prerequisite for true knowledge? The doctrine of the incarnation testifies that the eternal Son of God took on a human nature into His one person without laying aside His divine nature. How the infinite can combine with the finite without swallowing up the finite is a profoundly perplexing question, and the doctrine of the hypostatic union does not pretend to plumb exhaustively the depths of the union. But neither is the hypostatic union a nonsensical

---

[125]For a defense of the reliability of the Gospels, see, for example, *Gospel Perspectives*, ed. R. T. France, D. Wenham, C. L. Blomberg, vols. 1–6 (Sheffield: JSOT Press, 1981–1986); R. Bauckham, *Jesus and the Eyewitnesses: The Gospels as Eyewitness Testimony* (Grand Rapids: Eerdmans, 2006); C. L. Blomberg, *The Historical Reliability of the Gospels*, 2nd ed. (Downers Grove, IL: InterVarsity, 2008); G. R. Habermas, *The Historical Jesus: Ancient Evidence for the Life of Christ* (Joplin, MO: College Press, 1996); *Jesus Under Fire: Modern Scholarship Reinvents the Historical Jesus*, ed. M. J. Wilkins and J. P. Moreland (Grand Rapids: Zondervan, 1995); G. Boyd and P. Eddy, *The Jesus Legend: A Case for the Historical Reliability of the Synoptic Jesus Tradition* (Grand Rapids: Baker: 2007).

[126]Geivett and Phillips, "Response to John Hick," 73–74.

[127]For example, John Hick writes, "The . . . problem is that it has not proved possible, after some fifteen centuries of intermittent effort, to give any clear meaning to the idea that Jesus had two complete natures, one human and the other divine." Hick, "Pluralist View," 57. Hick would rather say that "Jesus embodied *as much* of the infinite divine moral qualities as could be expressed in a finite human life—rather than that 'in him the whole fullness of deity dwells bodily' (Col 2:9)." Ibid. Although the hypostatic union has no real meaning in history, it does have "powerful metaphorical meaning, in that Jesus was so open to divine inspiration, so responsive to the divine spirit, so obedient to God's will, that God was able to act on earth in and through him." Ibid., 58.

formulation that does not pass the test of intelligibility.[128] This interrelationship is difficult and mysterious, but mystery does not entail contradiction. As Clark Pinnock points out, the effort by pluralists to get rid of the incarnation "has less to do with evidence than with ideology."[129]

Both Hick and Knitter argue that the way forward is to move to theocentric criteria for evaluating religions rather than Christocentric criteria. The problem is that in the absence of revelation, God becomes so indeterminate that we end up with a vacant center. When a word can mean anything at all, it ultimately means nothing. It is no accident that the rise of religious pluralism in the West is concurrent with the rise of postmodernity, where the idea of certainty in truth claims is met with skepticism. For many who have embraced the postmodern criticism of truth claims, the indeterminacy of language, especially language about God, is a powerful argument for the pluralistic position.

Such argumentation is not peculiar to the postmodern setting. The late Wilfred Cantwell Smith, professor of comparative religion at Harvard Divinity School, argued that doctrine is of secondary importance when evaluating competing religions and that the legitimacy of religion is rooted in experience. Religious truth ought not to be thought of in propositional terms but in the personal "truth" of individual religious experience. Truth is therefore not static but personal and dynamic, the product of religious traditions. On this basis, Smith argued that all religions could be seen to be "true," even if their propositional content appears to be contradictory.[130]

---

[128]Chapter 8 will offer a cogent biblical explanation for the interrelationship between Jesus' human and divine natures manifest in His speech and actions. Also, for examples, see the helpful essays contained in *Jesus in Trinitarian Perspective*, ed. F. Sanders and K. Issler (Nashville: B&H, 2007).

[129]C. Pinnock, "Response to John Hick," in *Four Views on Salvation in a Pluralistic World*, ed. Okholm and Phillips, 63. As Geivett and Phillips point out, pluralists like Hick who deny the uniqueness of Christ because they do not understand the formulation are guilty of begging the question. Hick holds that the conjunction of deity and humanity in Jesus must be false, "since their conjunction entails the uniqueness of Christianity, and the uniqueness of Christianity is incompatible with our enlightened awareness of other faiths in the world. But this is little more than a shrill accusation that it is bad manners for God to act in a way that we cannot explain or in a way that offends our religious predilections." Geivett and Phillips, "Response to John Hick," 76.

[130]See W. C. Smith, *The Meaning and End of Religion: A Revolutionary Approach to the Great Religious Traditions* (San Francisco: Harper & Row, 1962); id., *Faith and Belief: The Difference Between Them* (Princeton: Princeton University Press, 1979).

I recently participated in a formal debate on the campus of a state university over the question "Are there many paths to one God?"[131] My opponent based her argument for pluralism on the indeterminacy of language. That is, because words can mean many things to different people, God intentionally inspires humans to use human words to describe Him so that the fullness of His being can be revealed. Such human words can be found in the Bible, the sacred texts of other religions, or other records of religious experience. Because words can have many different meanings, no one interpretation is to be privileged over another. God's use of human language in a pluralistic world enables better understanding of Him.

In a postmodern context, arguments for and against religious pluralism often come down to hermeneutics—not the interpretation of specific passages but the nature of interpretation itself. Is there a meaning in the text, and if so, who has the authority to teach, correct, or challenge the autonomous reader?[132] The pluralist's rejection of the idea that there is only one path to God, based on God's distinct revelation of Himself, has parallels in the postmodern rejection of the idea that authors control the meaning of texts. Both are ultimately a reaction against authority. Both are resistant to privileging one interpretation over another. The postmodern individual seeks to become an author in his own right, the maker of meaning. The pluralist's agenda is the same. He does not want anyone to tell him who God is because humans have no access to who God is in Himself. The individual only has access to his own personal experience of God. I cannot know who God is, the pluralist reasons. I can only know who God is *to me*. The autonomous individual becomes the maker of meaning, the determiner of divine reality.

Such arguments place the pluralist in a difficult position. To attempt to use human language to explain that human language is incapable of communicating true knowledge of God is self-refuting. To engage in a debate using rules of logic and rhetoric when those rules do not apply to the One about whom you are debating is an impossible position to maintain. Furthermore, the pluralist attempts to suspend the truth

---

[131]The logic and argumentation of this chapter is based largely on my opening monologue in that debate sponsored by the Oregon State University Socratic Club held 13 May 2008 on the campus of Oregon State University.

[132]See K. Vanhoozer, *Is There a Meaning in This Text? The Bible, the Reader, and the Morality of Literary Knowledge* (Grand Rapids: Zondervan, 1998), 43–97.

question due to the personal nature of religious truth is illegitimate. To do so is to confuse the nature of truth with the individual's response to truth. Despite pluralist protests, religious others are doing more than articulating their private or communal faith experience. They are making claims and judgments about the nature of reality.[133]

God Is a Particular Being

Thankfully, the God of the Bible is not indeterminate or subject to the ruminations and sensibilities of humanity. When Paul used the term God (*theos*), he was referring to the God and Father of the Lord Jesus Christ.[134] God is the Creator of the heavens and the earth and is separate from His creation (Gen 1:1). He created man and woman in His image from the dust of the earth, breathing into Adam the breath of life (Gen 2:7). He gives to humanity life and breath and all things (Acts 17:25). God is entirely self-sufficient and exists in utter independence from all that He created (Ps 50:1–15; Isa 40:12–31). His thoughts are higher than the thoughts of man, and His ways are not like the ways of man (Isa 55:8). God is not subject to humanity in any sense.

God's independence is grounded first and foremost in ontology, not epistemology. God is God, and all things He made (all things other than the Father, Son, and Holy Spirit) are not God (Gen 1:1–2; John 1:3; Rom 1:25). The Creator-creature distinction is fundamental to Christian theology, and any departure or denial of the distinction inevitably leads to confusion and error. Epistemological implications flow from the independence of God. He is infinite; humans are finite. He is omniscient; humans have limited, fallible knowledge. God does not have to be taught but knows all things. The list could be multiplied, but the fact that there are quantitative and even qualitative differences between the mind of God and the mind of humans does not entail that God is unable to reveal true particular information about Himself that can be truly understood by humans.

---

[133]Netland notes, "The various religions advance many different and even conflicting claims about the nature of reality. While undoubtedly such claims do serve a variety of functions, it is crucial to recognize that they are accepted by religious believers within the respective traditions as true." *Dissonant Voices*, 133.

[134]D. Howell, "The Apostle Paul and First Century Religious Pluralism," in *Christianity and the Religions: A Biblical Theology of World Religions*, ed. E. Rommen and H. Netland (Pasadena, CA: William Carey Library, 1995), 94. See also T. C. Tennent, *Theology in the Context of World Christianity: How the Global Church Is Influencing the Way We Think About and Discuss Theology* (Grand Rapids: Zondervan, 2007), 25–49.

God is also personal. He speaks, acts, and reveals to some His covenant name (Exod 3:14). He manifests the attributes and performs the actions of a person.[135] Though some may see these personal attributes and actions of God as anthropomorphic (emotions, speaking, hearing), the biblical presentation of the personal attributes of God suggests that we are personal beings because God is a personal, communicative being. The biblical teaching on God's creation of the first man and woman as *imago Dei* is clear and instructive. Pluralists may wish to argue the reverse, that we think of God as personal (usually masked in language of God being infinite and wholly other) because we ourselves are personal and particular. But where is the evidence for this assertion? Why should Christians accept such pluralist pronouncements when the biblical data leads to the opposite conclusion?

As a personal being, God is also particular; that is, He is one way and not another. The biblical presentation of God speaks to the particularity of God. When He spoke to Moses and commissioned him to approach Pharaoh, His directions were specific and particular (Exod 3–4). God commanded Moses to perform specific actions, and he was to speak a specific message. When God was angered at the Israelites' idolatrous worship of the golden calf, His reaction was specific and particular (Exod 32). He was not simultaneously angry and happy with the sin of the Israelites. Humans, as personal beings, are particularly one way and not another. For example, my wife is a personal and particular being. Imagine if in my quest to know her I made up facts about her and pursued her on the basis of my own speculation. I may even have admirable motives in doing so. Obviously, my wife would have little appreciation for such efforts. In fact, she would probably feel dishonored that I had ignored the reality of her being and chosen to pursue her on the basis of my idiosyncratic speculations and desires. After all, she is a real person and as such I can be right or wrong about her.

Why would we expect God to be any different? Do not the declarations of God's jealousy throughout Scripture teach that because God is a particular being, we are to know specific things about Him and approach Him in specific ways? When people pick and choose what

---

[135] J. Frame argues, "In the biblical view, the impersonal reduces to the personal. Matter, energy, motion, time, and space are under the rule of a personal Lord. All the wonderful things that we find in personality—intelligence, compassion, creativity, love, justice—are not ephemeral data, doomed to be snuffed out in cosmic calamity; rather, they are aspects of what is most permanent, most ultimate. They are what the universe is really all about." J. M. Frame, *The Doctrine of God* (Phillipsburg: P&R, 2002), 26.

of God they like and what of God they want to believe, they are engaging in idolatry, creating a god in their image. God is not an image that humans create. He has existence in and of Himself and does not derive that existence from human thoughts. At the risk of oversimplification, God is who He is, regardless of how or what I think about Him. I do not think Him into existence, nor do I have the right to pick and choose what I like about Him. When that is done, what is worshipped is not a real transcendent God but an avatar, a virtual god of the pluralist's own making before whom he worships. But a god of human making is not a god at all, and is certainly not worthy of worship. Worshipping such a god is tantamount to worshipping oneself. The biblical polemic against the foolishness of idolatry is applicable to such pluralist constructions. The Bible indicates that the supreme God is dishonored when we approach Him on our terms or by means of our own choosing. To suggest otherwise would fly in the face of simple logic and the biblical presentation of God.

THE CHRISTIAN RESPONSE

How are Christians to respond to pluralism? The biblical answer is proclamation of the God who saves and of His unique Son, the Lord Jesus Christ. The New Testament, from the ministry of Jesus to the Pauline letters, to the Apocalypse of John, does not offer any encouragement or endorsement of the Christless theocentrism of religious pluralism. When Jesus Christ encountered people from the surrounding nations, His call was to believe in Him and then to affirm the faith of individuals when it was directed at Him (Matt 8:5–13; 15:21–28; Mark 5:1–20). Paul, the apostle to the Gentiles, boldly proclaimed the gospel to communities and societies that did not know the living God and worshipped other deities and idols. Paul was intent on preaching the gospel of the cross in Corinth, even though "the Jews ask for signs and the Greeks seek wisdom" (1 Cor 1:22). There is no hint of accommodation, compromise, or syncretism in Paul's affirmation:

> We preach Christ crucified, a stumbling block to the Jews and foolishness to the Gentiles. Yet to those who are called, both Jews and Greeks, Christ is God's power and God's wisdom, because God's foolishness is wiser than human wisdom, and God's weakness is stronger than human strength (1 Cor 1:23–25).

179

When Paul addressed the church in Colossae that was facing the temptation of syncretism (Col 2:4–23), he proclaimed the uniqueness and unrivaled supremacy of Jesus Christ (Col 1:15–23). Don Howell summarizes, "Instead of rapprochement or accommodation there is displacement. Here is the dividing line for Paul, that is, anything that deprecates the full deity of Jesus and the adequacy of his redemptive work must be steadfastly rejected."[136]

In the face of pluralist calls to see the essential sameness in the great world religions, the Christian faith makes no such affirmations of equality. Jesus Christ did not offer Himself as one path among many, nor did He claim to be the best path. Christianity is not the fulfillment of other religious quests, nor is it based upon twenty-first-century sensibilities and judgments. The essence of Christianity is grounded in the reality that the God of grace is reaching out to those who have rebelled against Him, and He has done so uniquely and emphatically through Jesus Christ.

From the earliest days of the Church, Christians have been captured by the claims, actions, teachings, and life of Jesus. The accounts of Jesus' life, written in the Gospels, were written at most 40 to 70 years after the death and resurrection of Jesus. Paul's letters, which contain the critical events of Jesus' life, were written 15 to 25 years after the death and resurrection of Christ. In other words, there were living eyewitnesses to the events of Jesus' life at the time the biblical accounts were written (1 Cor 15:6). Those accounts include some strong statements by Jesus. He claimed to be the King of an eternal kingdom (Luke 22:29). He claimed sovereignty over life and death (John 5:21–24). He accepted worship that could only be directed toward God (Matt 28:17; Luke 24:52). He claimed sovereignty over eternal judgment and eternal reward (John 5:27). He said such things as "The one who has seen Me has seen the Father" (John 14:9) and "I am the way, the truth, and the life. No one comes to the Father except through Me" (John 14:6). And of course, Jesus opened the way to God when He, the perfect Son of God, suffered death for sinful humans, taking that which they deserved, so that those who believe in Him might live (John 3:16; 5:24).

The apostles remembered these things and preached from the very beginning, "There is salvation in no one else, for there is no other name under heaven given to people by which we must be saved" (Acts

---

[136]Howell, "Apostle Paul and First Century Religious Pluralism," 106.

4:12). When the apostle Paul stood before the Athenian Areopagus to explain Christianity to its members, he said the following to an utterly pluralistic society:

> Being then God's offspring, we ought not to think that the divine being is like gold or silver or stone, an image formed by the art and imagination of man. The times of ignorance God overlooked, but now He commands all people everywhere to repent, because He has fixed a day on which He will judge the world in righteousness by a man whom He has appointed; and of this He has given assurance to all by raising Him from the dead (Acts 17:29–31 ESV).

The apostle Paul was right. Pluralism falls apart in the face of the resurrection. The reality of the resurrection demands that Jesus be heard and His claims be taken seriously. As Tim Keller writes:

> The resurrection also puts a burden of proof on its nonbelievers. It is not enough to simply believe Jesus did not rise from the dead. You must then come up with a historically feasible alternate explanation for the birth of the church. You have to provide some other plausible account for how things began.[137]

Proclamation of the Lord Jesus Christ—His life, teaching, death, and resurrection—is the biblical response to pluralism. Such a course takes wisdom and boldness, for the more biblically faithful the gospel message is proclaimed, the more offensive it will be to those who have drunk deeply from the poisoned waters of religious pluralism. There is no way around this reality. Jesus made exclusive claims that are utterly incompatible with all other religious systems. For if Jesus is correct, then Muhammad and Buddha were wrong. If Jesus is incorrect, then Christians are wrong. People in our current cultural milieu might wish that this were not the case, but wishing does not make it so. To dismiss the truth claims of Jesus as self-evidently wrong because His statements offend cultural sensibilities is not an argument against those truth claims; it is only a complaint that His claims are offensive. Though postmodern sensibilities try to argue otherwise, palatability does not reflect on the validity of a truth claim. Christians, of all people, ought to realize this because they are told in Scripture that their

---

[137]Keller, *Reason for God*, 202.

message will be rejected precisely because it is offensive to blinded human sensibilities (John 3:19; 1 Cor 1:23; 2 Cor 4:1–5).

If one walks the route of religious and philosophical pluralism, intellectual honesty demands that the pluralist start with the claims of each religion. Christians must press this demand. The pluralist has to deal with the Bible's unique claims to be the Word of God. The truth contained in Scripture is not the product of naked religious experience or human intellectual construction; rather, it is revealed by God. In answer to the pluralist, the Christian can know things of this wonderful and mysterious God precisely and only because God has revealed them, through His Word and most fully through His Son, the Lord Jesus Christ. True knowledge of God, although not exhaustive knowledge, is possible because of His revelatory work.

The pluralist also has to deal with Jesus, what He said and did, before He can be dismissed as just another wise spiritual teacher who provided some insight into God. Approaches to religious pluralism have to deal with Jesus Christ. Who Jesus is and what He said have a controlling influence over one's approach to Christianity and other religions.[138] On analysis, Jesus' claims are fundamentally different from those of other religious leaders. Difference does not entail superiority, but it is illegitimate to assert that there are no essential differences in the religions when Christians believe that the claims and person of Jesus Christ are qualitatively different from those of other religious leaders.[139] If Christians compromise on this point, then they have no gospel to proclaim. If Jesus Christ is merely an extremely spiritual person with extraordinary ability to see and hear God, then the redemptive story chronicled in the Bible unravels, and the church has been guilty of perpetrating an unforgivable hoax. But if Jesus Christ is who He said He is, then there is hope for the world and urgency for the task of missions. Orthodox Christianity does not fit into a pluralistic scheme; it cannot do so and retain even a semblance of its essence. Jesus requires that every person close with Him, that every person answer the question that He asked His disciples: "What about you, who do you say that I am?" The apostle Peter gave the answer that must be given: "You are the Christ, the Son of the living God" (Matt 16:16 ESV).

---

[138] McGrath, "Response to John Hick," 67.
[139] Ibid.

Chapter Five

Inclusivism I:
Nonevangelical Expressions

INTRODUCTION

In February 1991, the World Council of Churches (WCC) held
its seventh general assembly in Canberra, Australia, under the theme,
"Come Holy Spirit—Renew the Whole Creation."[1] The presentations
to the WCC highlighted the re-creative work of the Holy Spirit with
special attention to universal aspects of the Spirit's work. The statements concerning the person and work of the Holy Spirit ranged from
orthodox to heretical to bizarre. This was nowhere more evident than
in the two keynote addresses surrounding the main theme. The first
address, written by the Greek Orthodox Patriarch Parthenios, characterized the ministry of the Holy Spirit as being always and everywhere. On that basis, dialogue with other religions should take on the
character of the Spirit and a dependence on the Spirit who is Himself
independent. According to Parthenios, the work of the Spirit and the
church is the pursuit of unity. Boundaries cannot be placed on the
Spirit because the Holy Spirit "blows where he wills, and we have no

---

[1]The purpose of the theme was to give voice to the awareness that the whole of creation is
"threatened by poverty, injustice, war and pollution" and that humanity is "woefully inadequate"
to fix things. M. Kinnamon, "Canberra 1991: A Personal Overview and Introduction," in *Signs
of the Spirit: Official Report, Seventh Assembly*, ed. M. Kinnamon (Geneva: World Council of
Churches Publications, 1991), 14.

right, nor is it an act of love, to restrict his movement and his breathing, to bind him with fetters and barbed wire."[2]

The second keynote address was delivered by Chung Hyun Kyung, who entered the assembly hall "accompanied by sixteen Korean and two Aboriginal dancers, complete with gongs, bells, drums, clap sticks and candles."[3] Her address began with "an invocation of the spirits of an eclectic collection of martyrs, from Hagar to the students in Tiananmen Square, from the 'spirit of Earth, Air, and Water' to 'our brother Jesus, tortured and killed on the cross.'"[4] She then invoked the voice of the Holy Spirit through the spirits of those who had died in their misery, explaining that "without hearing the cries of these spirits . . . we cannot hear the voice of the Holy Spirit. . . . I hope the presence of all our ancestors' spirits here with us shall not make you uncomfortable. For us they are the icons of the Holy Spirit."[5] The wild range of conclusions presented at the WCC Assembly is the product of two factors: over 30 years of theological drift concerning the possibility of salvation outside the church and speculation regarding the role of the Holy Spirit in effecting that salvation.[6]

Prior to the twentieth century, the response of the church to world religions was consistently negative with regard to their salvific potential. The development of a Christian theology of religions began, not in formal statements on world religions but in the response of the church fathers to schismatics. Ignatius, the bishop of Antioch, set the stage by declaring, "Be not deceived, my brethren: if anyone follows a maker of schism, he does not inherit the Kingdom of God; if anyone walks in strange doctrine he has no part in the passion."[7] Irenaeus, to whom current advocates of a pneumatological approach to theology of religions most often appeal, pronounced, "For where the Church is, there is the Spirit of God; and where the Spirit of God is, there is the Church, and every kind of grace; but the Spirit is truth."[8] The gravest condemnation of the possibility of salvation outside the church came from Cyprian: "For they cannot live out of it, since the house of God is

---

[2] Parthenios, "The Holy Spirit," in *Signs of the Spirit*, ed. M. Kinnamon, 36. Parthenios was not able personally to attend the meetings due to the Gulf War of 1991.

[3] Kinnamon, "Canberra 1991," 15.

[4] Ibid.

[5] Ibid. The reaction to Professor Chung ranged from stern protestations to enthusiastic support.

[6] An excellent summary can be found in H. Netland, *Encountering Religious Pluralism: The Challenge to Christian Faith & Mission* (Downers Grove, IL: InterVarsity, 2001), 23–54.

[7] Ignatius, *The Epistle of Ignatius to the Philadelphians* 3, *ANF*, 80.

[8] Irenaeus, *Against Heresies* 3,24.1, *ANF*.

one, and there can be no salvation to any except in the Church."[9] Thus the principle that guided the church for the better part of two millennia, *extra ecclesiam nulla salus* ("no salvation outside the church"), was articulated.

The past half-century has seen a dramatic shift away from *extra ecclesiam nulla salus* and with that a growing denial of the necessity of believing the gospel to be saved. Though this shift has been most dramatic in those denominations and traditions that do not share evangelical commitments to the authority and inspiration of Scripture, evangelicals have not been immune to the drift. The theology of nonevangelicals, developed and promoted as much as three decades earlier, has laid the foundation for the current proposals of pneumatological inclusivism offered by evangelicals such as Clark Pinnock and Amos Yong. Daniel Strange notes that Pinnock's inclusivism "is influenced more by traditions and communities outside evangelicalism than from within it (most notably the Roman Catholic statements of Vatican II, the Eastern Orthodox understanding of the Spirit and the theology of the early Greek Fathers)."[10] The purpose of this chapter is to describe those proposals for inclusive theologies of religions that have most influenced evangelical pneumatological inclusivists. Although not every nonevangelical contributor to a pneumatological theology of religions will be covered, significant writings by the Roman Catholic Church, Karl Rahner, Jacques Dupuis, and Georg Khodr will be summarized.

Roman Catholic Church

Until the late nineteenth century, the Roman Catholic Church held steadfastly to the requirement of membership in the church for salvation. For example, the Fourth Lateran Council, called by Pope Innocent III in 1215, declared, "There is one Universal Church of the faithful, outside of which there is absolutely no salvation."[11] Pope Boniface VIII, in his Papal Bull of 1302, *Unam Sanctum*, pronounced:

---

[9]Cyprian, *The Epistles of Cyprian* 61.4, *ANF*, 358. This statement comes in a discourse on whether to allow back into the church those women who had made a vow of chastity who were subsequently found in the same bed with a man but had maintained their chastity.

[10]D. Strange, *The Possibility of Salvation Among the Unevangelized: An Analysis of Inclusivism in Recent Evangelical Theology* (Waynesboro, GA: Paternoster, 2002), 43.

[11]"Medieval Sourcebook: Twelfth Ecumenical Council: Lateran IV 1215," Canon 1 [online]; accessed 8 September 2004; available from http://www.fordham.edu/halsall/basis/lateran4.html; Internet.

We are obliged by the faith to believe and hold—and we do firmly believe and sincerely confess—that there is one Holy Catholic and Apostolic Church, and that outside this Church there is neither salvation nor remission of sins. . . . Furthermore we declare, state, define and pronounce that it is altogether necessary to salvation for every human creature to be subject to the Roman pontiff.[12]

The first signs of departure from a strict exclusivism began to appear in the nineteenth and early twentieth centuries. Two popes, both choosing the name of Pius, planted the seeds for a theological inclusivism that would bloom at the Second Vatican Council in the mid-twentieth century. In 1856, Pope Pius IX demanded that those who fall under the witness of the church must enter the church to be saved, but he made provision for the one who was ignorant of the church "through ignorance beyond his control."[13] Shortly thereafter, he explained that it is a "grave error" to believe that one can be saved apart from the church, but those who live in "invincible ignorance" have hope:

> Here, too, our beloved sons and venerable brothers, it is again necessary to mention and censure a very grave error entrapping some Catholics who believe that it is possible to arrive at eternal salvation although living in error and alienated from the true faith and Catholic unity. Such belief is certainly opposed to Catholic teaching. There are, of course, those who are struggling with invincible ignorance about our most holy religion. Sincerely observing the natural law and its precepts inscribed by God on all hearts and ready to obey God, they live honest lives and are able to attain eternal life by the efficacious virtue of divine light and grace. Because God knows, searches and clearly understands the minds, hearts, thoughts, and nature of all, his supreme kindness and clemency do not permit anyone at all who is not guilty of deliberate sin to suffer eternal punishments.[14]

---

[12]H. Bettenson, ed., "The Bull 'Unam Sanctum,' 1302," in *Documents of the Christian Church*, 2nd ed. (New York: Oxford University Press, 1963), 115–16.

[13]Pius IX, *Singulari Quidem: On the Church in Austria* (17 March 1856), 7 [online]; accessed 23 September 2004; available from http://www.papalencyclicals.net/Pius09/p9singul .htm; Internet.

[14]Pius IX, *Quanto Conficiamur Moerore* (10 August 1863), 7 [online]; accessed 23 September 2004; available from http://www.papalencyclicals.net/Pius09/p9quanto.htm; Internet.

Two points are worthy of mention in Pius IX's encyclical. First, it explicitly ties the criteria for salvation to the church. The church is seen as the repository of the gospel, but it is surely significant that the encyclical is intentionally ecclesiocentric rather than gospel centered. Second, the evidences of the saving power of God in the life of the saved individual who is not a part of the church and confined in invisible ignorance of the church are obedience to natural law and an honest life. No criteria are given to aid in discernment of these virtues or from whence they spring.

In 1943, Pope Pius XII, in the papal encyclical *Mystici Corporis*, reaffirmed the principle of *extra ecclesiam nulla salus*, by emphasizing the necessity of unity in the body for participation in the Spirit. In particular he proclaimed that those who are "divided in faith" are not a part of the body of Christ and therefore are not living in the Holy Spirit:

> Actually only those are to be included as members of the Church who have been baptized and profess the true faith. . . . As therefore in the true Christian community there is only one Body, one Spirit, one Lord, and one Baptism, so there can be only one faith. And therefore, if a man refuse to hear the Church, let him be considered—so the Lord commands—as a heathen and a publican. It follows that those who are divided in faith or government cannot be living in the unity of such a Body, nor can they be living the life of its one Divine Spirit.[15]

Pius XII emphasized the unity of the body which flows from the unity of Jesus Christ and the Holy Spirit. In his statement, the one body and one baptism serve as ecclesiastical bookends to the union found in Christ and the Spirit. There is no salvation for those who do not participate in the church because one who is not part of the church has no part in the Spirit or in Christ.

In that same document, however, Pius XII left the door open when he implored those who were separated from the Catholic Church, but were unconsciously related to the church,

> to correspond to the interior movements of grace, and to seek to withdraw from that state in which they cannot be sure of their

---

[15]Pius XII, *Mystici Corporis Christi* (1943), 22 [online]; accessed 21 August 2004; available from http://www.vatican.va/holy_father/pius_xii/encyclicals/documents/hf_p-xii_enc_29061943_mystici-corporis-christi_en.html; Internet.

salvation. For even though by an unconscious desire and long-ing they have a certain relationship with the Mystical Body of the Redeemer, they still remain deprived of those many heavenly gifts and helps which can only be enjoyed in the Catholic Church. Therefore may they enter into Catholic unity and, joined with us in the one, organic Body of Jesus Christ, may they together with us run on to the one Head in the Society of glorious love.[16]

No definition is given as to exactly what this "unconscious desire" is or from whence it comes. Earlier paragraphs had taught that par-ticipation in the Holy Spirit is impossible apart from participation through baptism in the church, the body of Christ. In paragraph 103 of *Mystici Corporis*, Pius XII declares that a "certain relationship" with the body of Christ is possible apart from the church. Although neither the nature of this relationship nor how such a relationship is possible apart from participation in the Holy Spirit is explained, it is evident that Pius XII was allowing room for the possibility of salvation outside the church. Whereas Pius IX provided allowance for those who had never heard the gospel, Pius XII declared that no one was able to "set the boundaries" for that ignorance. The door left ajar by Pius IX and Pius XII was opened wide at the Second Vatican Council.

Vatican II

The import of Vatican Council II cannot be overemphasized.[17] Convened by Pope John XXIII during four consecutive autumns (1962–1965) and including over 2,000 bishops, the scope, mission, theology, and nature of the Catholic Church were redefined through the publication of 16 major documents. The most significant of these documents, for the purposes of the present discussion, are *Nostra Aetate* (the theology of religions), *Ad Gentes Divinitus* (the mission-ary task of the church), *Gaudium et Spes* (modern challenges to the church), and *Lumen Gentium* (the doctrine of the church).[18]

---

[16]Ibid., 103.

[17]Kärkkäinen suggests that "in the long history of the development of Catholic theology, no other event is of such transformative significance." V. Kärkkäinen, *An Introduction to the The-ology of Religions: Biblical, Historical and Contemporary Perspectives* (Downers Grove, IL: InterVarsity, 2003), 111.

[18]A. Flannery, ed., *Vatican Council II: The Conciliar & Post Conciliar Documents* (Wilm-ington, DE: Scholarly Resources, 1975).

At first glance the teaching of Vatican II concerning world religions is uncompromising. *Lumen Gentium*—while specifically mentioning Islam, Buddhism, and Hinduism—still declares that the church is "necessary for salvation." This pronouncement is rooted in the words of Christ who "explicitly asserted the necessity of faith and baptism, and thereby affirmed at the same time the necessity of the church which men enter through baptism as through a door."[19] Those who have entered into faith in Christ and have submitted to Christian baptism but do not "profess the Catholic faith in its entirety" are still joined to the Catholic Church "in some real way" by the Holy Spirit, who "stirs up desires and actions in all Christ's disciples in order that all may be peaceably united . . . in one flock under one shepherd."[20] But on examination, both *Lumen Gentium* and *Ad Gentes Divinitus* differentiate between those who have heard the proclamation of the Catholic Church and those who have not. Only those who know the necessity of the Catholic Church and consciously reject it cannot be saved.[21] Those who have not heard of the necessity of the church do not share such condemnation.

The disposition of the Vatican II documents toward those in other religions is somewhat favorable. Buddhism and Hinduism are specifically praised for "what is true and holy in these religions," and though the church is duty bound to proclaim the gospel to Buddhists and Hindus, the church declares that within these religions is "a ray of that truth which enlightens all men."[22] Those in any religion who have not heard the gospel "through no fault of their own" may "seek God with a sincere heart, and, moved by grace, try in their actions to do his will as they know it through the dictates of their conscience—those too may achieve eternal salvation."[23] It is evident from the rest of Catholic teaching that having a "sincere heart" and being "moved by grace" are considered evidence of the regenerative work of the Holy Spirit.[24] Though it is not explicitly stated, the inference of such a statement is that the Holy Spirit is at work salvifically, applying the work of Christ

---

[19]*Lumen Gentium* 14.

[20]Ibid., 15.

[21]"Hence they could not be saved who, knowing that the Catholic Church was founded as necessary by God through Christ, would refuse either to enter it, or to remain in it." *Lumen Gentium* 14. See also *Ad Gentes Divinitus* 7.

[22]*Nostra Aetate* 2.

[23]*Lumen Gentium* 15.

[24]See, for example, the teaching on the Holy Spirit in *Catechism of the Catholic Church* (New York: Doubleday, 1995), 684.

to those who have not heard the proclamation of the church.[25] This is accomplished by God, who, "in ways known to himself . . . can lead those who . . . are ignorant of the Gospel to that faith without which it is impossible to please him."[26] Though the inner workings of this salvation are known only to God, it is plainly accomplished through the work of the Holy Spirit.[27] In perhaps the most specific statement of the work of the Holy Spirit in world religions, *Gaudium et Spes* declares that among those who are being saved, there is a universal work of the Spirit that brings the benefits of redemption:

> This holds true not for Christians only but also for all persons of good will in whose hearts grace is active invisibly. For since Christ died for all, and since all are in fact called to one and the same destiny, which is divine, we must hold that the Holy Spirit offers to all the possibility of being made partners, in a way known to God, in the Paschal mystery.[28]

This is perhaps the earliest affirmation in official Catholic teaching of what has become the standard inclusivist position with emphasis on the role of the Spirit. The Holy Spirit is at work in *all* who are not Christians, including, then, those who have no knowledge of Christ or the teaching of the church, enabling them to become participants and beneficiaries of the work of Christ apart from gospel proclamation. According to *Gaudium et Spes*, because of the universal work of the Holy Spirit, one need not hear the gospel and embrace the Christian faith to be saved.

In summary, the role of the Holy Spirit, explicated in the Vatican II documents, has two key aspects. First, the Holy Spirit enables participation in the body of Christ, which is the church. Second, the Holy Spirit is at work in a universal sense applying the merits of Christ's

---

[25]The emphasis of Catholic teaching is on the proclamation of the church (see *Lumen Gentium* 14, *Ad Gentes Divinitus* 7, etc.). In Chapter 9 I address the necessity of human proclamation of the gospel.

[26]*Ad Gentes Divinitus* 7.

[27]How such a working is possible apart from conscious faith in Christ, or how that can be reconciled with the Catholic teaching on the person and work of the Holy Spirit, is not immediately evident. For example, the *Catechism of the Catholic Church* describes the joint mission of the Son and Spirit as follows: "When the Father sends his Word, he always sends his Breath. In their joint mission, the Son and the Holy Spirit are distinct but inseparable. To be sure, it is Christ who is seen, the visible image of the invisible God, but it is the Spirit who reveals him." *Catechism of the Catholic Church*, 689.

[28]*Gaudium et Spes*, 22.

atoning work to those who have not heard the gospel. It should also be noted that *Gaudium et Spes* offers a clear statement of pneumatological inclusivism—the Holy Spirit applying the work of Christ to those who do not possess conscious faith in Christ.

Roman Catholic Church Since Vatican II

Since the publication of the conciliar documents, the Catholic Church has sent out mixed messages with regard to the necessity of conscious faith in the gospel or participation in the Catholic Church for salvation. For example, in *Evangelii Nuntiandi*, given in 1975 by Pope Paul VI, there is an explicit statement of the necessity of belief in the gospel for salvation.[29] This affirmation is repeated as late as 1999 in the "Letter to Presidents of Bishops' Conferences on the Spirituality of Dialogue" by the Pontifical Council for Interreligious Dialogue.[30] But this has not been the norm for papal pronouncements since Vatican II, and the church has seen a steady drift from exclusivism since the Second Vatican Council.

The papacy of John Paul II saw the greatest departure from an exclusivist position. In the encyclical *Redemptoris Hominis* (1979), he elevated the role of the Spirit in the life of the church and mission.[31] He provided greater detail on the role of the Holy Spirit in mission in the encyclical *Redemptoris Missio* (1990), where the teaching on the Spirit in *Gaudium et Spes* was reaffirmed. The Spirit is at work outside the confines of the church, but discernment of that work is the responsibility of the church.[32]

---

[29]"This message is indeed necessary. It is unique. It cannot be replaced. It does not permit either indifference, syncretism or accommodation. It is a question of people's salvation." Paul VI, *Evangelii Nuntiandi* (8 December 1975), 5 [online]; accessed 10 September 2004; available from http://www.vatican.va/holy_father/paul_vi/apost_exhortations/documents/hf_p-vi_exh_19751208_evangelii-nuntiandi_en.html; Internet.

[30]"It is our firm conviction that God wants all persons to be saved (cf. 1 Tim 2:4) and that God can give his grace also outside the visible boundaries of the Church (cf. LG 16; *Redemptor Hominis* 10). At the same time the Christian is aware that Jesus Christ, the Son of God made man, is the one and only Saviour of all humanity, and that only in the Church which Christ founded are to be found the means of salvation in all their fulness." Francis Cardinal Arinze, "Letter to Presidents of Bishops' Conferences on the Spirituality of Dialogue" (Vatican City: 3 March 1999), 5 [online]; accessed 15 September 2004; available from http://puffin.creighton.edu/jesuit/dialogue/documents/articles/spirituality_of_dialogue.html; Internet.

[31]John Paul II, *Redemptoris Hominis* (Rome: 4 March 1979), 11–19 [online]; accessed 11 September 2004; available from http://www.vatican.va/holy_father/john_paul_ii/encyclicals/documents/ hf_jp-ii_enc_04031979_redemptor-hominis_en.html; Internet.

[32]John Paul II, *Redemptoris Missio* (12 December 1990), 28–29 [online]; accessed 11 September 2004; available from http://www.vatican.va/holy_father/john_paul_ii/encyclicals/documents/ hf_jp-ii_enc_07121990_redemptoris-missio_en.html; Internet.

The document *Dialogue and Proclamation*, a joint document of the Pontifical Council for Interreligious Dialogue and the Congregation for Evangelization of Peoples,[33] provides both the greatest movement in the disposition of the Catholic Church toward the possibility of salvation in other religions and the greatest specificity as to how God works savingly in peoples of other religions. As such, the document provides the clearest proposal on the salvific work of the Holy Spirit in peoples of other religions.

According to *Dialogue and Proclamation*, the basis for interreligious dialogue is the presence of the Holy Spirit in the hearts of all participants. The argument begins with the universal action of the Holy Spirit. Since the Holy Spirit was at work prior to the glorification of Christ, "these elements, as a preparation for the Gospel, have played and do still play a providential role in the divine economy of salvation."[34] Recognition of the Spirit's work "impels the Church to enter into 'dialogue and collaboration.'"[35] This dialogue is possible because the Holy Spirit is "mysteriously present in the heart of every person, Christian or otherwise" who engages in authentic prayer.[36] Although there is but "one plan of salvation for humankind, with its center in Jesus Christ," there is an "active presence of the Holy Spirit in the religious life of the members of the other religious traditions which causes a mystery of unity . . . in spite of the differences between religious professions."[37]

The Holy Spirit calls people into the unity of the body of Christ even if they remain "unaware" of this fact because their saving faith will manifest itself in a "sincere practice of what is good in their own religious traditions and by following dictates of their conscience."[38] Such practice constitutes a positive response to God's invitation to

---

[33]*Dialogue and Proclamation: Joint Document of the Pontifical Council for Interreligious Dialogue and the Congregation for Evangelization of Peoples* (Rome: 19 May 1991) [online]; accessed 21 August 2004; available from http://www.vatican.va/roman_curia/pontifical_councils/ interelg/documents/ rc_pc_interelg_doc_19051991_dialogue-and-proclamatio_en.html; Internet.

[34]*Dialogue and Proclamation*, 17.

[35]Ibid.

[36]Ibid., 27. This is a quotation taken from John Paul II's address to the Roman Curia after the World Day of Prayer for Peace in Assisi in January 2002. It was the second such gathering of religious leaders (the first being in October 1986) from around the globe representing many different faiths and traditions. John Paul was convinced that the basis for calling an interfaith day of prayer is the activity of the Holy Spirit in the lives of all those who seek God with sincerity.

[37]*Dialogue and Proclamation*, 28.

[38]Ibid., 29.

salvation in Christ, "even while they do not recognize or acknowledge him as their saviour."[39]

The above paragraph is a clear presentation of an inclusivist proposal that centers on the work of the Holy Spirit in applying the work of Christ to those who do not possess conscious faith in Christ. Such a "believer," being a possessor of the Spirit of God, will also display the fruit of the Spirit of God just as orthodox believers in Jesus Christ so do (Gal 5:28–29). This calls for a set of criteria for discerning the works of the Holy Spirit from the works of other spirits. According to *Dialogue and Proclamation*, discernment of the fruit of the Spirit in believers ("Christian or otherwise") is not overly problematic, but establishing a criteria for systematically identifying the work of the Spirit in other religious traditions presents far more obstacles:

> The fruits of the Spirit of God in the personal life of individuals, whether Christian or otherwise, are easily discernible (cf. Ga 5:22–23). To identify in other religious traditions elements of grace capable of sustaining the positive response of their members to God's invitation is much more difficult. It requires a discernment for which criteria have to be established. Sincere individuals marked by the Spirit of God have certainly put their imprint on the elaboration and the development of their respective religious traditions. It does not follow, however, that everything in them is good.[40]

The inclusion of individuals into the kingdom who do not possess conscious faith in Christ is possible because of the inchoate nature of the kingdom. The church must recognize that the unfinished nature of the kingdom allows the kingdom to extend beyond the boundaries of the church to those who "live evangelical values and are open to the action of the Spirit."[41] However, the unfinished nature of the kingdom also enables effective proclamation of the gospel. Because the Spirit is universally active, even prior to gospel proclamation, individuals may

> have already responded implicitly to God's offer of salvation in Jesus Christ, a sign of this being the sincere practice of their own religious

---

[39] Ibid.

[40] Ibid., 30.

[41] Ibid., 35. How one can be evangelical without believing the gospel is not explained?

traditions, insofar as these contain authentic religious values. They may have already been touched by the Spirit and in some way associated unknowingly to the paschal mystery of Jesus Christ.[42]

The teaching of the Roman Catholic Church on the possibility of salvation for those who do not express conscious faith in Christ and/ or participate in the Catholic Church has demonstrated a steady departure from the early position of *extra ecclesiam nulla salus*. The impact of Roman Catholic teaching on both nonevangelical and evangelical proponents of pneumatological inclusivism is unquestionably large. In a paper presented to the Evangelical Theological Society (ETS) in 2002, Clark Pinnock dedicated a significant portion of his address to the teaching of the Roman Catholic Church since Vatican II.[43] Pinnock was most impressed with John Paul's "respect for the presence and activity of the Holy Spirit among non-Christians, a presence and activity discernable in their religious life, in their practice of virtue, their spirituality, and their prayers."[44] The main point of departure for evangelical pneumatological inclusivists is on the question of discernment. Evangelical inclusivists are not nearly so optimistic about discerning the fruit of the Spirit in participants in other religions. This is discussed in detail in chapter 6.

KARL RAHNER AND ANONYMOUS CHRISTIANITY

Any discussion of the possibility of salvation in Christ apart from conscious faith in Christ would be incomplete without including the influential German-born Roman Catholic theologian Karl Rahner (1904–84) and his proposal of "anonymous Christianity."[45] Though his work takes him down a path toward pneumatological inclusivism that is not as well-developed as that of the others that follow in this chapter, his impact on advocates for a pneumatological inclusivism is significant.[46]

---

[42]Ibid., 68. This statement is an intentional elaboration on *Guadium et Spes*, 22.

[43]Approximately one-fifth of the paper discussed the teaching of the Catholic Church during the papacy of John Paul II. C. H. Pinnock, "Religious Pluralism: A Turn to the Holy Spirit" (paper prepared for the annual meeting of the Evangelical Theological Society, Toronto, Ontario, November 2002) [online]; accessed 15 September 2004; available from http://www.mcmaster.ca/mjtm/5–4.htm; Internet.

[44]Ibid.

[45]See, for example, K. Rahner, "Anonymous Christians," in *Theological Investigations*, vol. 6, trans. K. Kruger and B. Kruger (New York: Seabury, 1969), 390–98. Rahner believes his convictions on anonymous Christians are perfectly consistent with Vatican II. Ibid., 397.

[46]For example, P. Knitter is a former student of K. Rahner, and J. Dupuis engages Rahner as a primary conversation partner in the development of his Christological theology of religions.

Rahner's thesis is that salvation is available only through the work of Christ, but the salvific offer is mediated through the traditions of religious others. Therefore, there is salvation apart from gospel witness but not apart from Christ Himself.[47] Individuals are saved not in spite of their religious traditions but through their allegiance to them via the active presence of Christ in those religious traditions and practices. Rahner readily admits that the presence of Christ in other religious traditions is hidden from those adherents, and it does not compare to that of those who know the fullness of the historical Christ, but that does not deny the reality of His presence or the reality of their real, though anonymous, Christian experience. The anonymous Christian has a real and existential relationship based on his orientation to the grace of God. He faithfully follows the practices of his own religious tradition and is reached by Christ through these same traditions.[48] Rahner suggests that this is possible through elements of supernatural grace mediated by the Holy Spirit.[49] Rahner's emphasis, however, as indicated by the term "anonymous Christian," maintains a Christocentric focus because

the efficacy of the Spirit is directed from the very beginning to the zenith of its historical mediation, which is the Christ event (or in other words the final cause of the mediation of the Spirit to the world), it can be truly said that this Spirit is everywhere and from the very beginning the Spirit of Jesus Christ, the incarnate divine Logos. The Spirit communicated to the world has itself, as such, an inner relation to Jesus Christ (not merely in the divine intention which transcends the world, which would be external to the Spirit).[50]

This supernatural grace continues to be mediated to the anonymous Christian as long as no obligation is placed on the individual to follow

J. Dupuis, *Jesus Christ and the Encounter of World Religions* (Maryknoll, NY: Orbis, 1985), 129–30.

[47]See K. Rahner, *Foundations of the Christian Faith: An Introduction to the Idea of Christianity*, trans. W. V. Dych (New York: Seabury, 1978), 306.

[48]K. Rahner, *Theological Investigations*, vol. 17, trans. M. Kohl (New York: Crossroad, 1981), 41–42.

[49]Rahner explains, "Christ is present and efficacious in the non-Christian believer (and therefore in the non-Christian religions) through his Spirit. . . . If the non-Christian can have a redeeming faith and if it is permissible for us to hope that this faith really exists on a wide scale, then such a faith is . . . made possible and sustained by the supernatural grace of the Holy Spirit." Ibid., 43–44.

[50]Ibid., 46.

the traditions and practices of Christianity. Therefore, the anonymous Christian is a Christian without being conscious of his Christian state. It follows that the most significant difference between a Christian and an anonymous Christian is self-awareness.[51]

JACQUES DUPUIS AND CHRISTOCENTRIC RELIGIOUS PLURALISM

The Belgian-born Jacques Dupuis (1923–2004), after spending years in Asia as a Jesuit missionary, devoted the majority of his scholarly endeavors to the development of what he called a "theology of religious pluralism." The structure of his model was first introduced in *Jesus Christ and the Encounter of World Religions* and then fully developed in *Toward a Christian Theology of Religious Pluralism.*[52] Though Dupuis labeled his contribution "A Christian Theology of Religious Pluralism," his approach would not fall under the category of religious pluralism employed in this book. The Christocentric nature of his proposal resonates with the inclusivist proposals summarized to this point.

Dupuis's earlier thinking follows the same precommitments of most theological inclusivists, namely, a commitment and priority given to the universal salvific will of God, centered in the person and work of Jesus Christ. Dupuis explained, "Christians have no monopoly on the salvation bestowed by Jesus Christ."[53] The question is not whether Jesus Christ saves those outside the Christian faith. That was taken as axiomatic. The question is how Jesus Christ reaches those whom He saves outside the Christian faith. In particular, Dupuis investigated the instrumentality of world religions in securing the blessings of salvation made available through Jesus Christ. But he was adamant that religious others be given a dignity of their own; hence his refusal to call them "non-Christian religions." His goal was to posit "a living faith in Jesus Christ—not in Christianity as such—as the point of departure for reflection."[54]

Dupuis cited *Gaudium et Spes* as evidence that the Roman Catholic Church affirms the reality of salvation apart from gospel witness but criticized Vatican Council II for not explaining how such salvation is possible: "What the council leaves unexplained is *how* the saving

---

[51]See K. Rahner, *Theological Investigations*, vol. 5, trans. D. Bourke (New York: Seabury, 1966), 115–34.

[52]J. Dupuis, *Toward a Christian Theology of Religious Pluralism* (Maryknoll, NY: Orbis, 1997).

[53]Ibid., 125.

[54]Ibid., 3.

power of the Paschal mystery of Jesus Christ reaches the members of the other religious traditions. It is content to assert the fact. Theology, however, should ask this question, and answer it."[55]

To answer this question, Dupuis contrasted two different proposals. The first is a fulfillment theory that posits that all humans have an innate desire to fellowship with their Creator. This desire is worked out in the various religious traditions and cultures around the world. Christianity is seen as the fulfillment of this innate desire because "Jesus Christ and Christianity represent God's personal response to this universal human aspiration."[56] Thus while all other religions are varying expressions of *homo naturaliter religiosus*, and so of "natural religion," only Christianity, as the divine response to the human quest for God, is "supernatural religion."[57] Dupuis was critical of the fulfillment theory precisely at this point because it shifts the center of God's redemptive plan from Jesus Christ to Christianity and the Christian church.[58]

The second theory cited by Dupuis calls for recognition of the presence of Christ in world religions. In this theory the religious traditions of others are evidence of divine interventions into human history. Each tradition is positively oriented toward the Christ event, although not necessarily Christianity, and maintains a positive position in the order of salvation precisely because of the presence of Christ operating in and through them. Salvation can occur without the gospel but not without Christ.[59] This theory is advocated by such notables as Raimundo Panikkar and Gavin D'Costa.[60] Rahner designated this hidden presence of Christ in other religions with the term "anonymous Christianity." Dupuis was not fully satisfied with the anonymous Christianity model because it flattens significant differences between the conscious Christian and the anonymous Christian,[61] and it empties all significance of the practices of religious others by claiming that the saved individual is merely a Christian "unawares."[62]

---

[55] Ibid., 126 (italics original).
[56] Ibid., 127.
[57] Ibid.
[58] Ibid., 128.
[59] Ibid., 129.
[60] See, for example, R. Panikkar, *The Unknown Christ of Hinduism: Towards an Ecumenical Christophany* (Maryknoll, NY: Orbis, 1981); G. D'Costa, *The Meeting of Religions and the Trinity* (Maryknoll, NY: Orbis, 2000); and id., *Theology and Religious Pluralism: The Challenge of Other Religions* (Oxford: Blackwell, 1986).
[61] Dupuis, *Jesus Christ at the Encounter of World Religions*, 130.
[62] Ibid., 148.

According to Dupuis, reaching a conclusion on the Old Testament and New Testament disposition toward religious others is difficult because the evidence is ambiguous. Much in the Old Testament seems to condemn other religious traditions, but Dupuis thought this could be better explained perspectively.[63] The New Testament data is equally ambivalent, although Dupuis believed that Paul's message at the Areopagus does indicate that the "religions of the nations are not bereft of value, but find in Jesus Christ the fulfillment of their aspirations."[64]

Contrary to many current proposals, Dupuis sought a theology of religions that is Christological. He recommended three axioms for consideration in the development of his Christological theology of religions. First, any theology of religions must heed what he identified as the anthropological principle. The anthropological principle asserts that all of human existence is historical and that all humans live in community. The assertion that all of human existence is historical argues that all religious life will manifest itself in religious practice. Faith cannot exist apart from religion. That all humans live in community suggests that all religious human beings will exist in religious communities. Dupuis believed that this anthropological principle entails that in the institutions of religious others, there exists an authentic experience of God, pointing to "supernatural grace-filled elements."[65]

The second axiom is Christological and demands that any theology of religions must assert that all salvation is Christian, and it transpires only through Christ. Dupuis was able to avoid a traditional soteriological inclusivism by redefining Christ:

> Christ is the primordial sacrament, unique and necessary, of human beings' encounter with God. Once the mystery of Christ has been revealed, it is given to us Christians to recognize him in the human face of Jesus. Others are incapable of this discernment; however, they can encounter the mystery of Christ unconsciously and can attain salvation in this encounter. Indeed, in order to be saved, they

---

[63]The many judgments against idolatry found in the Old Testament were not condemnations of the traditions outside of Israel per se but are more descriptive of the special status that Israel enjoyed as chosen by the Lord. To turn away would constitute the supreme act of unfaithfulness. Ibid., 131.

[64]Ibid., 132.

[65]Ibid., 144.

must have this encounter, as there is no other way by which God turns to human beings in self-communication.[66]

The third axiom is ecclesiological and requires a commitment to the church as the eschatological community that proclaims and sacramentally represents the mystery of Christ. In and throughout redemptive history, the church is the perfect sign of the mystery of salvation, but this does not entail that imperfect signs of the mystery of salvation cannot and do not exist elsewhere.[67]

Dupuis was able to reconcile these three axioms and claim that other religions mediate the divine mystery of salvation by arguing that "every authentic experience of God, among Christians as among others, is an encounter of God in Jesus Christ with the human being."[68] This means that salvation occurs through a subjective experience with God in Jesus Christ that is mediated through the objective experience of the religions, of which Christianity is one of many. Therefore, Dupuis finds it necessary that God become personally present to religious others in Christ in the practice of their particular religious traditions.[69] Dupuis admits that it is difficult to quantify exactly how the traditions and practices of religious others mediate God's presence in Christ. Christianity enjoys pride of place and is qualitatively and quantitatively superior, but each religious tradition, Christianity included, mediates "distinct modalities" of God's presence in Christ.[70]

It was his commitment to the reality of the distinct modalities of God's presence in other religious practices that caused Dupuis to question the need for conscious faith in Christ. Such faith would necessitate that one cast off his own religious tradition with its distinct experience of God to enter into another distinct and different modality of experiencing Christ. To Dupuis, salvation occurs through the experience of God in Christ, not the experience of Christianity:

---

[66] Ibid.

[67] Ibid., 145–46.

[68] Ibid., 147. Because of the historical particularity of the gospel, Dupuis was also able to claim that in Christianity, God's personal presence to people is highest and most complete.

[69] To deny the reality of an encounter with God through Jesus Christ in other religious practices would be to commit the grave error of unduly separating subjective religious life and objective religious tradition. "Indeed, in their own religious practice is the reality that gives expression to their experience of God and of the mystery of Christ. It is the visible element, the sign, the sacrament of that experience. This practice expresses, supports, bears, and contains, as it were, their encounter with God in Jesus Christ." Ibid., 147–48.

[70] Ibid., 148.

Apart from Christianity, God encounters human beings in Christ, but the human face of God remains unknown. In Christianity, God encounters women and men in the human face of the human Jesus, who reflects for us the very image of the Father. While every religion contains an approach to the human being on the part of God, in Christianity God's advance toward the human being becomes fully human.[71]

Therefore, it is the presence of Christ and that alone that can bring harmony between commitment to the universal salvific will of God and the central role of Jesus Christ in salvation.[72]

A precommitment to the presence of Christ in other religions brings up the question of discernment, in particular how one differentiates between the presence and the lack of presence of Christ in other religious practices. Dupuis answered the question of discernment by turning to pneumatology. The experience of God in other religions is due to the "active presence and life-giving influence of the Holy Spirit."[73] Dupuis believed that the "eschatological outpouring of the Spirit that results from the glorification of Christ" cannot be limited to the Christian church. Rather, "the Holy Spirit gives life to the cosmos, transforming all within it."[74]

Though Dupuis desired to develop a strategy for finding the work of the Holy Spirit in the religious traditions of others, he cautioned that the two perspectives, the Christological and the pneumatological, must not be separated. They are, in fact, "inseparable in the Christian mystery, the cosmic influence of the Spirit being essentially bound up with the universal activity of the risen Lord."[75] So inseparable are the roles, that Dupuis rightly saw the work of the Spirit as focusing on the work of Christ, albeit a redefined Christ.[76] Dupuis was adamant that Christocentrism and pneumatology do not function as two distinct economies and stated unequivocally, "Christ, not the Spirit, is at the center as the way to God. To say it once more: Christocentrism and

---

[71] Ibid., 150.

[72] Dupuis refers to this mysterious presence as the "Christic mystery." Ibid., 150–51.

[73] Ibid., 152.

[74] Ibid.

[75] Ibid., 153.

[76] "The proper function of the Spirit is to center, by its immanent presence, the human being—and the church—on Christ, whom God has personally established as mediator and as the way leading to God. The Spirit is not at the center." Ibid.

pneumatology must not be set in mutual opposition as two distinct economies of salvation; they are two inseparable aspects of one and the same economy."[77] Christology and pneumatology are inseparable because the Spirit, who is the "point of entry" for divine-human communication, is at the same time the Spirit of Christ. Therefore,

> the cosmic influence of the Spirit cannot be severed from the universal action of the risen Christ. His saving function consists in "centering" people, through the medium of his immanent presence, on the Christ whom God has established as the mediator and the way leading to him.[78]

In a Christocentric model of salvation, Dupuis reasoned, the Holy Spirit becomes the point of contact between God, the person, and the church.[79] This is true for the Christian and for the members of other religious traditions, where the presence of Christ, though hidden in other religions, will be "manifested by the 'touches,' the personal imprint of the Holy Spirit in their members."[80]

This touch of the Holy Spirit will be found in religious others because at Pentecost the outpouring of the Holy Spirit, which birthed the church, also extends "beyond the community of Christian faith and consists in the re-creation by the Spirit of the whole of humanity and the entire cosmos."[81] Furthermore, the Spirit was active in the world prior to the incarnation "in view of, and in relation to, the historical event which stands at the center of the history of salvation."[82] Dupuis stopped short of an explicit Christocentric and Christ-glorifying work by the Spirit by limiting the specific function of the Spirit to "allowing persons to become sharers, whether before or after the event, of the paschal mystery of Jesus Christ's death and resurrection."[83] But does the Spirit bring His life-giving influence prior to the proclamation of

---

[77]Dupuis, *Toward a Christian Theology of Religious Pluralism*, 197.

[78]Ibid.

[79]Dupuis's Christocentric mission of the Spirit creates division between the pneumatological inclusivists C. Pinnock and A. Yong. Pinnock believes that Dupuis represents "how far one can go while still remaining within the bounds of orthodoxy." C. Pinnock, "Religious Pluralism." A. Yong believes that a robust Christological criterion will "mute the idea of the [religious] other and . . . act imperialistically toward other faiths." A. Yong, *Beyond the Impasse: Toward a Pneumatological Theology of Religions* (Grand Rapids: Baker, 2003), 103.

[80]Dupuis, *Jesus Christ at the Encounter of World Religions*, 153.

[81]Ibid., 154.

[82]Dupuis, *Toward a Christian Theology of Religious Pluralism*, 197.

[83]Ibid. Dupuis explicitly follows *Gaudium et Spes* in this regard.

the apostolic message? Dupuis was nonplused by the coming of the Spirit after gospel proclamation in Acts 8 and 10. Pointing to such passages as Rom 8:9 and 1 Cor 15:45, Dupuis suggested that the occasion of spiritual freedom is an "unequivocal sign of the presence of the Spirit of Christ in men and women. . . . Christians have no monopoly on these gifts."[84] He also pointed to the gift of faith in God, the fruit of the Spirit, and "the union and peace of human beings with God and among themselves" as further evidence of the work of the Spirit in religious others.[85]

Carrying these convictions into an analysis of world religions has implications at the most basic level of revelation. The prophet becomes one who is able to interpret correctly the present manifestation of salvation history. With this definition it is a small step to grant Muhammad the status of genuine prophet and the Qur'an as containing genuine prophecy.[86] Revelation occurs when God addresses the prophets "personally in the secret recesses of their hearts," thus willing to be "manifested and revealed to the nations in the divine Spirit."[87] Therefore, with some equivocation, Dupuis asserted that when the prophet writes, his word is a "word inspired by God," and when authentically recorded in their holy scriptures is a "word addressed by God to them."[88] Although he believed that the New Testament is unique in that it contains "the penultimate revelation of God which/who is Jesus Christ, . . . the holy scriptures of the nations, along with the Old and New Testaments, represent the various manners and forms in which God addresses human beings throughout the continuous process of the divine self-revelation to them."[89] Dupuis granted to the sacred writings of other traditions the status of divine self-revelation because of the universal influence of the Spirit. Though the words spoken in and through other religious traditions do not have the official character that is ascribed to the Old Testament, they are still the word of God, they are inspired, and they are holy Scripture because of the work of the Holy Spirit.[90]

---

[84]Ibid., 155.

[85]Ibid., 156.

[86]Dupuis notes, "The acknowledgment of Muhammad as a genuine prophet of God is no longer unusual in Christian theology." Ibid., 170. Dupuis admits to error in the Qur'an but suggests that the presence of error does not mean that the entire book is without revelation. It is revelation that is not complete or perfect, but it is revelation from God nonetheless.

[87]Ibid., 172.

[88]Ibid., 173.

[89]Ibid., 175.

[90]Ibid., 176.

Because the Spirit is universally active, it was axiomatic to Dupuis that the Spirit "reaches the members of other religious traditions precisely by the intervention of their traditions."[91] This again raises the question of differentiating the work of the Holy Spirit from that of other spirits. Dupuis recommended two presuppositions for recognizing divine intervention in other religions. First, "any personal experience of God is the vehicle of the presence and activity of the Holy Spirit."[92] Therefore, any authentic experience of God is necessarily an experience in the Spirit. Dupuis allowed that the grace of the Spirit will be different in the pre-Christian and Christian eras, but the very existence of grace points toward the active presence of the Spirit.[93]

The second presupposition necessary for distinguishing the work of the Holy Spirit is that the "Holy Spirit is at work throughout the economy of salvation."[94] The one constant throughout all the different dispensations of redemptive history is the gift of the Spirit. The economy of salvation is driving toward a plenary manifestation in Jesus Christ. In each dispensation the Spirit is the instrument of divine advance.

Though the Spirit plays an essential role in each dispensation, Dupuis stressed that the Christ event is the focal point of salvation history.[95] Because of this, he was able to affirm that the Holy Spirit has been working in the lives and traditions of religious others. How this can be so while affirming a strong Christocentrism is explained by following Rahner. "The Logos's preincarnational activity is oriented to the Christ-event, even as the Spirit can rightly be called the Spirit of Christ from the beginning of salvation history."[96] Thus, Dupuis was able to affirm both the universal activity of the Holy Spirit in history and world religions while affirming the centrality of Jesus Christ in redemptive history.

---

[91] Ibid., 165.

[92] This is based on the theological axiom that God encounters individuals as the triune God—Father, Son, and Holy Spirit—but the Holy Spirit is the point of entry into the divine life for humans. Ibid., 166.

[93] Dupuis argued that the "holy pagans" of the OT lived "by God's Spirit and responded in faith to the call of the Spirit." Ibid., 167.

[94] Ibid.

[95] Dupuis likewise cautions that "the Christocentrism of salvation history must not be construed into Christomonism." Dupuis, *Toward a Christian Theology of Religious Pluralism*, 221.

[96] Ibid., 222.

GEORG KHODR AND THE "TWO HANDS" METAPHOR

Georg Khodr grew up in Tripoli, Lebanon, studied theology in Paris, and was elected to the episcopate in 1970. He has been instrumental in the renewal of the Orthodox Church in Lebanon and Syria. His position in the archdiocese of Mount Lebanon has granted him unique access to the Muslim world, and Khodr has responded by active involvement in the ecumenical movement and Christian-Islam dialogue.

Paul Knitter credits Khodr for alerting the WCC to the advantages of starting a theology of religions with pneumatology in an address to the Baar Consultation in 1990.[97] Khodr, however, has long been an advocate of taking the Spirit as the starting point for a theology of religions. Doing so allows the Christian theologian to affirm the value and role of other religions without compromising the central role of Christ in salvation, while allowing for the possibility that world religions are "an all-comprehensive phenomenon of grace."[98] In fact, Khodr believes that by beginning with the Spirit, the entire shape of the debate can be altered by discarding the categories of exclusivism and inclusivism.

Shortly after being elected to the episcopate in 1970, Khodr had already begun reflecting on the rise of pluralism and the resistance of religious others to the gospel. This caused him to wonder about the legitimacy of maintaining an exclusive stance with regard to other religions, contending that soteriological exclusivism is "legalistic dogmatism" based on "ignorance."[99] In response, Khodr wanted to bring the Holy Spirit front and center in world religions and believes that evangelicals must follow:

> Moreover, if obedience to the Master means following Him wherever we find traces of His presence, we have an obligation to investigate the authentic spiritual life of non-Christians. This raises the question of Christ's presence outside Christian history. The strikingly evangelical quality of many non-Christians obliges us,

---

[97]P. Knitter, "A New Pentecost? A Pneumatological Theology of Religions," *CD* 19 (1991): 35.

[98]Ibid., 36.

[99]G. Khodr, "Christianity in a Pluralistic World—the Economy of the Holy Spirit," *ER* 23 (1971): 118.

moreover, to develop an ecclesiology and a missiology in which the Holy Spirit necessarily occupies a supreme place.[100]

To develop the central role of the Holy Spirit, Khodr turns to the book of Acts (e.g., Acts 10:35; 14:16–17; 17:23). He recognizes that Paul speaks with the rest of the New Testament and Old Testament writers in denying any theological status to the pagan world (Acts 19:16; 1 Cor 8:4; Rev 21:8; 22:15). Nevertheless, Khodr is confident that the Athenian worship of the unknown god demonstrated that they knew the true God although they did not recognize Him as the Creator. Such authentic worship is evidence that the Athenians were Christians, though unconsciously.[101]

Khodr is convinced that when genuine worship of the true God exists outside the church, then contemporary theology must broaden the boundaries of salvific inquiry. The Western church is involved only with itself, seeking illegitimately to narrow the scope of salvation history. Khodr believes that contemporary theology must go beyond the artificial restraints of salvation history to participate in the life of God. The economy of Christ cannot be reduced to a particular historical manifestation. Rather, the economy of God must be sought in eternity and in the life of the Holy Spirit.[102]

Khodr cites Pentecost as the beginning of the economy of the Spirit where the Holy Spirit was poured out on "all flesh" and was poured out "even on the Gentiles" (Acts 10:45). The Spirit is present everywhere and "fills everything by virtue of an economy distinct from that of the Son."[103] Khodr, in both his early writing and his 1991 address to the Baar consultation appealed to Irenaeus and the "two hands of God" metaphor to explain the distinct economies of the Spirit and the Son. Using this metaphor as a platform, he was able to affirm a "hypostatic independence" where the "advent of the Holy Spirit in the world is not subordinated to the Son, is not simply a function of the Word."[104] The economy of the Spirit is not to be confused with that of the Son; indeed, the Spirit is at work in the world in a way that is

---

[100]Ibid., 118–19.
[101]Ibid., 119.
[102]Ibid., 123.
[103]Ibid., 125–26.
[104]Ibid., 126.

"genuinely different from that made known to us through the Word incarnate in Jesus (in whom, of course, the Spirit was also active)."[105]

Different economies do not mean that there is division in the mind of God. The "two hands" metaphor enables Khodr to affirm the understanding of one economy with two different aspects, the salvific work of God through the separate works of the Spirit and Son, but he insists that these two aspects of God's redemptive plan are distinctly different. In particular, it is imperative that the activity of the Spirit not be seen as merely preparatory for the activity of the Son.[106]

The relative independence of the Spirit from the Son entails that the Spirit is at work in the world exercising His powers in accordance with His own distinct economy. This allows Khodr to speculate that non-Christian religions present evidence of the separate economies expressed in the Son and Spirit both of which fall under the overarching redemptive purposes of God. Non-Christian religions are seen as arenas in which the inspiration of the Holy Spirit is at work. Therefore, it follows that all who are "visited by the Spirit are the people of God."[107]

Khodr's understanding of redemptive history is still Christological, although this Christological focus does not entail conscious and active faith in the Christ of history. He argues that God has always been building His church, though sometimes this has happened outside the confines of conscious knowledge of Jesus (e.g., Old Testament Israel). Christ maintains His preeminent role in salvation even outside the confines of the gospel precisely because the economy of the Spirit and the economy of the Son are essentially related. Without granting any priority of the Son over the Spirit, Khodr is able to affirm that the Spirit exists through the Word and the Word exists in the Spirit.[108]

The relationship between the Spirit and Son is significant because it allows the Spirit to apply the gospel outside the particular witness of Christ:

This significant relationship to Christ is also applicable outside Israel inasmuch as the other nations have had their own types of the reality of Christ, whether in the form of persons or teachings. It is

---

[105]G. Khodr as quoted in Knitter, "A New Pentecost," 36.

[106]Ibid., 37.

[107]Khodr, "Christianity in a Pluralistic World," 126.

[108]Khodr as quoted in Knitter, "A New Pentecost," 36.

of little importance whether the religion in question was historical in character or not. It is of little importance whether it considers itself incompatible with the gospel. Christ is hidden everywhere in the mystery of his lowliness. Any reading of religions is a reading of Christ. It is Christ alone who is received as light when grace visits a Brahmin, a Buddhist or a Muhammadan reading his own scriptures. Every martyr for the truth, every man persecuted for what he believes to be right, dies in communion with Christ.[109]

Therefore, redemptive history will still culminate in Christ, and the Holy Spirit draws these together. In fact, the "economy of Christ is unintelligible without the economy of the Spirit."[110]

Khodr's understanding of the nature of the work of the Spirit in religious others is demonstrated by his conviction that the Holy Spirit illuminates the sacred writings of other religions in the same manner that He illuminates the Christian Scriptures. The Holy Spirit reveals Christ in the Old Testament. In the same way, the Spirit can reveal Christ in other religions and their scriptures:

> For just as the letter without the Holy Spirit can hide revelation from us in the case of the Old Testament Scriptures, Christ being the only key to them, so is it possible for us to approach other religions and their scriptures either in a purely critical frame of mind and as objective students of history and sociology, or else in order to discern the truth in them according to the breath of the Holy Spirit.[111]

Just as the Holy Spirit illumines the biblical text of the Old Testament so that the faithful reader might see Christ, so He illumines the sacred writings of religious others so that Christ might be encountered.

SUMMARY

The departure of nonevangelical Christian theology from the principle of *extra ecclesiam nulla salus* began in the Roman Catholic Church, which has moved from a commitment to active church participation to mystical inclusion in the body of Christ through union

---

[109]Khodr, "Christianity in a Pluralistic World," 124–25.
[110]Ibid., 125.
[111]Ibid., 127.

with the Holy Spirit. While affirming one way of salvation and one redeemed people, the Roman Catholic Church now allows the possibility that the Holy Spirit is applying the work of Christ to those who do not possess conscious faith in Christ. Other nonevangelical theologians have also looked to pneumatology, suggesting that the Holy Spirit is at work savingly in religious others. Pneumatological inclusivism requires the revision of many orthodox theological positions, many of which have recently been suggested in the evangelical community.

One of the most significant conceptions that nonevangelical theologians have put forward in support of pneumatological inclusivism—one that has been duplicated and/or followed by evangelical inclusivists—is a commitment to a hypostatic independence of the Spirit from the Son. The Holy Spirit must not be subordinated to Jesus Christ, nor can their economies be combined. This allows speculation that different world religions are evidence of the separate economies of the Son and the Spirit, both falling under the overarching revelatory and salvific purposes of God.

Second, formulation of a theology of religions must begin with pneumatology and not Christology. Beginning with pneumatology allows the inclusivist to affirm the value in other religious traditions while simultaneously holding to the centrality of Jesus Christ in salvation. When a theology of religions begins with pneumatology, it follows that discernment of the redemptive work of Christ in religious others hinges on pneumatology. The identification of religious practices that are the result of Spirit-indwelt individuals, however, is problematic. Most proposals for a set of criteria for discerning the work of the Spirit in religious others are ethical. Building a theology of religions from the foundation of pneumatology has enormous hermeneutical significance, as it conflicts with a Christological reading of Scripture.

Third, the events at Pentecost, where the outpouring of the Spirit extended beyond the boundaries of Israel, establish the biblical basis for the redemptive work of the Holy Spirit in religious others. Further, the active and central role of the Holy Spirit in creation provides the basis for the Holy Spirit's present universal re-creative work. The universality of the Spirit also suggests to some inclusivists that the sacred writings of religious others may attain the status of divine self-revelation.

Finally, because the Holy Spirit is universally at work in the world, including religious others, the Holy Spirit plays a foundational role in dialogue and interpretation. It is therefore necessary to be in community to hear the Spirit's voice, where community is multiethnic, multireligious, and multicultural.

As will be demonstrated in the following chapter, these four themes, the product of decades of nonevangelical thought, have been recently formulated by evangelical theologians. Our focus now shifts to their work.

Chapter Six

Inclusivism II: Evangelical Expressions

INTRODUCTION

Inclusivism has established a powerful presence in the evangelical church. At the popular, church, and academic level, evangelical voices are calling into question the necessity of believing the gospel to be saved.[1] Though still firmly committed to the work of Christ as the basis for salvation, some are suggesting that explicit faith in the death and resurrection of Christ is not necessary for salvation. According to inclusivist Amos Yong, inclusivism affirms "the distinction between salvation as ontologically secured (through the person and work of Christ) and as epistemically accessed (through the preaching of the gospel, among other providential means of God)."[2] Inclusivists do not all agree on how individuals are saved apart from conscious faith in Christ. However, all inclusivists agree that those who have never heard the gospel can be saved in a way analogous to the salvation of those

---

[1]An example of a denial of exclusivism in the popular literature can be found in the best-selling novel *The Shack*. In the fictional story Jesus explains His goal of transformation: "Who said anything about being a Christian? I'm not a Christian. . . . Those who love me come from every system that exists. They were Buddhists or Mormons, Baptists or Muslims, Democrats, Republicans and many who don't vote or are not part of any Sunday morning or religious institutions. . . . I have no desire to make them Christian, but I do want to join them in their transformation into sons and daughters of my Papa, into my brothers and sisters, into my Beloved." W. P. Young, *The Shack* (Los Angeles: Windblown Media, 2007), 182. Though there are significant questions regarding the convictions of the author William Young on the state of the unevangelized, the statement above captures the inclusivist ethos.

[2]A. Yong, *Beyond the Impasse: Toward a Pneumatological Theology of the Religions* (Grand Rapids: Baker, 2003), 23.

Old Testament figures who trusted God but were unable to believe the gospel because the death and resurrection of Christ was a future reality and therefore epistemologically inaccessible.[3] Inclusivist Clark Pinnock notes that even though it "has only seldom been proposed that the Spirit might be present in the religious sphere of human life," many inclusivists are currently suggesting that "non-Christian religions may be not only the means of a natural knowledge of God, but also the locale of God's grace given to the world because of Christ."[4] Other evangelical scholars who have proposed an inclusivist understanding of salvation include such notables as John Sanders, Veli-Matti Kärkkäinen, Terrance Tiessen, and the late Stanley Grenz.[5]

The purpose of this chapter is to summarize the inclusivist proposals of those who are intentionally turning to the work of the Holy Spirit as the means by which the salvific work of Christ is appropriated to those who have never heard or believed the gospel. Due to the current emphasis in theology on the Trinity and on the Holy Spirit, "pneumatological inclusivism" is also the most current and compelling of all inclusivist proposals. In fact, a turn to the Holy Spirit is the logical and necessary destination of all inclusivist models.[6] After all, the Holy Spirit is the primary member of the Trinity responsible for conviction of sin, regeneration, and sanctification. From an inclusivist perspective, who else but the Holy Spirit could possibly apply the work of Christ to those who have not heard or believed the gospel? If inclusivism of any stripe is going to maintain credibility, it must demonstrate that the regeneration of those who live on this side of the cross in redemptive history but who have not believed the gospel is consistent with the work of the Holy Spirit. Clark Pinnock and Amos

---

[3]This is the logic of Millard Erickson's cautious approach, for example. See M. J. Erickson, *Christian Theology*, 2nd ed. (Grand Rapids: Baker, 1998), 197.

[4]C. H. Pinnock, "An Inclusivist View," in *Four Views on Salvation in a Pluralistic World*, ed. D. L. Okholm and T. R. Phillips (Grand Rapids: Zondervan, 1996), 98.

[5]S. J. Grenz, "Toward an Evangelical Theology of Religions," *JES* 31 (1994): 49–65; V. Kärkkäinen, "Toward a Pneumatological Theology of Religions," *International Review of Mission* 91 (2002): 187–98; J. Sanders, *No Other Name: An Investigation into the Destiny of the Unevangelized* (Grand Rapids: Eerdmans, 1992); T. Tiessen, *Who Can Be Saved? Reassessing Salvation in Christ and World Religions* (Downers Grove, IL: InterVarsity, 2004). See also M. J. Erickson, "Hope for Those Who Haven't Heard? Yes, But . . . ," *EMQ* 11 (1975): 124; id., *How Shall They Be Saved? The Destiny of Those Who Do Not Hear of Jesus* (Grand Rapids: Baker, 1996).

[6]For example, though the role of the Holy Spirit is not as developed in Tiessen's model, the Holy Spirit still plays a critical role in Tiessen's system, particularly in the Spirit's necessary illumination of general revelation and special revelation. Tiessen, *Who Can Be Saved?*, 151–57.

Yong have provided the most developed investigations into the salvific role of the Holy Spirit outside the proclamation of the gospel, so their proposals will be explained in detail. My goal in this chapter is to explain, thoroughly and fairly, the inclusivist proposals that focus on the Holy Spirit. I will critique pneumatological inclusivism and provide a counterproposal in chapters 7 and 8. Rather than providing a legitimate possibility for the salvation of the unevangelized, I believe that when the person and work of the Holy Spirit are rightly understood on biblical-theological grounds, the case for the necessity of conscious faith in Christ for salvation will only be strengthened.

THE PNEUMATOLOGICAL LENS OF CLARK PINNOCK

Clark Pinnock's alignment with soteriological inclusivism is well known. His monograph *A Wideness in God's Mercy*, published in 1992, was a watershed book in the development of evangelical inclusivism.[7] In this work Pinnock formulates an inclusivist position in which the role of the Holy Spirit is mentioned but is not given significant attention. He continued to develop his position in the essay "An Inclusivist View" in the edited volume *Four Views on Salvation in a Pluralistic World*, originally published in 1995.[8] In this essay Pinnock expands on the role of the Spirit in salvation among the unevangelized. The priority of the salvific work of the Holy Spirit in religious others is formalized in Pinnock's volume on pneumatology, *Flame of Love*, published in 1996.

Inclusive Theology of Religions

Pinnock's inclusive theology of religions begins with the conviction that the work of Christ was intended to benefit the whole world. There is both universality (which Pinnock defines as God's love for all humanity) and particularity (which Pinnock sees as the reconciliation of sinners through the cross) in the work of Christ. The formal theology is constructed with two primary parameters.

Optimism of Salvation for the World   The first parameter, by order of priority, is an optimistic soteriological outlook for religious others based on the unbounded and universal love of God for all humanity.

---

[7]C. H. Pinnock, *A Wideness in God's Mercy: The Finality of Jesus Christ in a World of Religions* (Grand Rapids: Zondervan, 1992).

[8]Pinnock, "Inclusivist View," 95–123.

Citing such texts as Luke 13:29 and Rev 7:9, Pinnock maintains that "God's universal salvific will enables Christians to have deep hopefulness for the nations."[9] His optimistic outlook on salvation for the world is driven by two different impulses. The first impulse is based largely on his doctrine of God. Pinnock cannot conceive of a God who does not love all people equally. How can it be that a God of perfect love could condemn people who never had an opportunity to respond to the gospel?[10] Pinnock explains:

> We have to confront the niggardly traditions of certain varieties of conservative theology that present God as miserly, and that exclude large numbers of people without a second thought. This dark pessimism is contrary to Scripture and right reason. Not only does it contradict the prophetic hope of a large salvation, it is a cruel and offensive doctrine. What kind of God would send large numbers of men, women, and children to hell without the remotest chance of responding to his truth? This does not sound like the God whom Jesus called Father.[11]

Such pessimism has manifested itself in two primary errors on the part of the church: the denial of God's universal salvific will and an understanding of election as particular rather than corporate.[12]

The second impulse that drives Pinnock's inclusive theology of religions is more recent. Responding to the claims of religious pluralism, Pinnock is unable to believe that the grace of God is limited to the confines of the Christian church.[13] The rise of the global village and the accompanying relativistic mind-set of late modernity have caused a reevaluation of the doctrine of salvation as it pertains to those who have never heard the gospel.[14]

Clearly, the promise of the gospel is that multitudes will be saved and the nations will gather before the throne of God in the eschaton, but Scripture does not give any indication of relative proportions. In fact, Jesus gave more reason to be pessimistic regarding the percentage

---

[9] Pinnock, *Wideness in God's Mercy*, 13.

[10] The universal love of God is a "control belief" for Pinnock; that is, it is a "large scale conviction that controls many smaller issues." He cites such passages as 2 Pet 3:9; 1 Tim 2:4; and Rom 11:32 to justify what he calls his "hermeneutic of hopefulness." Ibid., 18–20.

[11] Ibid., 154.

[12] Ibid., 25.

[13] Ibid., 15.

[14] Pinnock, "Inclusivist View," 97.

of the saved. When teaching on the kingdom, Jesus instructed, "Enter through the narrow gate. For the gate is wide and the road is broad that leads to destruction, and there are many who go through it. How narrow is the gate and difficult the road that leads to life, and few find it" (Matt 7:13–14; cf. Luke 13:23–24). D. A. Carson is right to point out that no texts suggest the number of the saved will outnumber the unsaved and that it is hermeneutically invalid to set aside the biblical texts that explicitly address the question of relative proportions in favor of themes that do not speak to the question, regardless of how hopeful your hermeneutic.[15] Thus, Scripture does not support Pinnock's optimism for the unevangelized.

Christology and Theology of Religions   The second parameter in Pinnock's theology of religions is an affirmation of a high Christology.[16] Indeed, Pinnock has no patience with religious pluralists who would reject a high Christology.[17] Jesus Christ is the one mediator between God and man, but this does not entail that one should have a "negative attitude" toward world religions or cultures, nor does it require that Christians be exclusive in their interactions with religious others.[18] Pinnock is adamant that one is saved only on the basis of the work of Christ.[19] However, this does not mean that one need possess conscious faith in Christ in order to enjoy redemption through Jesus. A high Christology is mandatory, but it is important to "think in a trinitarian manner about these issues."[20] When one begins with

---

[15]D. A. Carson, *The Gagging of God: Christianity Confronts Pluralism* (Grand Rapids: Zondervan, 1996), 300. See also R. Richard, *The Population of Heaven: A Biblical Response to the Inclusivist Position on Who Will Be Saved* (Chicago: Moody, 1994), 31–33; D. Strange, *The Possibility of Salvation Among the Unevangelised: An Analysis of Inclusivism in Recent Evangelical Theology* (Waynesboro, GA: Paternoster, 2002), 271–73.

[16]Pinnock, *Wideness in God's Mercy*, 13. Pinnock proclaims, "God is healing the nations through the mediation of his Son, rather than in some other way. In his wisdom, God is reconciling the world to himself, not through religious experience, not through natural revelation, not through prophets alone, not through all the religions of the world, but through Jesus Christ." Ibid., 49.

[17]Pinnock scolds pluralists who make biblical appeals to support their soteriology. He accuses them of using the Bible as a strategy for "bringing on board more conservative Christians. . . . In actual fact, however, the reason for rejecting the finality of Christ is not exegetical but rather that Christ's finality does not fit into the modern mindset." Ibid., 70.

[18]Ibid., 13. Pinnock suggests that Col 1:16–17 establishes Jesus as "the cosmic Christ." Rom 5:18; 1 Cor 15:20–28; 2 Cor 5:18–21; Phil 2:6–11; and 1 Tim 4:10; 2:4–6 also supports the universal lordship of Christ. The resurrection of Christ, which establishes Jesus as a life-giving Spirit, points to the "global reach of God's salvation." When Christ comes into his kingdom, the nations that were once "smitten" by God in judgment will be healed (Rev 22:2). Ibid., 33–34.

[19]Ibid., 49.

[20]Ibid., 51.

the theocentric nature of the Bible, the church's confession of Jesus can be "compatible with an open spirit, with an optimism of salvation, and with a wider hope."[21] Pinnock appeals to Irenaeus's work on recapitulation as evidence of a wider hope. Citing Irenaeus, Pinnock argues, "God came into the world in Jesus in order [*sic*] save humanity from sin and death, to restore and perfect the creation. This indeed is a broad concept of redemption."[22] Pinnock also credits Vatican II as pointing the way toward a robust inclusivism that elevates the necessity of Christ's redemptive work while recognizing that people may be in different epistemological situations with regard to knowledge of that work.[23] It becomes necessary to distinguish between the ontological necessity of Christ's work of redemption from the epistemological situation of sinners: "There is no salvation except through Christ but it is not necessary for everybody to possess a conscious knowledge of Christ in order to benefit from redemption through him."[24]

Pagan Believers and Salvation History According to Pinnock, by ignoring the possibility of a "wider hope," Christians have undervalued the first 11 chapters of Genesis and the pre-Abrahamic history of humankind. These chapters demonstrate that God is the Lord of the whole earth and of all people, that He is concerned for the nations, and that outside of covenant Israel "pagan believers" such as Melchizedek and Job are held up as examples of men "who lived in the period of Israel's ministry, yet outside her sphere and covenant."[25] These examples of "holy pagans" demonstrate our need for dialogue with people outside the borders of Israel or the church.[26]

Such assertions are possible because Pinnock believes that "salvation history is coextensive with world history and its goal is the healing of all the nations."[27] Western theology is faulted for a narrowness that limited God's saving purposes to a "tiny thread of history

---

[21] Ibid., 74.

[22] Ibid., 36. Pinnock admits that Irenaeus was not open to salvation outside the church but argues that he cannot be blamed for this attitude. He was "unaware of the existence of a large number of unevangelized people and thus of our entire problem. We cannot say what he might have thought had he lived in our day." Ibid., 101.

[23] Ibid., 75.

[24] Ibid.

[25] Ibid., 26. Adam, Seth, Enoch, Noah, Abimelech, the king of Gerar, and the queen of Sheba are also cited as examples.

[26] Passages such as Ps 47:1,8–9; Jer 18:7–8; Mal 1:11 and Amos 9:7 and suggest that God "is in dialogue with the nations." Ibid., 27–29.

[27] Ibid., 23

and limited participation in salvation to the adherents of church and synagogue."[28] The biblical examples of the "pagan believers" are then cited as evidence that "God works outside so-called salvation history."[29] Pinnock then reads this wider hope into Paul's teaching in Romans 1–2:

> His point is that Jews and Gentiles alike possess the light of divine revelation and are responsible for knowing it, because God will judge them on the basis of it. It is not a negative thing to say that everyone in the whole world has access to God's truth, whether they know about Jesus or not. Granted, Paul is stressing the failure of sinners to respond to God in order to show why Jesus had to come. . . . But it is wrong to read into his words in Romans the idea that he is denying that many Jews and Gentiles in the past have responded positively to God on the basis of this light.[30]

In response, Pinnock's category of "pagan believers" is highly suspect. Each individual put forward by Pinnock as an example of a holy pagan had actually responded to special revelation. From Abel to Enoch to Daniel to Melchizedek, each had become a "saint" in response to particular revelation given by the Lord, either through personal encounter, ancient tradition, or through the covenant people of Israel.[31] Not one of them qualifies as a pagan, let alone one who had responded to general revelation alone in their search for God. As demonstrated in chapter 1, appeals to Cornelius actually strengthen the exclusivist case. Cornelius, though not Israelite, had aligned himself with the covenant people of Israel and was given the gospel in order that he would be saved. Not only is the entire narrative superfluous if he is already saved, but he is an invalid model for non-Christian

---

[28] Ibid.

[29] Ibid., 27. The accounts of Peter in Acts 10:34–35 and Paul's ministry in Lystra (Acts 14:16–17) and Athens (Acts 17:22–31) are further evidence that God is at work in pagan cultures. Ibid., 32.

[30] Ibid., 33.

[31] Pinnock's reference to Daniel is drawn from Ezek 14:14, where he assumes that the Daniel in question is not the exilic subject of the biblical book, Daniel, but is an entirely different man who preexisted Abraham. Ibid., 22. I disagree with Pinnock's identification of Daniel. The preponderance of evidence suggests that the Daniel referenced by Ezekiel is indeed the hero of the Babylonian exile and the subject of the book of Daniel. See D. B. Wallace, "Who is Ezekiel's Daniel?" http://bible.org/article/who-ezekiels-daniel (accessed 21 December 2009). See chapter 2 for a discussion of Melchizedek and where he received his knowledge of the Lord.

religions because the God whom he is said to fear and the God to whom he prays is the one true God. The acts of charity that he performs are done according to "piety derived from the Old Testament law."[32] If "pagan believers" exist, as Pinnock asserts, he will have to go somewhere other than the Bible to find them.[33]

The Pneumatological Inclusivism of Clark Pinnock

By 1995, Pinnock was moving toward a pneumatocentric understanding of inclusivism. His model of inclusivism was altered to one that "explores the possibility that the Spirit is operative in the sphere of human religion to prepare people for the gospel of Christ."[34] Pinnock continues to exhibit a degree of caution over the soteriological role of world religions. Because religions have the potential for error and are not in themselves vehicles of salvation, Pinnock labels his pneumatological inclusivism, which is also modeled by Vatican II, "cautious inclusivism."[35] But his understanding of inclusivism is based on the omnipresence of the Spirit, whose grace is at work "in some way among all people, possibly even in the sphere of religious life."[36] Because God is present everywhere as the triune Creator and Redeemer, "divine grace is also prevenient everywhere—since God has created the whole world, since Jesus Christ died for all humanity, and since the Spirit gives life to creation. Most specifically and crucially, inclusivists believe that the Spirit is everywhere at work in advance of the mission to prepare the way for Jesus Christ."[37]

Pinnock also refers to his approach to salvation in a pluralistic world as "modal inclusivism." By this Pinnock wants to leave room for the Lord to use world religions as He sees fit. God is not required always or ever to make positive use of world religions. Rather,

---

[32]W. J. Larkin, "The Contribution of the Gospels and Acts to a Biblical Theology of Religions," in *Christianity and the Religions: A Biblical Theology of World Religions*, ed. E. Rommen and H. Netland (Pasadena, CA: William Carey Library, 1995), 81. See also B. Demarest, "General and Special Revelation: Epistemological Foundations of Religious Pluralism," in *One God, One Lord: Christianity in a World of Religious Pluralism*, ed. A. Clarke and B. Winter (Grand Rapids: Baker, 1992), 191.

[33]See W. C. Kaiser, "Holy Pagans: Reality or Myth?" in *Faith Comes by Hearing: A Response to Inclusivism*, ed. C. W. Morgan and R. A. Peterson (Downers Grove, IL: InterVarsity, 2008), 123–41; Carson, *Gagging of God*, 297–99; and Strange, *Possibility of Salvation*, 176–89.

[34]Pinnock, "Inclusivist View," 96.

[35]Ibid., 99.

[36]Ibid., 98.

[37]Ibid. Note the priority given to the mission of the Son in this 1995 essay. Pinnock would begin to back away from the priority of the mission of the Son in future works.

God may use religion as a way of gracing people's lives and that is one of God's options for evoking faith and communicating grace. . . . Modal inclusivism then holds that grace operates outside the church and may be encountered in the context of other religions. My version of it is oriented to the Spirit as graciously present in the world among all peoples, even in non-Christian religious contexts.[38]

In Pinnock's theology, therefore, the Holy Spirit bridges the gap between the universal love of God, the unlimited extent of the atonement, and those who have never heard an explicit gospel proclamation.

The Spirit as Creator Pinnock turns to the first pages of Genesis to establish a biblical defense for the independent work of the Holy Spirit. He sees the role of the Holy Spirit in creation as the paradigm for work that the Spirit performed through all of redemptive history and continues today. Genesis 1:2 records the Holy Spirit hovering over the waters, bringing order where chaos once prevailed. Elihu takes up the role of the Holy Spirit in creation when he tells Job, "The Spirit of God has made me, and the breath of the Almighty gives me life" (Job 33:4). Pinnock points to other verses (Gen 2:7; Job 34:14–15; Ps 33:6; Acts 17:25) to establish that the Holy Spirit "gives life to creation at the most fundamental level. . . . The Spirit is present and active in creation—in its inception, continuation and perfection."[39] Pinnock goes on to identify the singular and penultimate work of the Holy Spirit in the creation of man: "Spirit, who facilitates God's relationship with the world, called forth a creature capable of loving God, a personal subject whose nature is to engage the world and its Maker."[40]

Few orthodox evangelicals would question the role of the Spirit in the creation of man and the cosmos. However, many would find the seeming autonomy in the work of creation that Pinnock establishes for the Spirit, apart from the Son, to be troubling. But for Pinnock, this is precisely the point in question. Having identified the unique role and work of the Holy Spirit in creation, Pinnock builds on this foundation to claim that the Holy Spirit has never ceased to fill the role that He began at creation. The Spirit's work around the world is consistent with

---

[38]Ibid., 100.

[39]C. Pinnock, *Flame of Love: A Theology of the Holy Spirit* (Downers Grove, IL: InterVarsity, 1996), 52–53.

[40]Ibid., 73.

His work in creation, and Pinnock refuses to "drive a wedge between what God does in creation and in redemption, because the Spirit is Lord and Life-giver in both spheres."[41] The Spirit's role in creation also establishes His omnipresence in the world. The Spirit, who is present everywhere, directs the world and moves it toward its eschatological hope, "bringing to completion first the creational and then the redemptive purposes of God."[42] For Pinnock, the Spirit is responsible for implementing God's purposes for creation from the beginning to the eschatological consummation and restoration of all things.[43]

The Spirit's role in creation and His omnipresence enables Him to have a sacramental role in the lives of humans, fostering the divine presence in the world.[44] Following Rahner, Pinnock sees the economic role of the Spirit as flowing out of His relationship of mutual indwelling within the Father and the Son. Because the Spirit is omnipresent, He is not only able to mediate the relationship between the Father and the Son, but He is able to mediate all relationships between the Father and His creatures.[45] The sacramental omnipresence of the Holy Spirit manifests God's desire to bless all people and is effectual to bring God's plans to fruition.[46] Because creation establishes the role of the Holy Spirit in redemption, any attempt to subordinate His efforts to the Son dishonors the third member of the Trinity. From this platform Pinnock launches the following critique of the theology and practice of the evangelical church:

> Let us stop demoting the Spirit, relegating him to spheres of church and piety. His role in the creation is foundational to these other activities. The whole creation is home to the Spirit's operations, and the cosmic fruits issue in new creation. The Spirit is the perfecter of the works of God in creation. . . . One does not properly defend the uniqueness of Jesus Christ by denying the Spirit's preparatory work that preceded his coming. Let us try to

---

[41]Pinnock, "Inclusivist View," 106. Pinnock appeals to John 6:63 to establish the Spirit as the life-giver.

[42]Pinnock, *Flame of Love*, 50.

[43]Ibid., 54.

[44]Ibid., 55.

[45]Ibid., 60.

[46]The Holy Spirit is "the power that brings God's plans into effect, as a gentle but powerful presence, communicating divine energies in the world and aiming at increasing levels of participating in the fellowship of love." Ibid., 60–61.

see continuity, not contradiction, in the relation of creation and redemption.[47]

In Pinnock's theology, the role of the Spirit in Creation establishes the nature of His relationship within the economic Trinity.

Pinnock and the Trinity   All of the preceding serves to sever the quality of relationship between the Son and the Spirit that the Western church sought to preserve with procession of the Spirit from the Father and the Son. Predictably, Pinnock is highly critical of the *filioque* clause and the theology it represents.[48] Not only does Pinnock see the *filioque* as an abuse of church authority, but he also denies the reality of double procession because he believes it subordinates the person and economic role of the Spirit to that of the Son. By denying double procession, Pinnock attempts to establish a measure of independence for the work of the Spirit from that of the Son, creating the relational autonomy necessary for the Spirit to fulfill His full range of creative and salvific work:

> God the Spirit also proceeds from the Father and is present in the whole world. God's breath flows in the world at large, not just within the confines of Christian movements. The Spirit of Jesus is at the same time a cosmic force hovering over the waters and giving life to every creature (Gen 1:2; Ps 104:30). The Spirit is the overflow of God's love. We see his activity in human culture and even in the religions of the humanity. The doctrine of the Trinity means that God, far from being difficult to locate in the world, can be encountered everywhere in it. One needs to take pains and be very adept at hiding *not* to encounter God.[49]

Pinnock sees the *filioque* as a threat to his understanding of the universality of the work of the Spirit. Pinnock suggests that the *filioque* promotes Christomonism by denying the truth that the divine

---

[47]Ibid., 63.

[48]*Filioque* is the Latin word translated "and the Son." The *filioque* controversy refers to the alteration of the Nicene-Constantinopolitan Creed (Latin form 381) by the Western church in 589 regarding the procession of the Holy Spirit. Prior to the alteration, the Holy Spirit was said to proceed from the Father. After the insertion of *filioque*, the Creed taught that the Spirit proceeds "from the Father and the Son." By the time of the great schism between the Western and Eastern churches in 1054, the *filioque* was a chief source of theological dissension between the two sides.

[49]Pinnock, *Wideness in God's Mercy*, 104.

mission of the Spirit is prior to and geographically larger than that of the Son:

> It might suggest to the worshiper that Spirit is not the gift of the Father to creation universally but a gift confined to the sphere of the Son and even the sphere of the church. . . . It does not encourage us to view the divine mission as being prior to and geographically larger than the Son's. . . . It undercuts the idea that Spirit can be active where the Son is not named and supports the restrictive reading of the axiom "Outside the church, no salvation."[50]

In Pinnock's economy, rejection of the *filioque* will help create the theological space to assert a relative independence for the Spirit.

In response, I believe that Pinnock misunderstands both church history and Eastern theology on this point. Rejection of the *filioque* will not create the theological space necessary to posit the relative independence of the Holy Spirit from the Son that Pinnock desires. He is convinced that the *filioque* has contributed to the subordination of the Spirit to the Son, at least in practice, in the West. By his thinking, the *filioque* insertion is "an impediment to a recognition of Spirit operations apart from and prior to Christ."[51] This is a fundamental error in Pinnock's understanding of the *filioque* and Eastern theology.[52] The *filioque* does not entail any sort of subordination, nor does rejecting the *filioque* establish any sort of autonomy for the Holy Spirit. Pinnock's argument is consistent with the accusation commonly leveled by the West against the East, namely, that the Eastern rejection of the *filioque* breaks the bond between the Son and the Holy Spirit, granting to the Spirit a relative autonomy. But Nick Needham argues that for Eastern theologians, such a separation is impossible because "Son and Spirit are united by the closest bond conceivable, the ontological bond of being the same God. Just as the Father is the same in essence (*homoousios*) as the Son, and the same in essence as the Spirit, so the Son and Holy Spirit are the same in essence as each other."[53] In

---

[50]Pinnock, *Flame of Love*, 196.

[51]Ibid., 260 n. 11.

[52]For a thorough critique of the inclusivist call for a rejection of the *filioque*, see T. L. Miles, "Severing the Spirit from the Son: Theological Revisionism in Contemporary Theologies of Salvation" (Ph.D. diss., Southern Baptist Theological Seminary, 2006), 134–51.

[53]N. Needham, "The *Filioque* Clause: East or West?" *SBET* 15 (1997): 159. Needham criticizes those who would accuse Eastern theology of seeking to sever the bonds between Christ and the Holy Spirit: "Ironically, the accusation itself bowls a pyrotechnic googly at fundamental

a fascinating rebuke of those who would accuse Eastern theology of severing the bond between the Son and Spirit, Needham writes:

> As far as their peculiar personal relationship is concerned, the Spirit rests upon and abides in the Son; or in John of Damascus' phrase, the Spirit is the Son's eternal companion. It may suit Western polemics to picture the East as having the Son fly off from the Father in one direction, and the Spirit in the opposite direction as fast as his wings will carry him; but you do not need a degree in Freudian or Jungian psychology to suspect that that says rather more about a Western imagination in wish-fulfilment mode than it does about actual Eastern theology.[54]

The primary concern of the East with the *filioque* is not that it subordinates the Holy Spirit to the Son; this concern is answered by the trinitarian doctrine of consubstantiality. Nor is the primary concern that the *filioque* teaches two separate sources of the procession of the Spirit; this concern is answered by an understanding of Augustine's locating the procession in the divine essence, not in the Father and Son *per se*. The chief concerns of the East are that the *filioque* compromises the monarchy of the Father and that the *filioque* confuses the Father and the Son. When it comes to relationship with the Holy Spirit, the *filioque* does not allow one to distinguish between the Father and the Son.[55]

Contrary to Pinnock, a rejection of the *filioque* does not create the theological space necessary for a relative independence of the Spirit from the Son. Pinnock's appeals to siding with the East in its rejection of the *filioque* will not advance his cause. A rejection of the *filioque* does not entail an affirmation of relative autonomy or hypostatic independence for the Holy Spirit. The East traditionally (with few exceptions) has not affirmed such a thing. Eastern theology, in fact, argues just the opposite: a close and unbroken relationship between the Son and the Spirit.[56]

---

trinitarian doctrine, and incidentally reveals an unfortunate absence of acquaintance with Eastern spirituality (which admittedly, seems almost universal among us Westerners, especially Protestants)." Ibid.

[54] Ibid.

[55] Ibid., 147. Cf. R. Letham, *The Holy Trinity: In Scripture, History, Theology, and Worship* (Phillipsburg, NJ: P&R, 2004), 206.

[56] For example, in writing on the procession of the Holy Spirit from the Father and how this relates to deification, the Eastern theologian Dumitru Staniloae writes, "The sending of the Spirit

The Relationship between Christology and Pneumatology How is the relationship of the Son and the Spirit to be characterized? Pinnock is quick to affirm the dependence of Christology upon pneumatology, and vice versa. "If it is true that the Spirit empowers the Son, it is also true that the Son is the criterion of manifestations of Spirit. The relationship is reciprocal through and through."[57] Pinnock rightly points out the integral role of the Holy Spirit in the life of Jesus. It was anointing by the Spirit that made Jesus the "Christ," and the Holy Spirit empowered His first advent ministry. It was "by the Spirit that Jesus was conceived, anointed, empowered, commissioned, directed and raised up."[58] But he cautions that a high Christology must not result in subordinating the Spirit to the Son because "the two are partners in the work of redemption."[59]

Pinnock calls for a pneumatological Christology to replace the *Logos*-Christology that he says has dominated Western theology. A paradigm shift is necessary because the Spirit who made the incarnation possible brings coherence to the kenosis, enabling Jesus "to live within the limits of human nature during his life."[60] In fact, Pinnock sees the incarnation as the fulfillment of the Spirit's universal and cosmic activity to save:

> God loves sinners, and the Spirit works in them that they may ultimately become obedient to Jesus Christ. Granted, such a goal can take much time to achieve. Yet instead of saying there is no salvation outside the church, let us simply say there is no salvation outside grace, or only finally outside Christ. . . . The truth of the incarnation does not eclipse truth about the Spirit, who was at work in the world before Christ and is present now where Christ is not named. The mission of the Son is not a threat to the mission of the Spirit, or vice versa. On the one hand, the Son's mission

---

by the Son to men rather signifies that the Spirit rests in those who are united with the Son, since he rests in the Son. The Spirit does not go beyond the Son, even when we say improperly that he is sent to men. The Son is the only and ultimate resting place of the Spirit. The Spirit dwells in us insofar as we are raised up in the Son. This saves us from a theological rationalism on the one side and a purely sentimental enthusiasm on the other." D. Staniloae, "The Procession of the Holy Spirit from the Father and His Relation to the Son, as the Basis for Our Deification and Adoption," in *Spirit of God, Spirit of Christ*, ed. L. Vischer (London: SPCK, 1981), 179.

[57]Pinnock, *Flame of Love*, 92.
[58]Ibid., 81–82.
[59]Ibid.
[60]Ibid., 88.

presupposes the Spirit's—Jesus was conceived and empowered by the Spirit. On the other hand, the mission of the Spirit is oriented to the goals of incarnation. The Spirit's mission is to bring history to completion and fulfillment in Christ.[61]

One arrives at a Spirit Christology by "placing Christology in the context of the Spirit's global operations, of which incarnation is the culmination."[62]

However, the strong reciprocity between Spirit and Son disappears when discussing the role of the Spirit in other religions. In fact, Pinnock argues that a shift in perspective is necessary to understand the relationship of the Spirit and the Son. He appreciates the Eastern view of the Son-Spirit relationship, where the Spirit is not tied to the Christ event exclusively but possesses a relative autonomy to operate in the whole world, which is the Father's domain. Following Georg Khodr, Pinnock appeals to Irenaeus's "two hands of God" metaphor to establish the theological space necessary to create a hypostatic independence between Son and Spirit.[63] The Son and Spirit have a joint mission that comes from the Father. With this theological and historical backing, Pinnock can then assert, "Let us see what results from viewing Christ as an aspect of the Spirit's mission, instead of (as is more usual) viewing Spirit as a function of Christ's."[64] Ironically, while Pinnock chastises evangelicals for subordinating the mission of the Spirit to that of the Son, his theology of religions is ultimately based upon subordinating the mission of the Son to that of the Spirit! For Pinnock, what was once out of bounds can now be given strong consideration by virtue of pneumatological freedom. Such a reversal is possible because God is active in His world through His Spirit.[65] This activity encompasses all of creation, throughout all of human history, even including the spheres of religion. The Spirit is able to overcome the historical particularity of the Son and become the Savior of all people.[66]

---

[61] Ibid., 194.

[62] Ibid., 82.

[63] Ibid. Pinnock cites the "two hands of God" metaphor without any explanation or context regarding Irenaeus's usage.

[64] Ibid., 80.

[65] Pinnock explains, "The breath of God is free to blow wherever it wills. The economy of the Spirit is not under our control, and certainly it is not limited to the church." Pinnock, *Wideness in God's Mercy*, 78.

[66] Pinnock, "Inclusivist View," 104.

Understood in context, Irenaeus's metaphor of the "two hands of God" does not at all imply what Pinnock and Khodr claim.[67] In the hands of inclusivists, the figure of speech becomes a statement of "hypostatic independence,"[68] but what Irenaeus had in mind gives no support to this concept. Irenaeus, the second-century bishop of the church in Lyons, developed the metaphor in a defense of the orthodox doctrine of creation against Gnosticism. The Gnostics taught a radical dualism: material existence was evil, and the active enemy of the spirit and spiritual living. Therefore, God could not be directly involved in the creation of the world but needed intermediaries (such as Archons or gods). Irenaeus argued that God had no need of intermediaries to create; He had His two hands, namely, the Son and the Spirit.[69] Irenaeus never used the metaphor to teach a hypostatic independence of the Spirit from the Son, and his theology does not even imply such an idea. With regard to the Son and the Spirit, Irenaeus consistently taught a symmetric order within the Godhead. The Father sent the Son to reveal the Father. The Son sent the Spirit to reveal the Son. The Spirit reveals the Son and brings people to Him. The Son in turn presents these same people to the Father.[70] Whether it was the doctrines of salvation, revelation, inspiration, or creation, Irenaeus consistently unites the ministry of the Holy Spirit to the ministry of the Son. When it came to the fate of the unevangelized, Irenaeus was even more direct. He consistently united the witness of the Spirit to the building of the church, the Body of Christ.[71]

Historiography is, by its very nature, somewhat subjective. Unless one is intentionally careful, references to history can be tendentious. Readers have a moral obligation to read and interpret in context.[72] Christian scholars, of all people, should recognize this. Irenaeus's

---

[67]For a thorough evaluation of inclusivism's tendentious use of metaphor, see T. L. Miles, "Irenaeus in the Hands of Soteriological Inclusivists: Validation or Tendentious Historiography?" *SBJT* 12/2 (Summer 2008): 4–17; id., *Severing the Spirit from the Son*, 116–33.

[68]P. F. Knitter, "A New Pentecost? A Pneumatological Theology of Religions," *CD* 19 (1991): 36.

[69]See Irenaeus, *AH*, 5.1.3; 5.5.1.

[70]Irenaeus, *Demonstration of the Apostolic Preaching*, trans. J. A. Robinson, in I. M. MacKenzie, *Irenaeus's Demonstration of the Apostolic Preaching: A Theological Commentary and Translation* (Burlington, VT: Ashgate, 2002), 6.

[71]Irenaeus wrote, "For where the Church is, there is the Spirit of God; and where the Spirit of God is, there is the Church, and every kind of grace; but the Spirit is truth." Irenaeus, *AH* 3.24.1.

[72]See K. J. Vanhoozer, *Is There a Meaning in This Text? The Bible, the Reader, and the Morality of Literary Knowledge* (Grand Rapids: Zondervan, 1998), 367–441.

"two hands" metaphor has become a playground of free interpretation in the hands of pneumatological inclusivists. They are free to use whatever metaphors that they wish, but when that use illegitimately leads their listeners to believe that their proposal enjoys the support of church history, then the metaphor is being used irresponsibly. Appeals to Irenaeus, when the context is ignored, claim the support of church history that is simply not there.[73]

The Salvific Work of the Spirit   With the Holy Spirit freed from a functional dependence on the Son, the Spirit is also freed from the constraints of the Son's church. Pinnock explains, "Spirit is not confined to the church but is present everywhere, giving life and creating community. . . . Because Spirit works everywhere in advance of the church's mission, preparing the way for Christ, God's will can be truly and credibly universal."[74] But preparation for Christ does not entail gospel witness because the Holy Spirit is able to "foster transforming friendships with God anywhere and everywhere."[75] To Pinnock the presence of the Spirit is always a presence of grace to bless and to save. General revelation and natural knowledge of God are always "gracious revelation and a potentially saving knowledge."[76] Therefore we need to view access to grace, not through the lens of the particularity of Christology but through the universality of the Spirit.[77] To Pinnock there is no way around this. If we want to have a wider hope in terms of salvation, we have to look to the "universal presence and activity of the Spirit."[78]

---

[73]Interestingly, Terrance Tiessen, who has offered an inclusivist proposal of his own, did his doctoral work on Irenaeus's teaching on the unevangelized. In a telling footnote, he writes, "The work of the Holy Spirit is given much attention in recent discussion of the state of the unevangelized. For this reason the paucity of material in Irenaeus is somewhat disappointing. However, it is not surprising when one considers the time in which he wrote and the Gnostic context he addressed." T. L. Tiessen, *Irenaeus on the Salvation of the Unevangelized*, ATLA Monograph Series 31 (Metuchen, NJ: Scarecrow, 1993), 258 n. 3.

[74]Pinnock, *Flame of Love*, 192. See also id., "Inclusivist View," 102.

[75]Pinnock, *Flame of Love*, 187.

[76]Ibid.

[77]"Here is the scenario. Christ, the only mediator, sustains particularity, while Spirit, the presence of God everywhere, safeguards universality. Christ represents particularity by being the only mediator between God and humanity (1 Tim 2:5–6), while Spirit upholds universality because no soul is beyond the sphere of the Spirit's operations. Spirit is not confined to the church but is present everywhere, giving life and creating community. Hovering over the waters of creation, Spirit is present also in the search for meaning and the struggle against sin and death." Ibid., 192.

[78]Ibid., 188.

The Holy Spirit and World Religions   Because the work of the Spirit is always potentially salvific, Pinnock suggests that it is legitimate to look for redemptive activity in other religions.[79] Jesus may not be named in other faiths, but the Holy Spirit is still present and He may be encountered there.[80] Any suggestion that the work of the Spirit could be confined by boundaries established by the explicit proclamation of the Christian gospel is an artificial ecclesiastical construct and is offensive to Pinnock. The Spirit is free to go wherever the Father wills: "The economy of the Spirit is not under our control, and certainly it is not limited to the church."[81]

Pinnock views all religions as subject to change at the will of God. He cites the rise of Wesleyanism and Pentecostalism as evidence of the changing nature of Christianity and suggests that, on the same basis, there is no reason to expect that Islam will be the same years from now. "We are obliged as Christians to regard religions as we ought to regard everything. They are in the context of the ongoing purposes of the Lord of history. This means change."[82] To Pinnock, "God is not going to leave out anything as important as the religions from the work of transforming all things."[83]

Pinnock understands that his model lacks strong biblical support. But given his commitment to the universal love of God, he cannot fathom any alternative. Lacking epistemological certitude, Pinnock appeals to hope. "There is no way around it—we must hope that God's gift of salvation is being applied to people everywhere. If so, how else than by the universal presence and activity of Spirit?"[84] Pinnock also appeals to epistemological uncertainty to justify his model. Because even the most godly, Spirit-filled Christian makes mistakes in theology, Pinnock reasons that adherents of other religions are only quantitatively, not qualitatively, different. Being almost completely wrong about the person and work of Jesus Christ is not qualitatively different from being marginally incorrect, and it certainly does not entail that

---

[79]Ibid., 201.

[80]Ibid., 204. Pinnock follows Dupuis's lead in noting that there are elements and evidences of grace in other religions traditions. We must hope that they mediate God's presence for people. Ibid., 206.

[81]Pinnock, *Wideness in God's Mercy*, 78.

[82]Ibid., 115.

[83]Ibid., 116.

[84]Pinnock, *Flame of Love*, 188.

the Holy Spirit cannot be working and speaking to a religious other just as He is to the Christian.[85]

Pinnock explains the existence of world religions on the basis of the prevenient grace of the triune God. This would include the Holy Spirit, whose activity can be seen in human culture and in the various religions of humanity.[86] Pinnock asks, "Why would God, who is present everywhere, absent himself so totally from the sphere of religion, the very realm in which people search for ultimate answers?"[87] He concludes that the Spirit is at work in the history of religions and that these religions play a part in redemptive history because the Holy Spirit is moving the world toward the kingdom of God.[88] It follows that we should find "saintly people and signs of truth in world religions"[89] because acceptance by God is based solely upon faith, which may have different content in different people. For Pinnock, it is the reality of faith, not the content of theology, that is decisive.[90]

Discernment of the Holy Spirit in Religious Others

How is one to discern the work of the Holy Spirit in world religions from the work of other spirits? Pinnock understands that not everything in world religions can be attributed to the Spirit. Furthermore, religions in and of themselves are not salvific.[91] Pinnock is convinced that the Holy Spirit is active in world religions, but he does not know "what role, if any, a given religion plays in the divine economy."[92] He does suggest that the key to discernment lies in "the universal operations of grace and the uniqueness of its manifestation in Jesus Christ."[93] Therefore, discernment must have a strong Christological component. That is, "The Paraclete is the Spirit of Jesus, and we orient ourselves by this insight. When we see Jesus' path, we know

---

[85] Ibid., 202.

[86] Pinnock, *Wideness in God's Mercy*, 104.

[87] Ibid., 79. Pinnock follows the lead of Vatican II (*Declaration on the Relationship of the Church to Non-Christian Religions*) and Pope John Paul II (*Redemptor Hominis*) in allowing and discerning the work of the Holy Spirit in non-Christian religions. See Pinnock, *Flame of Love*, 204.

[88] Ibid., 203.

[89] Ibid., 204.

[90] Pinnock, *Wideness in God's Mercy*, 105.

[91] Pinnock warns that the presence of the Spirit does not "make religions salvific as such, however. The Spirit is the power of God unto salvation, not to religion." Pinnock, "Inclusivist View," 116.

[92] Pinnock writes, "We are simply confident that the Spirit is operating in every sphere to draw people to God, using religion when and where it is possible and appropriate." Ibid., 106.

[93] Pinnock, *Flame of Love*, 202.

that the Spirit is near. As Lord of all, Jesus is the criterion of truth in religion, including the Christian religion."[94]

Pinnock suggests that there must be both a cognitive criterion and an ethical criterion. The cognitive criterion is simple: Does the person fear God?[95] The ethical criterion asks, "Do people pursue righteousness in their behavior?" For people lacking the opportunity to hear the gospel, this criterion becomes primary in Pinnock's economy.[96] Citing Matt 7:15–20, Pinnock argues that a legitimate faith response to the God of Jesus Christ can come in the form of actions of love and justice.[97] If an individual rejects the cognitive criterion while embracing the ethical criterion, Pinnock appeals to Vatican II to show that "God will save even the atheist who, though rejecting God (as he understands God), responds positively to him implicitly by acts of love shown to the neighbor."[98] Piety and accompanying Christlike works are evidence of the Spirit working in the life of the individual, regardless of whether he is a believer in Jesus Christ or a faithful adherent of another religion.[99]

Pinnock still has to do justice to the second of his axioms—commitment to a high Christology in salvation. He attempts to reintroduce Christology into his model of salvation by using the life and ministry of Jesus as the criterion for discerning the salvific role of the Spirit in other religions. The key to discerning the work of the Holy Spirit in world religions is found in the double mission of the Son and Spirit and the link between them:

> Truth incarnate is the criterion for testing spirits. The question to ask is christological (1 John 4:2–3). Spirit is in agreement with the Son and agrees with what he said and did. . . . Thus Spirit points to the criterion of incarnate wisdom. What the Spirit says and does cannot be opposed to revelation in Christ, because Spirit is bound to the Word of God. . . . To identify prevenience, we look for the fruit of the Spirit and for the way of Jesus Christ. . . . So wherever we see traces of Jesus in the world and people opening up to his ideals, we know we are in the presence of Spirit.[100]

---

[94]Pinnock, "Inclusivist View," 114.
[95]Pinnock, *Wideness in God's Mercy*, 96.
[96]Pinnock, *Flame of Love*, 211.
[97]Pinnock, *Wideness in God's Mercy*, 97.
[98]Ibid., 98. Pinnock also makes an appeal to C. S. Lewis's *The Last Battle*.
[99]Pinnock, *Flame of Love*, 210–11.
[100]Ibid., 209.

One can tell where the Spirit is at work around the world when one finds people who look like Jesus; that is, they exhibit the fruit of the Spirit and an ethic that matches Jesus' instruction on the kingdom.[101] Therefore, the sanctifying work of the Spirit is not limited to Christians. This also suggests that saving faith depends only ontologically on the work of Christ, not epistemologically.[102]

The inclusivism of Clark Pinnock must be challenged at a number of critical points. I have briefly touched on his historiography. Any appeal to Irenaeus to support pneumatological inclusivism distorts church history and the theology of Irenaeus. Further, contrary to Pinnock's assertions, rejection of the *filioque* will not create the theological space for a relative independence of the Spirit from the Son. Chapter 7 will critique Pinnock's theological method and assert that Scripture dictates how it is to be read. The Bible, by Jesus' own example, is to be read Christocentrically. To read Scripture pneumatocentrically, or to view Christ as an aspect of the Spirit's mission, is to destroy the fabric of the biblical story. Finally, a biblical theology of the Son and the Spirit will be developed in chapter 8, where many of Pinnock's assertions will be challenged on exegetical and biblical theological grounds.

THE "CHRISTOLOGICAL IMPASSE" OF AMOS YONG

If Clark Pinnock represents the old guard of evangelical inclusivism, then Amos Yong represents the younger generation of evangelical inclusivist scholars.[103] Yong's contributions to evangelical theology of religions began with *Discerning the Spirit(s): A Pentecostal-Charismatic Contribution to Christian Theology of Religions.*[104] He continued to develop his position in *Beyond the Impasse* and *The Spirit Poured Out on All Flesh: Pentecostalism and the Possibility of Global Theology.*[105]

---

[101] Ibid., 209–11.

[102] Ibid., 195. Pinnock's model entails that the Spirit begins transforming people into the image of the Son before they believe in the Son. Presumably the majority of these sanctified unbelievers will die in their unbelief yet enter eternity beginning to look like Jesus. The incoherence of Pinnock's soteriology and sanctification is staggering.

[103] Originally from Malaysia, Amos Yong is currently associate research professor of systematic theology at Regent University.

[104] A. Yong, *Discerning the Spirit(s): A Pentecostal-Charismatic Contribution to Christian Theology of Religions* (Sheffield, UK: Sheffield Academic, 2000).

[105] A. Yong, *The Spirit Poured Out on All Flesh: Pentecostalism and the Possibility of Global Theology* (Grand Rapids: Baker, 2005). *Beyond the Impasse* is cited in note 2.

Christianity and Theology of Religions

Amos Yong's religious, ethnic, and cultural background is significant in the development of his theology of religions.[106] Though a Christian theology of religions should seek its answers from the Bible, he is convinced that it must include a biblical understanding of history, society, and culture, and it must integrate a Christian theology of mission. This means that a Christian theology of religions can only happen as Christian theology engages the world religions in serious dialogue.[107]

A Christian theology of religions must also be trinitarian. Yong's Pentecostal background has made him particularly sensitive to the role of the Holy Spirit, and he believes that pneumatology will enable the theologian to develop a theology that meets current needs in both method and hermeneutics. He argues, "It is precisely because the Spirit is both universal and particular, both the Spirit of God and the Spirit of Jesus the Christ, that pneumatology provides the kind of relational framework wherein the radical alterity—otherness—of the religions can be taken seriously even within the task of Christian theology."[108]

Perhaps most significantly, a pneumatological theology of religions reframes the soteriological question. A pneumatological approach to religious others will still encourage serious regard for the person and work of Jesus, but it will not subordinate that work to the church. When the Spirit is not limited to the confines of the church (John 3:8), then the offer and application of salvation become available to those outside the reach of the church as well.[109]

The inclusivism of Amos Yong is based on three major areas of disagreement that he has with exclusivism: exegetical, practical, and soteriological. First, Yong is unconvinced by the primary proof texts of exclusivists, accusing exclusivist exegetes of question-begging. For example, should not Acts 4:12 be read as ontological rather than epistemological?[110] That is, even though "there is no other name under

---

[106]In the introductions to both *Discerning the Spirit(s)* and *Beyond the Impasse*, Yong outlines the importance that his religious and cultural backgrounds have played in the development of his theology. Regarding the Confucian values and Christian faith that were both passed down to him, Yong writes, "I have come to appreciate the truths, beauty, goodness, and values of other cultural-religious traditions, some of which I also received from them." Yong, *Beyond the Impasse*, 10.

[107]Ibid., 19.

[108]Ibid., 21.

[109]Ibid.

[110]See the discussion of this in chapter 1.

heaven given to people by which we must be saved," does this entail that the name must be consciously confessed? Yong also argues that passages such as John 3:17–18 speak to the fate of the evangelized, not the unevangelized. His conclusion, based on his exegesis of Scripture, is that the Bible is silent on the fate of the unevangelized.[111] Because of this silence, Yong suggests that exclusivism is a soteriological category, unique to Christian theology but not relevant to other religions. Therefore, exclusivism tells us how to deal with the evangelized but not the unevangelized. In addition to questioning its exegetical foundation, Yong has practical objections to exclusivism. He believes that the strongest argument for exclusivism is its appeal as the basis for motivation to missions. But Yong is convinced that this practical argument for exclusivism does not hold water because Christian mission should be motivated by obedience to the gospel rather than fear of hell.[112]

Yet Yong does not believe that the traditional inclusivist category is any more helpful for developing a theology of religions. As he sees it, most inclusivist proposals still have a Christological starting point, being focused on the fate of those who have never heard the Christian gospel. The main point of religious others in such inclusivist systems is that they are non-Christian. This will be the case for any theology of religions that begins with Christological assumptions. But like Pinnock, Yong asks, "What if one begins with pneumatology rather than christology?"[113]

Christology and Pneumatology

Yong finds the theological space necessary to construct his theology of religions in the procession and mission of the Holy Spirit, "because while the person of Jesus Christ is a historical symbol of God's reality in the world, the Holy Spirit is *par excellence* the symbol of divine presence and activity in the cosmic realm."[114] Yong recognizes that modifications to orthodox doctrines of the procession and mission of the Holy Spirit will have profound effects on virtually every

---

[111] Ibid., 25. Yong also takes on exclusivist interpretations of Rom 10:10–13, claiming that it must be read in light of Rom 2:12–16, which has a more universal thrust.

[112] Ibid., 26.

[113] Ibid., 27.

[114] Yong, *Discerning the Spirit(s)*, 29.

other doctrine of Christian theology.[115] But this is a risk that must be taken, provided one proceeds with caution:

> The whole christological question is, after all, whether or not Christ is *the* savior or just *a* savior. But what if we were to begin elsewhere, let's say, with the doctrine of Spirit? Surely, there is no doubt that the christological question would be merely postponed, not entirely dismissed. . . . Yet it would be intriguing to explore in that light how the Word and Spirit accomplish and mediate the salvific gift of the Father, both separately, if discernible, and in tandem. It is even the case that such may be a clue toward bringing together particularity and universality.[116]

The end result is that Yong wants to conduct a Christian investigation of other religions, not through the lens of Christology but through the lens of pneumatology. Doing so would mean that other religions are "no longer strangers residing outside the christological arena (Christ and church), but they can be legitimately recognized as dwelling within the province of the Spirit."[117]

Some will understand this approach to infer a lack of continuity or even coherence between the work of the Spirit and the work of Christ, but Yong, while disavowing any such inference, wants to emphasize the distinction between the economies of the Son and that of the Spirit in redemption.[118] Like Pinnock, he illegitimately appeals to Irenaeus's "two hands of God" metaphor for historical and theological support:

> The Word represents concreteness—as in for example, Jesus of Nazareth and the written Scriptures—historical particularity, and the human experience of objectivity; the Spirit represents the dynamism of the Anointed One—as in, for example, the Christ and the living, inspired, and illuminating word of God—cosmic relationality, and the human experience of the subjective.[119]

---

[115]Ibid., 57. Yong lists God's saving grace and love, the character of the kingdom of God, and Christian evangelism and missions, among others.

[116]Ibid., 58.

[117]Ibid., 62.

[118]Ibid., 61.

[119]Yong, *Beyond the Impasse*, 43.

This distinction has a twofold impact on pneumatology: It does not allow for the subordination of the work (or person) of the Spirit to that of the Son, and it also allows for a certain relational autonomy. The Spirit is not to be defined according to the Son, nor is the Son to be defined according to the Spirit.[120] Yong rejects any subordination of the Spirit to the Son because when the mission of the Spirit is subordinated to that of the Son, soteriology is defined ecclesiologically—that is, salvation is limited to those who belong to the church of Jesus Christ.[121]

The absence of subordination does not mean that the Holy Spirit is competing against the Son. Yong prefers to see the economies of the Word and Spirit as "overlapping dimensionally." Both work in different ways for a common goal: the salvation of the lost. This means that non-Christian faiths can be understood as "belonging to both economies, but in different respects. For starters then, it allows that they be conceived in pneumatological terms, related but not subordinated to or redefined by the economy of the Word."[122]

Yong's answer to concerns that his approach separates the Spirit from Christ and the church incorporates theological, hermeneutical, and eschatological perspectives. He argues theologically that in the past the distinction between the Son and the Spirit could be made by appealing to eternal generation and eternal procession, but such doctrinal constructs may not communicate beyond their Hellenistic and Scholastic contexts into our postmodern and pluralistic context. Therefore, Yong proposes that "in our time and religiously plural context, any understanding of the identities of both the Spirit and Christ, as well as the relationship of each to the other, has to pass through the crucible of the Christian encounter with other faiths."[123]

Yong's hermeneutical argument is that in any biblical passage about the Spirit testifying to and glorifying the Son the context is the building of the Christian church. Such passages in context, then, do not speak to the issue of the work of the Spirit in other religions. Yong argues that the Spirit's testimony to Christ is consistent with the Scriptures and religious traditions handed down, but is put into different

---

[120]Yong, *Discerning the Spirit(s)*, 69.

[121]Ibid., 64.

[122]Ibid., 62.

[123]A. Yong, "A P(new)matological Paradigm for Christian Mission in a Religiously Plural World," *Missiology* 23 (2005): 185. The similarities with the work of S. Samartha are apparent.

terms and categories depending upon the new context. Since the current context includes a plurality of religious traditions, Yong wonders whether or not it is possible that the Spirit's sowing of the Word in all people everywhere has come to fruition in the different religious traditions of the world.[124] In other words, the Spirit's testimony to Christ, in the context of the Church and Christian Scriptures, is explicit and unveiled. The Spirit's testimony to Christ in the other religious traditions of the world may be more difficult to discern, but it is still there, and the Holy Spirit can grant to us the necessary discernment to find His testimony.

Finally, Yong's eschatological defense against the charge that he is illegitimately severing the Spirit from the Son is to compare the glory of Christ in His first and second advents. Christ's second advent glory will so far exceed His first advent glory that He will be effectively unrecognizable. Appealing to Rev 21:22–26, Yong suggests that because every people and tongue will be in the Eschaton; and because culture, language, and religion cannot be arbitrarily separated, aspects of the religions will be redeemed and will contribute to the glory of God and Christ in the consummated state. Therefore, Yong asks, "Might not a pneumatological theology of religions facilitate historical discernment of that reality on this side of the eschaton?"[125] He is adamant that our conclusion must not be negative with regard to the salvific value of world religions: "Christians must remain agnostic on this side of the eschaton about the relationship of other faiths to salvation conceived in relation to the triune God."[126]

A Pneumatological Theology of Religions

Yong sees three advantages to his pneumatological approach to theology of religions. First, "pneumatology is the key to overcoming the dualism between christological particularity and the cosmic Christ."[127] Yong argues that because the Holy Spirit was instrumental in the work and person of Jesus of Nazareth, the Spirit provides the link between the historical Jesus and the coming Christ. Second, "pneumatology is the key to understanding the tension between what has traditionally been termed specific and natural revelation—that is,

---

[124]Ibid., 185–86.
[125]Ibid., 186.
[126]Ibid., 187.
[127]Yong, *Beyond the Impasse*, 47.

between the sacred and the profane or the church and the world."[128] Though these distinctions may still prove helpful, the Spirit flattens differences between those who will be saved, those who are being saved, and those who have been saved. Third, it offers alternatives to the impasse between the exclusivity of Christ and the reality of world religions. The universality of the Holy Spirit allows religious traditions to be viewed as serving divine purposes at different levels.

Pneumatology and Universality   Yong develops his theology of religions by looking to what the Bible says about religion and religious others. Like Pinnock, Yong concludes that the Bible both condemns and affirms the reality of religious others.[129] This conclusion is built in part on the presence of God through the Holy Spirit, who is "present and active, the power of God in creation, re-creation, and final creation."[130] God's presence and activity in creation speak to the universality of the Holy Spirit.[131] In fact, God's Spirit is the life-breath of the *imago Dei* in every human being and the presupposition of all human relationships and communities.[132] For Yong the presence of the Spirit is always a presence to bless. Because of the universality of the divine Spirit, God is not only Creator, but He is also Re-creator. The Spirit's role as re-creator is most evident in the life of Christ, so the work and role of the Holy Spirit in the life of Christ become "paradigmatic for the way in which God redeems and saves humankind individually and as a whole."[133]

Yong's pneumatological theology of religions proceeds in part from the Pentecost narrative in Acts 2 where the Holy Spirit is poured out on "all humanity" (Acts 2:17). Yong reads "all humanity" in a universal sense, and he believes that his reading is supported by the immediate context (which includes sons and daughters, young and old, slave and free), and by the broader context of the outpouring of the Spirit on all the different people from around the world who had gathered in Jerusalem that day. Contrary to traditional interpretations of Acts 2, Yong's universalist reading of "all humanity" implies that not just Christians receive the Spirit but all people. Furthermore,

---

[128] Ibid.
[129] Ibid., 36.
[130] Ibid.
[131] Ibid., 55.
[132] Ibid., 45.
[133] Ibid., 38.

he argues that a universal reading is preferred based on Luke's own narrative where a universalistic vision is supplied by Christ's imperative in Acts 1:8.[134]

Because the Pentecost narrative echoes the Tower of Babel narrative in Genesis 11, Yong makes a connection between language and culture that is then "extended to include the religious dimension of human life."[135] Language and culture cannot be arbitrarily separated from religious life, so just as God uses the language and cultures in the world, He also uses the religions of the world:

> Hence, the Pentecost narrative can be understood to redeem not only human languages and cultures, but also human religiosity. However, just as this does not mean that all human words and all aspects of human cultures are holy without qualification, so also it does not mean that all human religiousness is sanctified. Language, culture, and religion must all be discerned, even as each is potentially a vehicle for mediating the grace of God.[136]

Yong sees the reference to Joel 2:28–32 at Pentecost as important because it emphasizes the centrality of the Holy Spirit and the pneumatological character of the New Covenant, and because it makes clear that Pentecost emphasizes the eschatological Day of the Lord. The Day of the Lord inaugurates an age where people from "every tribe and language and people and nation" are redeemed by Christ (Rev 5:9). The eschatological vision of people from every tribe and tongue praising God is seen as evidence of the "universal presence and efficacious activity of the Spirit."[137]

Pneumatology and Understanding Religious Diversity   The second major aspect of Yong's pneumatological theology of religions is the benefit of providing dynamic categories for understanding religious diversity in salvific experiences. For Yong, conversion emphasizes the process of salvation; that is, he sees Christian conversion as a life-long journey through the various dimensions of life, including the

---

[134]Yong, "A P(new)matological Paradigm," 177. Yong admits that a traditional reading could probably be defended at the exegetical level but not at the theological level. Ibid.

[135]Ibid.

[136]Ibid. A common turn for many inclusivists is to expand eschatological promises of diverse language and cultures in the kingdom to include diverse religions.

[137]Yong, *Beyond the Impasse*, 40.

religious.[138] A pneumatological approach "would be better sensitized to the unfinished and dynamic character of religiosity . . . and religious life . . . and how each contributes to the religious shaping of human souls."[139] Tradition is also best understood pneumatologically. Viewing tradition through a pneumatological lens, "the Christian tradition and church not only exist, but are also becoming, because the tradition and church are the concrete expressions of human responses to and participation in the Spirit's outpouring upon—presence and activity in—the world."[140] Of critical importance in a pneumatological theology of religions is the elevation of religious praxis over doctrine.[141] That is, in the past, theology of religions was seen through the grid of doctrine and beliefs. A pneumatological approach is "much better able to account for the diversity of beliefs that are linked to and shaped by different social, moral, and religious practices."[142]

The Spirit of God providentially sustains all things for divine purposes. This preservation includes the religions of the world.[143] Religions, like all human endeavors, reflect "either God's permissive or active will toward ultimately divine purposes centered around the full revelation of Jesus Christ and the impending kingdom of God."[144] Therefore, Yong sees a benefit of his model in allowing an inclusive methodology rather than assuming *a priori* that religions "lie beyond the pale of divine presence and activity."[145]

Pneumatology and Judging Truth Claims   A pneumatological approach to the religions provides the capacity to engage religious truth intersubjectively; that is, it provides the means for adjudicating seemingly contradictory truth claims that can only be verified in the future. Yong explains:

> The problem here is twofold: either religious frameworks are incommensurable—based as they are on different semiotic and praxis systems—and hence apparently contrary claims are essentially non-adjudicable; or any attempt to adjudicate religious

---

[138]Yong, "P(new)matological Paradigm," 177.
[139]Ibid., 178.
[140]Ibid.
[141]Ibid.
[142]Ibid., 179.
[143]Yong, *Beyond the Impasse*, 46.
[144]Ibid.
[145]Ibid.

(doctrinal or truth) claims requires that one not only learns about or observes from a distance another tradition but also that one enters into and participates in its semiotic system.[146]

A pneumatological approach shows great promise in evaluating truth claims in other cultures because the Spirit, who gives the capacity to speak in other languages, can also grant the capacity to speak to and through foreign cultures and foreign religions.

Discernment of the Holy Spirit in Non-Christian Religions

How exactly are non-Christian faiths to be understood in terms of Christology and pneumatology? This is the question that most beleaguers pneumatological inclusivists. In an earlier publication Yong was unable to say specifically, but he was certain that the Spirit is at work in some sense in other religions:

> I think it is undeniable that the possible experience of the divine apart from an explicit knowledge of Christ supports the contention that there is an experience of the Spirit that is not explicitly christological. The ancient Israelite experience of Yahweh was certainly mediated by the Holy Spirit, whom they recognized only as the "divine breath." Can we be so certain that present day Jewish and Muslim experience of the divine is not that of the Holy Spirit?[147]

Establishing criteria for discerning the work of the Holy Spirit in religious others has become troublesome for inclusivists. Yong is not satisfied with the supposedly Christological criteria of fellow pneumatological inclusivist Clark Pinnock, who looks for traces of Jesus (ethical behavior) in religious others that reveal the presence of the Spirit. Yong wonders, if the criterion is going to be ethical, why import Christology?[148]

In *Beyond the Impasse*, Yong attempts to bypass what he sees as the Christological impasse by reconceiving spiritual discernment apart from Christological categories, turning instead to the categories of *logos* and *pneuma*. All determinate things contain both *logos* and

---

[146]Yong, "P(new)matological Paradigm," 179.
[147]Yong, *Discerning the Spirit(s)*, 68.
[148]Ibid., 200–3.

pneuma. Logos refers to concrete forms while the *pneuma* of any thing is the "complex of habits, tendencies, and laws that shape, guide, and in some way manifest and/or determine its phenomenal or concrete behavior."[149] Pneumatology can play a foundational role in a theology of religions because the exercise of human freedom is the domain of the Spirit. The combination of *logos* and *pneuma* in all things, according to Yong, shows that a return to Spirit Christology is necessary:[150]

> Apart from the inner dynamic of the Spirit, Jesus is not the Christ. Apart from the concrete form of the "Word made flesh," the Spirit remains hidden, ambiguous, ineffectual, and ultimately irrelevant. My point is that the person of Jesus of Nazareth himself is the Christ or Messiah, the Anointed One, pneumatologically defined. As such, Jesus the Christ is both the incarnate *logos* (or concrete form) and the anointed *pneuma* (inner dynamic field of force).[151]

Humans are qualitatively different from Jesus in that they struggle with their Spirit trajectory. But all of reality is this combination and interaction of concreteness and spirit.

Spiritual discernment, therefore, is a dynamic process concerned with recognizing the basic features of the outer world and the inner world.[152] According to Yong,

> There are, on the one hand, two kinds of discernments in Scripture—the charism of discernment of spirits more specifically and the exercise of spiritual discernment more generally, although both are enabled by the Spirit of God—and, on the other, that the means of discerning the spiritual or inner aspect of any thing is through careful perceptivity to its concrete or outer phenomenal features.[153]

Yong wishes to keep these two kinds of discernment in balance, affirming the role of both charismatic experience and reasoned

---

[149]Yong, *Beyond the Impasse*, 130.

[150]Ibid., 135. Yong appeals to American philosopher C. S. Pierce to describe the triadic nature of reality, focusing on the "secondness" and "thirdness" of a thing: "A thing's concrete form is that which is manipulable, sensible, perceptible, and phenomenologically encounterable. A thing's inner spirit is the laws, habits, tendencies, and energetic force that shape its processive actuality and direct its temporal trajectory." Ibid., 134.

[151]Ibid., 135.

[152]Ibid., 153.

[153]Ibid., 160.

examination in discerning the work of the Holy Spirit in the world. Therefore, he proposes specific criteria for discerning "greater or lesser divine presence and activity" in religious others.[154] Divine presence is marked by "truth, goodness, beauty, and holiness," while divine absence is marked by the "destructive, false, evil, ugly, and profane existence of the fallen and demonic world." Divine activity is thus "dynamic and mediational, calling attention to the fact that things move continuously either to or away from their divinely instituted reason for being."[155]

Yong recognizes that the challenge to his proposal arises from the dynamic complexity of human religious experience. He sees this dynamic complexity as due in part to the interrelatedness of divinity, humanity, and the demonic—each deriving part of its significance and reality from the other two.[156] Therefore, Yong suggests that Christians should build their criteria, norms, and means for discernment from the "normative life, death, and resurrection of Jesus . . . to discern the presence and activity of God in the world."[157] It seems that Yong is ultimately subordinating pneumatology to Christology when the criteria, norms, and means for discerning the presence and activity of God are focused squarely upon Jesus' person and ministry. But Yong claims that the problem of subordinating the Spirit to Christ can be overcome by means of a return to Spirit-Christology. Yong believes that any scriptural reference that seems to settle the impasse by subordinating pneumatology to Christology in discerning the activity of the Spirit of God needs to be read in context.[158] However, it is my conviction that a robust Spirit-Christology will lead to the opposite of Yong's conclusions. In chapter 8, I will demonstrate that a right understanding of the work of the Spirit in both the life of Christ and in the life of New Covenant believers will lead to the conclusion that any criteria for the discernment of the work of the Holy Spirit must be based upon the glorification of Jesus Christ, a profoundly Christological criterion.

---

[154]Ibid.

[155]Ibid., 165. See also, Yong, *The Spirit Poured Out on All Flesh*, 253–55.

[156]Yong, *Beyond the Impasse*, 166.

[157]Ibid., 167.

[158]Ibid., 169. Yong admits that 1 Cor 12:3 and 1 John 4:2–3 might appear to establish a Christological criteria for discerning the spirits, but he cautions that such passages ought not to be applied in a simplistic manner. Jesus warns that some who do not know Him will call Him "Lord" (Matt 7:21).

241

The real question Yong must address is whether the religions can mediate salvation. Establishing criteria is difficult and Yong cautions against either importing criteria that are established by other religions or exporting a Christian set of norms in the mutual evaluation of human religious experience. Yong therefore sees a dialogue between Christianity and other religions as necessary to establish "complex and sophisticated descriptive categories" in order to "respect the importances and the particularities of the different traditions, . . . which emerge during the course of interreligious engagement."[159] The sophistication that Yong calls for is exemplified with regard to the development of Christian Scripture. On the basis of the Bible's complex and variegated history, Yong rejects the idea that the sacred writings of religious others are not inspired by God and are therefore not revelatory.[160]

Yong seeks to establish criteria that will identify heterodoxy and heteropraxis. A Christian theology of religions must understand human religions as a diverse phenomenon, understand the relationship between the human and the divine in this phenomenon, and distinguish the divine and human from the demonic.[161] World religions can no longer be judged on the basis of *a priori* commitments, but a variety of disciplines, such as history of religion and philosophy of religion, must be brought to the dialogue.[162]

Dialogue and Conversion

According to Yong, the Christian must seek to understand world religions and must judge them by their own criteria. This points toward an internal critique, but it also suggests a coherence theory of adjudication. In this comparative process, he warns that bringing Christological criteria to the discussion at an early point could contaminate the purity of the comparison. A legitimate understanding is possible because of the Holy Spirit who continues his work at Pentecost of proclamation and dialogue.[163]

This Spirit-given ability manifests itself in the Christian evangelist who must "convert" to other religions, which is necessary for authentic dialogue. Yong describes conversion as an attitudinal change that

---

[159]Ibid., 173.
[160]Ibid., 181.
[161]Ibid., 175.
[162]The *a priori* commitments of which Yong speaks are presumably Christian doctrinal commitments.
[163]Yong, "P(new)matological Paradigm," 182.

occurs when the testimony of a religious other is taken seriously.[164] Conversion is predicated on the workings of the Spirit of God, therefore, "conversion to other faiths enabled by the Spirit will not contradict or compromise our commitment to Christ" because religious conversion "will emphasize the need to be led by and to discern the Spirit in and through the dynamic process of encounter with those in other faiths."[165] Furthermore, Yong is convinced that Christians can learn from religious others. Just as Christians have learned from the findings of science over the centuries and have adjusted their theology in light of those findings, so Christians should be open to adjusting their theology in light of the "dynamically reconstituting" religions of the world. To refuse to do so will deny Christians the ability to formulate a "Christian theology for the twenty-first century."[166]

According to Yong, authentic dialogue is necessary for a compelling contemporary theology because it results in religious "cross-fertilization."[167] Such cross-fertilization provides theological justification (not just missionary or pragmatic justification) for crossing over into other faiths to witness. True contextualization of the gospel is really a Spirit-wrought synthesis and is "the conversion of the gospel into terms provided by other linguistic-cultural-religious traditions."[168] Yong acknowledges that cross-fertilization could result in syncretism, but he is undaunted:

> In the synthesizing process, the gospel informs and enriches the other, and vice-versa (hence mutual transformation or cross-fertilization). On the other hand, the integrity of both Christian faith and other traditions are somehow dynamically preserved (otherwise, what we have would be syncretism). How is this possible except through the Spirit of God? The miracle of Pentecost—which preserves the authenticity of both the gospel and that of the diversity of tongues— is replicated on each occasion when the authentic cross-fertilization of gospel and culture and religion takes place.[169]

---

[164] Ibid.

[165] Ibid., 183.

[166] Yong, *The Spirit Poured Out on All Flesh*, 240. Yong also appeals to the infinitude of God, who cannot be "exhaustively conveyed in finite time and words" to justify learning from religious others.

[167] Yong, "P(new)matological Paradigm," 183.

[168] Ibid., 184.

[169] Ibid.

Ultimately, for Yong, dialogue with religious others is necessary, not just for the sake of religious others, but for the sake of the Christian. There is an "unfinished character" to Christian identity and learning from religious others can help expedite the process of transformation into Christlikeness. Yong reasons that if "others have something to say about God, should we not at least listen both sympathetically and critically?"[170]

Yong draws support for his thesis of learning from religious others by appeal to Jesus' parable of the Good Samaritan (Luke 10:25–37). In *The Spirit Poured Out on All Flesh,* after establishing the historical, social, and religious background of the Samaritans, Yong draws the following four conclusions from the parable: First, if Jesus' Jewish listeners could learn something from the Samaritan, then Christians can likewise learn from religious others. Second, if a Samaritan is capable of selfless love, then those of other religious faiths are likewise capable of selfless love. Third, because the Samaritan embodied God's "comradeship to human beings, does he also not show us the possibility of Jesus meeting us in religious others?" Finally, because Jesus told the parable in the context of the lawyer's question about how to inherit eternal life, Yong concludes that "it is possible that the Samaritan fulfilled both conditions in Jesus' initial response" (namely, to love the Lord your God and to love your neighbor as yourself).[171] Yong is careful to remind his readers of Eph 2:8–9, that "our salvation

---

[170]Yong, *The Spirit Poured Out on All Flesh,* 240.

[171]Ibid., 243. Yong's conclusions are fraught with hermeneutical difficulties. Jesus tells the parable in response to the question, "Who is my neighbor?" because the lawyer "wanted to justify himself" (Luke 10:29). It is not in direct response to the question of "What must I do to inherit eternal life?" (Luke 10:25). We must remember that every parable is made up of two parts: a fictional part (the story) and a real part (the comparison to which the story is likened). Because the story is fictional, it should not be compared to biblical narrative. Though the parable depends upon the historical reality of the antagonism between Jews and Samaritans, the story itself is fictional. The people in question may have existed in the abstract but did not exist in reality. Jesus made up a story about the least likely person (according to contemporary Jewish sensibilities) to show compassion when the most likely (according to contemporary Jewish sensibilities) had refused to show compassion. The point of the parable was to demonstrate that a neighbor is one who shows compassion to another who is in need. If the lawyer had asked a question about the possibility of salvation in the Samaritan religion or the work of the Holy Spirit in religious others, then Yong's conclusions would be justified. But it is questionable to draw theological conclusions from a parable when those theological affirmations are not attached to the specific purpose for which the parable was told. Furthermore, even though Yong references the dialogue between Jesus and the Samaritan woman in John 4 to establish the historical background for the parable, Yong fails to include Jesus' crucial correction of the Samaritan woman, "You Samaritans worship what you do not know. We worship what we do know, because salvation is from the Jews" (John 4:22). See my extended treatment of Jesus' dialogue with the Samaritan woman in chapter 2 for further details.

is by grace through faith as a gift from God."[172] But Yong asks, if the Samaritan (or any other religious other) is not working for his salvation nor is he boasting of attaining salvation through works, "then is it not still the loving prerogative of God to save this Samaritan (or any religious other)?"[173]

Pneumatological Inclusivism and Motivation to Missions

Yong admits that his proposal may remain under suspicion of undermining the logic of Christian mission. But he believes his proposal bolsters mission because Christology bespeaks particularity and the Spirit bespeaks universality. "In short, a pneumatological theology of revelation does not decide in advance about Christian uniqueness, but is willing to follow the Holy Spirit into history."[174]

SUMMARY

Chapter 5 traced the widespread departure of nonevangelical theology from the guiding principle of *extra ecclesiam nulla salus* to varying proposals of inclusivism and pluralism. Special attention was directed to those proposals that emphasized the role of the Holy Spirit over the person and work of Christ to establish the inclusivist position. The burden of chapter 6 has been to describe current proposals by evangelicals that also emphasize the role of the Holy Spirit over the person and work of Christ to establish their inclusivist positions.

The pneumatological inclusivism of evangelicals such as Clark Pinnock and Amos Yong is based on biblical and theological foundations that represent a departure from or revision of orthodox understandings. Theological commitments necessary to pneumatological inclusivism include the relative hypostatic independence of the Son and Spirit, pneumatology rather than Christology as the starting point for a theology of religions and missions, the redemptive touch of the universal Spirit reaching into world religions, and the concomitant necessity of religious others to hear the voice of the Holy Spirit. These

---

[172] Ibid., 244

[173] Ibid., 244. In response, the content of the faith in question is crucial (see chap. 2). While Eph 2:8–9 does not explicitly identify an object of the faith of the one who is saved, the book of Ephesians makes it clear that the faith that saves is faith in "the word of truth, the gospel of your salvation" (Eph 1:13). See chapter 1 for my understanding of the human condition, the character of God, His grace in salvation, and the gospel.

[174] Yong, "P(new)matological Paradigm," 189.

theological claims challenge traditional evangelical convictions, practices, and doctrines.

Challenging tradition with the possibility of reforming theology and doctrine is necessary to the health of Christ's church, provided the impetus for such challenge is rooted in the self-revelation of God. The purpose of the following chapters is to demonstrate that pneumatological inclusivism cannot stand up to the light of biblical scrutiny and fails on biblical-theological grounds. When the person and work of the Holy Spirit are understood in the light of the biblical presentation of the Spirit, speculation regarding an independent work of the Spirit, separated from the purpose of the glorification of the Son, will be demonstrated to be groundless. In fact, a proper understanding of the mission of the Spirit only serves to convince of the necessity of Christ-honoring trust in Jesus in order to be saved.

Chapter Seven

The Starting Point for a Biblical Theology of Religions— Christ or the Spirit?

INTRODUCTION

The inclusivist positions of Clark Pinnock and Amos Yong, described in chapter 6, are consciously pneumatological. In this regard they share much in common with the pluralist proposals of Peter Hodgson, Paul Knitter, and Stanley Samartha and the nonevangelical inclusivist proposals of the Roman Catholic Church, Jacques Dupuis, and Georg Khodr (see chap. 5). In order to posit an independent salvific work of the Holy Spirit apart from the proclamation of the gospel of Christ, a radical change in perspective in theological method is required. Pinnock summarizes this best by suggesting, "Let us see what results from viewing Christ as an aspect of the Spirit's mission, instead of (as is more usual) viewing Spirit as a function of Christ's."[1]

The question before us is whether such a change in perspective is permissible. Is reading Scripture pneumatocentrically a legitimate option, or is the Bible to be read Christocentrically? In this chapter I hope to demonstrate that moving Christ from the center of the Bible (a

---

[1]C. H. Pinnock, *Flame of Love: A Theology of the Holy Spirit* (Downers Grove, IL: InterVarsity, 1996), 80.

move necessary to justify pneumatological inclusivism) entails a fundamental misreading of Scripture and will result in theological positions that constitute illegitimate departures from orthodox doctrines. In short, reading the Bible as it presents itself leads to the inevitable conclusion that conscious Christ-glorifying belief in Jesus is necessary for salvation. In what follows, I will summarize the proposals of Pinnock and Yong. It is worth the time to summarize their proposals because while their theological conclusions may sound attractive to many, the methodology and hermeneutical gymnastics necessary to arrive at their inclusivist conclusions should cause concern. I will then offer a counterproposal for how to read and interpret the Bible to arrive at a faithful theology of religions.

PNEUMATOLOGICAL PROPOSALS

Clark Pinnock

Clark Pinnock cautions that although a strong theological method is necessary, its importance must not be exaggerated. From his perspective, "too much thinking about method spoils creativity."[2] Ultimately, Pinnock fears that a strong theological method can lead to what he terms "philosophical biblicism"—that is, the desire for "verifiable revelational data with which (if we had it) we could speak with absolute certainty to the world."[3] Instead, he prefers a "simple biblicism"—namely, the delight in the Word of God that does not require a Bible "that fits into an ideological agenda" or that is not "easily threatened by what exegesis might turn up and requires a more elaborate theory of truthfulness to fit the requirements."[4]

Earlier in his life Pinnock affirmed a Christocentric approach to reading the Bible and its interpretation: the central purpose of Scripture is to present Jesus Christ.[5] In order to arrive at his inclusivistic position, Pinnock has had to revise his approach to reading and interpreting Scripture. Today he celebrates the "growth" of evangelicals who are recognizing that there are other factors to consider in assessing

---

[2]C. H. Pinnock, "New Dimensions in Theological Method," in *New Dimensions in Evangelical Theology: Essays in Honor of Millard J. Erickson*, ed. D. S. Dockery (Downers Grove, IL: InterVarsity, 1998), 197.

[3]Ibid., 201.

[4]Ibid.

[5]C. H. Pinnock, *Biblical Revelation: The Foundation of Christian Theology* (Chicago: Moody, 1971), 103.

the meaning of Scripture. These factors include the role of tradition (Scripture may be primary, but tradition provides insight); reason (the need to cross-check the assertions of theology with reality—he points to the scientific advances in evolution); and culture and setting (the writers and the readers come to the text with questions and biases). On the last he credits the Spirit, stating that the theologian must overcome the "temptation . . . to stick with original meaning and not take risks discerning the mind of the Spirit for this moment."[6]

Pinnock's revision in method is rooted in his functional understanding of biblical authority. Whereas orthodox Protestants historically have based biblical authority upon ontology (the Bible is authoritative because of what it is), Pinnock understands that the authority of the Bible lies in its utilization by the Spirit: "The real authority of the Bible is not the scholarly exegesis of the text, open only to an elite, but the Word that issues forth when the Spirit takes the Word and renders it the living voice of the Lord."[7] All Christians are indwelt by the "Spirit of revelation" who "charges" the Bible with life and becomes "the living voice of God" to readers.[8]

Pinnock's understanding of the Spirit's role in biblical authority and revelation means that discernment of the ways of the Spirit is necessary to theological interpretation. For example, because cherished pluralism characterizes the current culture, it is incumbent upon theologians to "ponder what the Spirit is saying to us about it."[9] The proper tools for understanding the Spirit exceed the reading of Scripture. Because the Spirit cannot be "imprisoned in concepts," the Spirit is known by prayer and study.[10]

The need to discern the presence and work of the Spirit leads Pinnock to revisit the relationship between Christ and the Holy Spirit. Pinnock rightfully points out that because it was the anointing of the Holy Spirit that made Jesus the Christ, a healthy Christology must not lack for pneumatology.[11] He also points out that there has been neglect of both the Spirit as Creator and the Spirit in relation to Christ.[12] Both

---

[6]Pinnock, "New Dimensions in Theological Method," 204.

[7]C. H. Pinnock, *The Scripture Principle* (San Francisco: Harper & Row, 1984), 156.

[8]Ibid., 163.

[9]C. H. Pinnock, "An Inclusivist View," in *Four Views on Salvation in a Pluralistic World*, ed. D. L. Okholm and T. R. Phillips (Grand Rapids: Zondervan, 1996), 96.

[10]Pinnock, *Flame of Love*, 13.

[11]Ibid., 79.

[12]Ibid., 80.

of these statements are true. But Pinnock errs in his proposed correction by suggesting that Christ can be viewed as an aspect of the Spirit's mission rather than viewing the Spirit as an aspect of Christ's.[13]

Pinnock accomplishes this by placing Christology in the context of pneumatology, emphasizing the global operations of the Spirit. The activity of the Holy Spirit culminates in the incarnation, brings coherence to the kenosis, and is the background for the entire ministry of Christ.[14] From this perspective the Spirit is the "source of creation and redemption."[15] This reversal has an enormous effect on Pinnock's theology. For example, viewing Christ as an aspect of the Spirit's mission led to a shift in his understanding of the atonement from penal substitution to recapitulation.[16] Emphasizing Spirit-Christology directs Pinnock's attention to a participatory model of the atonement where we are united with the Christ who traces the human path as the last Adam.[17]

Amos Yong

Whereas the theological method of Clark Pinnock has to be culled from sources often not dedicated to the topic and there has been an obvious increase in Pinnock's perceived role of the Holy Spirit in interpretation and theology, the work of Amos Yong in hermeneutics and theological method is more intentional and developed.[18] Pinnock attempts to build his model of pneumatological inclusivism from Scripture. Yong is less certain that an explicit case can be made from Scripture, so he turns to epistemology, philosophy, and theological method to build his case, proposing a "foundational pneumatology." Just as beginning with the Spirit provides great potential for developing a theology of religions, Yong is convinced that beginning with pneumatology also "leads toward a robust trinitarianism, and that this movement reflects both the shape of a hermeneutical theology and the intuitions of a theological hermeneutics."[19] It is significant, therefore, that Yong's thesis for theological interpretation is conceived and

---

[13]Ibid.

[14]Ibid., 88.

[15]Ibid., 82.

[16]Ibid., 95. See also C. H. Pinnock and R. C. Brow, *Unbounded Love: A Good News Theology for the 21st Century* (Downers Grove, IL: InterVarsity, 1994), 99–110.

[17]Pinnock, *Flame of Love*, 100.

[18]See A. Yong, *Spirit-Word-Community: Theological Hermeneutics in Trinitarian Perspective* (Burlington, VT: Ashgate, 2003).

[19]Ibid., 219.

ordered as "the continuous interplay of Spirit, Word, and community,"[20] which he sees as reading Scripture through the three lenses of relationality, rationality, and the power of community.

Spirit and Word in Theological Method   Yong, who writes from a Pentecostal-Charismatic perspective, understands that theology, at least in the orthodox sense, should be bound by Scripture, but he wants to differentiate between theology and doctrine. In Yong's taxonomy, theology is "a provisional theoretical activity which attempts to correlate the biblical revelation with our experience of the world and vice versa."[21] Because theology is essentially second-order discourse about God, any attempt to circumscribe it within the parameters of the Christian church is artificial. Therefore, doctrinal distinctions are irrelevant in determining the legitimacy of a person's ability to speak about the divine. In other words, one cannot be dismissed from theological conversation on an *a priori* basis due to doctrinal differences.

Yong sees his work as being in basic continuity with ongoing developments in the trinitarian discussion of the Holy Spirit. If Jesus is the one mediator between God and man, then the Spirit is the means by which the mediation is brought about, the one who enables reconciliation between God and man.[22] A thoroughly trinitarian theology must be genuinely pneumatological, and Yong turns to Irenaeus and the "two hands of God" metaphor to establish his methodology.[23] In Yong's economy, all of reality hinges on Word and Spirit where the Word represents concreteness, objectivity, and particularity (e.g., the historical Jesus and the written Scripture), while the Spirit represents dynamism, relationality, and the subjectivity of human experience.[24] In theory Yong does not want to bifurcate the Word and Spirit by this paradigm, suggesting that "Word and Spirit are inseparable features of all things."[25] This understanding of Word and Spirit applies to hermeneutics as well, where Word and Spirit refer to the objective and subjective elements of hermeneutics. The subjective element of biblical interpretation, empowered by the Spirit, is manifest in illumination

---

[20]Ibid., 245.

[21]A. Yong, *Discerning the Spirit(s): A Pentecostal-Charismatic Contribution to Christian Theology of Religions* (Sheffield, UK: Sheffield Academic, 2000), 23.

[22]Ibid., 30–32.

[23]See ibid., 74–75, 258.

[24]A. Yong, *Beyond the Impasse: Toward a Pneumatological Theology of Religions* (Grand Rapids: Baker, 2003), 43, 135; id., *Spirit-Word-Community*, 51.

[25]Yong, *Beyond the Impasse*, 43. See also id., *Spirit-Word-Community*, 51–52.

and application. This element is critical to interpretation and in Protestant hermeneutics is often ignored, which Yong sees as further evidence of Protestant willingness to subordinate illegitimately the Spirit to the Son.[26] With an emphasis on the subjective work of the Spirit in interpretation, in what manner is the written Word authoritative? Yong can only conclude that "the Bible's authority (its normativeness) does not work in isolation, but in conjunction with the norms intrinsic to human engagement with reality in all its multidimensionality."[27] A significant implication of this position is that pneumatology becomes the key to understanding the tension between what he calls "specific and natural revelation," that is, the tension between the sacred and the profane, the church and the world.[28] In effect, there is no qualitative difference between the church and the world, the Scriptures and the sacred writings of religious others. The difference is quantitative, depending on the authoritative activity of the Spirit.

The foundation for such an assertion lies in Yong's understanding that the Spirit is the source of rationality itself and the mediator or communicator of rationality.[29] Specifically, the Spirit is the "wisdom of God."[30] Beginning at creation, Yong sees "woman-wisdom" as preexisting the world and bringing forth order out of chaos and nothingness.[31] Because of the work of the Spirit and the Word, the world and its inhabitants are "meaningful and intelligible."[32]

The Spirit's new covenant ministry is a continuation of His role as wisdom and rationality, with special emphasis on the incarnation. Jesus is the content of the wisdom of God, but the Spirit is "the one who mediates and communicates the message of the cross."[33] All interpretation is therefore a matter of Word and Spirit because truth is to be understood as the convergence of Word and Spirit.[34] Jesus is the truth, but it is the Spirit who guides us into all truth. Yong also suggests,

---

[26]Yong, *Beyond the Impasse*, 130.

[27]Yong, *Spirit-Word-Community*, 263.

[28]Yong, *Beyond the Impasse*, 47.

[29] Yong, *Spirit-Word-Community*, 123.

[30]Ibid., 35.

[31]Yong insists on using feminine pronouns in his Ashgate publication, *Spirit-Word-Community*, but not in his publications by the more evangelically mainstream Baker Publishing. In *Spirit-Word-Community*, Yong establishes the "femininity" of the Spirit by appeal to "woman wisdom" as being present at creation. Ibid., 35.

[32]Ibid., 37.

[33]Ibid., 39. Yong bases this on his interpretation of 1 Cor 2:10–16.

[34]Ibid., 40.

"The truth the Spirit communicates is not strictly circumscribed by Jesus' teachings. In short, the Spirit will expand, illuminate, apply, and communicate the truth which is embodied in Jesus."[35] In this economy the mediating contact between humanity and the divine is pneumatological.

The Holy Spirit, Interpretation, and Imagination   The Spirit is the source of rationality and the guide into all truth, but he uses the imagination in the interpretive process.[36] The role of the Spirit in the interpretation of the Word, particularly when imagination is used in a constructive way in the process, raises the issue of the relationship of the Spirit and the Word—pneumatology and Christology. Yong argues that both must retain their integrity for a fully trinitarian approach but that historically Protestant interpreters have consciously subordinated the Spirit to the Word. The result is that "the 'letter of the law' has stifled the vitality of the Spirit."[37] Therefore, Yong suggests that the role of the Spirit in interpretation be emphasized with particular regard given to the world-making task of the pneumatological imagination:

> My point is that while both elements are essential to a healthy hermeneutic, in practice, rarely is such balance accomplished or, more importantly, sustained. The relationality of Spirit requires nothing less than the thoroughly dialectical process of reading the world in the light of Scripture and vice-versa. Put theologically, while the content of the pneumatological imagination is effectively christomorphic and bibliocentric, the dynamic of the pneumatological imagination nevertheless remains distinctively charismatic and pneumatic.[38]

The pneumatological imagination is important in interpretation because of the subjective nature of the task. Interpretation involves signs and inferential abstractions, while the interpreter is motivated by subjective situations and goals.[39] It is the responsibility of the interpreter

---

[35] Ibid., 41.

[36] Yong points to Acts 17:28 and 1 Cor 2:9–16 as evidence that the pneumatological imagination is fueled by "life in the Spirit." He explains that the imagination is (1) the synthesis of passive and active components, (2) the cognitive blend of the affective and spiritual aspects of the human being, and (3) is valuational. Ibid., 123.

[37] Ibid., 138.

[38] Ibid., 138–39.

[39] Ibid., 221.

to be open to the Holy Spirit who "breaks into" the situation of the interpreter in unpredictable ways.[40] Yong is vague and unhelpful when it comes to recognizing the "breaking in" of the Spirit into the imaginative process. He suggests that the Spirit is recognized in such basic human expressions as a creative imagination, responsible exhibition of personal agency, and the human grasping of the transcendent.[41]

That the Holy Spirit is instrumental in the interpretive process is almost universally held by Christian interpreters, though the nature of that involvement may be disputed.[42] Yong's proposal differs from many because of the nature of the roles that he claims for the Spirit in theological interpretation. For example, the inspiration of Scripture is not a historical event, taking place at the time of the author's contemplation and writing, but is ongoing and dynamic, taking place at the level of hermeneutics.[43] When inspiration is severed from the historical act and is understood in this ongoing way, the number of potential revelatory sources is increased considerably. Therefore, Yong is clear that theological interpretation requires discernment of "the divine presence" in a wide range of areas, including culture and religious activity.[44]

A Foundational Pneumatology   Yong's proposal for hermeneutics is self-consciously subjective. He is therefore sympathetic with the postmodern critique of foundationalism, preferring a nonfoundationalist epistemology.[45] He develops his epistemology in dialogue with the Jesuit nonfoundationalist Donald L. Gelpi and the American pragmatist philosopher C. S. Pierce.[46] Eschewing the Cartesian foundationalism that bases all knowledge on *a priori* self-evident intuitions, Yong advocates what Pierce called a "'contrite fallibilism,' wherein

---

[40] Ibid., 222.

[41] Ibid.

[42] See, for example, G. D. Fee, *Listening to the Spirit in the Text* (Grand Rapids: Eerdmans, 2000).

[43] Yong, *Spirit-Word-Community*, 242–43.

[44] Ibid., 243.

[45] For insight into the discussion on the postmodern critique of foundationalism, see N. Wolterstorff, *Reason Within the Bounds of Religion* (Grand Rapids: Eerdmans, 1984); A. Plantinga and N. Wolterstorff, eds., *Faith and Rationality: Reason and Belief in God* (Notre Dame, IN: University of Notre Dame, 1983); and K. J. Vanhoozer, *Is There a Meaning in This Text?: The Bible, the Reader, and the Morality of Literary Knowledge* (Grand Rapids: Zondervan, 1998).

[46] See D. L Gelpi, *The Divine Mother: A Trinitarian Theology of the Holy Spirit* (Lanham, MD: University Press of America, 1984). The impact of Gelpi's thought on Yong is evident in A. Yong, "In Search of Foundations: The *Oeuvre* of D. L. Gelpi S. J., and Its Significance for Pentecostal Theology and Philosophy," *JPT* 11.1 (2002): 3–26. For an explanation of the influence of C. S. Peirce on Yong, see A. Yong, "The Demise of Foundationalism and the Retention of Truth: What Evangelicals Can Learn from C. S. Peirce," *CSR* 29 (2000): 563–89.

all knowledge is provisional, relative to the questions posed by the community of inquirers, and subject to the ongoing process of conversation and discovery."[47] Gelpi's methodology is foundational only in the sense that he sees conversion as absolutely necessary to truthful theology. One cannot speak truthfully about God, the world, or the self (from a Christian perspective) unless one is rightly related to God through the regeneration of the Holy Spirit. Gelpi's pneumatology is therefore foundational in that it serves as a "fundamental category of reality, including God, as descriptive of human experience, and as both prescriptive and normative for the ways in which Christians (and others) have experienced and should experience God."[48] The purpose of Gelpi's foundational pneumatology is to provide normative understanding of the Christian experience of the Holy Spirit.

But Yong has serious questions regarding Gelpi's proposal precisely because it seeks to provide a normative account of a Christian experience. Questioning Gelpi's assertion that regeneration is necessary for pneumatological understanding (because this limits the Holy Spirit to Christian experience only), Yong wants to expand the categories of pneumatological experience to those that are potentially universal in scope.[49] The proper audience for a pneumatological foundation is all of humanity. If it is to be foundational, it has to be true for all, not just Christians. According to Yong, it is not conversion that informs the foundation but a pneumatological imagination of seeing God, self, and the world in a way that is inspired by the Christian experience of the Holy Spirit:

> My own strategy, however, is to take this as a challenge to connect the theological articulation of our experience of the Holy Spirit with the experiences of others vastly different from ourselves in order to render claims of such experiences universally comprehensible (at least potentially) and to invite others toward deeper and more specifically understood experiences of the Spirit.[50]

Yong believes that a foundational pneumatology provides one avenue by which to adjudicate the differences in religions. He affirms

---

[47]Yong, *Beyond the Impasse*, 58.
[48]Ibid., 60.
[49]Ibid., 62.
[50]Ibid., 67.

a coherence test for truth, claiming that a foundational pneumatology is not simply content to be packaged systematically or to package the Bible. Any system that coheres and is internally consistent is meaningful on its own terms. "In Wittgensteinian terms, the Christian and Buddhist symbol systems . . . are subspecies of the religious language game, and their 'truths' are operative only within their respective frameworks and are meaningless without."[51] Yong also affirms a correspondence theory of truth in his pneumatological foundationalism. Therefore, it is both particular and universal, abstract and particular, etc.

This is the theological method that informs and shapes the theology of the pneumatological inclusivists Clark Pinnock and Amos Yong. The central thought in both is best summed up by a desire to read Scripture pneumatologically rather than Christologically and to construct theology from that perspective. The question before us is whether such an undertaking is legitimate.

JESUS CHRIST: THE CENTER OF BIBLICAL THEOLOGY

What does one do with the models outlined above? Yong advocates a cautious separation of the works of the Son and Spirit, although he is not entirely certain how to demonstrate the warrant for his proposal, while Pinnock attempts to ground his proposal on biblical proof texts.[52] Theological method is of primary concern in this discussion. The methodologies advocated by pneumatological inclusivists distort the relationship between the Son of God and the Holy Spirit that is integral to the biblical story built through the pages of Scripture. When Pinnock suggests that we ought to view "Christ as an aspect of the Spirit's mission, instead of . . . viewing Spirit as a function of Christ's,"[53] or when Yong asks what would happen if, in the construction of a Christian theology of religions, "one begins with pneumatology rather than christology,"[54] they have in fact subordinated Christology to pneumatology and reversed the roles of the Son and Spirit as they are developed in Scripture.

---

[51]Ibid., 70.

[52]A. Yong is critical of Pinnock's proposal for discerning the work of the Spirit, feeling that it does not stand up to the exclusivist critique. See A. Yong, "The Turn to Pneumatology in Christian Theology of Religions: Conduit or Detour?" *JES* 35 (1998): 437–54; and id., "Whither Theological Inclusivism? The Development and Critique of an Evangelical Theology of Religions," *EvQ* 71 (1999): 327–48. Pinnock responds in C. H. Pinnock, "Response to Daniel Strange and Amos Yong," *EvQ* 71 (1999): 349–57.

[53]Pinnock, *Flame of Love*, 80.

[54]Yong, *Beyond the Impasse*, 27.

Pinnock claims that "it lies within the freedom of theology to experiment with ideas."[55] But is such freedom actually permitted? Is theological inquiry and formulation a free play where the only boundaries are those of the theologian's imagination, or are there limits arising from the nature of the discipline itself and its subject matter? The development of any theological doctrine necessitates the justification of the resulting claims and conclusions. In other words, the theological method of a theologian is implicitly on trial with every proposal. When the object of investigation is Scripture, then it is incumbent on the interpreter to follow the lead of the Bible itself. Pneumatological inclusivism fails because it has been developed from an unwarranted and illegitimate theological method; that is, it fails on biblical-theological grounds. To demonstrate we turn first to the nature of biblical theology.

The Nature of Biblical Theology

Biblical theology is variously defined yet can be understood as "the theology of the biblical corpora as God progressively discloses himself, climaxing in the coming of his Son Jesus Christ, and consummating in the new heaven and the new earth."[56] Biblical theology seeks to discuss both the form and content of Scripture from the point of view of the revealing activity of God.[57]

The task of biblical theology is to investigate the themes presented in Scripture, to find the inner points of coherence, to define their interrelationships, and to set forth the "big picture" or "story" of Scripture.[58] As such, exegesis is of critical importance to biblical theology, but it must not be atomized.[59] That is, the task of biblical interpretation does not end with the exegesis of individual verses or texts, though that is the preceding and necessary step toward understanding the Bible as a unified whole. Biblical theology must be grounded in the entire canon, putting the texts in their proper contexts and focusing

---

[55]Pinnock, *Flame of Love*, 80. A. Yong also desires to do much the same thing with his foundational pneumatology. See, for example, Yong, *Beyond the Impasse*, 58–74.

[56]D. A. Carson, *The Gagging of God: Christianity Confronts Pluralism* (Grand Rapids: Zondervan, 1996), 502.

[57]See K. J. Vanhoozer, "Exegesis and Hermeneutics," in *NDBT*, 53.

[58]E. A. Martens, "Tackling Old Testament Theology," *JETS* 20 (1977): 123. See also S. J. Hafemann, "Biblical Theology: Retrospect and Prospect," in *Biblical Theology: Retrospect and Prospect*, ed. S. J. Hafemann (Downers Grove, IL: InterVarsity, 2002), 15–16.

[59]See G. Goldsworthy, "The Ontological and Systematic Roots of Biblical Theology," *RTR* 62 (2003): 152–64.

on the broad relationships between the themes and the two testaments. Biblical theology is concerned with "the horizon of the text" and seeks to interpret the structure of the Bible as a unit.[60] Rather than bringing extrabiblical categories to the text, the goal of biblical theology is to be intratextual, working inductively from the texts to synthesize and articulate the unity of the various biblical passages using the categories that arise from those texts themselves.[61]

Relationship of Biblical Theology to Systematic Theology In contrast to biblical theology, systematic theology seeks to articulate what the Bible says in a way that is culturally telling and culturally prophetic.[62] It will therefore bring categories, vocabulary, and questions to the biblical text,[63] seeking to "rearticulate what the Bible says in self-conscious engagement with (including confrontation with) the culture."[64] If systematic formulation is to reflect accurately the mind of God on any issue (including a theology of religions), it must be based on solid exegesis of Scripture, which both informs and is informed by an accurate biblical theology. In other words, whereas systematic theology is a culminating discipline, biblical theology serves as a bridge to systematic formulation.[65] If the biblical theology that undergirds systematic formulation is flawed, the systematic formulation will likewise be in error. This is evident in the theological formulations of pneumatological inclusivists such as Pinnock and Yong in that they are not being true to the categories of the Bible. In their desire to create a relative autonomy for the Holy Spirit, Pinnock and Yong do not follow the Bible's own presentation of the Son and the Spirit. Their theological proposals are wrong because they do not understand the Bible's own presentation of itself; that is, their biblical theology is flawed.

Is Biblical Theology Possible? Claiming to find a theology of the Bible begs the question of whether biblical theology as defined is

---

[60] C. H. H. Scobie, *The Ways of Our God: An Approach to Biblical Theology* (Grand Rapids: Eerdmans, 2003), 47.

[61] D. A. Carson, "Systematic Theology and Biblical Theology," in *NDBT*, 100.

[62] Ibid., 103.

[63] See G. Vos, "The Idea of Biblical Theology," in *Redemptive History and Biblical Interpretation: The Shorter Writings of Geerhardus Vos*, ed. R. Gaffin (Phillipsburg, NJ: P&R, 1980), 7; Carson, "Systematic Theology and Biblical Theology," 89–104; and Scobie, *Ways of our God*, 3–8.

[64] Carson, "Systematic Theology and Biblical Theology," 103.

[65] Ibid.

even possible.[66] The questions that surround biblical theology often rest upon the issue of whether the determination of a central theme or themes across the canon is feasible, given the varied nature of the two testaments.[67] Finding unifying themes would be impossible were Scripture merely a collection of religious works. However, Scripture can be read canonically because a single Author has performed a unified communicative act, despite the complexity and variegated nature of that single act.[68] The unity of the Bible is a necessary entailment of the divine inspiration of Scripture. Therefore, the faithful exegete will approach Scripture convinced that it presents a unified message expressed through diverse forms.[69]

Clearly, to read the Bible while assuming divine inspiration is to be guided by presuppositions.[70] According to Scobie, the biblical theologian must approach the text with a number of necessary presuppositions, in particular the beliefs that the Bible is divine revelation and that the "varied material in both Old and New Testaments can in some way be related to the plan and purpose of the one God of the whole Bible."[71] The doctrine of Scripture as the Word of God is dependent on the doctrine of the person and work of God. In particular, Scripture presents God as being personal, transcendent, omniscient, sovereign, faithful, and communicative.[72] The self-revealing God of the Bible has spoken in Scripture, and the Bible attests to its own divine nature.[73]

---

[66]For a summary of the history of biblical theology see G. F. Hasel, "The Nature of Biblical Theology: Recent Trends and Issues," *AUSS* 32 (1994): 203–15; Scobie, *Ways of Our God*, 9–45; id, "The Challenge of Biblical Theology," *TynBul* 42 (1991): 52–58; and B. S. Childs, *Biblical Theology in Crisis* (Philadelphia: Westminster, 1970).

[67]See P. Balla, "Challenges to Biblical Theology," in *NDBT*, 20–27.

[68]Vanhoozer, "Exegesis and Hermeneutics," 61. See also C. L. Blomberg, "The Unity and Diversity of Scripture," in *NDBT*, 65.

[69]D. L. Baker, *Two Testaments, One Bible: A Study of the Theological Relationships Between the Old and New Testaments*, rev. ed. (Downers Grove, IL: InterVarsity, 1991), 243.

[70]E. J. Schnabel writes, "The inspiration of Scripture forces us to recognize that theology is a discipline *sui generis* in which humans can participate only on the basis of adequate presuppositions." E. J. Schnabel, "Scripture," in *NDBT*, 41.

[71]Scobie, "Challenge of Biblical Theology," 50. Biblical theology is under the same attack from postmodernists as any other scholarly enterprise which engages in hermeneutical activity. For a postmodern analysis of biblical theology, see D. Penchansky, *The Politics of Biblical Theology: A Postmodern Reading* (Macon: Mercer, 1995). See also B. Ingraffia, *Postmodern Theory and Biblical Theology* (Cambridge: Cambridge University Press, 1995).

[72]See Schnabel, "Scripture," 37–38.

[73]E.g., 2 Sam 23:2; Isa 8:11; Jer 30:4; Mic 4:4; Acts 1:16; 3:18,21; 4:25; 2 Tim 3:16; 2 Pet 1:20–21; 3:16. Cf. Matt 5:17–18; John 10:35.

Biblical Theology and Hermeneutics   Commitment to the viability of biblical theology will necessarily impact the way the Bible is read and interpreted. Hermeneutics is typically described as the science and art of biblical interpretation.[74] It is the attempt to discover the meaning in the biblical text. Context has long been understood to be the primary determiner of meaning. In addition to historical context, the spheres of literary context surrounding any passage of Scripture include the passage itself, the immediate context, the book, the writer, the testament, and the Bible.[75] Since the largest context of any particular passage of Scripture is the Bible as a whole, each text should be consciously interpreted in the light of the themes that stretch across the canon, finding its place in the grand story. For this reason biblical theology must control hermeneutics. Just as violation of the immediate literary context or the historical context of a passage is an indicator of an invalid interpretation, so violation of the biblical theological context is also an indicator of invalid interpretation. Interpretation of Scripture can be no other way. Because biblical theology seeks to draw theological interpretation out of Scripture according to the language and categories that arise from the text, biblical theology and hermeneutics are necessarily inextricably linked.

Of course, one cannot discover the themes that stretch across the canon without first discerning the meaning of the passages that create those themes. That is, one cannot find the meaning of the whole without first finding the meaning of the parts that make up that whole. At the same time, the meaning of the parts is dependent upon their place in the whole. As the interpreter comes to understand the constituent parts of Scripture, his understanding of the whole will be enhanced, enabling an increased ability to interpret the parts. The result is a spiraling closer and closer to the true meaning of the text, both in part and in whole.[76]

The Progress of Revelation

According to Geerhardus Vos, a pioneer in the area of biblical theology, it is critical to theological understanding that divine

---

[74]See, e.g., W. Klein, C. Blomberg, and R. L. Hubbard Jr., *Introduction to Biblical Interpretation*, rev. ed. (Dallas: Word, 2004), 5.

[75]G. R. Osborne, *Hermeneutical Spiral: A Comprehensive Introduction to Biblical Interpretation* (Downers Grove, IL: InterVarsity, 1991), 21–22.

[76]This spiral toward meaning is much like that developed by Osborne in his *Hermeneutical Spiral*. Ibid., 22.

revelation be both progressive and organic. A characteristic feature of divine revelation is its historical progress. Truth does not come to us as a static entity; rather, it is dynamic. As redemptive history moves across time, the promises of God remain constant but "his progressive revelation of himself and his redemptive plan do take on different appearances in different periods."[77] It therefore follows that the degree to which one misunderstands the structure of the biblical plot is at least the degree to which one's exegesis will be inaccurate. Vos understands special revelation, with its progressive nature, to be inseparable from the activity of God which he calls redemption. He writes, "Now redemption could not be other than historically successive, because it addresses itself to the generations of mankind coming into existence in the course of history. Revelation is the interpretation of redemption; it must, therefore, unfold itself in installments as redemption does."[78]

The progress of divine revelation is also organic.[79] Each subsequent increase in revelation consisted in the unfolding of what was germinally there in the beginning of revelation.[80] Because there is a progress to revelation which moves toward a divine end, it follows that there is a consistent theme or actor in this divine drama.[81] For Vos, the central character in this drama is Jesus Christ:

> Hence from the beginning all redeeming acts of God aim at the creation and introduction of this new organic principle, which is none other than Christ. All Old Testament redemption is but the saving activity of God working toward the realization of this goal, the great supernatural prelude to the Incarnation and the Atonement. And Christ having appeared as the head of the new humanity and having accomplished His atoning work, the further renewal of the kosmos is effected through an organic extension of His power in ever widening circles.[82]

---

[77] R. Lints, *The Fabric of Theology: A Prolegomenon to Evangelical Theology* (Grand Rapids: Eerdmans, 1993), 301.

[78] G. Vos, *Biblical Theology: Old and New Testaments* (Edinburgh: Banner of Truth, 1975), 5–6.

[79] See Lints, *Fabric of Theology*, 276–79.

[80] Vos, "Idea of Biblical Theology," 11.

[81] See M. S. Horton, *Covenant and Eschatology: The Divine Drama* (Louisville, KY: Westminster John Knox, 2002), 99–120.

[82] Vos, "Idea of Biblical Theology," 12.

Though the pneumatological inclusivists Pinnock and Yong do not explicitly address the role of biblical theology in their theological method, they do interact with biblical theological themes.[83] Their work proposes a pneumatological center for understanding both redemptive history and the story of Scripture. But is this proposal legitimate? Biblical theology correctly understood must be Christocentric and precisely at this point pneumatological inclusivism fails.

The Christocentric Nature of Scripture

Pneumatological inclusivism rests upon a theological method demanding that Scripture be read through a pneumatological lens, but is this legitimate? Can redemptive history be seen and understood accurately in this light? I believe it is illegitimate to begin theological formulation with the universal work of the Spirit. It is speculative and illegitimate to view Christ "as an aspect of the Spirit's mission" because it ignores the categories, structure, and plot of the Bible. Furthermore, it runs contrary to the way that Jesus Himself and His apostles have told us to read Scripture.

Christ and the Interpretation of Scripture   The twenty-fourth chapter of Luke records two critical teachings by the Lord Jesus Christ on the nature of Scripture. Following His resurrection, Jesus Christ walked with two disciples who did not recognize him. Responding to Cleopas and his companion who were troubled over the events of the recent days, Jesus called them "unwise and slow" to believe in their hearts "all that the prophets have spoken" (Luke 24:25). The use of the word "unwise" (*anoētoi*) does not carry the sense of "moronic" in this context but of "obtuse."[84] The disciples were "slow of heart" because they did not understand the redemptive purposes of God. With this statement Jesus laid claim to being the center of the biblical prophetic ministry. He then seized the opportunity, "beginning with Moses and

---

[83]Although Amos Yong has written a book on theological method, *Spirit-Word-Community,* he does not offer any analysis on the role of biblical theology in his hermeneutical proposal. His work in *The Spirit Poured Out on All Flesh* (Grand Rapids: Baker, 2005) and *Beyond the Impasse* present his theology of religions, based upon a pneumatological starting point that is justified by his method. There is little to no explicit interaction with the discipline of biblical theology in his proposals for theology of religions. Likewise, neither Clark Pinnock's early work in *The Scripture Principle,* his theology of religions outlined in *A Wideness in God's Mercy* (Grand Rapids: Zondervan, 1992), nor his monograph on pneumatology, *Flame of Love,* offer any explicit interaction with the discipline of biblical theology.

[84]J. B. Green, *The Gospel of Luke,* NICNT (Grand Rapids: Eerdmans, 1997), 848.

all the Prophets," to interpret (*diermēneuō*) to them "the things concerning Himself in all the Scriptures" (24:27). Though we are not told which passages Jesus interpreted for His listeners, from Luke's perspective it does not matter. The ministries and teachings of Moses and all the prophets, just as all the Scriptures, point toward Christ and His glory through suffering. The two disciples had to have the Scriptures interpreted for them because they did not read them correctly.

In Luke 24:36–49, Jesus joined a larger gathering of disciples and and taught them the same lesson. In v. 44, Christ claimed that His ministry was the focal point of "the Law of Moses, the Prophets, and the Psalms" (metonymy for the entire Old Testament and its tripartite division).[85] Just as Jesus opened the eyes of the two disciples so that they could recognize Him in v. 31, so in v. 45, Jesus "opened their minds to understand the Scriptures."[86] The parallel establishes that one sees and understands Scripture correctly when one sees and recognizes Christ as pervasive throughout. Christ is the fulfillment of Old Testament prophecy, but He is also the central figure in a divine drama that dominates all of human history. This is demonstrated by Christ's statement, "This is what is written: the Messiah would suffer and rise from the dead the third day, and repentance for forgiveness of sins would be proclaimed in His name to all the nations, beginning at Jerusalem" (Luke 24:46–47). The use of the term "what is written" (*gegraptai*) indicates that Jesus is referring back to the Old Testament.[87] Jesus' statement, however, was not an explicit quotation of any biblical passage but was the implicit teaching of the entire Old Testament. The correct reading of Scripture, therefore, is not merely an academic exercise. Jesus claimed that the center and focus of the whole Scriptures was the proclamation of the forgiveness of sins through the

---

[85]A. Plummer, *A Critical and Exegetical Commentary on the Gospel According to S. Luke,* ICC (Edinburgh: T&T Clark, 1922), 562.

[86]So W. L. Liefeld, "Luke," in *EBC*, ed. F. E. Gaebelein (Grand Rapids: Zondervan, 1984), 8:1057.

[87]The term "what is written" (*gegraptai*) occurs 13 other times in Luke-Acts. Each time it is used to refer to an Old Testament quotation. The word *gegraptai* occurs 53 other times in the New Testament. In 49 of these uses, the passive verb is used to indicate an Old Testament quotation. With regard to the other four uses which are not clearly referring to Old Testament quotations, the use in 1 Cor 4:6 is ambiguous but probably refers to a scriptural quotation. The use in John 20:31 has interesting implications for the inspiration of the New Testament because it refers to New Testament writing. Only Rev 13:8 and 17:8 clearly do not refer to biblical quotation. They do, however, refer to divine writing in "the book of life."

work of the Messiah. Gerald Bray notes the revolutionary force of Jesus' instruction:

> He claimed that he was himself the interpretation of Scripture, that everything in the Old Testament pointed to him and to his work. During his lifetime very few people seem to have believed this, or even understood what he meant by it, but his resurrection from the dead changed everything. It was that event which ultimately justified his hermeneutical claims, and which led to the formation of a distinct body of Christians, whose gospel was to prove unacceptable to mainstream rabbinical Judaism.[88]

That the disciples understood this hermeneutical principle is evident from gospel proclamation in the book of Acts. Peter's sermon on the day of Pentecost in Acts 2:14–41 concludes, "Therefore let all the house of Israel know with certainty that God has made this Jesus, whom you crucified, both Lord and Messiah" (2:36). Peter did not arrive at this conclusion based on naked assertion from the Old Testament texts to which he referred.[89] But when the Old Testament is interpreted in the manner prescribed and modeled by Christ, then the Scriptures point in concert toward Christ. Toward the end of Acts, Paul summarizes his preaching ministry as "saying nothing but what the prophets and Moses said would come to pass: that the Christ must suffer and that, by being the first to rise from the dead, he would proclaim light both to our people and to the Gentiles" (Acts 26:22–23 ESV). A Christocentric hermeneutic leads Goldsworthy to conclude:

> We may conclude, then, that Christ authenticated himself and established the dogmatic basis upon which the first Christians engaged in the task of understanding and interpreting their Old Testament scriptures. From the outset, a fundamental Christology determines biblical theology. It is Jesus Christ, the Word incarnate, who informs the biblical theologian of what actually is happening in the whole expanse of revelation; that is, of what principles are at work. Only within this framework can we say that the biblical theological task is descriptive. The apostolic witness that Jesus

---

[88]G. Bray, *Biblical Interpretation: Past & Present* (Downers Grove, IL: InterVarsity, 1996), 54.

[89]So G. L. Goldsworthy, "'Thus says the Lord!'—The Dogmatic Basis of Biblical Theology," in *God Who Is Rich in Mercy*, ed. P. T. O'Brien and D. G. Peterson (Grand Rapids: Baker, 1986), 32.

fulfils the OT promise provides us with the substance of Jesus' own exposition of the way that all Scripture speaks of himself.[90]

Jesus Himself drives us back to the Old Testament, bequeathing to His church a hermeneutic that points to His person and work,[91] teaching us that it will lead us to Him. Vanhoozer states it well: "Scripture's own use of Scripture is of particular interest, for the cradle of Christian theology is perhaps best located in the interpretative practice of Jesus and the apostles."[92] We must read the Bible in the manner in which it specifies that we read it. It must begin with Christ. Goldsworthy summarizes:

> In doing biblical theology as Christians, we do not start at Genesis 1 and work our way forward until we discover where it is leading. Rather we first come to Christ, and he directs us to study the Old Testament in the light of the gospel. The gospel will interpret the Old Testament by showing us its goal and meaning. The Old Testament will increase our understanding of the gospel by showing us what Christ fulfills.[93]

The New Testament teaches that Jesus Christ Himself first taught His followers to read the Scriptures seeking Him. He offered to us a hermeneutic. C. H. Dodd asks an important question: "Are we compelled to reject the offer?"[94]

The Old Testament and the New Testament The path to reading the Old Testament in light of the Christ event is fraught with hermeneutical obstacles. Indeed, the Old Testament uses the term *Messiah* only nine times of the coming Anointed One who would arrive in the person of Jesus.[95] When seen in the light of the fabric of the Old

---

[90]Ibid., 32–33.

[91]Bock notes that the church has developed its understanding of the Old Testament from Jesus. D. L. Bock, *Luke,* NIVAC (Grand Rapids: Zondervan, 1996), 621.

[92]K. J. Vanhoozer, *The Drama Of Doctrine: A Canonical-Linguistic Approach To Christian Theology* (Louisville, KY: Westminster John Knox, 2005), 22.

[93]G. Goldsworthy, *According to Plan: The Unfolding Revelation of God in the Bible* (Downers Grove, IL: InterVarsity, 2002), 55.

[94]C. H. Dodd, quoted in M. Black, "The Theological Appropriation of the Old Testament by the New Testament," *SJT* 39 (1986): 8.

[95]W. C. Kaiser Jr., *Preaching and Teaching from the Old Testament: A Guide for the Church* (Grand Rapids: Baker, 2003), 22. Kaiser goes on to state, "Yet both the Jewish community (especially in pre-Christian days) and the early church found scores, if not hundreds, of texts supporting a messianic interpretation." Ibid.

Testament story, the challenge is not overly formidable. According to some rabbinical calculations, approximately 456 Old Testament texts refer either directly or indirectly to the Messianic age.[96] There is a fine line between faithful exegesis and overspiritualizing the text, inserting Christ and His work into every detail of the Old Testament text (e.g., Rahab's cord). One faithfully walks that line by recognizing that Christ is the focal point and true meaning of Scripture, and though every passage of the Bible may not speak directly of Him, every passage of the Bible is part of the Story which has its focus in Him.[97]

Brian Rosner agrees: "Biblical theology maintains a conscious focus on Jesus Christ, not in some naive and implausible sense, where Christ is found in the most unlikely places, but in noting God's faithfulness, wisdom and purpose in the progress of salvation history."[98] Witness Jesus' words to the Jews: "You pore over the Scriptures because you think you have eternal life in them, yet they testify about Me. And you are not willing to come to Me that you may have life" (John 5:39–40). The Bible tells a story, and though it may not be readily apparent from the beginning, the unity is perceived from the standpoint of its conclusion.[99] This is apparent from the first chapter of the first Gospel. The genealogy recorded in Matt 1:1–17 points to the Jewishness of Jesus and His position as the heir of David. These opening pages demonstrate what the Old Testament meant in the context of the gospel of Christ. The evangelists tell us the story of the real historical Jesus, but they weave their stories in such a way so as to emphasize specific points of interest. John Goldingay summarizes:

> As well as understanding Christ in the light of the Old Testament story, Matthew understands the Old Testament story in the light of the Christ event. Matthew's claim is that the story from Abraham to David and from the exile on into the post-exilic period comes to its climax with the coming of Christ, and needs to be understood in the light of this denouement. . . . The significance of Abraham's leaving Ur, the Israelites' exodus from Egypt,

---

[96]Ibid., 20.

[97]P. Misselbrook, "Biblical Theology and Biblical Interpretation," *Searching Together* 14.2 (1985): 25–26.

[98]B. S. Rosner, "Biblical Theology," in *NDBT*, 10.

[99]Misselbrook, "Biblical Theology and Biblical Interpretation," 25–26. See also Vanhoozer, *Drama of Doctrine*, 39.

David's capture of Jerusalem, and so on through the Old Testament story, emerges with fullest clarity only when you see these events in the light of each other and in the light of the Christ event which is their climax.[100]

Ties to the Old Testament are found not just in the words of Jesus but also in the literary strategy of the evangelists. For example, there are strong parallels in the Gospels between Jesus and Moses. In Luke-Acts, Jesus is portrayed as a prophet, lawgiver, and leader.[101] Matthew sees Jesus as recapitulating Israel's history (Matthew 1–7) and records Jesus as the one who is "greater than" all three major categories of Old Testament leaders: prophet, priest, and king (Matt 12:1–8,39–42).[102] The book of John clearly has Old Testament thematic echoes throughout the entirety of the Gospel. Themes such as creation, the "I Am" statements, miraculous signs, and the Jewish feasts act as organizing theological principles for John's writing.[103]

Prior to the incarnation there was a certain ambiguity inherent in Old Testament prophecy, but the first advent ministry of Christ and New Testament teaching on His return resolves that ambiguity and effectively limits interpretive options. "Now every part of the Old Testament must be seen in its relation to the complete picture; every part must be seen in its relation to the New Testament revelation of Jesus Christ."[104] The requirement of reading Old Testament texts in the context of the New Testament also follows from the reality of the progression of time through redemptive history. Jesus comes in "the completion of the time" (Gal 4:4); He is the one through whom God has spoken "in these last days" (Heb 1:2), which necessitates a Christological reading of all prior revelation.[105] Christ saw His mission outlined in the Old Testament as leading to glory through suffering, persecution, and death.[106]

---

[100]J. Goldingay, "The Old Testament and Christian Faith: Jesus and the Old Testament in Matthew 1–5, Part 1," *Themelios* 8.1 (1982): 5–6.

[101]See R. F. O'Toole, "The Parallels Between Jesus and Moses," *BTB* 20 (1990): 22–29.

[102]So C. L. Blomberg, *Matthew*, NAC 22 (Nashville, TN: Broadman, 1992), 31.

[103]A. J. Köstenberger, *John*, ECNT (Grand Rapids: Baker, 2004), 13–14.

[104]S. Greidanus, "The Necessity of Preaching Christ also from Old Testament Texts," *CTJ* 34 (1999): 193.

[105]Ibid., 193–94.

[106]"The Christology of the first Christians consequently followed this understanding of Jesus' mission. A biblical theology comprising both testaments should choose this understanding as its starting point." H. Graf Reventlow, "Between Theology of Covenant and Christology: Reflections of a Christian Old Testament Scholar on Biblical Theology," *Bangalore Theological Forum* 27 (1995): 39.

The centrality of Christ is manifestly evident in the New Testament. Even the closing of the biblical canon is based on the belief that Christ is the unique and final revelation of God.[107] As Vanhoozer concludes, "The canon appears as a function of Jesus' lordship over the church."[108] The Old Testament witness, which is devoted to the person and work of the one true God, is taken up in the New Testament and "made more precise Christologically."[109]

The goal of theology, therefore, is to know, see, and live Christ. It coalesces around the gospel of Jesus Christ. Evangelical theology, rightly understood, seeks to know the God of the gospel; the God who reveals Himself in redemptive history, recorded in Scripture, and is made known in Christ. Vanhoozer is correct when he states, "The Bible—not only the Gospels but all of Scripture—is the (divinely) authorized version of the gospel, the necessary framework for understanding what God was doing in Jesus Christ. Scripture is the voice of God that articulates the Word of God: Jesus Christ."[110]

A Short Proposal for Theological Method

It is necessary to outline those aspects of theological method that will differentiate my development of the doctrine of the Holy Spirit from that of pneumatological inclusivists in general, Clark Pinnock and Amos Yong in particular. Pneumatological inclusivism is based on a revision of the doctrine of the person and work of the Holy Spirit. The question before us is whether the case for such a revision is biblically sound. Because the theological methods of pneumatological inclusivists are flawed, their doctrines of the Holy Spirit cannot stand up to biblical scrutiny. I will present my doctrine of the Holy Spirit in chapter 8. This treatment of pneumatology will be substantially different from the pneumatologies of nonevangelical inclusivists (chap. 5) and evangelical inclusivists (chap. 6) for the following critical reasons. First, theology must treat Scripture as fully authoritative, first-order truth. Second, theological inquiry should rely heavily on biblical theology, picking up the categories and vocabulary from the

---

[107] So H. N. Ridderbos, *Redemptive History and the New Testament Scriptures* (Phillipsburg, NJ: P&R, 1988), 43; P. D. Wegner, *The Journey from Texts to Translations: The Origin and Development of the Bible* (Grand Rapids: Baker, 1999), 148; and Scobie, *Ways of Our God*, 57.

[108] Vanhoozer, *Drama of Doctrine*, 196.

[109] P. Stuhlmacher, "My Experience with Biblical Theology," in *Biblical Theology: Retrospect and Prospect*, ed. S. J. Hafemann, 188.

[110] Vanhoozer, *Drama of Doctrine*, 46.

text of Scripture itself. It should also be canonical, consciously asking throughout its development where and how the relevant texts fit into redemptive history. Finally, Christian theology should be consciously and intentionally Christocentric.

The Full Authority and Ontological Uniqueness of Scripture

Theological inquiry must be undertaken as a humble response to the self-revelation of God. As such, the proper attitude of both biblical exegesis and theological construction is humility; the proper posture is the bent knee. Any discussion of theological authority must begin with the absolute lordship of God the Father and His Son, Jesus Christ, and theological inquiry must submit itself to their lordship. Therefore, authority of any kind that resides in any other source is derivative.[111]

It follows, therefore, that the authority of Scripture is inextricably tied to its divine origin. The Bible alone is the written self-revelation and self-expression of an all-authoritative God. Reflecting on the apostles' understanding of divine revelation and authority, Carl F. H. Henry writes, "Any repudiation of divine inspiration as a property of the biblical text they would have considered an attack on the authority of Scripture."[112] The role of the Holy Spirit in the writing of Scripture must not be understated or diminished, for it is He, the third person of the Holy Trinity, who imparts to the Bible its unique status as revelation. Apart from the Spirit's movement in the human authors (2 Pet 1:20–21), Scripture can make no legitimate claim to divine authority.

Amos Yong affirms the Spirit's role in Scripture's authority but seeks to move the seat of the authority of Scripture from ontology to utility; that is, Scripture is authoritative not because of what it is but because of what it does.[113] This is a critical departure from the orthodox defense of the authority of Scripture with consequences that are borne out in the theology of Yong. For example, when Scripture's

---

[111]D. Clark elucidates, "Discussions of theological authority therefore typically begin with a basic ontological claim: God is the ultimate authority for defining our behaviors and beliefs. The authority inherent in any other source—Scripture, creeds, or church—is necessarily derived authority. It is derived from the Lord." D. K. Clark, *To Know and Love God: Method for Theology* (Wheaton, IL: Crossway, 2003), 62.

[112]C. F. H. Henry, *God, Revelation and Authority: God Who Speaks and Shows* (Wheaton, IL: Crossway, 1999), 4:68.

[113]See, for example, Yong, *Spirit-Word-Community*, 242–43; and S. J. Grenz and J. R. Franke, *Beyond Foundationalism: Shaping Theology in a Postmodern Context* (Louisville, KY: Westminster John Knox, 2001), 65.

authority is based on how the Spirit uses the Bible in a given community, then the distinction between Scripture and other sacred writings, including the sacred writings of religious others, moves from qualitative to quantitative. Any unique status or authority granted to Scripture is not based upon its divine origin or essential qualities. Rather, the Bible is privileged over other writings because the Holy Spirit chooses to use it more that He does other writings.

We have already seen how nonevangelicals such as Jacques Dupuis grant to the sacred writings of other traditions the status of divine self-revelation because of the universal influence of the Spirit or Stanley Samartha who believes that the Holy Spirit continually breathes life into the sacred writings of different religions. Yong does not go this far, but when inspiration is severed from a historical act and becomes part of the interpretive or illuminating process, then the number of potential sources for revelation is increased dramatically.

Yong rightly wants to emphasize the present role of the Holy Spirit in the process of illumination and interpretation. But blurring illumination and interpretation into inspiration effectively severs inspiration from its historical roots, which leads to an impoverished doctrine of Scripture. The Bible is not merely a record of redemptive history but is in fact part of redemptive history. Scripture, not just its message, but also its origin, is a vital part of redemptive history and must be seen in light of the historical gospel.[114]

The Spirit's role in illumination is necessary for taking the interpretive process through understanding to application, its right and necessary culmination. Without the activity of the Spirit, one can understand the grammatical sense of the text but not possess the understanding that comes from faith. But the Holy Spirit's vital role of illumination should not overshadow His historical act of inspiration. Nor should the authority of Scripture hinge on understanding by the interpreter, as Yong in effect concludes. Concerning the functional authority of Scripture, Darrell Bock writes:

> However, the fact that the Spirit inspires the Word and helped to create it suggests that the product and its narrative, propositions and promises possess authority not only in how the Spirit makes use of them but also in what they affirm. There is an authority in

---

[114]So Vanhoozer, *Drama of Doctrine*, 45.

the text because it is Spirit-induced, whether or not that product is "deputized" or "appropriated."[115]

It is ironic that those who advocate an increased role for the Holy Spirit by basing the authority of Scripture on illumination do so at the expense of the Holy Spirit's role in inspiration. There is an organic unity between inspiration and illumination, not due to the blurring of categories but because the Holy Spirit is responsible for both. The Spirit who inspired the biblical text is the one who brings illumination of that same text to the interpreter.[116] Calvin reminds us,

> Therefore, the Spirit promised to us has not the task of inventing new and unheard-of revelations, or of forging a new kind of doctrine, to lead us away from the received doctrine of the gospel, but of sealing our minds with that very doctrine which is commended by the gospel.[117]

It is critical to understand this distinction: the ontological authority of the Bible is not the same as its epistemic authority. The ontological ground of authority is objective and lies in the Scripture principle, identifying the Bible fully as the Word of God. Epistemic authority is the subjective recognition of the Scripture principle by the interpreter, a personal or community response to what the Bible is. Both ontological and epistemic authority are critical for the Word of God to accomplish what God desires.[118] But focusing on the epistemic authority (even if Spirit grounded) while ignoring the ontological authority of Scripture effectively denies the work of the Spirit in the writing of Scripture and in the formation of the canon. It elevates the subjective, depending on each interpretive community to guard against faulty theology without an objective standard. Theological inquiry must begin with a humble respect for the authority of the Word of God prior to interpretation.

---

[115]D. L. Bock, *Purpose-Directed Theology: Getting Our Priorities Right in Evangelical Controversies* (Downers Grove, IL: InterVarsity, 2002), 18.

[116]This fact makes untenable Yong's complaint that when the Spirit is subordinated to the Word, the result is that the "letter of the law" has stifled the vitality of the Spirit.

[117]J. Calvin, *Institutes of the Christian Religion*, trans. F. L. Battles, ed. J. T. McNeill (Philadelphia: Westminster, 1960), 1.19.1.

[118]See Clark, *To Know and Love God*, 65.

A Biblical Theology That Is Canonical

Theological formulation that submits to the lordship of the triune God must speak with unmoving conviction where Scripture is explicit and speak with thoughtful humility where Scripture is silent. The best route for the theologian to achieve this goal is to rely heavily on biblical theology, picking up the themes, categories, vocabulary, and storyline from the text of Scripture itself.

Because Scripture comes with its own themes and categories, indeed an entire storyline, it cannot be said that the Bible is pre-theoretical. It provides both the forms and the content for its own interpretation. When addressing typically systematic issues such as the role of the Holy Spirit in culture and world religions or the relationship between Christ and the Holy Spirit, our theological paradigm and method must depend on the content of Scripture the theological inquiry is seeking to illumine.[119] As Richard Lints affirms, "The Bible, in its form and its content, records the dramatic story of God reaching into human history and redeeming a people for himself. The form and content of our theology must reflect this."[120] Closely related to the concept of biblical theology, evangelical theology must be self-consciously canonical. If redemptive history constitutes the organizing structure of Scripture, then theological inquiry must reflect that structure by reading any text of Scripture across the canon in that context. D. A. Carson is correct when he notes, "That stance is most likely to be deeply Christian which attempts to integrate all the major biblically determined turning points in the history of redemption."[121]

The problem with the methodologies of pneumatological inclusivists such as Yong and Pinnock is that they effectively treat the Bible as pre-theoretical, ignoring the form, content, and themes given in Scripture for doing theology, seeking to provide their own. Pinnock seeks to "view Christ as an aspect of the Spirit's mission" and explains that "it lies within the freedom of theology to experiment with ideas."[122] This

---

[119]Horton, *Covenant and Eschatology*, 1.

[120]Lints, *Fabric of Theology*, 64. Lints follows the practice of Jonathan Edwards: "Theology was not supposed to be merely a rational framework placed over the scriptural revelation in order to make the Scriptures intelligible to modern man, he believed. Rather, he saw the aesthetic harmony of the Scriptures as the underlying fabric for the theological framework. Beauty was a structural concept for Edwards, held primarily not in the eye of the beholder but in the very mind of God. As the mind of God was discovered in the Scriptures, the beauty of his revelation became apparent, and an aesthetic or structured theology was possible." Ibid., 175–76.

[121]D. A. Carson, *Christ and Culture Revisited* (Grand Rapids: Eerdmans, 2008), 83.

[122]Pinnock, *Flame of Love*, 80.

would be fine except that the Spirit-inspired Scriptures do not allow for that theological framework. The theologian cannot mine the Bible as if it were a sterile source book for theological construction, looking to find answers to a set of questions that arise out of the ambient cultural climate. Rather, the "interpretive matrix should be the interpretive matrix of the Scriptures" and "the structures of systematic theology ought to mirror in some important way the structure of biblical theology. The theological framework ought to be linked to the actual structure of the biblical text itself and not merely to the content of the Bible."[123]

It is illegitimate to suggest that the theologian, the church, or the interpretive community can claim relative autonomy in determining a theological framework. Prolegomena does not stand apart from the authority of Scripture. It is not on a different epistemological category from the theology that comes from it. The biblical texts, to which the theologian is beholden, do not stand in isolation from one another but are organically linked. Yong and Pinnock err at this point because they are guilty of ignoring the organic unity of the text, thereby tearing the fabric of Scripture.

In the tradition of Vos and Lints, I propose that recognition of the progress of redemptive history is crucial to understanding Scripture. Beginning with creation and culminating in the eschatological return of Christ and the new creation, the fundamental framework of the Bible is the creative and redemptive activity of God, of which Christ is the apex.[124] It follows that theology must begin with an understanding of the history of redemption.[125] Any interpretation or theological construction must not rend the overall fabric of redemptive history. Pneumatological inclusivists approach the text with an agenda that runs contrary to God's revelation of the flow of His redemptive acts. Their proposals fail because they ignore redemptive history even though they work with biblical texts. As will be demonstrated in the next chapter, a theology of the Holy Spirit must take its cues from both the structure and content of the Bible.

The current work of the Holy Spirit falls into the epoch between the first and second advents of Christ, that is, the church age. Present readers of Scripture, therefore, though separated from the New Testament writers by over 2,000 years and large differences in geography and culture, are

---

[123]Lints, *Fabric of Theology*, 270–71.
[124]Ibid., 264–65.
[125]Ibid., 268.

nevertheless on the same page of redemptive history. Just as Paul, Peter, and John wrote letters, inspired by the Spirit, to the churches, informing them of things that presently were and things to come, so current readers read those letters, guided by the Spirit, and learn of things that presently are while they look ahead to those same things to come. The kingdom of God, inaugurated with the first advent of Christ, will be consummated in the future. The Spirit inspired the apostles to write of that kingdom, guided the church through the canonization of those writings to build that kingdom, and acts as the agent of sanctification in the context of that inaugurated kingdom. This is the purpose of the divine canon, to grow the kingdom, both quantitatively and qualitatively, and neither that purpose nor the words have changed since they were written.

A Christocentric Theology

If theology must follow the structure of redemptive history, and the apex of redemptive history is Jesus Christ, it follows that theology should be Christocentric. All things in Scripture point to Christ, and Christ is the hermeneutical principle given by Christ Himself. This does not mean that the exegete should attempt to find Jesus in every verse of the Old Testament by virtue of his imagination or creative interpretive skill. Rather, as Christopher Wright explains, "The person and work of Jesus become the central hermeneutical key by which we, as Christians, articulate the overall significance of these texts in both Testaments. Christ provides the hermeneutical matrix for our reading of the whole Bible."[126] This is not to establish a canon within the canon because "it is a canonical center that Jesus' identity and mission represents."[127] Therefore, as one works through the divine canon, all of Scripture must be read on a Christological basis. Lints explains the danger of ignoring Christology in interpretation: "God revealed the identity of the Messiah in the person and work of Christ, but the process of revelation began much earlier, with Moses and Abraham and even back to Adam. Our own understanding of Christ will be greatly impoverished if we fail to relate it to the stories of Moses and Abraham and Adam."[128] Lints is correct but states only the half of it. Because Scripture is structured around redemptive history, of which Christ is

---

[126]C. J. H. Wright, *The Mission of God: Unlocking the Bible's Grand Narrative* (Downers Grove. IL: InterVarsity, 2006), 31.

[127]Horton, *Covenant and Eschatology*, 18.

[128]Lints, *Fabric of Theology*, 268.

274

the apex, our understanding of the stories of Moses and Abraham and Adam, or any other critical actors in redemptive history, will also be "greatly impoverished" if we fail to relate them to Christ.

Amos Yong objects that limiting the Holy Spirit to Christian proclamation illegitimately narrows the scope of the Holy Spirit's ministry and thereby diminishes our understanding of Christ:

> The Spirit's living testimony to Christ always translates the scriptural and received ecclesial witnesses into the terms and categories of the new context. This context today involves the plurality of religious traditions. Put christologically, then, is it possible that the seeds of the Word sown into the hearts and lives of all persons everywhere (cf. John 1:9) have germinated, at least in part, in the world's religious traditions? . . . In the first century, Jesus was not recognized as the . . . Messiah by (most of) his fellow Jews, even as he was said to be embodied in the prisoner, the naked, the hungry and the sick, and even the (demonized) Samaritan. Do not the prisoners, the naked, the hungry and the sick of today include not only the Samaritans but also those in other religious traditions? Might we come to a deepened and transformed understanding of Christ when viewed through the prisms of other faiths?[129]

Ignoring Yong's exegesis for the time being, we must ask, are we really in a new context? Is a "plurality of religious traditions" new? I doubt it. Religious pluralism, manifest in humanity's rebellion against and reaching out for its Creator, is the continuous backdrop to the drama of redemptive history from Genesis to Revelation. The reality of religious pluralism was part of Paul's mission to take the gospel to the nations. Cherished pluralism, which is subjective, may be new, but empirical pluralism, which is objective, is not. This current cultural value does not change the purposes of the inaugurated kingdom, nor does it change the role of the Spirit in growing that kingdom. As was established earlier, we inhabit the same place in redemptive history as the apostles who wrote, by inspiration of the Holy Spirit, the Scriptures. Bruce Ware summarizes well:

---

[129]A. Yong, "A P(new)matological Paradigm for Christian Mission in a Religiously Plural World," *Missiology* 23 (2005): 185–86.

But as the authors of Scripture were moved by the Spirit to write what the Spirit moved them to write, what was the central subject and focus of their writing? Jesus. He's the centerpiece of the Bible. He is what everything points to in the Old Testament, and he is what the New Testament expands upon. All Scripture is given to us by the Spirit. And what the Spirit wants to talk about, most centrally, is Jesus.[130]

Pneumatological inclusivism fails on biblical theological grounds, and I have demonstrated from the nature of biblical theology why this is the case. The culmination of this project is to explore the actual relationship between the Son of God and the Holy Spirit. In so doing, it will be demonstrated that the Holy Spirit seeks to glorify the Lord Jesus Christ; and any proposal that grants a relative autonomy to the Spirit, independent of the Son, fails on Christological and pneumatological grounds.

---

[130]B. A. Ware, *Father, Son, & Holy Spirit: Relationships, Roles, & Relevance* (Wheaton, IL: Crossway, 2005), 112.

Chapter Eight

Son and Spirit: The Christ-Glorifying Work of the Holy Spirit

INTRODUCTION

On the night that Jesus was betrayed, He gathered His disciples and told them that He would soon be sending the Spirit to them. Jesus explained, "When the Spirit of truth comes, He will guide you into all the truth. For He will not speak on His own, but He will speak whatever He hears. He will also declare to you what is to come. He will glorify Me, because He will take from what is Mine and declare it to you." (John 16:13–14). The thesis of this chapter is that Jesus' declaration of the Spirit's mission to glorify the Son describes the priority of the Spirit throughout the entirety of redemptive history. Any attempts to assert a relative autonomy for the Spirit or a hypostatic independence between Son and Spirit cannot be sustained by biblical theology or exegesis.

We will first analyze the work of the Spirit prior to the incarnation. We will demonstrate that even though the Son is not explicitly mentioned, the activity of the Spirit, according to Scripture, was to drive redemptive history toward the incarnation, crucifixion, and resurrection of the Son of God. The Spirit came upon people at critical junctures in salvation history to effect necessary events in God's redemptive plan. We will also show that many of the references to the Spirit in the Old Testament relate not to what the Spirit was doing during the old covenant but to what the Spirit would do during the messianic age.

We will look then at the incarnation and discover that Jesus of Nazareth was the Christ, the anointed one of God, precisely because of the unique presence of the Spirit in His life. The Spirit led and empowered Jesus Christ throughout all aspects of His life and ministry from birth (incarnation) to crucifixion, resurrection, and ascension. During this time the Spirit directed people's attention and praise toward the Son and never to Himself.

Finally, we will see that, following the ascension of Christ, the role of the Spirit has been exactly what Jesus said it would be, namely, to glorify the Son of God. Since Pentecost the Spirit's ministry has been a quantitative and qualitative expansion of the Son's first advent ministry. As Leon Morris avers, "The work of the Spirit is Christocentric. He will draw attention not to Himself, but to Christ. He will glorify Christ. It is the things of Christ that he takes and declares, that is, his ministry is built upon and is the necessary sequel to that of Christ."[1] According to both the explicit testimony of Scripture and its overall storyline, the Spirit works toward the glorification and magnification of the Son. When the Spirit is at work in the world, the Son is glorified.

What follows is a brief biblical theology of the Son and Spirit. Most of the attention is focused on passages that describe the activity of the Holy Spirit. We begin where Scripture begins—the book of Genesis and creation.

THE SON AND THE SPIRIT: PREINCARNATION

The Hebrew word for "spirit" (rûaḥ) occurs in noun and verb form approximately 388 times in the Old Testament.[2] Much like its Greek counterpart pneuma, rûaḥ can also denote the movement of air.[3] This creates a difficulty in both translation and theology. The movement

---

[1]L. Morris, *The Gospel According to John*, rev. ed., NICNT (Grand Rapids: Eerdmans, 1995), 622.

[2]L. J. Wood, *The Holy Spirit in the Old Testament* (Grand Rapids: Zondervan, 1976), 16–17. Wood breaks down the 388 occurrences as follows: "wind" (101), "breath" (18), "odor" (13), "space" (6), "spirit" of man (84), "Spirit" of God (97), emotional center of man (28), life principle of man (11), angels (4), evil spirits (18), the spirit of a beast (1), and uncertain in meaning (7).

[3]See the range of meanings in *A Hebrew and English Lexicon of the Old Testament*, ed. F. Brown, S. R. Driver, and C. A. Briggs (Oxford: Clarendon, 1951), 924–26. For a comparison of the use of rûaḥ and pneuma see Wood, *Holy Spirit in the Old Testament*, 20–22.

of air can be either outside a man, as in "wind," or inside a living being, suggesting "breath."[4] These three meanings, "spirit," "wind," and "breath" are not mutually exclusive.[5] "Wind" in Scripture, though invisible, is often a mysterious force and can be the instrument of God's action and judgment (e.g., Exod 10:13; Isa 27:8). "Breath" is likewise linked with God who is Himself the source of breath and life (e.g., Gen 6:17). Though it can carry the meaning of a light wind, in the Old Testament the term usually emphasizes an animating energy (e.g., Isa 31:3). Humans have a spirit, which is the life force that animates them. The meaning is determined by the context, but it is often difficult to ascertain. In the Old Testament the term is often used synonymously with the presence of God (e.g., Ps 51:11). The divine *rûaḥ* grants life; it also grants vital powers that surpass the normal capacity of men (e.g., Gen 6:3; 45:27; Num 16:22; Job 12:10; Ps 104:29–30; Ezek 2:2). Eichrodt develops the Old Testament usage to explain the utter dependence of all creation on the divine *rûaḥ*:

> Hence every living thing in the world is dependent on God's constantly letting his breath of life go forth to renew the created order; and when its vital spirit from God is withdrawn every creature must sink down in death. Thus *ruach* is at all times plainly superior to Man, a divine power within his mortal body, subject to the rule of God alone.[6]

Wood suggests that Old Testament reference to the Spirit of God occurs about 97 times, approximately one quarter of all uses of the Hebrew word *rûaḥ*.[7]

Creation

With Jesus' instructions on the Christ-glorifying nature of the Spirit's ministry to guide us, we begin to develop our biblical theology of the Spirit at the beginning of the Canon, and it is in the context of the beginning that the Spirit of God is first encountered. Genesis 1:2

---

[4]S. Ferguson suggests that both *pneuma* and *rûaḥ* are onomatopoeic terms whose sound and meaning convey the same meaning: the forced movement of air. S. Ferguson, *The Holy Spirit* (Downers Grove, IL: InterVarsity, 1996), 16. See Job 9:18; 19:17; Ps 135:17.

[5]So J. H. Walton, *Genesis*, NIVAC (Grand Rapids: Zondervan, 2001), 74.

[6]W. Eichrodt, *Theology of the Old Testament*, trans. J. A. Baker (Philadelphia: Westminster, 1967), 2:47–48.

[7]Wood, *Holy Spirit in the Old Testament*, 17.

recounts that the *rûaḥ elōhîm*[8] was already present "hovering over the face of the waters." This implies that God's Spirit has been involved in His works from the very beginning, establishing the cosmic order, preparing the world for human habitation.[9] The activity of the Spirit in creation is fundamental to the biblical narrative because it establishes the active role of the Spirit in redemptive history.[10] The Spirit hovering over the waters in Gen 1:2 is the same picture of God in Deut 32:11, where He is depicted as an eagle who "hovers over its young" (NIV),[11] This *inclusio* suggests that the picture of the Spirit of God at work is intended throughout the Pentateuch.[12]

Though the language of Genesis 1 makes attribution of creation to the action of the Holy Spirit a contested assertion, the role of the Holy Spirit in creation is developed throughout the Old Testament (e.g., Job 26:13; 33:4; Ps 104:30; Isa 40:12–14). Ferguson sees a series of connections between creation, the Exodus, and the Spirit in the Old Testament. Isaiah 63:7–14 attributes the Exodus to the execution of the Holy Spirit, while Deut 32:10–11 identifies the executor of the Exodus as one who hovers over the people like an eagle. Therefore, an analogy is drawn "between the 'hovering' of the *rûaḥ elohîm* over the inchoate creation and the presence of the Spirit of God in the as-yet-incomplete

---

[8]There is debate over how to translate this term. Proposals include "mighty wind" (G. von Rad, *Genesis*, rev. ed., trans. J. H. Marks [Philadelphia: Westminster, 1972], 49); "wind of God," (C. Westermann, *Genesis 1–11: A Commentary*, trans. J. J. Scullion [Minneapolis: Augsburg, 1984], 107–8; Walton, *Genesis*, 74–78; G. J. Wenham, *Genesis 1–15*, WBC 1 [Waco, TX: Word, 1987], 17; and "Spirit of God" (B. K. Waltke, *Genesis: A Commentary* [Grand Rapids: Zondervan, 2001], 60; J. J. Sailhamer, *The Pentateuch as Narrative: A Biblical-Theological Commentary* [Grand Rapids: Zondervan, 1992], 85–86; id., "Genesis," *EBC*, ed. F. E. Gabelein [Grand Rapids: Zondervan, 1990], 2:25; V. P. Hamilton, *The Book of Genesis: Chapters 1–17*, NICOT [Grand Rapids: Eerdmans, 1990], 111–17). "Spirit of God" is to be preferred, due to the verb *mērahepet*, that is best translated "was hovering" and the fact that *rûaḥ* is seen to have a beneficent force in the verse. Hamilton prefers to translate it "spirit" as opposed to "Spirit" because to choose the latter is to superimpose "trinitarian concepts on Gen 1 that are not necessarily present." Hamilton, *Book of Genesis*, 114–15. Talmudic interpretation rendered the collocation a wind created by God on the first day, but U. Cassuto found this interpretation inconsistent with Talmudic interpretation of the second and third days when separation of the waters occurs. Cassuto believed the collocation has an identical meaning as Job 33:4, which is rendered Spirit of God. U. Cassuto, *A Commentary on the Book of Genesis*, trans. I. Abrahams (Jerusalem: Magnes, 1961), 24.

[9]So Ferguson, *Holy Spirit*, 19; cf. Waltke, *Genesis*, 60.

[10]The presence of the Spirit coupled with the creative speech acts of God through his Word is the first hint in Scripture of the trinitarian nature and activity of God. This allows theologians to assert that the role of the Spirit in the creation narrative indicates that the Spirit is assisting the Father in the works of creation. B. A. Ware, *Father, Son, & Holy Spirit: Relationships, Roles, & Relevance* (Wheaton, IL: Crossway, 2005), 105.

[11]The only other place where the verb is used is Jer 23:9.

[12]So Sailhamer, *Pentateuch as Narrative*, 87.

work of redemption."[13] Sailhamer sees a parallel between the creation of the world in the first two chapters of Genesis and the construction of the tabernacle in Exodus. He notes that in both accounts of the work of God in Gen 1:2 and Exod 31:3 the work is established by the Spirit of God.[14] The creation narrative, therefore, marks the first stage of God's interaction in history. Ferguson highlights the importance of this beginning: "What is of interest is that the activity of the divine *ruach* is precisely that of extending God's presence into creation in such a way as to order and complete what has been planned in the mind of God."[15]

While the creation narrative includes the role of the Spirit, it also introduces the speech of God. God spoke creation into existence, and everything exists by that word. In the creation narrative, the creative Word of God is preceded by the *rûaḥ* of God. This establishes, from the very beginning, a close association between the Spirit and the Word of God. Boris Bobrinskoy comments, "In the work of creation, the Word of God is not only preceded by the Spirit; the latter accompanies it and ensures that it resounds. In the order of creation, therefore, there is a simultaneity between the Word and the Spirit."[16] The psalmist summarizes well the close relation between the Word and Spirit in creation in Ps 33:6. It is "by the word of the Lord" and "by the breath of His mouth" that the heavens and all their host were made.[17] Eichrodt notes that the association of the spirit of life with the creative word asserts the sovereignty of God over the dominant forces of nature: "It is, therefore as the possessor of the spirit of life that God utters the creative word."[18]

---

[13] Ferguson, *Holy Spirit*, 20.

[14] Sailhamer, *Pentateuch as Narrative*, 87.

[15] Ferguson, *Holy Spirit*, 21. This is evident from Ezek 39:29 where the manifestation of the Spirit is promised "with a view to fulfilling a variety of goals in redemptive history" (ibid.). Keil and Delitzsch see the Spirit of God as the principle of all life who quickens and prepares all living forms which were called into being by the creative word. C. F. Keil and F. Delitzsch, *The Pentateuch*, Commentary on the Old Testament, trans. J. Martin (Grand Rapids: Eerdmans, 1969), 1:49.

[16] B. Bobrinskoy, *The Mystery of the Trinity: Trinitarian Experience and Vision in the Biblical and Patristic Tradition*, trans. A. P. Gythiel (Crestwood, NY: St. Vladimir's Seminary Press, 1999), 28.

[17] The LXX translates Ps 33:6 with the terms *tō logō tou kuriou* ("word of the Lord") and *pneumati* ("spirit" or "breath"). There is a strong connection between the LXX translation of Ps 33:6 and John 1:1–3, where the *logos* is the subject of creation.

[18] Eichrodt, *Theology of the Old Testament*, 2:49.

The language of the creation narrative sows the seeds of trinitarian thought that come to full bloom in the New Testament. The New Testament writers interpret the Genesis narrative's record of the activity of the divine Word in creation as a recognition of the preeminence of the Son of God in creation.[19] The relationship between the prologue to John's Gospel and Genesis 1 is readily apparent. John sees the Word as both the agent in creation—"All things were created through Him"—and the indispensable element in creation—"apart from Him not one thing was created" (John 1:1–5).[20] In Col 1:15–20, Paul applies to Christ the title of "the beginning," while teaching that all things were created by, for, and through Him. Jesus Christ, who is the *Logos* of God, powerfully illustrates how God's Word binds all elements of creation to Himself and to one another.

Precisely at this point, the creation narrative, Pinnock illegitimately separates the Word from the Spirit, ignoring the active roles of both the Spirit and the Son together. Pinnock affirms the work of the Son in creation in the sense that the Son is the pinnacle or archetype of creation. Creation "exists in the space between the Father and Son."[21] That is, the Son models the "other as distinct but in relationship" to the Father, and it is this "self-differentiation of the Son from the Father" that is the "basis of creation."[22] The Son is also the model of what creation is meant to be, giving focus and glory to the Father. The Son is the exemplar of creation, "independent from but in relationship with God."[23] The Spirit, on the other hand, is the dynamic creative agent of power in creation. The Spirit energizes and perfects creation as the life-giving force.[24] Pinnock's concern is that the Spirit's role in creation has been ignored, "relegating him to spheres of church and piety."[25] He suspects that the motivation for ignoring the Spirit's work

---

[19]The objection is often raised that the New Testament authors are reading their trinitarian theology into the text and that the Old Testament only hints in this direction. Such an objection fails on two grounds. First, even if the creation narrative only "hints" at trinitarian thought, if the New Testament authors say that it is there, then it is there, even if not fully developed. Second, the inspired New Testament authors were reading the Old Testament exactly the way that Jesus, who is the very Word of God, taught them. Such an approach to the Old Testament was developed in chapter 7 of this work.

[20]So Hamilton, *Book of Genesis*, 144.

[21]C. H. Pinnock, *Flame of Love: A Theology of the Holy Spirit* (Downers Grove, IL: InterVarsity, 1996), 59.

[22]Ibid.

[23]Ibid.

[24]Ibid., 60–61.

[25]Ibid., 63.

in creation is "the desire to protect the uniqueness of salvation through Christ."[26] But Pinnock's description of the Trinity's work in creation ignores a crucial aspect of the role of the Son. While the incarnation of the Son establishes Jesus Christ as the prototype of the new humanity, the firstborn of all creation (Col 1:15), He is also an active agent in creation (John 1:3; Col 1:16; Heb 1:2) and in the preservation of creation (Col 1:17; Heb 1:3). By reducing the role of the Son in creation to that of "model," Pinnock effectively establishes the Spirit as the sole dynamic agent. Pinnock then uses the role of the Spirit in creation, relatively autonomous from the Son, to justify the same relative autonomy of role in the Spirit's actions in redemptive history. But the affirmation of such a separation is illegitimate. The works of the Word and Spirit are irreducibly linked. From the beginning, as Ps 33:6 intimates, there is no work of the Son in creation apart from the Spirit, and there is no work of the Spirit in creation apart from the Son. Ironically, affirmation of the dynamic roles of both the Son and Spirit was Irenaeus's intention in his "Two hands of God" metaphor, an intention ignored or misunderstood by Pinnock. The interrelationship between the Son and the Spirit in creation establishes the pattern for the Spirit's activity, namely, to prepare creation (ultimately, man, the pinnacle of God's creative work) to receive the Word of God.[27] This is the biblical teaching, but the interrelationship between the two is severed in Pinnock's model.

The Creation of Man

The Spirit is an active participant in the creation of man. The Lord God breathed into the man formed from the dust of the earth the breath of life and man was thereby created *imago Dei*, in the image of God (Gen 1:26–27; 2:7). Pneumatological inclusivists are surely correct to draw attention to the role of the Spirit in the creation of man. The trouble occurs when, in their zeal to assert the activity of the Spirit, they ignore the importance of the Son.[28] Because Jesus Christ is the image of the invisible God (Col 1:15), He is also the image of perfected humanity (1 John 3:2). Jesus Christ is the fulfillment of all that

---

[26] Ibid.

[27] See Bobrinskoy, *Mystery of the Trinity*, 26.

[28] See Pinnock, *Flame of Love*, 73–74. Yong is more careful to see the parallelism between the Spirit and the Word. A. Yong, *Spirit-Word-Community: Theological Hermeneutics in Trinitarian Perspective* (Burlington, VT: Ashgate, 2002), 40, 45.

humanity was created to be, in that He was in His Father's mind the prototype of that perfect humanity.[29]

Furthermore, the pneumatological aspects of the *imago Dei* find their place within the context of the Trinity as a whole. The social aspects of the Trinity as related to creation in the image of God have been well documented recently.[30] However, the *imago Dei* includes more than community implications but also encompasses aspects of dominion and stewardship. The mandate of Gen 1:26–29 to multiply and subdue the entire earth "embraces the whole creation" and is the "basic building block for the unfolding structure of salvation after the Fall."[31] The creation of man in the image of God makes possible the incarnation of the Son of God, who is also the Spirit-empowered Davidic heir. The prophesied destiny of Jesus is to exercise dominion throughout the cosmos (2 Sam 7:13–16; Isa 9:6–7; 11:1–5; Dan 7:13–14; Phil 2:9–10), and the destiny of all men and women redeemed by Him, regenerated, sealed, and empowered by the Spirit, is to reign with Him (Rom 8:22–23; 2 Tim 2:12; Rev 20:4). Therefore, there is continuity between creation as trinitarian and salvation as trinitarian. Both are ultimately in Christ.[32] Letham explains, "Since Genesis . . . is to be read in the context of the whole of Scripture, we can see references in the New Testament to the role of Christ and the Holy Spirit in creation as reinforcing this interpretation (Col 1:15–20; Heb 1:3; 11:3; John 1:1ff)."[33] Hughes describes salvation as the "reintegration within man of the image of God at the heart of his being," and that this salvation is "necessarily effected through the Second Person of the Holy Trinity for the reason that he himself is the Image after whom man was created."[34]

The Holy Spirit played a vital and life-giving role in the creation of the first man from the dust of the ground. But the creation of man,

---

[29]See P. E. Hughes, *The True Image: The Origin and Destiny of Man in Christ* (Grand Rapids: Eerdmans, 1989), 10–50, 213–23.

[30]See, for example, S. J. Grenz, *The Social God and the Relational Self: A Trinitarian Theology of the Imago Dei* (Louisville, KY: Westminster John Knox, 2001); S. R. Holmes, "Image of God," in *Dictionary for Theological Interpretation of the Bible*, ed. K. J. Vanhoozer (Grand Rapids: Baker, 2005), 319; K. Barth, *Church Dogmatics*, ed. G. W. Bromiley and T. F. Torrance, vol. 3, *The Doctrine of Creation*, pt. 1, trans. J. W. Edwards, O. Bussey, and H. Knight (Edinburgh: T&T Clark, 1958), 185–86.

[31]R. Letham, *The Holy Trinity: In Scripture, History, Theology, and Worship* (Phillipsburg, NJ: P&R, 2004), 21.

[32]It will be established later in this chapter that even the mere reference to "Christ" or "Messiah," rightly understood, assumes a powerful working of the Spirit.

[33]Ibid.

[34]Hughes, *True Image*, 213.

as are all the works of God, was a trinitarian act—a joint effort of the Father, the Son, and the Holy Spirit. Furthermore, humanity was created by the triune God with a special view toward the incarnation of the Son. Humanity was created *imago Dei* so that the redemptive purposes of God could be accomplished in Christ. When one elevates the role of the Spirit in creation to the exclusion of the Son, as pneumatological inclusivists do, the entire purposes of God in creation and, ultimately, redemption, are distorted.

Special Empowerment

As redemption is progressively revealed in the history of Israel, so the work of the Spirit is also progressively revealed. From the patriarchs to the high point of the monarchy in Solomon to the work of the prophets during the era of the divided kingdom, the Spirit's work was primarily a special endowment granted to God's chosen people for the purpose of mediating God's salvation, in all its various manifestations.[35] The Old Testament is replete with examples of the Spirit coming upon people, empowering them for acts of service that figure prominently in God's redemptive plan.[36] Eichrodt summarizes well:

> God's activity of history, aimed at the creation of a consecrated people of God, was discerned not only in isolated marvelous events, but also in the emergence of specially equipped men and women whose leadership in word and deed, by wars of liberation without and by the establishment of the will of God in the social and moral order within, dragged the dull mass of the people with them, again and again smashing and sweeping away all the obstacles which the incursion of heathen morals and ways of thought raised against them. In the activity of these mediators and instruments of the divine covenant purpose of salvation the Israelite people recognized afresh the irruption of God's transcendent life into the paltry patchwork of this world.[37]

---

[35] G. Goldsworthy, *According to Plan: The Unfolding Revelation of God in the Bible* (Downers Grove, IL: InterVarsity, 2002), 214. See also M. A. Inch, *Saga of the Spirit: A Biblical, Systematic, and Historical Theology of the Holy Spirit* (Grand Rapids: Baker, 1985), 32.

[36] E.g., Gen 41:38; Exod 28:3; 31:1–11; 35:30–35; Num 11:17; 27:18. Ferguson notes, "But already, from the beginning, the ministry of the Spirit had in view the conforming of all things to God's will and ultimately to his own character and glory." *Holy Spirit*, 22.

[37] Eichrodt, *Theology of the Old Testament*, 2:50.

There are approximately 60 references to the work of the Holy Spirit in approximately 100 individuals in the Old Testament. These occurrences are commonly broken into four categories of people: The Holy Spirit came upon craftsmen, civic leaders, judges, and prophets. In each case the primary purposes of God in the sending of the Spirit are concurrent and synergistic: the protection and care for the chosen people of God and the active guiding of redemptive history toward the incarnation, cross, and the consummation of all things.[38]

Craftsmen　The first category of Spirit-empowered individual is the craftsman. Bezalel was "appointed by name" by the Lord who "filled him with God's Spirit, with wisdom, understanding, and ability in every craft" (Exod 31:2–3).[39] Bezalel appears to have been temporarily empowered for the specific activity of designing and creating the tabernacle. The craftsmanship necessary to make the implements for the sanctuary was enormous (e.g., the intricate instructions for the lampstand in Exod 25:31–37). To Bezalel was given the task of making those items described to Moses by the Lord Himself. But Bezalel was not merely making beautiful things. He was designing and crafting the tabernacle—the center of Israelite religious, political, and social life.[40] The implements of worship were "copies of the things in the heavens" (Heb 9:23), placed in a sanctuary that was "a model of the true one" (Heb 9:24). All these things were meant to teach the people of Israel of a higher reality: the one who "appeared one time, at the end of the ages, for the removal of sin by the sacrifice of Himself" (Heb 9:26). The Holy Spirit uniquely gifted Bezalel to create artifacts that would serve to point the people of God to Jesus Christ. Far from asserting a relative autonomy from the Son, this empowerment of the Holy Spirit was working toward the glorification of the Son.

Judges　After the entrance into the promised land but prior to the development of Israel's monarchy, God raised up individuals to rescue the tribes of Israel. The Spirit came upon four of these judges. Judges

---

[38]So C. H. H. Scobie, *The Ways of Our God: An Approach to Biblical Theology* (Grand Rapids: Eerdmans, 2003), 272.

[39]See 1 Kgs 7:13–14. Hiram from Tyre, a worker in bronze "was full of wisdom, understanding, and skill for making any work in bronze" (ESV). The same verb in Exod 31:3, *mālēʾ*, "fill," is here a passive form, indicating that the action was wrought upon Hiram. Wood writes, "In view of the context, the only likely way for him thus to be wrought upon was by being 'filled' by the Spirit." Wood, *The Holy Spirit in the Old Testament*, 42.

[40]So B. S. Childs, *The Book of Exodus*, OTL (Philadelphia: Westminster, 1974), 540.

3:10 states concerning Othniel, "The Spirit of the LORD was on him." This statement is critical for understanding the role of the judges and the source of their authority and gifting. In this case "the empowering presence of the Spirit of God transforms this minor Israelite officer from Debir into the ruler . . . of Israel and the conqueror of a world-class enemy."[41] He was empowered to prevail in war against Cushan-rishathaim, the king of Mesopotamia. Likewise, when the Ammonites oppressed the eastern tribes, "the Spirit of the LORD came on Jeph-thah" (Judg 11:29). He was enabled to raise up and lead a victorious army to rescue the people of Israel from the Ammonites.

In Judg 6:34, "the Spirit of the LORD enveloped [Hb. "clothed"] Gideon," as he raised up an army to defeat the Midianites. The idiom "enveloped" is a more dramatic representation of that which occurred with Othniel and illustrates how a man doing all he could to avoid the leadership role can become courageous enough to destroy a Baal cult site and become a victorious military leader. Judg 14:6 records that "the Spirit of the LORD rushed upon" Samson, empowering him with enormous strength to tear a lion apart "as one tears a young goat" (ESV). A short time later in the narrative, "the Spirit of the LORD rushed upon" Samson again, and he slaughtered the male residents of a Philistine town (Judg 14:19 ESV). In Judg 15:14, the Spirit rushed upon Samson, enabling him to escape the Philistines and kill 1,000 men. So the Spirit "rushed upon" Samson on three different occasions. In each of these cases, the Spirit coming upon Samson is intentional, purposeful, and of limited duration.

The active role of the Spirit as the instrument of salvation history is most apparent with the judges. The judge needed special empowerment to carry out his assigned tasks and bring about the result that God wanted, namely, the saving of Israel. In the case of the four judges mentioned above, the Spirit came upon them, leaving no doubt that the Lord was at work to save His people according to His plan. Eichrodt notes,

> The unifying factors behind all these varied phenomena were first, that in them men saw the radiance of a higher kind of life, translating Man into direct contact with the divine world, and secondly,

---

[41] D. I. Block, *Judges, Ruth*, NAC 6 (Nashville: B&H, 1999), 155.

that they all occurred in the service of the establishment of the kingdom of God in Israel.[42]

The judges were empowered by the Spirit to rescue the tribes of Israel from their oppressors. In these cases the Spirit of the Lord came upon a man who led a violent uprising. The presence of the Spirit therefore was the personal manifestation of divine deliverance for the Israelites and divine judgment on the Canaanite nations. What then can be made of assertions by pneumatological inclusivists that the omnipresence of the Spirit represents the "power of love at work in the world"?[43] In many cases the presence of the Spirit may bring blessing, but it may also bring judgment. Pinnock and Yong are guilty of reducing the Spirit to a presence of blessing in their haste to affirm both the uniform love of God for all people and God's universal salvific will manifest in the omnipresence of the Spirit. Such a reduction flattens the biblical narratives of judgment and cursing, and it distorts the activity of the Holy Spirit.

With the judges the Spirit came upon men at critical junctures in salvation history to rescue Israel in order to further God's grand redemptive purposes. Empowerment of the judges was not an arbitrary, independent, or *ad hoc* activity. Rather, the Spirit was driving redemptive history toward the incarnation, the crucifixion, and the glorification of the Son.

Civil Rulers   Four individuals are specified in the Old Testament as uniquely empowered by the Holy Spirit for the express purpose of governing and leading the people of Israel: Moses (Num 11:17–29), Joshua (Num 27:18; Deut 34:9), Saul (1 Sam 11:6; 16:14), and David (1 Sam 16:13; Ps 51:11). The Spirit-empowerment of Moses is made

---

[42]Eichrodt, *Theology of the Old Testament*, 2:51. Interestingly, Eichrodt believes that, given the supernatural nature of Spirit empowerment to save, it would be easy for the nation of Israel to lapse into an intrusive mysticism. What kept the nation within the boundaries of truth was the "close association of the spirit and the word" (2:64).

[43]Pinnock, *Flame of Love*, 52. A further example of a reductionistic generalization that cannot account for all the biblical data is Pinnock's assertion that the Spirit is "the power that brings God's plans into effect, as a gentle but powerful presence, communicating divine energies in the world and aiming at increasing levels of participating in the fellowship of love." Ibid., 61. While this is certainly true in some cases, it cannot account for the work of Spirit in all cases, and it therefore cannot be used as a controlling idea in interpreting the ministry of the Spirit. Cf. A. Yong, *Beyond the Impasse: Toward a Pneumatological Theology of the Religions* (Grand Rapids: Baker, 2003), 37. Yong cites Ps 139:7–10 with reference to the omnipresence of the Spirit but says only that "because the divine Spirit is universally present and active that God is not only Creator, but also Re-creator, or Redeemer and Savior" (ibid., 38).

clear by the fascinating account of the 70 elders of Israel being empowered during the desert wanderings in Numbers 11. In this pericope the grumbling of the children of Israel over their food situation became too great for Moses, and he cried out for help. The Lord responded by telling Moses to gather 70 elders of Israel and that He would "take some of the Spirit who is on you and put the Spirit on them. They will help you bear the burden of the people" (Num 11:17).

Two initial observations must be made. First, the Spirit of the Lord was already "on" Moses.[44] Though the immediate context gives no indication as to whether the Spirit was continuously on Moses, the Spirit given to the elders was already in some sense on Moses. Second, Moses appears to be the only individual at this time empowered by the Spirit for this ministry. Endowing the Spirit was not a simple reference to the wisdom of Jethro in Exod 18:25–26. The purpose was not merely a sharing of administration but a sharing of the Spirit necessary to attend to such matters. In the plan of God, Moses was the key figure in the revelatory work of God at this time. The sharing of the Spirit is significant because it indicates that the endowment that had previously been only on Moses was to be given to the elders as well.[45]

Standing at the traditional place of revelation, the entrance to the tent of meeting, Moses gathered the 70 men around the tent, where the Lord came down in a cloud and spoke to him. At this time that the Lord "took some of the Spirit that was on Moses and placed the Spirit on the 70 elders" (Num 11:24–25).[46] The elders immediately began to prophesy as validation that the Spirit had come upon them, but such ecstatic utterance did not characterize their ministry for "they never did it again." The Spirit also rests upon Eldad and Medad, two elders

---

[44]So T. R. Ashley, *The Book of Numbers*, NICOT (Grand Rapids: Eerdmans, 1993), 211.

[45]So R. Dennis Cole, *Numbers*, NAC 3b (Nashville: B&H, 2000), 189.

[46]There is some debate over whether the endowment of the Spirit to the elders caused a reduction in Moses' Spirit-endowment. Cole is representative of those who believe otherwise when he writes, "This distribution of the Spirit was carried out by God and as such did not diminish that portion of the Spirit that had rested upon Moses previously. . . . This impartation was a unique gift of God upon the leaders and scribes that would enable them to assist Moses in giving spiritual oversight and supervision to this large rebellious congregation." Ibid., 192–93. Levine believes that the passage indicates that God withdrew some of the Spirit from Moses and gave it to the elders. B. A. Levine, *Numbers 1–20*, AB 4A (New York: Doubleday, 1993), 313. Calvin believed that Moses was being punished when the Lord divided his Spirit between Moses and the elders. J. Calvin, *Commentaries on the Four Last Books of Moses*, trans. C. W. Bingham (Grand Rapids: Eerdmans, 1950), 4:25. Moses' statement in Num 11:29 makes it very difficult to accept any interpretation that sees the giving of the Spirit as somehow punitive toward Moses or that it diminishes Moses' share of the Spirit in any way.

who had not gathered at the tent of meeting, who prophesied in turn in the camp (Num 11:26). Joshua prevailed upon Moses to make them stop, but Moses responded, "Are you jealous on my account? If only all the LORD's people were prophets, and the LORD would place His Spirit on them" (Num 11:29).

The purpose behind the prophesying of the elders is clear from the context, in particular the duration of the prophesying and Moses' response. The basic meaning of the verb *nb'* is "to behave like a prophet, act prophetically, appear as a prophet,"[47] so little can be discerned about the nature of their activity from the word itself. In 1 Samuel 10 and 19 the verb form is connected with behavior that "might be called abnormal or, better, 'ecstatic.'"[48] The author of Numbers is clear that the elders did not continue to prophesy.[49] It follows that the execution of their office and ministries did not require or include the exercise of prophetic utterance, regardless of the form. The prophesying, therefore, served as visible validation that the Spirit who had previously rested only upon Moses was also manifested on the 70 elders. The elders were gifted by the Holy Spirit to assist Moses in the leading of God's covenant people as they progressed toward the promised land in the short term and toward God's greater redemptive purposes in the long term. The prophesying was a one-time experience associated with their installation into office that served as a sign to the community that the same gifting that enabled Moses' authoritative leading had also been given to the 70.[50]

The response of Moses is telling with regard to the then-present and future ministry of the Holy Spirit, both then and later. Because the elders did not continue to prophesy, it must be concluded that it was not God's intention that everybody be a prophet. Moses' stated desire, "If only all the LORD's people were prophets" must be seen in light of the role of the elders' one-time prophesying and the rest of Moses' wish, where he explicitly declares what was implicit in the first part: "and the LORD would place His Spirit on them." In other

---

[47]E. Jenni and C. Westermann, *Theological Lexicon of the Old Testament* (Peabody, MA: Hendrickson, 1997).

[48]Ashley, *Book of Numbers*, 214. See also Levine, *Numbers 1–20*, 325; Keil and Delitzsch, *Pentateuch*, 3:71; G. J. Wenham, *Numbers: An Introduction and Commentary*, TOTC (Downers Grove, IL: InterVarsity, 1981), 109.

[49]So Ashley, *Book of Numbers*, 214; Keil and Delitzsch, *Pentateuch*, 3:71; R. B. Allen, "Numbers," in *EBC*, ed. Gaebelein, 2:796.

[50]So P. J. Budd, *Numbers*, WBC 5 (Waco, TX: Word, 1984), 128. See also Keil and Delitzsch, *Pentateuch*, 3:70.

words, Moses' desire was not that all of the Lord's people would hold office as prophets but that all of the Lord's people would be "prophets" in the sense of having the Spirit of the Lord resting upon them.

The eschatological implications of Moses' desire must not be missed. The experiences of the Holy Spirit under the old covenant became the basis for a greater work in the new covenant. The bestowal of the Holy Spirit and the response of the elders reflect "a pattern of God's working that is carried out in ultimate fashion in the outpouring of the Holy Spirit upon those who were gathered in Jerusalem on the Day of Pentecost."[51] It was Moses' prayer that all the Lord's people would one day have the Spirit.[52] This desire of Moses would later bloom into prophetic promise in Joel 2:28–29, where God would pour out His Spirit "on all humanity." Ezekiel prophesied of a time when the Lord would put His Spirit within the house of Israel and cause the people to walk in His statutes (Ezek 36:22–32). Jeremiah looked forward to the time when a new covenant would be inaugurated and the law no longer would be written on tablets of stone but would be written on the hearts of the whole nation (Jer 31:31–34). Sailhamer suggests that the narrative begins to introduce a different style of leadership at this point, a movement toward the Spirit-controlled office of the prophet.[53] What was only a "pious but vain hope" at this point in redemptive history would one day become the normative experience of all of the Lord's people following the events of Pentecost when Jesus Christ sent the Holy Spirit.[54]

The Spirit-empowerment of civic leaders is further illustrated in the accounts of Saul and David. When Saul was anointed king of Israel, Samuel prophesied that "the Spirit of the LORD will rush upon you, and you will prophesy with them and be turned into another man" (1 Sam 10:6 ESV). Shortly thereafter, he met a group of prophets, and "the Spirit of God rushed upon him, and he prophesied among them" (1 Sam 10:10 ESV). The transformative work of the Spirit, making this timid man "into another man," was evident almost immediately

---

[51]Cole, *Numbers*, 193. Cf. Allen, *Numbers*, 794.

[52]At this point in redemptive history, the total number of individuals the Bible makes a specific claim that the Spirit rested upon includes (perhaps) Joseph (Gen 41:38), Bezalel, Moses, Joshua (Num 27:18), Balaam (Num 23:5), and the 70 elders. The only place in the Old Testament where there is any mention of an experience of the Spirit by all the people of God is in the form of eschatological promise in Joel 2.

[53]Sailhamer, *Pentateuch as Narrative*, 386.

[54]Scobie, *Ways of Our God*, 274.

in the narrative, and it is clear that the coming of the Spirit was the efficient cause of all that ensued. When Saul learned about the plight of his kinsmen, the inhabitants of Jabesh Gilead, who were besieged by the Ammonite army of Nahash, "the Spirit of God rushed upon Saul . . . and his anger was greatly kindled" (1 Sam 11:6 ESV).[55] He rallied the disparate tribes of Israel (1 Sam 10:27), led them to a mighty victory over the Ammonites, and rescued the people of Jabesh Gilead (1 Sam 11:5–11), thus fulfilling his mandate as king over Israel and demonstrating his kingly worth. Saul's actions also united the tribes of Israel, and he was installed as king at Gilgal (1 Sam 11:12–14). All of this was done by the power of the Spirit of God who had rushed upon him.

When Saul sinned by not destroying the Amalekites, the Lord rejected Saul as king and Samuel was instructed to anoint David as king. When David was anointed, "the Spirit of the LORD rushed upon David from that day forward" (1 Sam 16:13 ESV). Concurrently, "the Spirit of the LORD had left Saul, and an evil spirit from the LORD began to torment him" (1 Sam 16:14). David's experience of the Spirit was therefore quantitatively different from that of Saul and serves to demonstrate the superiority of David's Spirit endowment.[56] With this in the background, the events of 1 Samuel 17 make perfect sense. Saul, from whom the Spirit had departed, refused to engage the Philistine champion, Goliath, in battle. By refusing to fight the enemies of Israel, Saul was in effect reneging on his responsibilities as king (1 Sam 9:16), thereby demonstrating his lack of kingly worth. David, in contrast, upon whom the Spirit of the Lord had come, engaged and defeated the Philistine champion so that "all the world will know that Israel has a God, and this whole assembly will know that is not by sword or by spear that the LORD saves" (1 Sam 17:46–47). With this one act he demonstrated his kingly worth by defeating the enemies of Israel and began to shepherd the people of Israel by teaching them the ways of the Lord.[57] All of this was done by the power of the Spirit of God who rushed upon him.

---

[55]Davis makes the point that the placement of the Spirit rushing upon Saul (10:6) in the middle of the narrative emphasizes the primary role of the Spirit in the deliverance of Jabesh and the leadership of Saul. D. R. Davis, *1 Samuel: Looking on the Heart* (Ross-Shire, UK: Christian Focus, 2000), 94.

[56]So R. W. Klein, *1 Samuel*, WBC 10 (Waco, TX: Word, 1983), 162; R. D. Bergen, *1, 2 Samuel*, NAC 7 (Nashville: B&H, 1996), 180.

[57]So Bergen, *1, 2 Samuel*, 196.

When we consider the place of this account in redemptive history, it is evident that the work of the Spirit was necessary to save the people of God. Because of the role of the Spirit in the lives of Saul and David, it is clear that the monarchy was not a merely human institution, but its efficacy rested in the ministrations and power of the Spirit of God.[58] The salvation of Israel, through the Spirit-empowered work of the first kings, was absolutely necessary for the plot line of redemptive history to advance and the Messianic line to continue. The monarchy, more than just the human choice of a fickle people, established, through the Spirit, a throne upon which the coming Christ would reign. David, far more than a godly man and great king, was established by the work of the Spirit as a type of the one whose reign would endure forever (2 Sam 7:8–17).

Another instance of Spirit-empowerment in redemptive history occurred when the exiles returned to the land. Zerubbabel, the governor, and Joshua, the high priest, led the people in their efforts to rebuild the temple. Their incentive to persevere in the work of repair was the promise of the Lord: "Work, for I am with you, declares the LORD of hosts, according to the covenant that I made with you when you came out of Egypt. My Spirit remains in your midst. Fear not" (Hag 2:4–5 ESV). Likewise, the prophet Zechariah encouraged Zerubbabel with the same promise of the Spirit's empowering presence: "'Not by strength or by might, but by My Spirit,' says the LORD of hosts" (Zech 4:6).

Prophets   The fourth and most significant classification of Spirit-empowered person was the prophet. As was demonstrated in the earlier discussion of Numbers 11, the Holy Spirit was especially identified with the prophets who were filled with the Spirit of God. Like the judges, the Spirit of the Lord came upon the prophet temporarily or for extended periods (e.g., Elijah, 2 Kgs 2:15), inspiring him to speak a specific message to God's intended audience, whether kings, leaders, or citizens of a nation.[59] With the prophets the Word-Spirit link is developed even further. God spoke to and through the prophet, and

---

[58] So W. Brueggemann, *First and Second Samuel*, Interpretation (Louisville, KY: John Knox, 1990), 75.

[59] Scripture is specific concerning the temporary empowerment of Azariah (2 Chr 15:1–7), Jahaziel (2 Chr 20:14–17), Zechariah (2 Chr 24:20), Balaam (Num 24:2), and Amasai (1 Chr 12:18). In each of these cases, the pattern is consistent: "The Spirit of the Lord came upon . . ." or "the Spirit of the Lord clothed . . . ."

when the Word came, it invaded and captured the prophet (Jer 20:7–9).[60] Often the Spirit empowered the prophets to do mighty deeds, usually in the context of authenticating their message (e.g., 2 Kgs 2:9,15–16). At times the Spirit of God would enable the interpretation of dreams and visions (Gen 41:38; Dan 4:8–9,18; 5:11–14). As with the judges, the coming of the Spirit signified that the empowerment of God had come upon an individual to accomplish something that God wanted done. The primary task of the prophet was to call the people of Israel back to the covenant.[61] It was the Spirit of the Lord who inspired, empowered, and authenticated his message.[62] The relationship between the Spirit of God and the Word of God is seen most explicitly in the Old Testament prophet (e.g., Moses in Num 11:17–29; 24:2). The link is sometimes only implicit, as when Jeremiah argues in 5:13 that the prophets are nothing but wind and that the breath of the Lord is not in them, but this reference only reinforces the necessary link between Word and Spirit.[63] For example, in Isa 59:21, God said to the prophet Isaiah, "My Spirit who is on you, and My words that I have put in your mouth, will not depart out of your mouth."[64] Indeed, this passage (Isa 59:15–21) speaks to the need of a great covenant mediator, one in whom is the Spirit and the Word of God. Many of the prophetic messages were inscripturated, again under the inspiration of the Holy Spirit (2 Tim 3:16; 1 Pet 1:10–12). With the prophets, "in the marvelous world of the *ruach*, by far the most prominent feature was the spiritual and personal operation of the covenant God, with his call to commitment and decision. For among all the wonders of the Spirit the proclamation of the word of Yahweh came more and more to take the central place."[65]

---

[60]So Bobrinskoy, *Mystery of the Trinity*, 31.

[61]For a description of the OT prophetic task, see P. R. House, *Old Testament Theology* (Downers Grove, IL: InterVarsity, 1998), 251.

[62]Ezekiel and Micah are the only inscripturated prophets who make an explicit claim of Spirit-empowerment like the judges do. Ezekiel is "unusually conscious" of his Spirit empowerment when he writes, "And as he spoke to me, the Spirit entered into me and set me on my feet" (Ezek 2:2 ESV; cf. 3:12,14; 37:1), while Micah claims, "I am filled with power, with the Spirit of the Lord" (Mic 3:8 ESV). Wood, *Holy Spirit in the Old Testament*, 46. That the other inscripturated prophets are inspired by the Holy Spirit is evident from Zech 7:12 and 2 Tim 3:16. Joseph and Daniel are attributed by pagan leaders as having the Spirit of God based on their ability to interpret dreams and visions (Gen 41:37; Dan 5:14).

[63]So G. D. Badcock, *Light of Truth & Fire of Love: A Theology of the Holy Spirit* (Grand Rapids: Eerdmans, 1997), 17.

[64]See also Isa 42:1–4; 49:1–6; 50:4.

[65]Eichrodt, *Theology of the Old Testament*, 2:53.

Whereas the giving of the Spirit in the Old Testament was an exceptional occurrence, much of the eschatological vision granted by the Spirit to the prophets focused on the future work of the Spirit. The promise of relationship with God by the Spirit was extended to the people of God in the messianic age. Such a relationship could not be based on human effort or obedience; it had to be the work of the Spirit. His coming in the messianic age would bring renewal and life. For example, in the context of judgment, Isaiah offered a word of hope when "the Spirit from heaven is poured out on us. Then the desert will become an orchard, and the orchard will seem like a forest" (Isa 32:15; cf. 34:16; Ezek 39:29).[66] What was once barren and under condemnation will flourish with "justice" and "righteousness" (Isa 32:16–17). The Spirit who worked in creation (Gen 1:2) and is the life-giver (Isa 40:7; 42:5) is the "Agent in the regeneration which will mark the messianic future."[67] When God sends His Spirit in the future age, the whole world will be made fruitful and abundant.

The coming of the Spirit will cause personal transformation, a change in personal dispositions. God promised, "For I will pour water on the thirsty land, and streams on the dry ground; I will pour out My Spirit on your descendants and My blessing on your offspring" (Isa 44:3). Even though the Lord will give up Israel to "total destruction" (Isa 43:28), the promises of the covenants had not been abrogated. God will send "his own Spirit, the energy and vitality that made the world."[68] The future, which had heretofore been in doubt, was assured because the Lord will act by sending His Spirit. Because of the Spirit's work, a day will come when many will be anxious to identify themselves with the Lord, to call on the Lord. People will delight in the Lord, claiming "I am the LORD's" (Isa 44:5; cf. 1 Cor 12:3).

The personal transformation the Spirit will bring is the sign of the renewal of the covenant. Just as the prior covenants had signs (e.g., a rainbow for the Noahic covenant and circumcision for the Abrahamic covenant), so the sign of the new covenant was the sending of

---

[66]The use of the word "until" (*'ad*) in Isa 32:15 serves to demonstrate the contrast between the present age and the age to come. God will pour his Spirit on the people and a change will come. See B. S. Childs, *Isaiah*, OTL (Louisville, KY: Westminster John Knox, 2001), 241.

[67]J. Alec Motyer, *Isaiah: An Introduction and Commentary*, TOTC (Downers Grove, IL: InterVarsity, 1999), 206.

[68]J. N. Oswalt, *The Book of Isaiah: Chapters 40–66*, NICOT (Grand Rapids: Eerdmans, 1998), 166. See also id., *Isaiah*, NIVAC (Grand Rapids: Zondervan, 2003), 493; and P. D. Hanson, *Isaiah 40–66*, Interpretation (Louisville, KY: Westminster John Knox, 1995), 83.

the Spirit.[69] In fact, the power of the new covenant promise coalesced around a unique and expansive sending of the Spirit that was also tied to cleansing with water:

> I will also sprinkle clean water on you, and you will be clean. I will cleanse you from all your impurities and all your idols. I will give you a new heart and put a new spirit within you; I will remove your heart of stone and give you a heart of flesh. I will place My Spirit within you and cause you to follow My statutes and carefully observe My ordinances (Ezek 36:25–27; cf. 11:19; Jer 31:33–34).[70]

The sprinkling with water calls to mind the external rites necessary for priestly worship (Num 19:13,20), but it is symbolic of an inward cleansing.[71] Behavior modification is not enough. There has to be a personal transformation that is brought about by the will of God. He who was formerly rebellious or unresponsive to the Lord will be given a new heart of vital, warm flesh, rather than dead, cold stone. In short, he will be given an entirely new nature and the Lord's own Spirit to animate and motivate him. The Spirit will cause those He indwells to walk in the statutes of the Lord; they will have both the will and the ability to follow the commands of the Lord.[72] Bobrinskoy notes that, "The Word becomes a walkable path for the human being, prepared and renewed by the Spirit."[73]

The Word-Spirit interrelationship is dramatically represented in Ezekiel's Spirit-inspired vision of a valley full of dry bones. The Lord asked Ezekiel, "Can these bones live?" (Ezek 37:3). The question is rhetorical. There was no trace of life in the dry bones, nor was there hope. Israel was the same—dead, lifeless, and without hope, until God promised to "put breath in" them (Ezek 37:6). The prophet was instructed, "Prophesy to the breath, prophesy, son of man. Say to it:

---

[69] So W. VanGemeren, *The Progress of Redemption: The Story of Salvation from Creation to the New Jerusalem* (Grand Rapids: Baker, 1988), 303.

[70] This connection between cleansing with water and the sending of the Spirit is picked up by Jesus in John 3:5 and Paul in Titus 3:5–6. See Ferguson, *Holy Spirit*, 122.

[71] See L. E. Cooper Sr., *Ezekiel*, NAC 17 (Nashville: B&H, 1994), 316.

[72] See I. M. Duguid, *Ezekiel*, NIVAC (Grand Rapids: Zondervan, 1999), 415. See also L. C. Allen, *Ezekiel 20–48*, WBC 29 (Waco, TX: Word, 1990), 179.

[73] Bobrinskoy, *Mystery of the Trinity*, 33. Bobrinskoy elaborates, "Thus prophecy, marked in some elect by an extraordinary presence of the Word and the Spirit, announces an outpouring of the Spirit, to know and fulfill the Word of God—an effusion simultaneously upon the entire people and upon each person; upon each and all, inseparably" (ibid.).

This is what the Lord GOD says: Breath, come from the four winds and breathe into these slain so that they may live!" (Ezek 37:9). Ezekiel prophesied to the bones, the breath entered them, and they lived (Ezek 37:10). The same Spirit who inspired the word of the prophet would bring life to a dead people. When the prophet prophesied, the bones heard the Word of God, and life came when the Spirit entered them. Only the *rûaḥ* of God can bring life, and this will be accomplished when God fulfills His promise to "put My Spirit in you, and you will live, and I will settle you in your own land" (Ezek 37:14).

The expansiveness of this divine action—without age, gender, or class distinction—is clarified by the prophet Joel with the Lord's incredible promise:

> After this I will pour out My Spirit on all humanity; then your sons and your daughters will prophesy, your old men will have dreams, and your young men will see visions. I will even pour out My Spirit on the male and female slaves in those days (Joel 2:28–29).

The context of this prophecy is a discourse on the day of the Lord. God's saving presence will manifest itself in something far greater than restored crops and material wealth (Joel 2:23–26); the blessing of the Lord will be evidenced by the granting of His presence in the pouring out of His Spirit.[74] One cannot read this promise without hearing echoes of Numbers 11 in the background.[75] Consistent with the Numbers 11 pericope, endowment of the Spirit will manifest itself in prophetic utterance.[76] In Moses' time the Spirit fell on 70 men in Israel, causing Moses to proclaim, "If only all the LORD's people were prophets, and the LORD would place His Spirit on them" (Num 11:29). On this future day Moses' wish will be fulfilled: the Spirit will be poured out on "all

---

[74]L. C. Allen, *The Books of Joel, Obadiah, Jonah, and Micah*, NICOT (Grand Rapids: Eerdmans, 1976), 98.

[75]See D. A. Garrett, *Hosea, Joel*, NAC 19A (Nashville: B&H, 1997), 368; Allen, *Books of Joel, Obadiah, Jonah, and Micah*, 99; D. Stuart, *Hosea-Jonah*, WBC 31 (Waco, TX: Word, 1987), 230; and J. Barton, *Joel and Obadiah: A Commentary* (Louisville, KY: Westminster John Knox, 2001), 95.

[76]Finley suggests that the prophesying, dreaming, and seeing of visions denotes "a new era of revelation." T. J. Finley, *Joel, Amos, Obadiah*, WEC (Chicago: Moody, 1990), 72–73. As will be demonstrated below, the Messianic Age and new covenant era are marked by a radical qualitative and quantitative increase in the activity of the Spirit. Nevertheless, I do not believe that Joel was attempting to give a taxonomy of the Spirit's future work. Rather, consistent with the validating work of prophecy for Spirit-endowment in Numbers 11, the primary purpose behind the prophesying, dreaming, and seeing of visions is the demonstration of the reality of the coming of the Spirit.

flesh," encompassing the young and old, male and female, slave and free (cf. Gal 3:28). Though the distinguishing mark of this promise is its expansiveness, it is universal in that the Spirit is poured out on all Israel, not all humanity.[77] The promise will be fulfilled in "your sons and your daughters," "your old men," and "your young men."

The Old Testament prophecies about the Spirit focus on the saving deeds of God and in the human agents upon whom the Spirit will rest to carry out these deeds. Centrality is given to the Messiah, the one anointed by the Spirit of God to save finally the people of God and effect lasting change, ushering in the final age. Isaiah records many prophecies of the Spirit-filled Messiah:

> Then a shoot will grow from the stump of Jesse, and a branch from his roots will bear fruit. The Spirit of the LORD will rest on Him—a Spirit of wisdom and understanding, a Spirit of counsel and strength, a Spirit of knowledge and of the fear of the LORD. His delight will be in the fear of the LORD. He will not judge by what He sees with His eyes, He will not execute justice by what He hears with His ears, but He will judge the poor righteously and execute justice for the oppressed of the land. He will strike the land with discipline from his mouth, and He will kill the wicked with a command [*rûaḥ*] from His lips. Righteousness and faithfulness will be a belt around His waist (Isa 11:1–5; cf. Isa 11:1–10; 28:5; 42:1; 48:16; 59:21; 61:1).

This prophecy focuses on the gifts, attributes, and acts of the Messiah. He will be given a Spirit of wisdom, understanding, counsel, might, knowledge, and the fear of the Lord. These are all characteristics of the Lord and are attributes that a king must have if he is to rule wisely and justly. The Spirit-anointed one will also exemplify all that is promised in personal transformation when the Spirit comes, for He will have a capacity for delight that is completely absorbed in the Lord (Isa 44:5). If Messiah is able to obey the Word of God, it is because the Spirit rests upon Him. He will perceive correctly and rule wisely with correct motivations. He will minister not by fallen human nature but by the power of Spirit.

---

[77]Garrett, *Hosea, Joel*, 369. "For Joel, the gift of the Spirit to Israel was vindication of their status as the people of God as well as the source of their power to reconstitute as a community of obedience under God's favor."

The Messiah's dependence on the Holy Spirit is again prophesied in Isaiah:

The Spirit of the Lord GOD is on Me, because the LORD has anointed Me to bring good news to the poor. He has sent Me to heal the brokenhearted, to proclaim liberty to the captives, and freedom to the prisoners; to proclaim the year of the LORD's favor (Isa 61:1–2).

The promise of the Spirit-anointed one does not begin a new chapter in God's interaction with humanity but is a major thread in the fabric of redemptive history. Throughout Isaiah, the Spirit is seen as the conveyor of justice and righteousness (e.g., Isa 11:2; 32:15–16; 42:1; 44:3; 48:16; 59:21).[78] The promise of the Servant reaffirms the covenant given to David in 2 Samuel 7. The Spirit and Servant come together in the Spirit-anointed one, the Messiah. He is anointed by the Spirit for the ministry of the word, the preaching of "good news," the proclamation of favor and vengeance.[79] Vos comments on the hope surrounding the coming of the Messiah and the Spirit: "Still the prophet does not mean to describe what the Spirit is for the Messiah Himself, but what through the Messiah He is for the people."[80]

The Holy Spirit is the one who heralds the coming of the future world which is ruled by Messiah, the Spirit-anointed one. It is the Spirit who inaugurates that age (Joel 2:28–32). The Holy Spirit is also the source of the future new life. The Spirit becomes characteristic of the eschatological state itself (Isa 32:15–17; 44:3; 59:21; Ezek 36:27; 37:14; 39:29). In that age the sending of the Spirit is explicitly designated not of the Messiah but from God, although the statements occur in prophecies that speak of the Messiah.[81] In Rabbinic theology, the role of the Messiah with respect to the Spirit is broadened. He is not merely the Spirit-anointed one, but the one through whom the Spirit will be communicated to others. The Messiah pours out on

---

[78]Oswalt, *Book of Isaiah: Chapters 40–66*, 564.

[79]Oswalt notes that the Servant's "most potent instrument is the word of his mouth." Oswalt, *Book of Isaiah: Chapters 40–66*, 563–64.

[80]G. Vos, "Paul's Eschatological Concept of the Spirit," in *Redemptive History and Biblical Interpretation: The Shorter Writings of Geerhardus Vos*, ed. R. Gaffin (Phillipsburg, NJ: P&R, 1980), 95.

[81]Vos, "Paul's Eschatological Concept of the Spirit," 95–97.

people the Spirit of grace so that henceforth they walk in the ways of God.[82]

Pneumatological inclusivist Stanley Samartha suggests that the inspiration of the Old Testament prophets by the Holy Spirit opens the door to the Spirit working in world religions. Samartha writes, "By acknowledging that the Spirit was at work and spoke through the prophets of Israel before Christ, the door is perhaps a little more open for the prophets of other faiths to be smuggled into God's *oikoumene*."[83] But Samartha is mistaken because he fails to recognize the clear reciprocity between the Word of God and the Holy Spirit in the prophets. This relationship will become fully manifest in the person and ministry of Jesus Christ, in whom the Holy Spirit constitutes the "messianic unction."[84] Furthermore, Samartha does not recognize that the prophetic burden of the prophets was ultimately Christocentric. Pneumatological inclusivists cannot appeal to the work of the Spirit in the lives of the prophets to assert any form of hypostatic independence or relative autonomy for the Spirit. The prophets were empowered by the Spirit to act as change agents among God's covenant people to the end that redemptive history continued toward the incarnation, crucifixion, and resurrection of the Son of God. The prophets were inspired by the Spirit to speak of a future where the Messiah, the incarnate Son of God, would reign in glory.

THE SON AND THE HOLY SPIRIT: INCARNATION

Though the Holy Spirit was active from creation through the old covenant, empowering particular individuals who were critical to God's redemptive plan, the promise of future restoration involved a far greater work of the Spirit than what had been previously experienced. That which was anticipated, even yearned for, by the prophets would find fulfillment in the Messianic Age. The Gospels offer a record of the coming of the Messianic King. Jesus is the one to whom the biblical story had been pointing from its beginning pages (e.g., Gen 3:15; 12:1–3; 49:8–12). Because the incarnation, ministry, crucifixion, resurrection, and ascension of Jesus Christ are the hinges upon which human and redemptive history turn, the work of the Holy Spirit had

---

[82]Ibid., 98. Vos is interacting with biblical texts such as Joel 2:28–29 and apocryphal texts such as Judith 24:2.

[83]S. J. Samartha, "The Holy Spirit and People of Other Faiths," *ER* 42 (1990): 256.

[84]Bobrinskoy, *Mystery of the Trinity*, 35.

been focused on driving history toward the advent of Christ. Jesus fulfills the promise of a restored kingdom (cf. Isa 9:6–7; Ezek 37:24–28; Mic 5:1–5; Mal 3:1–6), and in Christ—the Spirit-anointed one *par excellence*—the promise of the Holy Spirit is inaugurated.

The Use of *Pneuma* in the New Testament

Evidence for the fulfillment of the promise of increased activity of the Spirit in the Messianic era can be obtained by comparing references to the Spirit in the New Testament and the Old Testament. Both *rûaḥ* and *pneuma* carry the same ambiguity of multiple meanings: "wind," "breath," or "spirit." Whereas there are just 388 uses of *rûaḥ* in the Old Testament and only approximately 100 of them refer to the *rûaḥ* of God,[85] there are 379 uses of *pneuma* in the New Testament with over 260 referring to God's *pneuma*. Furthermore, though there are only two passages in the entire Old Testament that use the collocation "Holy Spirit" or "Spirit of Holiness" (Ps 51:11; Isa 63:10–11), the Spirit of God is referred to as the "Holy Spirit" 90 times in the New Testament.[86] Implications of the increase in references to the Holy Spirit will be discussed in "The Son and the Holy Spirit: Church Age."

The Holy Spirit and the Conception and Birth of Christ

It is no mere tautology to state that it is not by virtue of the deity of Jesus but rather by the anointing of the Holy Spirit that Jesus is the Christ. Hawthorne comments on the importance of the Holy Spirit in the life of Jesus:

> The Holy Spirit in the life of Jesus is but one additional proof of the genuineness of his humanity, for the significance of the Spirit in his life lies precisely in this: that the Holy Spirit was the divine power by which Jesus overcame his human limitations, rose above his human weakness, and won out over his human mortality.[87]

The involvement of the Holy Spirit in the life of the Anointed One in the Synoptic Gospels begins with the conception of Jesus Christ. In

---

[85]Of those 100 references to the Spirit of God in the Old Testament, approximately 40 refer to future pneumatological activity in the messianic age.

[86]The number increases to 91 if you include "the Spirit of holiness" in Rom 1:4.

[87]G. F. Hawthorne, *The Presence & the Power: The Significance of the Holy Spirit in the Life and Ministry of Jesus* (Dallas: Word, 1991), 35.

Matt 1:18, Mary was told that she will come to be with child "by the Holy Spirit," that is, by the agency of the Holy Spirit.[88] When Mary asked Gabriel how she could conceive, she was told, "The Holy Spirit will come upon you, and the power of the Most High will overshadow you. Therefore the holy One to be born will be called the Son of God" (Luke 1:35).[89] The essential interrelationship of pneumatology and Christology is evident from the beginning of Christ's life and ministry, and His divine conception marked Him out as the Son of God.[90] The activity of the Holy Spirit in the conception parallels the creation account where the Spirit was "hovering over the surface of the waters" (Gen 1:2; cf. Exod 40:34–35; Num 9:18).[91] Significantly, the angel Gabriel attributes the holiness of Christ to the agency of the Holy Spirit. "Wisdom" and "understanding" were prophesied as characteristic of the Spirit-filled Messiah in Isa 11:2. Even with a relative lack of information concerning the boyhood of Jesus, Luke does tell us that the young Jesus was said to be "filled with wisdom" (Luke 2:40; 2:52) while the temple teachers were "astounded at His understanding" (Luke 2:47).

The work of the Holy Spirit in glorifying Christ even occurred while Jesus was *in utero*. When Elizabeth, the mother of John, the Messiah's forerunner, saw Mary, John leaped in Elizabeth's womb, while she herself was "filled with the Holy Spirit" (Luke 1:41). By inspiration of the Spirit, she confessed the baby carried by Mary as "my Lord" and pronounced a blessing upon Mary (Luke 1:42–45). Zechariah, the father of John, was likewise "filled with the Holy Spirit" (Luke 1:67), and he also prophesied concerning the advent of Messiah, a "horn of salvation" who would one day redeem His people (Luke 1:68–69). The Spirit also oversaw the dedication of the baby Jesus. Simeon, "guided by the Spirit," went into the temple, took Jesus

---

[88]This is the first reference in the NT to the Spirit of God as "Holy." Morris notes that this adjective is not applied to the Spirit by Philo or Josephus. It is a distinctively Christian idea. L. Morris, *The Gospel According to Matthew*, PNTC (Grand Rapids: Eerdmans, 1992), 27.

[89]Compare the announcement of Elizabeth's conception of John: Whereas John was "filled with the Holy Spirit" from the womb (Luke 1:15), Jesus is conceived by the Spirit. This activity of the Holy Spirit points to the superiority of Christ over John. R. H. Stein, *Luke*, NAC 24 (Nashville: B&H, 1992), 85.

[90]D. A. Hagner, *Matthew 1–13*, WBC 33A (Waco, TX: Word, 1993), 17. See also C. L. Blomberg, *Matthew*, NAC 22 (Nashville: Broadman, 1992), 58; I. H. Marshall, *Commentary on Luke*, NIGTC (Grand Rapids: Eerdmans, 1978), 70–71.

[91]D. L. Bock, *Luke 1:1–9:50*, ECNT (Grand Rapids: Baker, 1994), 121. Stein denies any allusion to the covering of the Shekinah glory here. Stein, *Luke*, 85.

in his arms, blessed God, and prophesied over the child concerning His future salvific work (Luke 2:27–35). Even prior to His public ministry, the Holy Spirit was working to draw attention and bring honor to Jesus.

The Holy Spirit and the Baptism of Christ

The next reference to Christ and the Holy Spirit comes in the preaching ministry of John the Baptist. Luke 1:13–17 makes clear that John was "filled with the Holy Spirit" from the womb for the purpose of making "ready for the Lord a prepared people"; that is, the Holy Spirit filled John to enable him to preach a message of repentance that made the people ready for Christ and His kingdom, and then he was to point out Jesus when he began His ministry (John 1:29,36). Whereas John baptized with "water for repentance," the coming one would "baptize . . . with the Holy Spirit and fire" (Matt 3:11; cf. Mark 1:7–8; Luke 3:16–17). Jesus' baptism was to be no mere ritual. He brought the gift of the Spirit. It was prophesied that the Davidic Messiah would have the Spirit (Isa 11:1–2), but "no mere mortal could pour out the Spirit."[92] While echoes of the pouring out of the Spirit prophesied in Isaiah and Joel whispered in the background, John informed the crowds that the one who brings the Holy Spirit will also bring judgment. The risen Christ repeated the Baptist's words just prior to His ascension: "John baptized with water, but you will be baptized with the Holy Spirit not many days from now" (Acts 1:5). Jesus kept His promise on the day of Pentecost.

John's baptism of Jesus, where the "Holy Spirit descended on Him in a physical appearance like a dove" (Luke 3:22), is prominently recorded in all four Gospels (Matt 3:13–17; Mark 1:9–11; Luke 3:21–22; John 1:29–34).[93] When Jesus was baptized by John, the one who was to "baptize with the Holy Spirit" was anointed by the Holy Spirit. This remarkable event witnessed the simultaneous presence of all three members of the Trinity. The Christ-centered nature of redemptive history is evident in that while all three members of the Trinity were present, the Spirit served to identify the Son, while the Father proclaimed Jesus to be His Son (Luke 3:22; Matt 3:17). Killian

---

[92]C. S. Keener, *A Commentary on the Gospel of Matthew* (Grand Rapids: Eerdmans, 1999), 130. Keener suggests that this and John's declarations reveal a high Christology.

[93]Although John does not record the baptism event *per se*, he does refer to the anointing of the Spirit that took place at the baptism as the identifying mark of the Messiah.

McDonnell summarizes the Christocentrism of the Spirit's mission: "The Spirit who begets and the Spirit who is communicated in baptism comes from above, from the Father, but there is no act or manifestation of the Spirit which is not through Christ."[94]

Significantly, the Spirit was seen as coming down on Jesus (Matt 3:17).[95] The Baptist testified that the Spirit "rested" (*emeinen*, the aorist of *menō*; cf. John 15:4–10) on Him (John 1:32). In a manner completely in keeping with the identification of the Messiah as the Spirit-anointed one (Isa 11:1; 61:1), John was told to look for the one on whom the Spirit remains. Carson comments, "Small wonder, then, that some visible descent of the Spirit on Jesus served as the God-given sign by which the Baptist would know that this was the long-awaited Coming One."[96] Jesus was not only anointed with the Spirit, but the Spirit remained on Him.[97] Indeed, Jesus is the one to whom God gave the Spirit "without measure" (John 3:34). The Baptist was able to recognize the Messiah by His unique and close relationship with the Spirit. The Spirit-anointed one had arrived. John had witnessed the dawning of the Messianic Age.[98]

The Holy Spirit and the Temptation of Christ

Immediately after His baptism, Jesus was "full of the Holy Spirit, and was led by the Spirit in the wilderness for 40 days to be tempted by the Devil" (Luke 4:1; cf. Matt 4:1; Mark 1:12). All three Synoptists record the guidance of the Holy Spirit in the temptation narrative, indicating the importance of both the role of the temptation in Jesus' ministry and the role of the Holy Spirit in Jesus' trial. Jesus had just been anointed by the Spirit and declared by divine proclamation to be the Son of God. Each of the satanic temptations was therefore directed

---

[94] K. McDonnell, "A Trinitarian Theology of the Holy Spirit?" *TS* 46 (1985): 205.

[95] The Spirit-anointing of Jesus at His baptism raises the following question: What was the nature of the relationship between Christ and the Holy Spirit prior to his baptism? Hawthorne suggests that "this coming of the Spirit 'into' Jesus was something more, something even greater—a greater filling yet." Hawthorne, *Presence and the Power*, 127.

[96] D. A. Carson, *The Gospel According to John*, PNTC (Grand Rapids: Eerdmans, 1991), 151. See also T. Schreiner, *New Testament Theology: Magnifying God in Christ* (Grand Rapids: Baker, 2008), 437.

[97] Köstenberger notes that it is therefore "reasonable to assume that the Spirit remained with Jesus continually throughout his ministry." A. J. Köstenberger, *John*, ECNT (Grand Rapids: Baker, 2004), 70. See also G. M. Burge, *John*, NIVAC (Grand Rapids: Zondervan, 2000), 74; B. Witherington III and L. M. Ice, *The Shadow of the Almighty: Father, Son, and Spirit in Biblical Perspective* (Grand Rapids: Eerdmans, 2002), 112.

[98] G. T. Montague, *Holy Spirit: Growth of a Biblical Tradition* (Peabody, MA: Hendrickson, 1976), 242.

at Jesus' Sonship. The process of resisting Satan's temptations demonstrated how His incarnate Sonship was to be lived out.[99] Luke is careful to identify the activity of the Spirit prior to and after the temptations. Jesus was "led by the Spirit in the wilderness" (Luke 4:1) and "Jesus returned . . . in the power of the Spirit" (Luke 4:14). These two verses in Luke, which highlight the active role of the Holy Spirit, serve as an *inclusio* to the narrative. Bookended by statements affirming the guidance of the Spirit, the clear implication is that the Spirit was also active during the temptations themselves.[100] Jesus Christ, filled with the Spirit, stood up to Satan's temptations by quoting Scripture, which was inspired by the Spirit (2 Tim 3:16; Eph 6:17). In this response Jesus Christ, as the Spirit-filled one *par excellence*, also provides a trustworthy model for believers who must face temptation.

Jesus' time in the wilderness recalls the nation of Israel's sojourn in the wilderness where the people repeatedly failed to believe and honor God in the face of trial and temptation. Even the Scriptures that Jesus quoted demonstrate that the temptation narrative is to be seen as antitypical of Israel's sojourn in the desert. Each of His three quotations is taken from a section in Deuteronomy reminding Israel of its experience of testing in the wilderness (Deut 6:13,16; 8:3;). Where Israel, God's son, failed (Deuteronomy 8), Jesus, the Spirit-anointed Son, was victorious. Through the power of the Spirit of God and the Word of God, Jesus defeated Satan in the wilderness and began His public ministry.

The Holy Spirit and the Ministry of Christ

Fresh off His victory over Satan and temptation, Jesus returned to Galilee "in the power of the Spirit," and "news about Him spread throughout the entire vicinity" (Luke 4:14; literally, the "fame" of Jesus grew). As He taught in the synagogues in this Spirit-empowered state, the result was that He was "glorified by all" (Luke 4:15 ESV). The connection between Christ, the Holy Spirit, and glory ought not to be missed. When Jesus Christ ministered in the power of the Holy Spirit, the result was that Jesus Christ was glorified.[101]

---

[99]So R. T. France, *The Gospel of Matthew*, NICNT (Grand Rapids: Eerdmans, 2007), 127–28.

[100]See Hawthorne, *Presence and the Power*, 139; Stein, *Luke*, 145.

[101]The verb *doxazomenos* ("being glorified") is usually reserved for God alone. Only here does Luke use it of Jesus. Bock, *Luke 1:1–9:50*, 393.

Christ affirmed the critical role of the Holy Spirit in His life and work by inaugurating His public ministry by reading of the Spirit-anointed Messiah in Isa 61:1–2 (Luke 4:17–19). Looking back to His baptism (Luke 3:22), Jesus declared that "as you listen, this Scripture has been fulfilled" (Luke 4:21). In doing so, Jesus identified Himself not just as a prophet but as the fulfillment of messianic hope. Jesus was not merely the herald, but He was the one who would accomplish and bring salvation.[102] He was the one upon whom the Spirit rested and who had been anointed to preach, to heal, and to bring freedom. In quoting Isaiah, Jesus described the whole of His ministry. Every dimension of His work was dependent upon the empowering anointing of the Spirit. Again the reaction to Jesus' proclamation was that "they were all speaking well of Him and were amazed by the gracious words that came from His mouth" (Luke 4:22).[103]

In the Gospels, particularly the Synoptics, the Holy Spirit played a prominent role in the ministry of Jesus. Immediately following Jesus' announcement in Nazareth, Jesus taught with great authority (Luke 4:31) and exorcised a demon (Luke 4:33–35). The result is again significant: all the people were amazed at His authority and power (Luke 4:36). Jesus also healed Simon's mother-in-law (Luke 4:39) and all those who were "sick with various diseases," including other demon-possessed individuals (Luke 4:40–41). Ferguson notes, "Nothing is outside his dominion. The wonders He performs are accomplished in the energy and by the presence of the Holy Spirit."[104] The Holy Spirit did far more than empower and guide Jesus; He affected the totality of Jesus' being, including intelligence and emotions (e.g., Luke 2:40,52; 10:21; John 3:34–35).

The Gospels make numerous references to the power (*dunamis*) of Christ, which are implicit references to the power and authority of the Holy Spirit in Jesus.[105] The connection between the power of Christ and the presence of the Holy Spirit is clear in Luke. Mary was told, "The Holy Spirit will come upon you, and the power [*dunamis*] of the Most High will overshadow you" (Luke 1:35). Here, the Holy Spirit and the power of the Most High stand in synonymous parallel-

---

[102]Stein, *Luke*, 156.

[103]Ferguson therefore sees a connection between the Holy Spirit and the character of Jesus. Jesus was seen to be gracious because the Spirit of the Lord was upon him. *Holy Spirit*, 51.

[104]Ibid., 50.

[105]See Hawthorne, *Presence and the Power*, 54–60.

ism with one another.[106] Following His temptations in the wilderness, Jesus returned to Galilee and began His public ministry "in the power of the Spirit" (4:14). Thus when statements are made that Jesus had "the Lord's power to heal" (5:17) or that He exorcised demons and healed the masses because "power was coming out from Him" (6:19), it is evident that the source of that power was the Holy Spirit.[107]

The clearest statement made by Christ that He attributed His miraculous power to the Holy Spirit came in His dispute with Pharisees who had accused Him of being in league with Satan (Matt 12:22–32; cf. Mark 3:22–27; Luke 11:14–23). The literary context for this narrative is particularly informative. In Matt 12:9–14, Jesus healed a man with a withered hand on the Sabbath. The Pharisees, infuriated by their confrontation with Jesus and His subsequent healing action, began to plot His destruction. Jesus withdrew, but many people continued to follow Him (Matt 12:15–17). Significantly, Matthew ties that sequence of events to Isa 42:1–3, which identifies the Servant of the Lord as the one upon whom the Spirit is given. The Isaiah reference has the twofold purpose of tying Christ's power to the Spirit, which will be the point of confrontation in Matt 12:22–29, and to speak to the gentle and humble character of the messianic Servant, which will play a significant role in Christ's response to the Pharisees.

When Jesus delivered the demoniac, the people were amazed and rightly asked if the one who can do such things is the Messiah (Matt 12:23). The Pharisees acted quickly to stifle any talk of the Messiah, claiming that the miraculous healing should be attributed to Beelzebul, the prince of demons. Jesus responded by questioning the logic of such a strategy and then made an unequivocal statement: "If I drive out demons by the Spirit of God, then the kingdom of God has come to you" (Matt 12:28).[108] Jesus viewed His capacity to restore sight to the blind, heal the mute, and drive out the demonic as empowered by the Spirit of God. Such Spirit empowerment was constitutive of the prophesied messianic identity. The crowd had seen what the Pharisees refused to believe, that the miraculous ability of Jesus signaled

---

[106] So Stein, *Luke*, 85; Marshall, *Commentary on Luke*, 70; Bock, *Luke 1:1–9:50*, 121.

[107] So Stein, *Luke*, 176; see also Luke 1:17, 4:36; 8:46; 9:1; and 10:19; cf. Mark 5:30; Acts 10:38.

[108] Keener suggests that the Greek construction is better rendered, "Since I drive out demons by the Spirit, the kingdom has come on the scene." Keener, *Commentary on the Gospel of Matthew*, 364. In any case the contrast is absolute. Jesus substitutes the "Spirit of God" for "through Beelzebul" in 12:27 for the true agency of his work. Hagner, *Matthew 1–13*, 343.

the beginning of the Messianic Age. Years later the apostle Peter, in proclaiming the gospel to Cornelius, would introduce Jesus as the one whom "God anointed . . . with the Holy Spirit and with power, and how He went about doing good and curing all who were under the tyranny of the Devil, because God was with Him" (Acts 10:38). In summarizing the life and ministry of Christ, Peter points to the unique presence of the Holy Spirit.

For this reason Jesus' response to the Pharisees was so strong. Sin and blasphemy against Christ will be forgiven (Matt 12:31–32); the Spirit-anointed one "will not argue or shout" (12:18–21). But those who witnessed the working of the Spirit and attributed it to Satan, those who took the sign that constituted the Messiah *qua* Messiah and perverted it into a Satanic act, were confirmed in their unbelief, and there would be no forgiveness for them.[109] Sin against the Spirit was "not just a personal reaction to Jesus, but a rejection of the Spirit's ministry and therefore of the evidence that the kingdom has come and the new age has dawned."[110]

The role of the Holy Spirit in the ministry of Christ extended even to His death and resurrection. "Through the eternal Spirit" Christ "offered Himself without blemish to God" (Heb 9:14).[111] John Calvin provides the strongest interpretation of this passage when he declares that the death of Christ is to be regarded from the perspective of the power of the Spirit:

> Christ suffered as man, but in order that His death might effect our salvation it came forth from the power of the Spirit. The sacrifice

---

[109]So Morris, *Gospel According to Matthew*, 320; Hagner, *Matthew 1–13*, 347; Keener, *Commentary on the Gospel of Matthew*, 365.

[110]Ferguson, *Holy Spirit*, 51.

[111]This is the only verse that speaks of the Spirit's role in the death of Christ, and its interpretation is contested. It could refer to the Holy Spirit or to Christ's eternal spirit. The evidence is fairly balanced. W. L. Lane suggests that the relative clause "implies that he had been divinely empowered and sustained in his office" and "may be understood as a designation for the Holy Spirit." *Hebrews 9–13*, WBC 47b (Dallas: Word, 1991), 240. See also F. F. Bruce, *The Epistle to the Hebrews*, NICOT (Grand Rapids: Eerdmans, 1964), 216–17; and D. A. Hagner, *Hebrews*, NIBC (Grand Rapids: Eerdmans, 1977), 139–40. H. W. Attridge sees "eternal Spirit" as referring "to Christ and to the interior or spiritual quality of his sacrificial act." *The Epistle to the Hebrews* (Philadelphia: Fortress, 1989), 251. See also G. A. Cole, *He Who Gives Life: The Doctrine of the Holy Spirit* (Wheaton, IL: Crossway, 2007), 166–67; P. E. Hughes, *A Commentary on the Epistle to the Hebrews* (Grand Rapids: Eerdmans, 1977), 359; and B. F. Westcott, *The Epistle to the Hebrews: The Greek Text with Notes and Essays* (London: MacMillan, 1929), 261–62. See C. C. Ryrie, *The Holy Spirit* (Chicago: Moody, 1965), 49, for a brief discussion of interpretive options. Even if it does refer to Christ's spirit, the distinction between Christ's eternal spirit and the Holy Spirit is difficult to sustain.

of eternal atonement was a more than human work. He calls the Spirit eternal so that we know that the reconciliation which he effects is eternal.[112]

Finally, the New Testament associates the resurrection of Jesus with the Holy Spirit. It was according to the "Spirit of holiness" by His "resurrection from the dead" that Christ was declared to be "the powerful Son of God" (Rom 1:4; cf. 1 Cor 6:14). Peter writes that Christ was made alive in (Gk. *en*) the Spirit (1 Pet 3:18).[113] The Holy Spirit, the breath of God who brings life to dead bones (Ezek 37:13–14), is given as the guarantee of a resurrection similar to that of Christ to those who are in Christ. "And if the Spirit of Him who raised Jesus from the dead lives in you, then He who raised Christ from the dead will also bring your mortal bodies to life through His Spirit who lives in you" (Rom 8:11).

The Holy Spirit actively empowered every aspect of the ministry of Jesus Christ. The response of witnesses to that ministry was that they glorified God and marveled at Christ. When Jesus preached in the power of the Spirit, "the crowds were astonished" because He taught them "like one who had authority" (Matt 7:28–29). When Jesus healed in the power of the Spirit, the "fame" of Jesus spread (Matt 4:24). When Jesus went to the cross, suffered, and died by the power of the Spirit, the centurion proclaimed, "This man really was God's Son" (Matt 27:54). When Jesus was raised from the dead by the power of the Spirit, Thomas proclaimed, "My Lord and my God" (John 20:28).

Christ, the Holy Spirit, and the Kenosis

The active presence of the Holy Spirit in the life of Christ could also provide the key to the Christological question of the *kenosis* raised in Phil 2:5–8:

---

[112]J. Calvin, *The Epistle of Paul the Apostle to the Hebrews and the First and Second Epistles of St Peter*, Calvin's New Testament Commentaries 12, trans. W. B. Johnston (Grand Rapids: Eerdmans, 1963), 121.

[113]Exegetes differ on the correct interpretation of 1 Pet 3:18, which uses two dative nouns to describe the death ("put to death in the body," *en sarki*) and resurrection ("made alive by the Spirit," *en pneumati*) of Christ (NIV). The dative *pneumati* could be translated "in the spiritual realm" (HCSB), "in the spirit" (ESV), or "by the Spirit" (NIV). I agree with Schreiner that the parallel in 1 Tim 3:16 is instructive. He writes, "The deadlock can be broken if we recognize that the two dative nouns are not used in precisely the same way; the first is a dative of reference, and the second is a dative of agency. Christ was put to death with reference to or in the sphere of his body, but on the other hand, he was made alive by the Spirit." T. R. Schreiner, *1, 2 Peter, Jude*, NAC 37 (Nashville: B&H, 2003), 184; see also Ryrie, *Holy Spirit*, 50.

Make your own attitude that of Christ Jesus, who, existing in the form of God, did not consider equality with God as something to be used for His own advantage. Instead He emptied Himself [*heauton ekenōsen*] by assuming the form of a slave, taking on the likeness of men. And when He had come as a man in His external form, He humbled Himself by becoming obedient to the point of death—even to death on a cross.

The critical Christological issue involves the phrase in 2:7, "He emptied Himself."[114] How can Christ, who exists "in the form of God," empty Himself to take on the "form of a slave"? Theological proposals that seek to answer this question abound.[115] The passage begins with an exhortation to have the mind of Christ. The most satisfactory understanding is that we are to follow the ethical example of Christ Jesus who possessed and possesses the kind of mind-set described in vv. 6–8.[116] "Form of God" in 2:6 is parallel with "equality with God," which points to the preexistence of Christ who, because He is

---

[114]See N. T. Wright, *The Climax of the Covenant: Christ and the Law in Pauline Theology* (Minneapolis, MN: Fortress, 1993), 56–98, for a summary of the interpretive proposals.

[115]The Christological heresies of the fourth and fifth centuries, such as Docetism, Ebionism, Apollinarianism, Nestorianism, Monphysitism, and Adoptionism, all dealt with the issue at hand, but space does not allow a rehearsal of these heresies. During the nineteenth century, German theologian Gottfried Thomasius proposed what is known as kenotic theory. He argued that in becoming incarnate, Jesus divested Himself of the external attributes of omniscience, omnipotence, and omnipresence but maintained the internal attributes of love and holiness. S. M. Smith, "Kenosis: A Kenotic Theology," in *Evangelical Dictionary of Theology*, ed. W. A. Elwell (Grand Rapids: Baker, 1984), 600. This kenotic theory had many variations. For example, W. Friedrich Gess expanded the theory to suggest that Jesus gave up His divine attributes, thereby essentially ceasing to be God, changing from God to man. See M. J. Erickson, *Christian Theology*, 2nd ed. (Grand Rapids: Baker, 1998), 789. A. M. Fairbairn suggested that by divesting Himself of the external attributes such as omnipotence and omniscience, Jesus was able to reveal the internal attributes of love and holiness in a manner impossible apart from the *kenosis*. See Smith, "Kenosis," 602. The formulations of Thomasius, Gess, and Fairbairn are all deficient because they run contrary to the truth of Col 2:9 ("For in him the whole fullness of deity dwells bodily"). C. Gore, a twentieth-century Anglican, argued for a different form of kenoticism. He taught that Jesus refrained from the exercise of His divine powers, while at other times Gore used language of abandoning divine prerogatives. Jesus lived His life entirely within the limitations of humanity. See D. Macleod, *The Person of Christ* (Downers Grove, IL: InterVarsity, 1998), 206–7. H. R. Mackintosh argued that the incarnation consisted of an exchange of particular divine attributes for human attributes. See Erickson, *Christian Theology*, 749. P. T. Forsyth modified kenoticism still more by writing that it is impossible for a being to lay aside an attribute, though there are "accidental relations which determine the form in which the attribute exists." P. T. Forsyth, *The Person and Place of Jesus Christ* (London: Hodder & Stoughton, 1910), 296. Therefore, Jesus could not lay aside any of his divine attributes, though the exercise of those attributes is inconsistent with true humanity.

[116]So M. Bockmuehl, *A Commentary on the Epistle to the Philippians*, Black's New Testament Commentaries (London: A. & C. Black, 1997), 121; P. T. O'Brien, *The Epistle to the Philippians: A Commentary on the Greek Text*, NIGTC (Grand Rapids: Eerdmans, 1991), 205.

310

divine, enjoyed the essence and existence of deity. He possessed, prior to the incarnation, divine equality. The parallel construction describes Jesus Christ, "in his pre-existent state, as one who is indeed, and fully, *capax humanitatis*, but at the same time different from all other human beings in his nature and origin."[117]

But Jesus did not consider equality with God a thing "to be used for His own advantage." That is, He chose not to exploit His equality with God for self-aggrandizement or personal advantage.[118] The manner of Christ's self-emptying is identified in the remainder of the verse: by "taking the form of a slave, taking on the likeness of men." The Son of God emptied Himself, not by divesting Himself of divine attributes but by adding the attributes of humanity, a human nature. "Emptying" in the Pauline corpus is never literally the emptying of something of the qualities it possesses but is a figurative expression for nullifying something or making something of no account.[119] There was no transfer of the divine attributes in the *kenosis*. Jesus did not exchange the attributes of God for the attributes of a servant; rather, He manifested the perfect attributes of God that are commensurate with humanity in the manner and existence of a servant.[120]

The question remains, What happened to the divine attributes such as omnipotence, omniscience, and omnipresence, those attributes that are incompatible with authentic human experience, at the incarnation? Scripture presents the true humanity of Jesus not only as fact but also as necessity (Heb 2:17–18; 4:15; 5:8–9). However, the biblical testimony also demands that Jesus be recognized as fully divine (John 1:1; Heb 1:1–3; 1 John 1:1–2). Therefore, the divine attributes— including omniscience, omnipotence, and omnipresence—cannot be thought of as being laid aside or divested when Jesus became human, lest He cease to be divine. Rather, it is best to think of Jesus as fully possessing the attributes of deity yet choosing to rely upon the Holy Spirit for expression of those divine attributes that are inconsistent

---

[117]Wright, *Climax of the Covenant*, 82. Cf. G. F. Hawthorne, *Philippians*, WBC 43 (Waco, TX: Word, 1983), 83; Bockmuehl, *Commentary on the Epistle to the Philippians*, 129.

[118]I. H. Marshall, *The Epistle to the Philippians*, Epworth Commentaries (London: Epworth, 1991), 50; R. R. Melick Jr., *Philippians, Colossians, Philemon*, NAC 32 (Nashville: Broadman, 1991), 103, G. D. Fee, *Paul's Letter to the Philippians*, NICNT (Grand Rapids: Eerdmans, 1995), 208; and Wright, *Climax of the Covenant*, 79.

[119]F. Thielman, *Philippians*, NIVAC (Grand Rapids: Zondervan, 1995), 117.

[120]F. F. Bruce, *Jesus, Lord and Savior* (Downers Grove, IL: InterVarsity, 1986), 164.

with authentic human existence.[121] As has been demonstrated above, Jesus, as the Spirit-anointed one, lived in complete dependence upon the Holy Spirit (Acts 10:38 is Peter's summary of Christ's life and ministry). Jesus received guidance throughout His ministry by the Spirit (Matt 4:1). Jesus was empowered for ministry by the Spirit (Matt 12:28; Acts 1:8). This explains why there were occasions when Christ did not know something or was unable to do something (e.g., Matt 13:58; 24:36).[122] Rather than exercising the full prerogatives of His deity, Jesus lived as a human, dependent on the Holy Spirit.

THE SON AND THE HOLY SPIRIT: CHURCH AGE

On the night Jesus was betrayed, He gathered His disciples and told them that soon He would be leaving them. He next explained to His sorrowful followers that it was to their advantage that He was going away, for unless He went, He would not be able to send the Helper to them (John 16:7).[123] Prior to His ascension, Jesus again committed to send "what my Father promised. As for you, stay in the city until you are empowered from on high" (Luke 24:49). The promise was reaffirmed when He told them, "But you will receive power when the Holy Spirit has come upon you" (Acts 1:8). Just as Jesus ministered by the power of the Holy Spirit, He would send them the Spirit so that they too would be empowered for ministry (e.g., Acts 3:12; 4:7; 4:33; 6:8,10). The Spirit bearer became the Spirit giver.

Jesus Promises to Send the Holy Spirit

The explicit testimony of Scripture is that Jesus has revealed the Father to us (John 1:18; 10:30; 14:9). But it is also evident that Jesus has revealed the Holy Spirit to us as well. Ferguson comments:

---

[121] See B. Ware, "Christ's Atonement: A Work of the Trinity," in *Jesus in Trinitarian Perspective: An Introductory Christology*, ed. F. Sanders and K. Issler (Nashville: B&H, 2007), 179–86. See also Hawthorne, *Presence and the Power,* 208.

[122] In Matt 24:36, the day of the Second Advent had not been revealed to Christ from the Father. I take it that had it been revealed to Christ, such revelation would have occurred through the Spirit. In contrast, it seems likely that in John 1:48, the Spirit had revealed knowledge of Nathaniel to Christ.

[123] It is not because they cannot both simultaneously minister for ontological reasons that Jesus must depart before the Spirit can be sent. As Carson explains, the reason is eschatological: "The many biblical promises that the Spirit will characterize the age of the kingdom of God (*e.g.* Isa 11:1–10; 32:14–18; 42:1–4; 44:1–5; Ezk 11:17–20; 36:24–27; 37:1–14; Joel 2:28–32; *cf.* notes on John 3:5; 7:37–39) breed anticipation. But this saving reign of God cannot be fully inaugurated until Jesus has died, risen from the dead, and been exalted to his Father's right hand, returned to the glory he enjoyed with the Father before the world began." Carson, *Gospel According to John,* 533–34.

It is recognized that there is a partial character about the work of the Spirit which will reach its fullness only in the Messiah (Isa 11:1ff.), and therefore in the inner and widespread experience of the Spirit (Ezek 36:25–27; Joel 2:28ff.). We therefore ought to expect a strong element of the enigmatic about the Old Testament witness to the Spirit parallel to what the authors of messianic prophecy discovered in their own prophecies about Christ (cf. 1 Pet 1:10–11). Only through the revelation of the Spirit in the Messiah does the enigmatic testimony of the Old Testament come into its true light, so that the Spirit's activity is seen to have been more than merely an extension of the presence of God.[124]

The Father demonstrated His love for His Son by lavishing the Spirit upon Him "without measure" (John 3:34–35). In contrast to the prophets who were only given a measure of the Spirit, Jesus has the Spirit in all of His fullness.[125] It is out of that fullness that Jesus sent the Spirit.

Jesus instructed Nicodemus that unless he was born of "water and the Spirit," he could not enter the kingdom of God (John 3:5). Though the reference to water has been the subject of some debate,[126] the best understanding is that Jesus was linking the cleansing effect of water with the regenerative work of the Spirit. Nicodemus was rebuked for not understanding the teaching of Jesus (John 3:10), so it is preferable to draw understanding from the Old Testament context with which Nicodemus should have been familiar. The importance of regeneration by water and the Spirit finds its antecedents in the prophetic anticipation of the coming of the Spirit where the prophets often linked water and Spirit (e.g., Isa 44:3; Ezek 36:25–27). The relationship between water and the Spirit is also found in John 7:37–39. Water-pouring ceremonies were a prominent feature of the Feast of Tabernacles,[127] and

---

[124]Ferguson, *Holy Spirit*, 29.

[125]Carson records that rabbinic teaching rightly commented that the Holy Spirit was given to the prophets only in measures. John's statement stands in strong contrast; Jesus is given the Spirit without measure. *Gospel According to John*, 213.

[126]Some interpret John 3:5 as a reference to physical birth, seeing "water" as a reference to the amniotic waters of birth or even as an allusion to semen which brings physical birth. It is doubtful that Jesus would make such an obvious statement to Nicodemus, that in order to enter the kingdom one must be born physically and then be born spiritually. Others see an allusion to Christian baptism, but Nicodemus could not have been expected to know about an ordinance that had not been instituted at the time.

[127]See Köstenberger, *John*, 239–40.

on the last day of the feast, Jesus proclaimed that those who were in thirst ought to come to Him. John 7:39 explains that the "streams of living water" that "flow from deep within" the believer refer to the Spirit. But the Spirit is not separable from Christ because, as John explains, only those who put their trust in Jesus receive the Spirit, whose sending could not take place until Jesus was glorified.

Perhaps the most important aspect of the pneumatological character of Christ's ministry was the revelation and sending of the Spirit. In the upper room discourse, recorded by John, Jesus taught on the sending and ministry of the Spirit in five *Paraclete* passages (14:15–17,26; 15:26; 16:7–15).

The Nature of the Paraclete   John had previously explained that the Spirit had not been sent because Christ had not been glorified (John 7:39). With the glorification that would take place at the cross immanent, Jesus introduced the Spirit by promising to ask the Father to send "another Counselor" (*allon paraklēton*, John 14:16). The term *paraklētos* is notoriously difficult to define, but it can carry the meaning, depending on the context, of "advocate," "lawyer," "comforter," "helper," or, literally, "one who comes alongside."[128] Jesus Himself is a *Paraclete* (1 John 2:1), and the Father sent one whose ongoing work would be a continuation of the Son's work.[129] There is such continuity between the Son and the Spirit—Jesus' identification with the Spirit is so strong—that He could say, "I am coming to you" in the person of the Spirit (John 14:18).[130] In this instance the Son says he will ask the Father to send the Spirit (14:15), but later during the same discourse, He says that He will send the Spirit from the Father (John 15:26), that the Spirit proceeds from the Father (15:26),[131] and that the Spirit will be sent by Christ (John 16:7).

Jesus named the *Paraclete* the Spirit of truth (John 14:17). He is the Spirit of truth because He speaks the truth and testifies to the

[128] Köstenberger, *John*, 435; Carson, *Gospel According to John*, 499; Burge, *John*, 397; Morris, *Gospel According to John*, 576, 587–91. Each agrees that the term "advocate," though not exhaustive of the range of meaning implied by *paraclete* in John 14–16, best captures what is intended by Christ in the context.

[129] So Burge, *John*, 396; Köstenberger, *John*, 436; Schreiner, *New Testament Theology*, 468.

[130] Köstenberger, *John*, 435.

[131] In context John 15:26 refers to economic procession rather than "to some ontological 'procession.'" Carson, *Gospel According to John*, 529. Morris states plainly, "The passage is not concerned with the eternal mutual relationships of the Persons of the Trinity but with work the Spirit would do in this world as a continuation of the ministry of Jesus." Morris, *Gospel According to John*, 606.

one who is the Truth (John 14:6). When the Spirit of truth comes, the result would not be ecstatic experience. Burge comments, "The truth (this Spirit of truth) is not a compelling spiritual experience in the first instance; it is the capacity to point faithfully to what is known about Jesus' historic ministry from its onset."[132] For this reason "the world cannot receive" the Spirit. Given the Christological character of the Spirit's mission, this makes perfect sense. As Carson explains, "In terms of the Spirit's responsibility to replace Jesus as Paraclete to the disciples, it would be a profound contradiction of their fresh, eschatological, new covenant experiences of God mediated by the Spirit . . . if these experiences were shared with those who had not yet closed with Jesus."[133] Moreover, the disciples were already familiar with the Spirit. Throughout Israel's past, the presence of the Lord had been mediated to Israel in the person of the Spirit dwelling among the people. During the age of the new covenant, the Spirit who once dwelled among the people of God would now dwell in them, to the glory of Christ who sends the Spirit (John 14:17).[134]

The unity of the Godhead does not eliminate distinction between the roles of the divine persons, as is evident from Jesus' teaching. The Father sends the Son and the Spirit, but the Father is never sent (John 3:16; 14:16). The Spirit is sent by both the Father and the Son, but the Spirit is never the sender (John 16:7). Only Jesus fulfills both roles: He is the sent one and the sender.[135] Christ sends the Holy Spirit to His sent ones, the apostles and other disciples, to empower them to deliver His message to the world. Further, the sending language of John 16 indicates that there is a relational differentiation between the Father, Son, and Spirit in the immanent Trinity that manifests itself in different roles. The priority of the Spirit to glorify the Son in redemptive history is consistent with the nature of their eternal relationships.[136]

---

[132]Burge, *John*, 422.

[133]Carson, *Gospel According to John*, 500.

[134]J. M. Hamilton Jr., *God's Indwelling Presence: The Holy Spirit in the Old and New Testaments* (Nashville: B&H, 2006). See also G. E. Ladd, *A Theology of the New Testament*, rev. ed. (Grand Rapids: Eerdmans, 1993), 326.

[135]Köstenberger, *John*, 442.

[136]See B. A. Ware, "Tampering with the Trinity: Does the Son Submit to His Father?" *Journal for Biblical Manhood and Womanhood* 6/1 (2000): 4–12; and S. D. Kovach and P. R. Schemm Jr., "A Defense of the Doctrine of the Eternal Subordination of the Son," *JETS* 42 (1999): 461–76. In contrast, see G. Bilezikian, "Hermeneutical Bungee-Jumping: Subordination in the Godhead," *JETS* 40/1 (1997): 57–68.

The Holy Spirit and Revelation   Understanding the nature of the Spirit's revealing ministry is critical for a faithful theology of religions. Jesus promised His disciples that the Holy Spirit would teach them and "remind [them] of everything" He had said to them (John 14:26); that is, the Spirit would "help them grasp its significance and thus to teach them what it meant."[137] In doing so, the Spirit would not bring "qualitatively new revelation"[138] but would complete, explain, and enable the disciples to understand the words of Christ as they fit into the larger picture of redemptive history. That is, the Spirit does not operate in the world as an independent source of truth. He teaches truth in that He testifies about Jesus (John 15:26). The words the Spirit would speak are the words of Christ. Just as Jesus spoke only what the Father told Him, so the Spirit speaks only what He hears from the Son. Köstenberger notes, "Hence, the Spirit's mission is a continuation of Jesus' mission . . . which continues the emphasis on the unity among the different persons of the Godhead in this Gospel."[139]

Even though Jesus is the Word of God, the Holy Spirit guides Christ's followers "into all the truth" (John 16:13). But the discharge of this duty is done under the authority of Jesus Christ. The Spirit speaks only what He hears. Such submission is consistent with the centrality of Christ in revelation, the self-disclosure of God. As Carson avers:

> We are to understand that Jesus is the nodal point of revelation, God's culminating self-disclosure, God's final self-expression, God's "Word" (1:1,14). All antecedent revelation has pointed toward him, and reaches its climax in him. That does not mean he himself provides all the details his followers will need; it does mean that "extra" bits the Holy Spirit provides after he is sent by Christ Jesus, consequent upon Jesus' death/exaltation, are nothing more than the filling out of the revelation nodally present in Jesus himself.[140]

For this reason, at the beginning of the book of Acts, Luke summarizes his own Gospel, or "first narrative," as dealing with "all that Jesus began to do and teach" (Acts 1:1). As F. F. Bruce explains, "The impli-

---

[137]Carson, *Gospel According to John*, 505.

[138]Ibid.

[139]Köstenberger, *John*, 442. See also Burge, *John*, 399.

[140]Carson, *Gospel According to John*, 539. See also Burge, *John*, 439; Ware, *Father, Son, & Holy Spirit*, 109.

cation of Luke's words is that his second volume will be an account of what Jesus *continued* to do and teach after His ascension—no longer in visible presence on earth but by his Spirit in his followers."[141]

The Ministry of the Holy Spirit   The major aspects of the Spirit's church-age mission (convicting the world of sin, righteousness, and judgment; guidance into truth; and glorifying the Son) provided by Jesus in John 15:26–16:15 are all specifically related to the ministry of the Son.[142] The nature of the Spirit's work of conviction is debated,[143] but it is clear that Christ sees Himself at its center.[144] In fact, the Spirit will not be known apart from Christ. Ferguson notes the Christocentric nature of the revelation and conviction of the Spirit:

> For it is not only because of Christ that we come to know the Spirit more fully, but actually in Christ. Indeed, it is apparently a principle of the divine Spirit's working that he declines to disclose himself in any other way (Jn 16:13–15). He will not be known as he is in himself apart from Christ. Before the Spirit rests permanently on all the faithful children of God, he first must rest on the uniquely faithful Son of God (cf. Jn 1:33).[145]

The Holy Spirit Glorifies the Son   The entirety of all that the Son sends the Spirit to do is summed up in the glorification of the Son (John 16:14). Just as the Son brought glory to the Father (John 7:18; 17:4), so the Spirit brings glory to Jesus.[146] The means by which the Spirit will do this are by revealing all that Jesus is and did: "He will take from what is Mine and declare it to you" (John 16:14).[147] That the central purpose of the Spirit is the glorification of the Son is no slight

---

[141]F. F. Bruce, *The Book of Acts*, NICNT, rev. ed. (Grand Rapids: Eerdmans, 1988), 30.

[142]Burge writes that the "foremost feature of Johannine pneumatology was its christocentric basis." G. M. Burge, *The Anointed Community: The Holy Spirit in the Johannine Tradition* (Grand Rapids: Eerdmans, 1987), xvi.

[143]For different views, see, for example, Carson, *Gospel According to John*, 538; Köstenberger, *John*, 472; Burge, *John*, 438; and J. Aloisi, "The Paraclete's Ministry of Conviction: Another Look at John 16:8–11," *JETS* 47:1 (March 2004): 55–69.

[144]So G. C. Berkouwer, *Sin* (Grand Rapids: Eerdmans, 1971), 224.

[145]Ferguson, *Holy Spirit*, 30.

[146]Ladd believed it is noteworthy "that John attributes nothing of the ecstatic or marvelous to the coming of the Spirit. His primary function is to exalt Jesus and to interpret his work of salvation." Ladd, *Theology of the New Testament*, 333.

[147]Carson explains that this "does not simply mean that the Paraclete passes on what Jesus declares, but that all the revelation bound up in Jesus' person and mission are pressed home on the disciples." Carson, *Gospel According to John*, 541.

to God the Father. Everything the Son has belongs to the Father, and the glorification of the Son redounds to the glory of the Father (1 Cor 15:28; Phil 2:11). It is appropriate and consistent with the work of the Holy Spirit in redemptive history to bring glory to the Son.

Inclusivists are anxious to recognize the presence and activity of the Spirit in others, but the establishment of criteria for such discernment has proven elusive. In Pinnock's quest to identify the activity of the Spirit, he reduces the criteria to the ethical realm by speaking in terms of "the criterion of incarnate wisdom" and seeing "traces of Jesus in the world and people opening up to his ideals."[148] But when Jesus said that the Holy Spirit would glorify Him, He was speaking of more than ethical behavior. Scripture itself presents criteria for discerning the work of the Spirit, and those criteria transcend ethical behavior. In 1 John 4:1–6, John is adamant that any alleged experience with the Spirit that denies either the full humanity or full deity of Christ is not an experience with the Spirit of God. Glorification of the Son involves the proclamation of the gospel (Rom 10:13–17) and lordship of the person of Christ (1 Cor 12:3). For Paul, Christology was at the heart of discerning the work of the Holy Spirit.[149]

Clearly there is a strong relationship between Christ and the Holy Spirit in the life and ministry of Jesus. Pneumatological inclusivists are quick to affirm the dependence of the Son on the Spirit during the incarnation.[150] But Jesus' teaching on the Spirit reaches beyond the incarnation. Jesus establishes a Christocentric nature to the mission of the Spirit that extends into the age of the church and beyond.

The Present Work of the Holy Spirit

Promise Fulfilled at Pentecost   In Acts 1:4, Jesus reiterated the statement made by John the Baptist that He would baptize with the Holy Spirit (cf. John 1:33). The events of Pentecost fulfilled the promise of Christ, when the Spirit descended upon the disciples and they were "all filled with the Holy Spirit" (Acts 2:4). Each began to speak in tongues, attracting a crowd of people where "each one heard them speaking in his own language" (Acts 2:6). When Peter stood to preach,

---

[148]Pinnock, *Flame of Love*, 209. Yong criticizes Pinnock for providing criteria that have the appearance of a natural morality. Yong, *Beyond the Impasse*, 120.

[149]Cole, *He Who Gives Life*, 274.

[150]Pinnock, *Flame of Love*, 79–112.

he explained that the speech of the disciples was in fact the long-awaited fulfillment of Joel's prophecy:

> And it will be in the last days, says God, that I will pour out My Spirit on all humanity; then your sons and your daughters will prophesy, your young men will see visions, and your old men will dream dreams. I will even pour out My Spirit on My male and female slaves in those days, and they will prophesy. I will display wonders in the heavens above and signs on the earth below: blood and fire and a cloud of smoke. The sun will be turned to darkness, and the moon to blood, before the great and remarkable day of the Lord comes; then whoever calls on the name of the Lord will be saved (Acts 2:17–21).

Jesus had fulfilled what He promised in the upper room (John 14:16–17; 16:7), pouring out the Spirit whom He had received from the Father (Acts 2:33). It is surely significant that the immediate result was that Peter proclaimed the gospel of Jesus Christ (Acts 2:22–39), exhorting the crowd, "Repent . . . and be baptized, each of you, in the name of Jesus the Messiah for the forgiveness of your sins, and you will receive the gift of the Holy Spirit" (Acts 2:38). Peter was convinced that the pouring out of the Spirit had inaugurated the "last days," the Messianic Age. The first post-Pentecost, Spirit-empowered sermon resulted in 3,000 trusting in Christ.

Significant to this project is the question raised with regard to Acts 2:17: what does it mean that the Spirit would be poured out on all flesh? Pneumatological inclusivists, such as Amos Yong, caution "against reading the 'all' of Acts 2:17 in an exclusively ecclesiological sense."[151] Yong instead prefers to interpret "all flesh" in a universalist sense.[152] But such an understanding of all flesh (*pasan sarka*)

---

[151]Yong, *Beyond the Impasse*, 40. Yong explains, "The Spirit's activity across the dimensions of both space—the Spirit's being poured out upon all people—and time—'in the last days,' stretching from the Day of Pentecost to the coming of the kingdom of God—begs to be understood in a universal sense that transcends (at least the institutional boundaries) of the church." Yong also uses Acts 2:17 as a proof text to establish the universal presence of the Holy Spirit in parallel with Ps 139:7–12. Ibid., 131.

[152]Amos Yong, "A P(new)matological Paradigm for Christian Mission in a Religiously Plural World," *Missiology* 33 (2005): 177. Yong admits that a traditional reading could probably be defended at the exegetical level but not at the theological level. The people upon whom the Spirit is poured become Christians after the Spirit comes. Yong also defends his universalistic reading of "all flesh" by the fact that the proselytes are not full converts; that is, they "embody in their lives multiple traditions and cultures in various degrees." He also argues for universality

can hardly be sustained biblically. Acts 2:17 must be read in light of Num 11:29 where, prior to the work of Christ, the coming of the Spirit was limited to a few. Under the new covenant, "the boundaries of the Mosaic economy within which the Spirit had, by and large, previously manifested himself are rendered obsolete."[153] Isaiah 32:15 also speaks of "the Spirit from heaven" being "poured out on us." This prophecy of the Messianic times can hardly be taken as a proof text of the Spirit's universal outpouring because the recipients are specifically identified as "My people" in Isa 32:18.[154] Likewise, the text in question, Acts 2:17–18, specifically limits the reception of the Spirit to "your sons and your daughters," "your young men," "your old men," and "My male and female slaves." Acts 1:8 ties Spirit-empowered witness "to the ends of the earth" to the witness of Christ. The remainder of the book of Acts demonstrates that the pouring out of the Spirit extends inclusively outside the boundaries of ethnic Israel, without race, gender, age, or class distinction but exclusively only to those who believe in Jesus Christ.[155] Moses' dream had become reality; the Spirit had been poured out on all of God's people, manifest in those who had heard and believed the gospel.

Because of the mutual relationship between the Son and the Spirit, the "pouring out" of the Spirit at Pentecost is far more than a pneumatological event; it is profoundly Christological.[156] The coming of the Spirit is the fulfillment of Christ's promise that He would be with His disciples always (Matt 28:20), that He would "abide" or "remain" (*meinate*) in His disciples (John 15:4; cf. 1:33).[157] The New Testament writers understood this relationship and referred to the Spirit of God as the Spirit of Christ (Rom 8:9; 1 Pet 1:11). The coming of the Spirit is the life-giving bond between the physically absent King and

on the basis that the summary list of regions and languages encompasses most of the known, first-century world.

[153] Ferguson, *Holy Spirit*, 62.

[154] A. Yong quotes Isa 32:15–17 to demonstrate that the Spirit is "thereby the universal presence and activity of God." Yong, *Beyond the Impasse*, 42. But Yong ignores the designation of "My people" in 32:18.

[155] J. B. Polhill, *Acts*, NAC 26 (Nashville: Broadman, 1995), 109.

[156] So J. D. G. Dunn, *Jesus and the Spirit: A Study of the Religious and Charismatic Experience of Jesus and the First Christians as Reflected in the New Testament* (Grand Rapids: Eerdmans, 1997), 194.

[157] McDonnell explains it thus: "Every experience of the Spirit is materially, not formally, the experience of Christ." "A Trinitarian Theology of the Holy Spirit," 206.

His subjects.[158] The Holy Spirit ensures the uninterrupted presence of Christ in the church.[159]

The Present Work of the Holy Spirit in the Church Age   The work of the Spirit in the church age continues the story of redemption without alteration to the interdependence of the roles between Spirit and Son. Jesus promised that the Holy Spirit would lead His disciples into all truth. Because Jesus Christ is Himself the truth, the role of the Spirit is to lead others to testify of and glorify Christ (John 14:6; 16:3,14). The Spirit's role in inspiration is here implicitly if not explicitly tied to the testimony of Jesus. Revelation 19:10 makes this explicit: "Worship God, because the testimony about Jesus is the spirit of prophecy." That is, the testimony about Jesus is what constitutes Spirit-inspired prophecy.[160] The entire book of Revelation bears testimony to this fact. Though the book is called the "revelation of Jesus Christ" (Rev 1:1), John emphasizes in four places that he was "in the Spirit" when he received the revelation (Rev 1:10; 4:2; 17:3; 21:10). The letters to the churches in chapters 2 and 3 close with the admonition, "Anyone who has an ear should listen to what the Spirit says to the churches" (Rev 2:7,11,17,29; 3:6,13,22). But each letter claims to be the words of the Son of Man (Rev 2:1,8,12,18; 3:1,7,14). Clearly the words of Jesus Christ are simultaneously the words of the Holy Spirit.

In Pauline theology, being filled with the Spirit and being filled with the Word of Christ are complementary (Eph 5:18; Col 3:16).[161] As Schreiner notes, "There is no such thing as being filled with the Spirit if one is not filled with the external word of Christ."[162] This is demonstrated throughout the narratives of Acts. When Peter was queried by the Jewish leaders on account of the healing of a lame man, he was "filled with the Holy Spirit" (Acts 4:8). The result was a bold and

---

[158]Dawson states, "The Spirit, who gives himself to be so poured, becomes the bond between the still-incarnate Son in heaven and his people still sojourning on earth. By this boon, the physically absent King establishes a living tie between himself and his subjects." G. Scott Dawson, *Jesus Ascended: The Meaning of Christ's Continuing Incarnation* (Phillipsburg, NJ: P&R, 2004), 54.

[159]See Bobrinskoy, *Mystery of the Trinity*, 72.

[160]See Schreiner, *New Testament Theology*, 420.

[161]There is a strong parallel between the promises of the new covenant and the commands to be filled with the Spirit and to be filled with the Word of Christ. Jeremiah 31:33 describes the new covenant as a time when God would put His law within His people (cf. Col 3:16), while Ezek 36:27 describes the new covenant as a time when God will put His Spirit within His people (cf. Eph 5:18).

[162]T. R. Schreiner, *Paul: Apostle of God's Glory in Christ* (Downers Grove, IL: InterVarsity, 2001), 310.

uncompromising gospel proclamation (Acts 4:8–12). Acts 4:31 summarizes well: "They were all filled with the Holy Spirit and began to speak God's message with boldness." The same pattern is repeated in the bold witness of Stephen (Acts 6:10) and in the life and ministry of Paul. Paul received the Spirit through the laying on of hands by Ananias (Acts 9:17). This filling of the Spirit is the basis by which the gospel is disseminated to the Gentile world throughout the book of Acts (e.g., 8:29; 10:19–20; 11:12; 13:2,9–11; cf. 16:6,7). At each critical juncture in the book of Acts, the Holy Spirit is impelling and empowering the spread of the gospel and the ministry of the church.[163]

The preaching of the gospel for salvation is performed through the power of the Spirit (Rom 15:19; 1 Thess 1:5; 1 Pet 1:12).[164] But what is the gospel? What are its priorities? The gospel is the good news of salvation in Christ, focused on the proclamation of the death and resurrection of Christ, a thoroughly Christocentric message (1 Cor 15:1–6) that objectively altered the course of redemptive history for everybody, not just those who hear of Christ. Therefore, when Amos Yong claims that Acts 4:12 should be read as ontological rather than epistemological, or that John 3:17–18 refers to the fate of the evangelized but is silent on the fate of the unevangelized, he misunderstands the nature of redemptive history and the work of the Spirit.[165] This is evidenced by the account of Peter and Cornelius in Acts 10–11. Even though Cornelius was a God fearer, he had to hear the gospel for salvation. Cornelius was told that he must hear from Peter who "will speak words to you by which you and all your household will be saved [sōthēsē]" (Acts 11:14). Cornelius's salvation was a future event contingent on hearing and believing the gospel.[166] The crucifixion and resurrection of Christ were defining events in redemptive history that changed the soteriological landscape for every person in every place, even for the unevangelized.

---

[163]Cole, *He Who Gives Life*, 213.

[164]See G. D. Fee, *God's Empowering Presence: The Holy Spirit in the Letters of Paul* (Peabody, MA: Hendrickson, 1994), 629; T. R. Schreiner, *Romans*, ECNT (Grand Rapids: Baker, 1998), 768.

[165]Yong, *Beyond the Impasse*, 25.

[166]Pinnock rejects any notion that Cornelius was not saved prior to Peter preaching the gospel to him. "As Job in the Old Testament story, Cornelius did not need a special messenger to make him a believer. He was a believer already and not hellbound. True, he needed to become a Christian to receive messianic salvation, including assurance and the Holy Spirit, but not to be saved from hell." C. H. Pinnock, *A Wideness in God's Mercy: The Finality of Jesus Christ in a World of Religions* (Grand Rapids: Zondervan, 1992), 166.

The giving, work, and presence of the Spirit in the life of the believer in Jesus are irreducibly related to the person and work of Christ. Badcock is surely correct when he writes:

> After the coming of Christ, the Spirit cannot be understood apart from its relation to him, for the canon of authentic experience of the Spirit is defined christologically by Paul, precisely because the new existence in Christ is something pneumatological. . . . The Spirit, in short, is given to the community through the glorification of Jesus in his passion, but the Spirit could not in fact be what it is in the life of the Christian community without or apart from the glorification of Jesus in his passion.[167]

Sanctification, washing, and regeneration are accomplished "in the name of the Lord Jesus Christ and by the Spirit of our God" (1 Cor 6:11). Consider the act of regeneration. Only those who believe in Jesus are born again (John 3:5–16). Paul speaks of the same regenerative work in 2 Corinthians 3–4. Prior to regeneration the unbeliever is blinded by "the god of this age" so that he "cannot see the light of the gospel of the glory of Christ" (2 Cor 4:4). But "the Lord who is the Spirit" (2 Cor 3:18) opens blind eyes so that Jesus can be seen. Bruce Ware comments, "Amazingly, when the Spirit works in our hearts to bring us salvation, his central purpose is to show us the beauty and glory of Jesus, not himself. Although the Spirit plays this crucial role in our salvation, his goal is to open our eyes to behold the wonder and glory of Christ."[168]

Only by the Spirit can one confess that Jesus is Lord, while "no one speaking by the Spirit of God says, 'Jesus is cursed'" (1 Cor 12:3). For Paul, "the ultimate criterion of the Spirit's activity is the exaltation of Jesus as Lord,"[169] and apart from the enabling and transforming power of the Spirit, no one can live under the lordship of Christ.[170] To be in Christ is to be set free by the Spirit (Rom 8:2,14–15). The freedom to keep God's commands is the result of the Spirit's work, but the liberty was secured by Christ at the cross (Rom 8:1–8). Those who are "in Christ Jesus" are to walk "according to the Spirit" (Rom 8:1–4). On

---

[167]Badcock, *Light of Truth & Fire of Love*, 26–28.
[168]B. Ware, "Christ's Atonement," 186.
[169]Fee, *God's Empowering Presence*, 157–58.
[170]Schreiner, *Paul*, 164.

the other hand, those who willfully sin or spurn the gospel of Christ have "trampled on the Son of God" and "insulted the Spirit of grace" (Heb 10:29). The New Testament identifies the Spirit as "the Holy Spirit" 90 times, compared to just three times in the Old Testament. This surely speaks to the priority of the Spirit under the new covenant to effect holiness in those in whom He resides (cf. Luke 1:35). In fact, the entire goal of sanctification, which is an act of the Spirit, is to be transformed into the image of Christ (Rom 15:16; 2 Cor 3:18; 1 John 3:2).

Those who are sons of God in Christ Jesus have received not a spirit of bondage but a Spirit of sonship that cries out to God both on our behalf and with us (Gal 3:26; Rom 8:16).[171] Indeed, it is not merely the Spirit that has been sent to us, but the "Spirit of His Son . . . crying, 'Abba, Father!'" (Gal 4:6). The same Son of God whose death secured sonship for all believers now dwells in their hearts through the Spirit. It is the Spirit's indwelling that makes union with Christ possible, and the benefits of this union extend to worship and prayer. The Spirit that led the Lord Jesus Christ is now to guide and control the believer in Christ (Eph 5:18). Because Jesus is our great High Priest (Heb 7:23–26; 8:1–2), Graham Cole writes, "The Spirit of the Son enables us to pray like the Son, as far as Paul is concerned in Romans and Galatians."[172] The fruit of the Spirit (Gal 5:22–24) manifests the presence of Christ who lives in the church and in the heart of the believer.

The church belongs to Jesus, and she is to submit to His headship (Matt 16:18; Eph 5:22–24). Jesus is the chief cornerstone of the church (Eph 2:20). So close is the relationship between Christ and the church that a common image of the church in Paul is "the body of Christ" (e.g., 1 Cor 12:12; Eph 1:23; cf. Acts 9:4). But the coming of the Spirit inaugurated the church (Acts 2), and by the Spirit believers "are being built together for God's dwelling" (Eph 2:22). To that end the Spirit appoints leaders for the church of Christ (Acts 20:28) and strengthens them for the purpose that they might guard the gospel of Christ (2 Tim 1:14). The Spirit apportions gifts and empowers their use to the end that the body of Christ, the church of which Christ is the head, might be built up (1 Cor 12:4–11). These gifts and abilities are Spirit enabled

---

[171] Ferguson, *Holy Spirit*, 183.
[172] Cole, *He Who Gives Life*, 235.

and Spirit selected, but the entire discussion of the gifts of the Spirit is "subsumed under the banner of the lordship of Christ."[173]

Before going to the cross, Jesus prayed that His believers would be unified (John 17:20–23). His cross work made that unity possible (Eph 2:13), but it is by the instrumentality of the Spirit that Jews and Gentiles "both have access . . . to the Father" (Eph 2:18; cf. 1 Cor 12:13). The result of this Spirit-enabled unity is that the world recognizes and believes that God the Father sent Jesus into the world (John 17:20–21).

The Proleptic Work of the Holy Spirit A unifying theme within the Bible is new creation or regeneration. Since the fall, God has been in the process of restoring creation. This restoration has been enacted on the stage of human history, playing out the divine drama of redemptive history. The Holy Spirit has a revelatory role to play in this drama (e.g., 1 Cor 2:12–13). Scripture teaches that the primary sphere of the Holy Spirit in the believer is eschatological; that is, as the Spirit works in believers in Christ, He is moving the Christian toward what the believer shall one day be perfectly.[174]

Of primary importance in New Testament theology, and indeed in the experience of believers, is the doctrine of resurrection. Those who participate in Christ are partakers of regeneration, re-creation, and look forward to the resurrection (Rom 6:4–11; 1 Cor 5:17; 15:12–49). Paul makes clear that the resurrection is no small part of the Christian life but rather essential to it. If there is no resurrection of the dead, Paul's teaching is false; and the lives of Christians, let alone their truth claims, are pitiable (1 Cor 15:14–19). But the Spirit is given to the believer as "the firstfruits," an anchor of the soul, to guarantee perseverance and bolster hope of what will one day be (Rom 8:19–25). Paul's use of the term "firstfruits" (*aparchēn*) elicits eschatological imagery of the harvest, demonstrating that for Paul, the ministry of the Holy Spirit was an essentially eschatological reality.[175] The indwelling presence of the Spirit provides a taste of the glory of sonship that is to come, tantalizing the believer so that he groans in anticipation of his adoption.[176]

---

[173]Schreiner, *New Testament Theology*, 488.
[174]Vos, "Paul's Eschatological Concept of the Spirit," 120.
[175]Fee, *God's Empowering Presence*, 573.
[176]Schreiner, *Romans*, 438.

Christ has been raised from the dead, and the renewal, sanctification, and resurrection of the believer share a vital connection to what was transacted in Christ. Jesus is the firstfruits of those who have died (1 Cor 15:20). As the resurrected Lord, He becomes the life-giving Spirit (1 Cor 15:45). This latter point is instructive because it brings the entire redemptive story full circle. The role of the Holy Spirit under the new covenant is not an interruption in the biblical story but is perfectly consistent with it. As was demonstrated above, a primary role of the Spirit in the Old Testament is that of life giver. In the end the interrelationship of Son and Spirit is reaffirmed by the declaration of Jesus Christ as the life-giving Spirit.

An important implication of this relationship is that to be joined to the Lord is to be one Spirit with Him (1 Cor 6:17). If the spiritual life of the believer shares in the spiritual life of Jesus Christ, then "it must to some extent partake of the eschatological character of the latter."[177] The Spirit that led and empowered Christ's kingdom proclamation and ethic is the one who leads and empowers the kingdom proclamation and ethic of Christians today.

Paul taught that the Spirit is the seal and guarantee of the inheritance that all people who hope in Jesus will receive (Eph 1:12–14; 2 Cor 1:22). The giving of the inheritance entails that believers are made joint heirs with Christ (Rom 8:17; Eph 3:6). Those who are thus sealed by the Spirit are assured of the resurrection of their bodies and their future life with Christ (2 Cor 5:5). In the New Testament possession of the Holy Spirit is the sign of acceptance from God, of participation in the privileges of the Christian state (Acts 10:45–47). The Spirit is the Spirit of promise (Eph 1:13), whose presence in the lives of believers today guarantees life in the eschatological day of redemption (Eph 4:30). The new covenant work in the hearts of believers is written not with ink but with "the Spirit of the living God," and Jesus Christ is the author (2 Cor 3:3).

The Holy Spirit, who is closely associated with the resurrection of Jesus, is also the permanent ground of the resurrection life. The presence of the indwelling Spirit guarantees the future resurrection of believers in Christ.[178] The Spirit as down payment verifies that the salvific process previously inaugurated will be completed.[179] He who

---

[177]Vos, "Paul's Eschatological Concept of the Spirit," 114.
[178]So Fee, *God's Empowering Presence*, 552.
[179]Schreiner, *Paul*, 262.

raised Jesus from the dead is the one who keeps, empowers, and will one day raise those in Christ (Rom 8:9–11; 2 Cor 13:4).

CONCLUSION

The interrelationship between the Son and Spirit cannot be severed. To emphasize the role of the Spirit to the detriment of the Son is to misunderstand the role of the Spirit, ignore biblical teaching, distort redemptive history, silence the gospel, and pervert eschatological promises. The Christological center of the Spirit's ministry renders any attempts to posit even an ecumenism around anything but the person and work of Christ illegitimate.[180]

The burden of this chapter has been to demonstrate that the role of the Holy Spirit described by Jesus Christ in John 16:14, that the Spirit would glorify the Son, is representative of the relationship between the Son and the Spirit. The Holy Spirit was active in the creation of the cosmos (Gen 1:1–2). He came upon individuals at critical junctures to move redemptive history toward the cross of Christ. During the incarnation, "God anointed Jesus of Nazareth with the Holy Spirit and with power" (Acts 10:38). The Spirit empowered Jesus to live sinlessly, preach the kingdom of God, and go to the cross. Christ's resulting glorification enabled Him to send the Spirit so that all who believe in the Lord Jesus Christ might be indwelt by His Spirit and empowered to glorify Christ. The Holy Spirit always seeks to glorify the Son. In denying this, pneumatological inclusivism fails on Christological grounds and ultimately, ironically, distorts pneumatology.

---

[180]Reitsma explains, "There can be a Christ-less spirituality in which the Spirit receives attention in a way that does not honor the Spirit and contradicts his essence. Whenever a renewal does not lead us back to the cross of Christ, it is not from the Spirit." B. Reitsma, "The Power of the Spirit: Parameters of an Ecumenical Pneumatology in the 21st Century," *TR* 23 (2002): 23.

Chapter Nine

A Christian Theology of Religions and Mission

INTRODUCTION

The purpose of a Christian theology of religions is to guide and inform the individual's and the Church's interaction with other religions. When Christians interact with religious others, they do so out of their convictions based on their study of Scripture, exposure to teaching, experiences, and a host of other factors. The question is not whether one has a theology of religions. Be it conscious or subconscious, examined or unexamined, every Christian has a working theology of religions that guides his interaction with religious others. The question is whether one's theology of religions is faithful to Scripture and the gospel. For some, their theology of religions is eclectic, incoherent, inconsistent, and driven more by the whims of the world than the authority of Scripture, guided more by the cultural spirit than the Holy Spirit. Such *ad hoc* thinking is sub-Christian and dishonoring to Christ.

While the world struggles to make sense of the reality of religious pluralism and its conflicting truth claims, the Christian has been commissioned by the Lord Jesus Christ to declare the good news of his death and resurrection. Only the Christian is reconciled to the Creator of heaven and earth. Of all people the Christian alone can have a coherent and consistent theology of religions that is simultaneously honoring to the Lord. Therefore, the Christian must be intentional in "taking every thought captive to the obedience of Christ" (2 Cor 10:5) by thinking rightly about religious others. As in all things, we are to submit our thinking to Scripture, being ever mindful of the wonderful privilege and extraordinary responsibility to herald the good news of Christ to a world alienated from its Creator, Sustainer, and Judge.

When a Christian's theology of religions moves from exclusivism to inclusivism, pluralism, or universalism, the result is a diminished commitment to missions and evangelism. Historically, the conviction that those who have not heard and believed the gospel are lost has been a major motivation to Christian missionary endeavor. As Harold Netland observes:

> One simply cannot understand the remarkable Protestant missionary effort of the nineteenth century, including the work of missionary pioneers such as William Carey, Adoniram Judson, David Livingstone and Hudson Taylor, without appreciating the premise underlying their efforts: salvation is to be found only in the person and work of Jesus Christ, and those who die without the saving gospel of Christ face an eternity apart from God.[1]

When Christians begin to doubt that conscious faith in Christ is necessary for salvation, the inevitable result will be lack of conviction to share the gospel with religious others.[2] As David Wells warns, "In the Western world, the single greatest cause for diminished interest in and support for evangelism is the erosion of confidence in the uniqueness of Christian faith."[3] If a theology of religions causes people to ignore the clear biblical mandate to proclaim the gospel, then it cannot be called Christian, and its validity must be questioned.

---

[1] H. A. Netland, *Encountering Religious Pluralism: The Challenge to Christian Faith & Mission* (Downers Grove, IL: InterVarsity, 2001), 27.

[2] Christian inclusivists are conscious of this concern but deny that it is a valid refutation of the inclusivist position. See, for example, T. L. Tiessen, *Who Can Be Saved? Reassessing Salvation in Christ and World Religions* (Downers Grove, IL: InterVarsity, 2004), 259–94; C. Pinnock, *A Wideness in God's Mercy: the Finality of Jesus Christ in a World of Religions* (Grand Rapids: Zondervan, 1992), 176–80. Inclusivist Clark Pinnock denies that the conviction that the lost will suffer eternal separation from God in hell is a legitimate motivation to mission. C. Pinnock, "Response to John F. Walvoord," in *Four Views on Hell*, ed. W. Crockett (Grand Rapids: Zondervan, 1996), 39. But valid, demonstrable implications of the inclusivist, pluralist, and universalist positions must be considered, particularly when these implications run contrary to the heart of the biblical message and mission.

[3] D. F. Wells, *God the Evangelist: How the Holy Spirit Works to Bring Men and Women to Faith* (Grand Rapids: Eerdmans, 1987), 63.

KEY QUESTIONS A CHRISTIAN THEOLOGY OF RELIGIONS MUST ANSWER

In this chapter we will consider six questions crucial to a Christian theology of religions. (1) Is general revelation sufficient for salvation? (2) Does special revelation require a human messenger? (3) Is there truth in other religions? (4) Is there salvation in other religions? (5) Is interreligious dialogue beneficial? (6) Is interreligious social cooperation legitimate? Answering these questions in fidelity to the Spirit-inspired Scriptures is critical if the Church is to carry out the Great Commission in a Spirit-empowered and Christ-honoring way. The answers to these questions will have a guiding influence on the mission strategy of the Church.

Is General Revelation Sufficient for Salvation?

Theologians have long differentiated between general and special revelation. Although these two categories are not explicitly biblical, they do serve to bring attention to the broad differences in the different kinds of revelation described in Scripture. General revelation is that knowledge of God the Lord has revealed to humanity as a whole and which contains general truths of and about God. It is general in scope and general in content. God is rich in mercy and not stingy with knowledge of Himself. He has woven true knowledge of Himself in all that He has made. Psalm 19:1 states, "The heavens declare the glory of God, and the sky proclaims the work of His hands." Consistent with this, the apostle Paul wrote that God's invisible attributes such as His "eternal power and divine nature" have been clearly perceived ever since the creation of the world (Rom 1:20). The providential care of God bears testimony to His power and nature (Matt 5:45; Acts 17:26). God has written His moral law on the consciences of all humans (Rom 2:15). God has also communicated that He is the judge before whom sinful humanity will be condemned or acquitted, and the human conscience both accuses and excuses its bearer (Rom 2:15–16). Those who violate God's laws know they deserve to die (Rom 1:32). Finally, it is clear to all humanity that God is merciful and patient because the just and deserved judgment warranted by sinful action does not come as soon as it should (Rom 2:4). These examples fall under the category of general revelation, so named because they are general truths about God that go out to a general audience.[4]

Special revelation is aptly named because it is revelation of God that is specific in scope and specific in substance. It is particular information about God and His redemptive purposes and activities that goes to a particular audience. Avenues of special revelation found in Scripture include personal encounter with the Lord through dreams, visions, or theophanies (e.g., Exod 3:1–6; Matt 1:20–23; 2:13), mighty acts (Exod 14:21–31; 2 Kgs 14:19–35), the verbal word of God (2 Tim 3:16; 2 Pet 1:20–21), and the incarnation of the Son of God (John 1:14). By this definition, Jesus Christ embodies personal encounter, mighty act, and verbal truth.

The reputation of general revelation has been sullied by discussion of its salvific potential. An unfortunate result is that God's character is often called into question. For years conservative Christian systematic theologians have spoken of general revelation mainly in contrast to special revelation. The conclusion is that general revelation is insufficient to save but sufficient to condemn. Many balk at this conclusion and question the character of One who would give revelation for the purpose of condemnation. Why would God give just enough revelation to damn a person but not enough to save that person? But that is hardly a fair question. The inference that God gives general revelation merely for the sake of providing a basis for condemnation will not bear the test of biblical scrutiny. Scripture identifies several reasons God provides general revelation, including glorifying Himself (Ps 19:1), informing His image-bearers of His attributes and nature (Rom 1:19–21), enabling them to make sense of the world around them and to grow in their knowledge of it (Ps 36:9), motivating people to seek Him (Acts 17:27), transmitting His moral will (Rom 2:14–15), and providing a just basis for acquittal and judgment (Rom 2:16).

Further, what we call general revelation and special revelation were never meant to be separated. In particular, God's general revelation of

---

[4] One problem with the title "general" as opposed to "special" revelation" is that it may unwittingly communicate to some that there is revelation of God that is ordinary and mundane. Of course, this is not the case. The Bible is clear that revelation of God is not a matter of human discovery or construction, but is always the product of personal divine disclosure. When it comes to knowledge of God, humans are absolutely dependent upon the merciful disclosure of God. The one who looks at a snowy mountain peak or watches the ocean surf crashing against the shore is confronted with the power, creativity, artistry, and majesty of God. There is nothing ordinary about that knowledge, even though we may categorize it as "general."

Himself in creation, providence, and conscience was not meant to be received in a self-interpreting manner.[5] In the beginning, God walked with Adam and Eve and interpreted for them what they saw in His creation. Sin entered the world when Adam and Eve chose to ignore the instruction of God, choosing rather to evaluate God's creation by a standard other than God and His words to them (Gen 3:1–6). As Cornelius Van Til concludes, general revelation and special revelation are "mutually meaningless without one another" but "mutually fruitful when taken together."[6]

Even before the fall there was a hermeneutical ambiguity to general revelation. God's words have always been necessary to interpret God's works.[7] But the need for divine interpretation of general revelation is made more acute by the fall of man. Daniel Strange explains, "First, there is an increased complexity and potential hermeneutical ambiguity in the objective external revelation; for what is revealed now is not only God's glory and goodness but His wrath and judgment as well (Rom 1:18). Second, this revelation of wrath is revealed both externally in the world and internally within mankind."[8] Fallen humanity is in desperate need of regeneration, a transformation that comes through the Holy Spirit with the gospel of Christ. General revelation does not, nor can it, contain this knowledge.

Whereas pluralists are certain and inclusivists are hopeful that saving knowledge of God is found in general revelation, exclusivists see no reason from Scripture to share such hope. The response of sinful humanity to the general revelation of God is to suppress that truth in unrighteousness (Rom 1:18). Although the fact that God withholds judgment for a time is a demonstration of His "kindness, restraint and patience" that is supposed to lead the world to repentance, the result is hypocrisy and greater sin due to the hardness of the human heart (Rom 2:1–5). Whereas the Lord exercises His sovereign governance over the

---

[5]That general and special revelation are not to be separated is demonstrated in Psalm 19. It is no mere convenience that this psalm includes six verses explicating general revelation (Ps 19:1–6) immediately followed by five verses celebrating special revelation (Ps 19:7–11). Daniel Strange notes that the nature psalms are to be understood "within the context of the already regenerated, redeemed, and particular community of Israel." D. Strange, "General Revelation: Sufficient or Insufficient?" in *Faith Comes by Hearing: A Response to Inclusivism*, ed. C. W. Morgan and R. A. Peterson (Downers Grove, IL: InterVarsity, 2008), 57.

[6]C. Van Til, "Nature and Scripture," in *The Infallible Word*, ed. N. B. Stonehouse and P. Woolley (Philadelphia: Presbyterian and Reformed, 1946), 269.

[7]Strange, "General Revelation," 66.

[8]Ibid., 67.

nations so that "they might seek God" (Acts 17:27), the result is that "there is no one who understands, there is no one who seeks God" (Rom 3:11). Even if active suppression of the truth did not take place, general revelation is not sufficient to save because it does not tell of God's specific redemptive acts. In particular, general revelation does not tell of God's plan for salvation in Jesus Christ, who is the greatest revelation of God.

In the hands of pluralists and inclusivists, general revelation is asked to bear the salvific burden to the "unevangelized," while special revelation carries the salvific message to the evangelized. Such a bifurcation of tasks is not legitimate because general revelation and special revelation are not separate categories that are intelligible and effective apart from each other.[9] General revelation, which is not salvific because it does not tell the story of Jesus, was never meant to carry the message of salvation alone. Rather, general revelation provides "the background or scaffolding for God's redemption in Christ."[10]

The entrance of sin into the world, coupled with the suppression of the truth of general revelation, has consequences for the accessibility of revelation. Strange explains, "Instrumentally the withdrawal of special revelation from a people, with its important corrective to salvifically insufficient general revelation, is already a demonstration of God's righteous judgment, a cyclical degenerative process of sin and judgment continuing over generations."[11] Therefore, far from some individuals not having access to special revelation, "through no fault of their own," the absence of special revelation is an indication of initial judgment upon fallen humanity. In a demonstration of God's grace and mercy, some undeservedly receive the special revelation of the good news of Christ. Some of that group believe and are saved.

In summary, general revelation and special revelation were never meant to be separated. Even before sin entered the world, humanity was dependent on God's special revelation to interpret rightly God's general revelation. This need was made more acute with the fall of humanity in Genesis 3. The fall also introduced the need for God's

---

[9]Greg Bahnsen draws out the apologetic implications of this: "The epistemological defense of natural revelation and the epistemological defense of special revelation must even now continue to be integrated and work together, rather than treated as separate religious claims that are intelligible and justifiable apart from each other." G. L. Bahnsen, *Van Til's Apologetic: Readings and Analysis* (Phillipsburg, NJ: P&R, 1998), 195.

[10]Strange, "General Revelation," 69.

[11]Ibid., 72.

redemptive action in the world and God's announcement of those redemptive acts. General revelation, which has always been dependent on special revelation for right understanding, cannot carry the good news of Christ's salvific work. The absence of special revelation that interprets general revelation and announces redemption through Christ is evidence of God's just judgment on sinful humanity.

Does Special Revelation Require a Human Messenger?

Scripture must guide the Church's thinking on this question because of its importance to missions. There is no explicit statement in Scripture that people must respond to the Church's proclamation of the gospel in order to be saved. People are converted by the Word of God (Rom 10:17). The sinner is saved by the Lord when he repents and believes the gospel. The emphasis is on the object of faith, namely the gospel, not the agency by which the gospel is made known. However, the typical manner in which the gospel is spread, as described in the biblical narratives and teachings, is through human proclamation. The book of Acts, for example, records narratives and gospel proclamations to large and small groups (e.g., 2:14–40; 3:12–26; 4:8–12; 10:34–43; 13:16–41; 16:25–34; etc.), as well as to individuals (e.g., 8:26–40).

The case of Paul's conversion does seem to make allowance for other means of gospel proclamation. Emphasis is placed upon Paul's encounter with Christ (Acts 9:1–8; 26:12–18), what he called his "heavenly vision" (Acts 26:19). But Paul's encounter, ironically, came in the context of his appointment as a "witness of the things" he had seen (Acts 26:16; cf. 9:15–16). Paul himself saw the uniqueness of his conversion and appointment as an apostle (1 Cor 15:8; Gal 1:12). Also, whereas both Paul and Ananias received visions during the time surrounding Paul's conversion (Acts 9:10–12), the Lord still required Ananias to physically visit Paul to effect his healing (Acts 9:13–14). The story of the conversion of the Ethiopian eunuch is also instructive (Acts 8:26–40). Although an angel intervened in human events to the degree of sending Philip to the eunuch (8:26) and the Spirit of God gave further guidance to Philip (8:29) and remarkable transport away from the scene (8:39), it was to Philip that the privilege was given of telling the eunuch "the good news about Jesus" (8:35). Surely the Lord could have sent the angel directly to the eunuch to preach the gospel or even could have appeared to the eunuch Himself. Yet it was the Lord's plan to use the redeemed Philip for the important task of proclamation. The results of the gospel encounter are telling: The eunuch believed the "good news about Jesus," requested baptism, and "went on his way rejoicing" (8:36–39), while Philip continued his ministry from Azotus to Caesarea, "evangelizing all the towns" (8:40).

The Church has been given a mandate to take the gospel to the ends of the earth. Paul's own logic in Rom 10:14–15 assumes human proclamation of the gospel. Sinners cannot believe and call on the Lord unless they are told, and they cannot hear unless a preacher is sent. The logic is that only those who hear the preaching of a sent one will be able to hear and believe. The Lord may use whatever means He chooses to spread the gospel, but the Church has been directed to go and preach the good news to the nations, not wait for Jesus or His angels to appear to the unevangelized.

Recent testimony of the role of dreams and visions among Muslims, pointing them to Christ or Scripture,[12] is evidence that the Holy Spirit is at work in advance of gospel proclamation, preparing people to receive the message. Such a work by the Holy Spirit would be consistent with both Scripture (Acts 10:30–32; 11:13–15) and the Christ-glorifying role of the Holy Spirit taught in Scripture and developed in chapter 8 of this book. In a 2001 survey of approximately 600 Muslim-background Christian believers, over one-fourth stated "quite emphatically that dreams and visions were key in drawing them to Christ and sustaining them in difficult times."[13] Randal Scott, a field director with Frontiers, writes that at least 50 percent of Muslim-background believers "had an extraordinary dream as a part of their pilgrimage of faith."[14] J. Dudley Woodberry and Russell Shubin categorize the dreams and visions as being either empowering or preparatory.[15] Empowering dreams are given to believers to strengthen them in the face of persecution. Preparatory visions are given to elicit curiosity in the gospel.

---

[12]See, for example, B. Sheikh, *I Dared to Call Him Father* (Waco, TX: Word Books, 1978); P. Parshall, *New Paths in Muslim Evangelism: Evangelical Approaches to Contextualization* (Grand Rapids: Baker, 1980), 24, 152–53; R. Love, *Muslims, Magic and the Kingdom of God* (Pasadena, CA: William Carey Library, 2000), 156ff.; J. D. Woodberry and R. G. Shubin, "Why I Chose Jesus," *Mission Frontiers Magazine* (March 2001) [journal online]; accessed 28 January 2006; available from http://www.missionfrontiers.org/pdf/2001/01/200101.htm; Internet.

[13]Woodberry and Shubin, "Why I Chose Jesus."

[14]R. Scott, "Evangelism and Dreams: Foundational Presuppositions to Interpret God-given Dreams of the Unreached," *EMQ* (April 2008): 176.

[15]Woodberry and Shubin, "Why I Chose Jesus."

Typically, "a Man in white" confronts the Muslim who then directs the recipient of the vision to seek understanding of Himself. In most cases this involves being directed toward a Christian who can then explain the meaning of the dream and the meaning of the gospel. Significantly, Scott concludes, "Dreams prepare people to believe and repent; however, they never (in my experience) contain a clear gospel message. God uses followers of Jesus to explain the gospel so that dreamers can believe and repent."[16] We observe, based on this anecdotal evidence, that even when the Lord uses an extraordinary event like a dream or vision, the usual practice is still to involve human proclamation of the gospel. The Church may pray that the Lord would send dreams and visions to religious others to arouse curiosity in Christ, but only the poorest and laziest of mission strategies would end there. The Church must mobilize and send proclaimers to minister to those recipients of dreams and visions so that they may hear of and believe in Jesus.

Is There Truth in Other Religions?

God has made known truths of Himself through general revelation, but that knowledge does not include the story of redemption in Christ. Is there any truth, then, in the beliefs and dogmas of religious others? As established above, Scripture is clear that general revelatory knowledge is granted to all of humanity through creation, providence, and conscience. As was noted in chapter 2 with the case of Melchizedek, Scripture also allows for residual knowledge of special revelation passed down through the generations. This truth of God, what Ajith Fernando calls "reminiscent knowledge," was originally given to Adam and Noah and has not been entirely lost by the human race.[17] Contrary to evolutionary models of religions that posit a progress in religious understanding, the Scriptures instead teach a devolution in knowledge of the Lord as people have exchanged the truth of God for a lie and chosen to worship the creature rather than the Creator (Rom 1:25).

With the exposure of Christians to individuals of non-Christian faiths has come an increased familiarity with the sacred writings of

---

[16]Scott, "Evangelism and Dreams," 183. Woodbury and Shubin agree: "Dreams and visions may have been used by God in part because there is a dearth of flesh-and-blood witnesses for Christ willing to articulate and demonstrate the power of the Gospel in person." Woodbury and Shubin, "Why I Chose Jesus."

[17]A. Fernando, *The Christian's Attitude Toward World Religion: Responding to the Idea that Christianity Is Just Another Religion* (Wheaton, IL: Tyndale House, 1987), 104.

non-Christian religions. Perhaps in the past an uncritical dismissal of non-Christian writings would have seemed acceptable, but today societal pressure and intellectual honesty demand that the sacred writings of religious others be evaluated on their own merits. At best, these sacred writings and the traditions from which they flow are a combination of accuracy and inaccuracy.[18] Christians, therefore, ought not to embrace the extremes of either broad condemnation or naïve acceptance of non-Christian texts.[19] The hardness of the human heart and the devolution over time of reminiscent truth in the traditions of religious others, exacerbated by the ongoing lack of special revelation to correct errors, inevitably leads to misunderstandings, inaccuracies, and distortions of God's attributes and actions in the beliefs of religious others. Fallen human wisdom and darkened human hearts result in theology and worship that does not honor God as God (Rom 1:21–25). Further, the role of the demonic in other religions, explained in chapter 2, is a reality and ought not to be ignored. These different sources and influences result in a curious mixture of truth and error. Chapter 2 demonstrated that the result of misconceptions of God is idolatry. Further, Heb 1:1–2 teaches that God, who in times past spoke to the fathers "in the prophets . . . in these last days has spoken to us in his Son [*en huiō*]" (NASB). The prepositional phrase *en huiō* communicates the

---

[18]Gerald McDermott argues that the insight other religions have about God cannot be chalked up to human insight, but neither will the typical general/special revelation taxonomy work. Such religious insight, which varies from religion to religion, is not special revelation because it does not tell of the saving work of God in Christ. But it is not general revelation either because it is not generally available to all people. McDermott borrows from Jonathan Edwards's work on types to suggest that there is revelation from God to people in their customs and religions that provides traces of Himself and His plan (however diminished by sin). McDermott explains, "If the types in the religions give only broken and partially distorted access to divine realities, they are similar to Old Testament types—which point to truth but sometimes obscurely." G. R. McDermott, *Can Evangelicals Learn from World Religions? Jesus, Revelation & Religious Traditions* (Downers Grove, IL: InterVarsity, 2000), 114. McDermott does not equate the sacred texts of other religions with the Christian Bible. Scripture is categorically different because it mediates the reality of God in Christ. But McDermott does believe "the Bible itself suggests that there are 'little lights' in the religions that help illuminate the realities that the Light of the World more clearly displays. . . . My claim is that among the religions are scattered promises of God in Christ and that these promises are revealed types planted there by the triune God." McDermott does not go into detail as to how God "plants" these types in other religions, though the avenues of general revelation, reminiscent knowledge, as well as special intervention through dreams and visions are plausible options. McDermott's proposal is speculative because to suggest that God has placed types in the traditions and religions of the world is to go further than Scripture affirms. But his proposal does provide an explanation for why some people groups are more prepared for the gospel than are others.

[19]T. C. Tennent, *Theology in the Context of World Christianity: How the Global Church Is Influencing the Way We Think About and Discuss Theology* (Grand Rapids: Zondervan, 2007), 68–69.

qualitative difference between speaking "in the prophets" and "in (His) Son." The revelation of God through Jesus is qualitatively different from any speech of God. That it comes "in these last days" indicates the finality of God's speech through His Son. Therefore, any teaching that does not elevate the Son is by definition inferior and, given the progression of redemptive history that culminates in the Son, untrustworthy.

But Christians ought not to write off the sacred texts of religious others as "a pack of lies" in a blanket fashion for two biblical reasons. First, we have already established that non-Christian religions may contain a mixture of truth and error through general revelation and reminiscent truth, so it should come as no surprise when we find true statements of God or even of Jesus in the teachings of other religions. For example, the Qur'an teaches that Jesus was born of a virgin, while Pure Land Buddhism contains teaching on the need of grace to attain enlightenment. This is, after all, our Father's world, and He will not be shut out of it. Some people groups are more prepared for the gospel than others.[20] Therefore, Christians should expect to find some truth in all areas of the world, including non-Christian philosophies and religions, even where the gospel has not been preached. This is so, not because these non-Christian philosophies and religions have any independent insight into the nature of God and His redemptive purposes but because the God and Father of the Lord Jesus Christ created humans in His image and speaks clearly and loudly through general revelation. Second, the biblical writers themselves felt the freedom to affirm the truth content of certain non-Christian writings. For example, the apostle Paul, in his address at the Areopagus, quoted the words of pagan poets that he neither accepted as authoritative nor believed to be inspired by God (Acts 17:28). The apostolic use of nonbiblical sacred texts ought to inform and guide our use of these texts.

Timothy Tennent provides the following three guidelines for using nonbiblical sacred texts.[21] First, use of the texts should be limited to

---

[20]For example, speaking of Hindu-background Christians, Timothy Tennent writes, "When many of them look back on their past life in Hinduism and reflect on it, they are aware of profound discontinuity as well as surprising continuity. They see not only deliverance from demonic deception, but also, quite remarkably, they see little windows of God's grace in preparing and drawing them, even while they were still Hindus, for the day when they would receive the full light and glory of the Christian gospel and live their new lives in the presence of the living Christ." Ibid., 69–70.

[21]Ibid., 71–73.

evangelistic outreach where the intended audience consists predominately of individuals who would be familiar with those texts. Whereas Paul strategically quoted Greek poets to his audience in Athens, quoting Greek poets to a predominately Jewish audience would have been nonsensical. Is it not likely that if Paul were speaking to a Muslim audience that he would quote from Arab or Muslim sources? For example, quoting the Qur'an's affirmation of the virgin birth of Jesus (19:15–22) or the Qur'an's record of Jesus' miraculous works (3:49–50; 43:63) would be a legitimate use of the Muslim sacred text in an evangelistic encounter with Muslims.

Second, non-Christian texts should be used only to corroborate Christian truth, not to serve as an independent source of truth. As the Creator and the Architect of redemption, God has revealed in Christ not a set of isolated facts about Himself but a complete picture of reality. Religions that deny the supremacy and salvation of Christ may be correct about certain facts about God and reality (because of general revelation), but those truth claims will be independent and discontinuous. The arbitrary nature of those verities renders other religions untrustworthy sources of truth. Only in Christ are "hidden all the treasures of wisdom and knowledge" (Col 2:3 ESV). The search for truth must begin with Scripture, must be submitted to Scripture, and must honor the One to whom Scripture points. Where non-Christian sacred texts corroborate the truths of Scripture, they may be used apologetically or evangelistically.[22] The Christian ought not to privilege any text above Scripture or treat it as equal to Scripture because only the Bible is the Spirit-inspired Word of God and a trustworthy source of divine words.

Third, any nonbiblical sacred text that is quoted should be "lifted out of its original setting and clearly reoriented within a new Christocentric setting."[23] World religions do not present themselves as disinterested sources of facts about the Almighty. Rather, as chapter 4 established, religions present total views of metaphysics, epistemology, and ethics. In short, world religions offer worldviews of varying degrees of coherence and internal consistency. The truth claims of religious others are

---

[22]Tennent provides a quotation from the Hindu Upanishads and writes, "Using a nonbiblical sacred text as a corroborative witness serves to sharpen the biblical message and helps to demonstrate that Jesus does not arrive in India as a stranger, but in answer to the prayers of Hindu hearts." Ibid., 72.

[23]Ibid., 71–72.

part of their particular worldview that does not tell the story of Jesus or submit to His lordship. Therefore, even where religious others make an accurate truth claim, due to God's powerful voice in general revelation, that claim must be reoriented toward Christ. Paul does this very thing in Acts 17 when he takes the statements of Epimenides and Aratus, statements in context given in praise to Zeus, and accurately reorients them toward the God and Father of Jesus.

In summary, the right-thinking Christian will evaluate the truth claims of religious others according to their own claims, but he must recognize that those claims make up a worldview that does not exalt Christ. Because all things were made by, through, and for Christ (Col 1:16), any worldview that does not submit to the lordship of Christ is necessarily false. With that recognition the Christian can redeem truths of God from religious others by taking those thoughts captive in obedience to Christ, that is, reorienting them toward Christ in apologetic and evangelistic encounters (2 Cor 10:4–5).

Is There Salvation in Other Religions?

If one understands the essence of Christianity to be facts about God, cultivation of personal devotion, advocacy of social justice, or development of the nuclear family, then other religions may bring their own set of credentials to the discussion. But Christianity, at its core, is not any of these things. A Christian is one who trusts the gospel of Jesus Christ and is thereby justified by God, reconciled to God, indwelt by God's Spirit, and is being progressively transformed into the image of Christ in anticipation of Christ's return to consummate His kingdom. Sympathetic attempts to seek salvific potential in non-Christian knowledge of God are misguided because other religions are not centered around the saving work of Jesus Christ. Gospel-believing Christians should know better than to evaluate religions by any standard other than the gospel. When Jesus commissioned His disciples, He called and empowered them to bear witness to Himself, not to establish a religion (Matt 28:18–20; Luke 24:46–49; Acts 1:8). The nature of the Great Commission dictates that any comparison between Christianity and the religions of the world are to be based upon the gospel.[24] The world, including the adherents of other religions, stands

---

[24]For an excellent discussion that makes the same point, see J. Goldingay and C. Wright, "'Yahweh Our God Yahweh One': The Oneness of God in the Old Testament," in *One God, One*

condemned before God because of sin and rebellion (John 3:18). Jesus Christ came that those who believe in Him might be saved (John 3:16–17). There is no basis in Scripture for evaluating the religions of the world according to any other criterion. Only those who believe in the gospel will be saved.

Is Interreligious Dialogue Beneficial?

Because salvation is found only in Christ and not in any religion that is not centered on the gospel of Christ, Christians must engage in dialogue with religious others.[25] The proclamation of Jesus and the apostles must guide our interaction with the world religions. Encounters with religious others provide many of the boldest examples of gospel witness in the Bible. Chapter 2 highlighted Jesus' confrontation with the nations and with the religious leaders of Israel. His interaction with "religious others" included dialogue but never for the purpose of learning something new about God or His redemptive purposes. His dialogue was always for the purpose of relationship and to drive the conversation to the truth He was proclaiming. The gospel proclamation of the apostles was no different. Paul's strategy with religious others was always one of respectful confrontation, even with idolaters.[26] He looked for points of contact with those to whom he

Lord: Christianity in a World of Religious Pluralism, ed. A. D. Clarke and B. W. Winter, 2nd ed. (Grand Rapids: Baker, 1992), 53–55.

[25]Gerald McDermott, who has written on these issues perhaps more than any other evangelical, says that we can learn from religious others in the following three ways: "placing a new emphasis on a part of the revelation of Christ so that revelation as a whole takes on a new light; seeing an old concept, which has previously helped us understand Christ from a new perspective; and developing ideas further by way of new application, relationship or implication." G. R. McDermott, *Can Evangelicals Learn from World Religions*, 14. In each of these three areas the Christian does not learn new truths of God, nor does a religious other expose him to truth that is not available in Scripture; rather, McDermott emphasizes the subjective appropriation of revelation. Ibid., 71–72. Fernando makes much the same point when he explains that though God's revelation may be complete, our perception of it is incomplete. Because of cultural conditioning, some Christians may be hindered from learning things that are clearly taught in Scripture or are evident through creation, conscience, or providence. Other cultures may not have these cultural barriers. Dialogue may expose that cultural conditioning, enabling the Christian to see an ancient truth for the first time or in a fresh way. As an example, Fernando tells of a friend of his, a Christian convert from Hinduism, who brought a "meditative, devotional reverence" to prayer that he brought with him from his Hindu background. Fernando also points out that much of the core of his friend's Hindu convictions on prayer had to be altered and transformed (including the subject, purpose, and value of prayer). Fernando, *Christian's Attitude toward World Religions*, 111–12.

[26]William Larkin calls Luke's strategy in writing the book of Acts, "respectful integrity." His common ground is not that of fellow searcher but of fellow human (14:15). "Acts seems to avoid two extremes: direct confrontation with the particulars of a religion and treating the religion as fulfilled in Christianity." I do think that Paul did confront the particulars of other religions (see my discussion in chap. 2 of Acts 14 and 17), but he did so in such a way that did not strip the

was witnessing. These points of contact were not "neutral ground," as though such a thing exists for the Christian, but they were occasions of common experience where the apostle and the unbeliever could speak together. Paul's interaction with non-Christians was always driven by the Great Commission as a mandate to persuade others to repent and believe the gospel of Christ. As Eckhard Schnabel writes, "Paul was a missionary, not a religionist involved in a dialogue that proceeds from the assumption that God is present in all religions, that salvation is possible through all faiths and ideologies, and that God's Spirit is at work in all religions, faiths, and ideologies."[27]

With this background, I offer four guidelines to interfaith dialogue for the disciple of Jesus. First, *Christians must engage in dialogue with people of other faiths*. The current pluralistic and postmodern context has placed a premium value on authentic discussion. Where true tolerance is cherished, dialogue must follow. Regardless of the Christian's personal ambivalence toward dialogue or his level of confidence in speaking with people of other faiths, the cultural context demands that believers engage in dialogue if they are going to witness faithfully to Christ. The apostle Paul was willing to "become all things to all people" in order that he might save some (1 Cor 9:22). Becoming "all things" will require the Christian to learn something of the backgrounds and faiths of those around him. An effective way of doing this is through dialogue.

Second, *Christians engaged in dialogue must be listeners*. We cannot dismiss the truth claims of religious others as being "simply false." In our current climate a sure way to disqualify oneself from the roundtable of discussion is to communicate a stubborn and intellectually proud heart that refuses to listen. Make no mistake, the response against the truth claims of the gospel, apart from the grace of God, will be strong and at times antagonistic. Sufficient for the moment is the inherent offense of the cross to the sinful heart (1 Cor 1:23). The Christian ought not to add to that offense or distract from the gospel through an elitist, proud, or condescending attitude. We should listen to religious others attentively and sympathetically and then do all we can to

Athenians of their essential human dignity. W. J. Larkin, "The Contribution of the Gospels and Acts to a Biblical Theology of Religions," in *Christianity and the Religions: A Biblical Theology of World Religions*, ed. E. Rommen and H. Netland (Pasadena, CA: William Carey Library, 1995), 85.

[27] E. J. Schnabel, "Other Religions: Saving or Secular," in *Faith Comes by Hearing*, ed. Morgan and Peterson, 121.

provide a Christ-honoring response to their religious affirmations and faithful answer to their legitimate questions. The Christian ought not to fear dialogue. The gospel is robust and powerful (Rom 1:16). Paul felt no need to shrink from his responsibility as a minister of the new covenant or to peddle the word of God, making it more palatable for a finicky audience (2 Cor 2:17; 4:2). Instead, he preached Christ and reasoned with his audiences (Acts 17:17), being fully persuaded of the truth of the gospel. He also recognized the spiritual essence of his ministry, knowing that those who reject the gospel are blind to the reality of Christ's glory (2 Cor 4:3–6). Because the gospel is true, it can stand up to the toughest questions and most vehement criticism. We do not need to have all the answers. A simple "I do not know" response is not a rejection of Christ, nor is it a denial that an answer to a specific question exists. Stereotypes will disappear and misunderstandings will be corrected when both sides listen to each other. The truth of the gospel will be communicated by both the content of the proclamation and the manner in which the gospel is proclaimed. Remember the words of Jesus: "It is more blessed to give than to receive" (Acts 20:35), and "Whatever you want others to do for you, do also the same for them" (Matt 7:12).

Third, while listening with humility, *Christians must not abandon their Christian convictions.* Pluralist sensibilities would demand that Christians place the truth question in abeyance for the purpose of authentic dialogue, but the Christian is under no obligation to participate in this manner. In fact, the opposite is true. The Christian has been commanded to take every thought captive in obedience to Christ (2 Cor 10:4–5). To check your Christian convictions at the door in the name of "authentic dialogue" is to dishonor the Lord who bought you and to ensure that you have nothing of value to say at the religious roundtable. First Peter 3:15 teaches as a prerequisite for giving a defense of the Christian faith, "In your hearts set apart Christ as Lord" (NIV). Further, the Christian ought not to be ashamed of his faith in Christ, nor of its intellectual fortitude. Recall that Peter proclaimed that Israel could "know with certainty" that Jesus was the Messiah (Acts 2:36), while Paul "kept confounding the Jews . . . by proving" that Jesus is the Christ (Acts 9:22). Timothy Tennent, who has written perhaps the best book on Christian dialogue with religious others, notes that most of those who are setting the agendas for interreligious dialogue, even though they claim to speak for Christianity, are not in fact Christians.[28] In interreligious discussions, faith commitments must not be suspended. Interreligious discussion void of convictions is little more than disinterested chatter. When transcendent truth is abandoned for the sake of "authentic dialogue," theology devolves into anthropology and sociology, a vapid interchange of personal feelings and experiences. When personal experience replaces the objective reality of God in interreligious dialogue, the participants engage in idolatry, the public promotion of private avatars. Praise be to God, the Christian has a far more compelling and powerful message precisely because of the real glory and transcendent majesty of the Lord Jesus Christ.

Finally, and most importantly, *the goal of Christians in interreligious dialogue must be the conversion of their conversation partners to Christ.* This is an unpopular notion because many assume that dialogue is its own point, that is, the exchange of ideas without persuasion is the goal of the day. But to accept this understanding of dialogue is to accept the relativistic worldview that it presupposes. If truth were relative, if God were unknowable, then calls for conversation without persuasion might be legitimate. But such is not the case. God does exist. He has sent His Christ. Jesus has commissioned His disciples to be His witnesses. The gospel is powerful to save. Authentic dialogue and passionate witness are not mutually exclusive. In fact, you cannot have one without the other—not if the topic of discussion focuses on ultimate reality. Pluralists may pretend that they are disinterested parties, evaluating the evidence in an unbiased manner. In fact, they themselves are active and interested participants seeking a solution to the problem that besets them and all of fallen humanity. Their culpable refusal to submit to Christ demonstrates how biased (or blinded) they actually are. They will not surrender their false worldview for the sake of "authentic dialogue." Why should Christians, who alone possess the hope for reconciliation with God, surrender both their worldview and their mission?

Is Interreligious Social Cooperation Legitimate?

The question of interreligious cooperation is particularly significant given the pluralistic world that most Christians inhabit. Christians

---

[28]T. C. Tennent, *Christianity at the Religious Roundtable: Evangelicalism in Conversation with Hinduism, Buddhism, and Islam* (Grand Rapids: Baker, 2002), 10.

live with religious others in the same cities and share common cause for the welfare of the city and state. Can the church join with Muslims, Buddhists, or Hindus to fight hunger, homelessness, or illiteracy? Included in this question would be the legitimacy of the church joining with secular governments or accepting tax dollars to perform ministries of help and compassion.

The answers to these questions may seem obvious on the surface. Why should the church not partner with those whose cause is the same? If Buddhists are concerned about the welfare of others and there is opportunity for effective partnerships, then would it not be arrogant for Christians to refuse to cooperate? If cities seek the help of the church, should not the church gladly do what she can to serve?

The issue becomes decidedly less clear when Scripture, motivations, and theology are considered. Jesus' statement in Matt 12:30, "Anyone who is not with Me is against Me," is instructive, as is His teaching in Mark 9:39–40: "There is no one who will perform a miracle in My name who can soon afterwards speak evil of Me. For whoever is not against us is for us." In both cases Jesus thrusts Himself into the middle of the works done, and He becomes the test of whether the work is Christian. The Christian's capacity to serve others is borne out of a compassion and kindness that is the result of the sanctifying work of the Holy Spirit (Gal 5:22–23). As in all things, the Christian's motivation for service is to be the glory and praise of God (1 Cor 10:31). Christians are to exercise their service gifts according to the direction of 1 Pet 4:11: "If anyone serves, his service should be from the strength God provides, so that in everything God may be glorified through Jesus Christ." The motivation to glorify Christ is not only distasteful to and impossible for religious others (1 Cor 12:3), but it is fundamentally impossible to please God unless one is in the Spirit (Rom 8:7–8).

My biggest concern with interreligious partnerships and partnerships with secular groups is that identification with Christ and gospel proclamation are often not allowed as a precondition for the partnership. For example, in 2009, a group of evangelical churches in Portland, Oregon, began officially partnering with the city of Portland on a number of specific tasks. Some churches had previously been volunteering to mentor students in the public schools. *The Oregonian*, the city and state's largest newspaper, ran an article essentially reassuring the public that evangelism would not take place in these partnerships.

> Talk to the church's school volunteers and you'll realize that they're keenly aware of the concern and committed to playing by the rules. Phrases like "no strings attached" and "no agenda" came up repeatedly at a recent organizing meeting of school-partnership coordinators from participating churches.

One of the students working closely with a church volunteer confessed that she did not know the name of the mentor's church, nor did she know "much about her mentor's beliefs, other than a commitment to 'helping people.'"[29] When the Christian has to agree not to identify himself with Christ in order to partner with others, then is that a partnership appropriate to pursue? Is any theological cost too high to pay in the pursuit of interreligious partnerships?

The Emergent church, a movement of left-leaning younger church leaders, seems willing to make any theological revision necessary to partner with religious others.[30] The movement has generated much publicity with a commitment to missional living that has challenged the evangelical church to rethink its views on culture, world religions, preaching, and social action. The works of Emergent leaders such as Brian McLaren, Rob Bell, Dan Kimball, Doug Pagitt, and Tony Jones have had significant influence upon many, including evangelical churches that do not formally identify with the Emergent movement.

In particular, a growing number of young leaders are challenging the nature of the gospel, redefining it in such a way so as to open the church to inclusivism, pluralism, and universalism. Reacting against a gospel focused only on the afterlife, Emergent leaders redefine the

---

[29]T. Krattenmaker, "Church Volunteers Walk a Fine Line in Public Schools," *The Oregonian*, 3 August 2009, D1–2.

[30]The "Emerging" and "Emergent" nomenclature is confusing to some. The term *Emerging church* commonly refers to churches that are intentionally and missionally engaged with the emerging culture. There is a continuum of beliefs represented in the Emerging church ranging from conservative to something far less so. In 2001, the term *emergent* was first used by the Young Leaders Network of Leadership Network. Those who participated in this group eventually started another group, coalescing under the Internet domain name, emergentvillage.com. Generally speaking, the Emergent movement represents a more liberal aspect of the Emerging church continuum. For a helpful history of the Emergent movement, see D. Kimball, "Origin of the terms 'Emerging' and 'Emergent Church,'" http://www.the-next-wave-ezine.info/issue100/index.cfm?id=23&ref=ARTICLES_EMERGING%20CHURCH_347 (accessed 26 December 2009).

gospel to be about "social transformation arising from the presence and permeation of the reign of Christ."[31] McLaren writes:

> But now I wonder if this gospel about how to get your soul into Heaven after death is really only a ghost of the real gospel that Jesus talked about, which seemed to have something to do with God's will being done on earth now, not just in Heaven later. . . . Yes, I believe that the gospel has facts that deal with forgiveness of sins, but I feel unfaithful to Jesus to define the gospel by that one facet when I see our contemporary churches failing to address so many other essential gospel concerns—justice, compassion, sacrifice, purpose, transformation into Christlikeness, and ultimate hope.[32]

Many Christian leaders have chosen to use the kingdom of God as the paradigm for their revisioning of theology and praxis,[33] rightly noting the biblical emphasis on the kingdom of God. To them, the kingdom offers the theological space necessary to overcome the particularity of Jesus' incarnation, and the sooner the church understands that the kingdom is bigger than Christ's church, the sooner the church can fully embrace the inclusive mission of the kingdom. For example, McLaren uses the supposed inclusive nature of the kingdom of God to interpret Gal 3:28 in the modern context as saying that reconciliation demands that "Christians with Jews and Muslims and Hindus" must live together in the kingdom.[34] Samir Selmanovic, coleader and founder of Faith House Manhattan, argues,

> The emergent church movement has come to believe that the ultimate context of the spiritual aspirations of a follower of Jesus

---

[31] E. Gibbs and R. K. Bolger, *Emerging Churches: Creating Christian Community in Postmodern Cultures* (Grand Rapids: Baker, 2005), 60.

[32] B. D. McLaren, "The Method, the Message, and the Ongoing Story," in *The Church in Emerging Culture: Five Perspectives*, ed. L. Sweet (Grand Rapids: Zondervan, 2003), 213. Michael Horton, commenting on the same essay, points out that most of what is on McLaren's list are human works and, therefore, cannot be identified with the gospel.

[33] As one Emerging church leader explained, "We have totally reprogrammed ourselves to recognize the good news as a means to an end—that the kingdom of God is here. We try to live into that reality and hope. We don't dismiss the cross; it is still a central part. But the good news is not that he died but that the kingdom has come." Gibbs and Bulger, *Emerging Churches*, 54.

[34] B. D. McLaren, *The Secret Message of Jesus: Uncovering the Truth That Could Change Everything* (Nashville: Word, 2006), 99. There are limits to Brian McLaren's inclusiveness. "For example, if we deny the Trinity or the full humanity and deity of Christ, I believe we have turned from the path." Id., "Seeking to Do One Thing Well: A Response to Three Helpful Reviews," *Reformation and Revival Journal* 14:3 (2005), 123.

Christ is not Christianity but rather the kingdom of God. This realization has many implications, and the one standing above all is the fact that, like every other religion, Christianity is a non-god, and every non-god can be an idol.[35]

According to Salmanovic, the kingdom of God is "better than Christianity" because it "supersedes Christianity in scope, depth and expression. . . . The Christian religion is still an entity in the human realm."[36] With regard to the gospel, Salmanovic explains, "The gospel is not our gospel, but the gospel of the kingdom of God, and what belongs to the kingdom of God cannot be hijacked by Christianity. God is sovereign, like the wind. He blows wherever he chooses."[37] Dave Sutton of New Duffryn Community Church in Newport, UK, says, "My understanding is that if the kingdom is what God is about, then God might be involved in other faiths. . . . We very much see our work in relation to the unique person and work of Christ. If other religions are involved in that work, that is fine."[38]

Clearly priority is given to the kingdom of God in the Bible. The prophets predicted the kingdom, Jesus inaugurated it, and He will one day return to consummate His kingdom. The problem is that the Emergent church's understanding of the kingdom of God is woefully deficient to the point of distortion.[39] The Emergent church ignores the Bible's presentation of the kingdom, especially the Old Testament anticipation of the kingdom and the New Testament testimony to the necessity of the cross for the consummation of the kingdom.[40] In the hands of the Emergent church, the kingdom is reduced to a "dream"

---

[35]S. Selmanovic, "The Sweet Problem of Inclusiveness: Finding God in the Other," in *An Emergent Manifesto of Hope*, ed. D. Pagitt and T. Jones (Grand Rapids: Baker, 2007), 192.

[36]Ibid., 194.

[37]Ibid. Salmonovic explains, "My friend Mark from New York serves Jesus in substance rather than in words, living out a wordless faith in God. This is only to say that there are no indications in the Bible that this dynamic applies only to individuals and not to groups. Religions live under the spiritual laws of the kingdom of God." Ibid., 195.

[38]Gibbs and Bolger, *Emerging Churches*, 133.

[39]For a thorough critique of the kingdom theology of the Emerging church movement, see T. L. Miles, "A Kingdom Without a King? Evaluating the Kingdom Ethic(s) of the Emerging Church," *SBJT* 12/1 (2008): 88–103.

[40]McLaren's *The Secret Message of Jesus*, which is framed around his understanding of the kingdom of God, is a deeply troubling work because the gospel cannot be found in it. The Holy Spirit is conspicuously absent from the book, including His work of regeneration. The new covenant is hardly mentioned, if at all. The human dilemma is one of laziness and bad education, rather than a heart that is fallen. At the end of the day, McLaren's message is essentially a call for humanity to try to be like Jesus by pulling itself up by its own moral bootstraps.

for a politically correct version of the twentieth-century social gospel: the parenthood of God and the siblinghood of humanity. Jesus Christ is demoted to a spokesperson and exemplar for kingdom values, effectively severed from His kingdom as described in the Bible. In the place of a full-orbed, Spirit-empowered, Christ-honoring biblical kingdom, the Emergent church offers a kingdom without a King and no legitimate explanation, other than human effort, as to how the kingdom can come. History has emphatically demonstrated the impotence of humans to usher in the kingdom of God. Unless God intervenes in human history, deals with human sin and guilt, and then establishes His Christ upon the throne, there can be no consummated kingdom of God. When humans attempt to bring in the kingdom while ignoring the biblical presentation of the kingdom and the proclamation of the King, the entire affair quickly devolves into just another failed Social Gospel experiment.

Jesus expects that His disciples will serve and love others in material tangible ways, just as He did. Jesus told His disciples that they would be "the salt of the earth" (Matt 5:13) and "the light of the world" (Matt 5:14). He instructed His followers, "Let your light shine before men, so that they may see your good works and give glory to your Father in heaven" (Matt 5:16). Jesus' words are instructive because the object of others' praise is not God in the abstract or "the god of our many understandings"; rather, people will praise the God of Jesus' disciples who is specifically identified as the disciples' Father. The disciples' right and ability to call God "Father" presupposes the work of Christ that makes their adoption possible (Gal 4:4–7). How will people know whom to praise unless disciples make some sort of positive identification with the God and Father of Jesus Christ (see Matt 10:42)? When Christians do acts of service, they must do them in Jesus' name, explicitly identifying themselves with Christ (see Acts 3:6,16; 4:30; 16:18; 19:13). Otherwise, the One who empowers your service is neither honored nor thanked, and God the Father is robbed of glory that is rightfully His. Our ministry model must be that of the apostles, who preached "the good news about the kingdom of God and the name of Jesus Christ" (Acts 8:12). When the church is not allowed to identify herself explicitly with Christ, let alone to share the gospel, then the church ought not to participate officially in such interreligious or secular partnerships (Acts 4:18–20).

A CALL FOR IDENTIFICATION WITH CHRIST AND
PROCLAMATION OF THE GOSPEL

The church is situated at a critical stage in redemptive history. The cultural climate is such that bold, uncompromising proclamation of the gospel is looked upon as culturally insensitive, politically incorrect, morally offensive, and intellectually deficient.[41] The world will not offer incentive or encouragement to faithful gospel proclamation. This should come as no surprise since Jesus warned that the world would hate His followers as it had hated Him (John 15:18). Therefore, the Church must be particularly diligent to safeguard her fidelity to her biblical mandate to take the gospel to the nations.

"Preach the gospel at all times and when necessary use words," a saying commonly attributed to Francis of Assisi, has become axiomatic to many Christians. In its purest form it is a call for consistency between words and deeds. Too often, it has become an excuse to avoid evangelism. Far from a legitimate biblical strategy for kingdom expansion, it has become an ointment to assuage the consciences of those not interested in sharing the gospel with others. Unfortunately, too many Christians find it easier to share food occasionally than to share Christ.

Missiologist Michael Jaffarian reports on giving and sending trends in North American mission agencies that relate to this issue. In a survey of 820 mission organizations from the United States and Canada, 45.1 percent of the nearly $6 billion donated to mission organizations annually was given to agencies whose primary ministry was in the area of evangelism and discipleship, while 49.1 percent was given to agencies whose primary ministry areas were relief and development.[42] More troubling are the giving trends. Jaffarian observes:

---

[41]Consider the claim of T. Tilley: "Radical exclusivism which claims that all who do not believe in Jesus' name are bound for hell is as intolerable to orthodox theology as indifferentist pluralism which finds that all religions are equally valid or invalid paths to a single transcendent goal." "Christian Orthodoxy and Religious Pluralism," *Modern Theology* 22/1 (January 2006): 51.

[42]M. Jaffarian, "The Statistical State of the North American Protestant Missions Movement, from the *Mission Handbook*, 20th Edition," *International Bulletin of Missionary Research* 32/1 (January 2008): 37. Evangelism and discipleship mission agencies were involved in activities such as church planting, evangelism, national church nurture, and Bible distribution. Relief and development activities include agricultural programs, justice issues, medicine, and public health. Seven of the top 10 North American mission agencies by income are devoted almost entirely to relief and development. World Vision alone, with an annual income of over $1 billion, accounts for over one-sixth of the total income given in North America for overseas missions.

The total income given for overseas ministries . . . grew by more than $1.27 billion between 2001 and 2005, or 27.5 percent in this span of four years. Most of that growth took place in the relief/development area. American agencies focused on evangelism/discipleship saw combined income grow by 2.7 percent during those four years; those focused on relief/development saw theirs grow by a whopping 74.3 percent.[43]

The numbers indicate a growing commitment to social concerns over against gospel proclamation and church planting.

Few churches in North America have not been influenced by this trend. Service weekends and seasons of service are commonplace in the evangelical community. The call to social action is a needed corrective to the church that for decades was suspicious of attempts to engage in helping ministries for fear of being thought sympathetic to the Social Gospel movement. Concern for the poor and oppressed is evidence that the Spirit of God, who spoke through the Old and New Testament prophets, is at work in the hearts of those who love Christ. But social justice issues, as significant as they are, do not replace the Great Commission. Hunger, poverty, oppression, sickness, and death are evidences of a fallen world. Christ came to redeem that world and inaugurate His kingdom, where such evils will have no place. As such, any good works of service must be done with an explicit identification with Jesus Christ, not with a vague or unspoken nod to the "god of our many understandings." How else will others know what God to praise (Matt 5:16)? Feeding the hungry is a necessary treatment of a symptom and it gives evidence of the current manifestation of the inaugurated kingdom of Christ where one day hunger, illness, and death will be wiped away forever. But the gospel forever remains the only hope for a lasting solution. Only when people are regenerated and reconciled to God through belief in the gospel will social transformation occur. Healing and relief of poverty are effects of the gospel; they are not the gospel themselves. Concern for the poor should never replace the biblical mandate to witness to the crucified and risen King.

Scripture will not allow us to think in terms other than proclamation. The apostles were sent to witness to the risen Christ. The biblical writers were earnest missionaries whose goal was to take the gospel to

---

[43]Ibid.

the whole world in obedience to Jesus (Acts 10:42). Urgency to preach Christ marked Paul's life from immediately after his conversion (Acts 9:20) to his imprisonment in Rome (Acts 28:30–31). His life's ambition was to preach the gospel wherever Christ had not already been named (Rom 15:20) because he was gripped by the biblical conviction that unless people hear, they cannot believe and be saved (Rom 10:14–15; 15:21). That is, Paul's desire was to spend himself for the cause of the gospel because he was convinced from the Scriptures that Christ's death and resurrection is the only hope for sinners and that they must hear and believe the gospel in order to be saved.[44]

The gospel is good news. It is the announcement that the God who created the heavens and the earth has sent His Son to save sinners. Jesus invited "anyone" who heard Him to believe in Him to escape condemnation (John 5:24). He said, "I am the way, the truth, and the life. No one comes to the Father except through Me" (John 14:6). He also claimed, "Anyone who does not honor the Son does not honor the Father who sent Him" (John 5:23). If the Lord wanted to communicate that one must believe in Christ to be saved, how much clearer could He have been? The apostles made the point in this way: "There is salvation in no one else, for there is no other name under heaven given to people by which we must be saved" (Acts 4:12). Jesus promised His attending presence, through His Spirit, to His disciples to empower their Christ-glorifying gospel witness to the end of the age (Matt 28:18–20; John 16:14; Acts 1:8).

What about those who have never heard the good news of God's salvation in Christ? The biblical response is a clear and decisive command: Go tell them! The Spirit-inspired biblical authors did not spend time philosophizing or theologizing over the state of the unevangelized. Gathering support for a shared optimism concerning the fate of those who have never heard does not help anybody, least of all the unevangelized.[45] In their quest to muster support for a "wider hope," inclusivists and pluralists effectively treat the mandate to share the gospel as though it was an embarrassing problem to be overcome, something that impugns the justice and fairness of God. Of course, far from problematic, the gospel is actually the God-given and grace-

---

[44]See J. N. Jennings, "God's Zeal for His World," in *Faith Comes by Hearing*, ed. Morgan and Peterson, 223.

[45]See C. W. Morgan and R. A. Peterson, "Answers to Notable Questions," in *Faith Comes by Hearing*, ed. Morgan and Peterson, 253.

saturated solution to the world's problems. Only in our twisted world would proclamation of Jesus Christ be seen as problematic by those who claim to be Christians. The gospel is the good news, the power of God for salvation to all who believe—a demonstration of the love, mercy, power, righteousness, and wisdom of God. By God's grace, may the Church embrace her mission, and may the Spirit embolden our witness as we testify to the love of God in Christ.

Bibliography

Books

Badcock, G. D. *Light of Truth & Fire of Love: A Theology of the Holy Spirit*. Grand Rapids: Eerdmans, 1997.

Baker, D. L. *Two Testaments, One Bible: A Study of the Theological Relationships Between the Old and New Testaments*, rev. ed. Downers Grove, IL: InterVarsity, 1991.

Baker, D. W., ed. *Biblical Faith and Other Religions: An Evangelical Assessment*. Grand Rapids: Kregel, 2004.

Bartholomew C. and A. C. Thiselton, eds. *Out of Egypt: Biblical Theology and Biblical Interpretation*. Grand Rapids: Zondervan, 2004.

Bobrinskoy, B. *The Mystery of the Trinity: Trinitarian Experience and Vision in the Biblical and Patristic Tradition*. Trans. A. P. Gythiel. Crestwood, NY: St. Vladimir's Seminary Press, 1999.

Carson, D. A. *The Gagging of God: Christianity Confronts Pluralism*. Downers Grove, IL: InterVarsity, 1996.

Clark, D. K. *To Know and Love God: Method for Theology*. Wheaton: Crossway, 2003.

Clarke D. and B. W. Winter, eds. *One God, One Lord: Christianity in a World of Religious Pluralism*, 2nd ed. Grand Rapids: Baker, 1992.

Clendenin, D. B. *Many Gods, Many Lords: Christianity Encounters World Religions*. Grand Rapids: Baker, 1995.

Cole, G. A. *He Who Gives Life: The Doctrine of the Holy Spirit.* Wheaton: Crossway, 2007.

Crockett, W., ed. *Four Views on Hell.* Grand Rapids: Zondervan, 1996.

D'Costa, G. *The Meeting of Religions and the Trinity.* Maryknoll, NY: Orbis, 2000.

———. *Theology and Religious Pluralism: The Challenge of Other Religions.* Oxford: Blackwell, 1986.

———, ed. *Christian Uniqueness Reconsidered: The Myth of Pluralistic Theology of Religions.* Maryknoll, NY: Orbis, 1996.

DiNoia, J. A. *The Diversity of Religions: A Christian Perspective.* Washington, DC: Catholic University of America Press, 1992.

Dupuis, J. *Jesus Christ and the Encounter of World Religions.* Maryknoll, NY: Orbis, 1985.

———. *Toward a Christian Theology of Religious Pluralism.* Maryknoll, NY: Orbis, 1997.

Edwards, D. L. *Evangelical Essentials: A Liberal-Evangelical Dialogue.* Downers Grove, IL: InterVarsity, 1988.

Eichrodt, W. *Theology of the Old Testament*, vols. 1–2, trans. J. Baker. Philadelphia: Westminster, 1961, 1967.

Erickson, M. J. *How Shall They Be Saved? The Destiny of Those Who Do Not Hear of Jesus.* Grand Rapids: Baker, 1996.

Ferguson, S. *The Holy Spirit.* (Downers Grove, IL: InterVarsity, 1996.

Fernando, A. *The Christian's Attitude Toward World Religions.* Wheaton: Tyndale, 1987.

Ferré, N. *The Christian Understanding of God.* New York: Harper, 1951.

———. *Evil and the Christian Faith.* New York: Harper & Brothers, 1947.

Fudge, E. *The Fire That Consumes: A Biblical and Historical Study of the Doctrine of Final Punishment.* Lincoln: iUniverse.com, 1982, 2000).

Fudge E. W. and R. A. Peterson. *Two Views on Hell: A Biblical & Theological Dialogue.* Downers Grove, IL: InterVarsity, 2000).

Gaffin, R., ed. *Redemptive History and Biblical Interpretation: The Shorter Writings of Geerhardus Vos.* Phillipsburg, NJ: Presbyterian and Reformed, 1980.

Goldsworthy, G. *According to Plan: The Unfolding Revelation of God in the Bible.* Downers Grove, IL: InterVarsity, 2002.

Gray, T. and C. Sinkinson, eds. *Reconstructing Theology: A Critical Assessment of the Theology of Clark Pinnock.* Carlisle, UK: Paternoster, 2000.

Grenz, S. J. and J. R. Franke, *Beyond Foundationalism: Shaping Theology in a Postmodern Context.* Louisville: Westminster John Knox, 2001.

Hamilton, Jr., J. M. *God's Indwelling Presence: The Holy Spirit in the Old and New Testaments.* Nashville: B&H, 2006.

Hawthorne, G. F. *The Presence & the Power.* Dallas: Word Publishing, 1991.

Hess, R. *Israelite Religions: An Archaeological and Biblical Survey.* Grand Rapids: Baker, 2007.

Hick, J. *Disputed Questions in Theology and Philosophy of Religion.* New Haven, CT: Yale University Press, 1993.

———. *God and the Universe of Faiths: Essays in the Philosophy of Religion.* New York: St. Martin's, 1973.

———. *The Myth of God Incarnate.* Philadelphia: Westminster, 1976.

Hick, J. and P. F. Knitter, eds. *The Myth of Christian Uniqueness: Toward a Pluralistic Theology of Religions.* Maryknoll, NY: Orbis, 1987.

Horton, M. S. *Covenant and Eschatology: The Divine Drama.* Louisville: Westminster John Knox, 2002.

House, P. R. and G. A. Thornbury, eds. *Who Will Be Saved? Defending the Biblical Understanding of God, Salvation, & Evangelism.* Wheaton: Crossway, 2000.

Kärkkäinen, V. *An Introduction to the Theology of Religions: Biblical, Historical and Contemporary Perspectives.* Downers Grove, IL: InterVarsity, 2003.

Knitter, P. *Jesus and Other Names: Christian Mission and Global Responsibility.* Maryknoll, NY: Orbis, 1996.

———. *No Other Name? A Critical Survey of Christian Attitudes Toward the World Religions.* Maryknoll, NY: Orbis, 1985.

Ladd, G. E. *A Theology of the New Testament*, rev. ed. Grand Rapids: Eerdmans, 1993.

Letham, R. *The Holy Trinity: In Scripture, History, Theology, and Worship*. Phillipsburg, NJ: P&R, 2004.

Lints, R. *The Fabric of Theology: A Prolegomenon to Evangelical Theology*. Grand Rapids: Eerdmans, 1993.

McDermott, G. R. *Can Evangelicals Learn from World Religions? Jesus, Revelation & Religious Traditions*. Downers Grove, IL: InterVarsity, 2000.

Miles, T. L. *Severing the Spirit from the Son: Theological Revisionism in Contemporary Theologies of Salvation*. Ph.D. dissertation. Louisville: The Southern Baptist Theological Seminary, 2006.

Montague, G. T. *Holy Spirit: Growth of a Biblical Tradition*. Peabody, MA: Hendrickson, 1976.

Morgan C. W. and R. A. Peterson, eds. *Faith Comes by Hearing: A Response to Inclusivism*. Downers Grove, IL: InterVarsity, 2008.

————. *Hell Under Fire: Modern Scholarship Reinvents Eternal Punishment*. Grand Rapids: Zondervan, 2004.

Nash, R. H. *Is Jesus the Only Savior?* Grand Rapids: Zondervan, 1994.

Netland, H. *Dissonant Voices: Religious Pluralism and the Question of Truth*. Grand Rapids: Eerdmans, 1991.

————. *Encountering Religious Pluralism: The Challenge to Christian Faith & Mission*. Downers Grove, IL: InterVarsity, 2001.

Okholm D. L. and T. R. Phillips, eds. *Four Views on Salvation in a Pluralistic World*. Grand Rapids: Zondervan, 1995, 1996.

Panikkar, R. *The Unknown Christ of Hinduism: Towards an Ecumenical Christophany*. Maryknoll, NY: Orbis, 1981.

Pinnock, C. H. *Biblical Revelation: The Foundation of Christian Theology*. Chicago: Moody, 1971.

————. *Flame of Love: A Theology of the Holy Spirit*. Downers Grove, IL: InterVarsity, 1996.

————. *The Scripture Principle*. San Francisco: Harper & Row, 1984.

————. *A Wideness in God's Mercy: The Finality of Jesus Christ in a World of Religions*. Grand Rapids: Zondervan, 1992.

Rahner, K. *Foundations of the Christian Faith: An Introduction to the Idea of Christianity*. Trans. W. V. Dych. New York: Seabury, 1978.

———. *Theological Investigations*, vol. 5. Trans. D. Bourke. New York: Seabury, 1966.

———. *Theological Investigations*, vol. 6. Trans. K. Kruger and B. Kruger. New York: Seabury, 1969.

———. *Theological Investigations*, vol. 17. Trans. M. Kohl. New York: Crossroad, 1981.

Richard, R. *The Population of Heaven: A Biblical Response to the Inclusivist Position on Who Will Be Saved.* Chicago: Moody, 1994.

Robinson, J. A. T. *In the End God.* New York: Harper & Row, 1968.

Rommen E. and H. Netland, eds. *Christianity and the Religions: A Biblical Theology of World Religions.* Pasadena, CA: William Carey Library, 1995.

Rosner, B. S. et al, eds. *New Dictionary of Biblical Theology.* Downers Grove, IL: InterVarsity, 2000.

Samartha, S. J. *Courage for Dialogue: Ecumenical Issues in Inter-Religious Relationships.* Geneva: World Council of Churches, 1981.

———. *One Christ—Many Religions: Toward a Revised Christology.* Maryknoll, NY: Orbis, 1991.

Sanders, F. and K. Issler, eds. *Jesus in Trinitarian Perspective.* Nashville: B&H, 2007.

Sanders, J. *No Other Name: An Investigation into the Destiny of the Unevangelized.* Grand Rapids: Eerdmans, 1992.

Scobie, C. H. H. *The Ways of Our God: An Approach to Biblical Theology.* Grand Rapids: Eerdmans, 2003.

Stackhouse, J. G., ed. *No Other Gods Before Me? Evangelicals and the Challenge of World Religions.* Grand Rapids: Baker, 2001.

Strange, D. *The Possibility of Salvation Among the Unevangelised: An Analysis of Inclusivism in Recent Evangelical Theology.* Waynesboro, PA: Paternoster, 2002.

Tennent, T. C. *Christianity at the Religious Roundtable: Evangelicalism in Conversation with Hinduism, Buddhism, and Islam.* Grand Rapids: Baker, 2002.

———. *Theology in the Context of World Christianity: How the Global Church Is Influencing the Way We Think About and Discuss Theology.* Grand Rapids: Zondervan, 2007.

Tiessen, T. L. *Who Can Be Saved? Reassessing Salvation in Christ and World Religions.* Downers Grove, IL: InterVarsity, 2004.

Vanhoozer, K. J., ed. *Dictionary for Theological Interpretation of the Bible.* Grand Rapids: Baker, 2005.

———. *The Drama of Doctrine: A Canonical-Linguistic Approach To Christian Theology.* Louisville: Westminster John Knox, 2005.

———. *Is There a Meaning in This Text? The Bible, the Reader, and the Morality of Literary Knowledge.* Grand Rapids: Zondervan, 1998.

Vos, G. *Biblical Theology: Old and New Testaments.* Edinburgh: Banner of Truth, 1975.

Wood, L. J. *The Holy Spirit in the Old Testament.* Grand Rapids: Zondervan, 1976.

Wright, C. J. H. *The Mission of God: Unlocking the Bible's Grand Narrative.* Downers Grove, IL: InterVarsity, 2006.

———. *Salvation Belongs to Our God: Celebrating the Bible's Central Story.* Downers Grove, IL: InterVarsity, 2007.

Wright, N. T. *The Climax of the Covenant: Christ and the Law in Pauline Theology.* Minneapolis: Fortress, 1993.

———. *Paul: In Fresh Perspective.* Minneapolis: Fortress, 2005.

———. *What Saint Paul Really Said: Was Paul of Tarsus the Real Founder of Christianity?* Grand Rapids: Eerdmans, 1997.

Yong, A. *Beyond the Impasse: Toward a Pneumatological Theology of Religions.* Grand Rapids: Baker, 2003.

———. *Discerning the Spirit(s): A Pentecostal-Charismatic Contribution to Christian Theology of Religions.* Sheffield, UK: Sheffield Academic Press, 2000.

———. *The Spirit Poured Out on All Flesh: Pentecostalism and the Possibility of Global Theology.* Grand Rapids: Baker, 2005.

———. *Spirit-Word-Community: Theological Hermeneutics in Trinitarian Perspective.* Burlington, VT: Ashgate, 2003.

Articles

Bauckham, R. "Universalism: A Historical Survey." *Themelios* 4/2 (1979): 48–54.

Erickson, M. J. "Hope for Those Who Haven't Heard? Yes, But . . ." *EMQ* 11 (1975): 122–26.

Fudge, E. "The Final End of the Wicked." *JETS* 27/3 (September 1984): 325–34.

Grenz, S. J. "Toward an Evangelical Theology of Religions." *JES* 31 (1994): 49–65.

Hodgson, P. "The Spirit and Religious Pluralism." *Horizons* 31/1 (2004): 22–39.

Kärkkäinen, V. "Toward a Pneumatological Theology of Religions," *International Review of Mission* 91 (2002): 187–98.

Khodr, G. "Christianity in a Pluralistic World—the Economy of the Holy Spirit." *ER* 23 (1971): 118–28.

Knitter, P. "A New Pentecost? A Pneumatological Theology of Religions." *CD* 19 (1991): 32–41.

Lindsell, H. "Universalism Today: Part Two." *Bibliotheca Sacra* 122 (January, 1965): 31–40.

McDonnell, K. "A Trinitarian Theology of the Holy Spirit?" *TS* 46 (1985): 191–227.

McGrath, A. E. "The Challenge of Pluralism for the Contemporary Christian Church." *JETS* 35/3 (September 1992): 361–73.

———. "The Christian Church's Response to Pluralism." *JETS* 35/4 (1992): 487–501.

Miles, T. L. "Irenaeus in the Hands of Soteriological Inclusivists: Validation or Tendentious Historiography?" *SBJT* 12/2 (Summer 2008): 4–17.

Packer, J. I. "The Way of Salvation: Part III, The Problems of Universalism." *Bibliotheca Sacra* 130 (January, 1973): 3–14.

Robinson, J. A. T. "Universalism—Is It Heretical?" *SJT* 2 (1949): 139–55.

Samartha, S. J. "The Holy Spirit and People of Other Faiths," *Ecumenical Review* 42 (1990): 250–63.

Wright, N. T. "Towards a Biblical View of Universalism." *Themelios* 4/2 (1979): 54–58.

Yong, A. "A P(new)matological Paradigm for Christian Mission in a Religiously Plural World," *Missiology* 23 (2005): 175–91.

———. "The Turn to Pneumatology in Christian Theology of Religions: Conduit or Detour?" *JES* 35 (1998): 437–54.

———. "Whither Theological Inclusivism? The Development and Critique of an Evangelical Theology of Religions." *EvQ* 71 (1999): 327–48.

Name Index

Allen, K.   *100*
Allen, L. C.   *296, 297*
Allen, R. B.   *290, 291*
Aloisi, J.   *317*
Anderson, G. H.   *5*
Ashley, T. R.   *289, 290*
Attridge, H. W.   *308*
Augustine   *1, 99, 222*

Badcock, G. D.   *294, 323, 355*
Bahnsen, G.   *333*
Baker, D. L.   *259, 355*
Baker, D. W.   *355*
Balla, P.   *259*
Bartholomew, C.   *355*
Barton, J.   *297*
Bauckham, R.   *50, 51, 52, 53, 56, 60, 62, 78, 84, 97, 99, 101, 174, 360*
Beale, G. K.   *38, 89*
Bell, R.   *346*
Beougher, T. K.   *119*
Bergen, R. D.   *292*
Berkouwer, G. C.   *317*
Bettenson, H.   *186*
Beverley, J. A.   *141*
Bilezikian, G.   *315*
Block, D.   *42, 50, 54, 62, 65, 123, 287*
Blomberg, C. L.   *174, 259, 260, 267, 302*
Boa, K. D.   *121*

Bobrinskoy, B.   *281, 283, 294, 296, 300, 321, 355*
Bock, D. L.   *23, 93, 265, 270, 271, 302, 305, 307*
Bockmuehl, M.   *310, 311*
Bolger, R. K.   *347, 348*
Bosch, D. J.   *7*
Bowman, R. M., Jr.   *121*
Braaten, C. E.   *3, 8*
Bray, G.   *41, 50, 81, 264*
Brow, R. C.   *250*
Bruce, F. F.   *108, 121, 308, 311, 316, 317*
Brueggemann, W.   *293*
Budd, P. J.   *290*
Burge, G.   *304, 314, 315, 316, 317*
Burke, S.   *30*

Calvin, J.   *271, 289, 308, 309*
Caputo, J. D.   *140*
Carson, D. A.   *6, 12, 13, 21, 25, 28, 88, 115, 116, 121, 130, 131, 139, 165, 214, 217, 257, 258, 272, 304, 312, 313, 314, 315, 316, 317, 355*
Cassuto, U.   *280*
Chamberlain, M. T.   *100*
Childs, B. S.   *259, 286, 295*
Chisholm, R.   *54, 59, 67*
Clark, D. K.   *269, 271, 355*
Clarke, A. D.   *3, 355*
Clendenin, D. B.   *3, 355*

Cole, G. A.   *308, 318, 322, 324, 356*

Cole, R. D.   *289, 291*

Cooper, L. E.   *296*

Crockett, W. V.   *121, 125, 356*

Crouzel, H.   *99*

Cyprian   *184, 185*

Davids, P. H.   *114*

Davis, D. R.   *292*

Dawson, G. S.   *321*

D'Costa, G.   *356*

Delitzsch, F.   *281, 290*

Demarest, B.   *76, 89, 99, 217*

DiNoia, J. A.   *3, 167, 168, 356*

Dodd, C. H.   *265*

Duguid, I. M.   *296*

Dunn, J. D. G.   *78, 84, 320*

Dupuis, J.   *146, 147, 185, 194, 195, 196, 197, 198, 199, 200, 201, 202, 203, 227, 247, 270, 356*

Duthie, C. S.   *96, 103*

Edwards, D. L.   *101, 103, 104, 105, 126, 356*

Edwards, J.   *10, 95, 96, 272, 337*

Eichrodt, W.   *37, 39, 41, 49, 279, 281, 285, 287, 288, 294, 356*

Erickson, M. J.   *5, 211, 310, 356, 360*

Fee, G. D.   *86, 118, 254, 311, 322, 323, 325, 326*

Ferguson, S.   *279, 280, 281, 285, 296, 306, 308, 312, 313, 317, 320, 324, 356*

Fernando, A.   *3, 90, 92, 336, 341, 356*

Ferré, N.   *103, 104, 356*

Finley, T. J.   *297*

Flannery, A.   *188*

Forsyth, P. T.   *310*

Frame, J.   *39, 178*

France, R. T.   *174, 305*

Franke, J. R.   *269, 357*

Fudge, E.   *97, 126, 127, 129, 130, 356, 361*

Funk, R. W.   *166*

Garrett, D. A.   *297, 298*

Geivett, R. D.   *21, 23, 166, 170, 172, 174, 175*

Gelpi, D. L.   *254, 255*

Gess, W. F.   *310*

Gibbs, E.   *347, 348*

Gilkey, L.   *167*

Goldingay, J.   *41, 43, 44, 45, 47, 48, 51, 54, 60, 61, 62, 65, 66, 81, 266, 267, 340*

Goldsworthy, G.   *257, 264, 265, 285, 357*

Goodstein, L.   *1*

Gray, T.   *357*

Green, J. B.   *262*

Green, M.   *129*

Greidanus, S.   *267*

Grenz, S.   *159, 211, 269, 284, 357, 361*

Grossman, C. L.   *139*

Grudem, W.   *10*

Habermas, G. R.   *174*
Hagner, D. A.   *302, 307, 308*
Hamilton, J. M., Jr.   *315, 357*
Hamilton, V. P.   *280, 282*
Hanson, P. D.   *295*
Harris, M. J.   *14*
Hasel, G. F.   *259*
Hawthorne, G. F.   *301, 304,*
    305, 306, 311, 312, 357
Heim, S. M.   *168, 169*
Henry, C. F. H.   *269*
Hess, R.   *35, 41, 48, 49, 52, 55,*
    57, 58, 69, 357
Hick, J.   *98, 141, 142, 143, 144,*
    145, 146, 147, 148, 149,
    150, 153, 166, 168, 172,
    173, 174, 175, 357
Hodgson, P.   *28, 150, 151, 152,*
    247, 361
Holmes, S. R.   *284*
Horton, M. S.   *261, 272, 274,*
    347, 357
House, P. R.   *37, 49, 63, 72,*
    294, 357
Howell, D.   *84, 86, 87, 177,*
    180
Hubbard, R. H., Jr.   *260*
Hughes, P. E.   *130, 284, 308*

Ignatius   *184*
Inch, M. A.   *285*
Ingraffia, B.   *259*
Irenaeus   *184, 205, 215, 224,*
    225, 226, 230, 233, 251
Issler, K.   *359*

Jaffarian, M.   *350*
Jennings, J. N.   *352*

Johnston, P. S.   *123*
Jones, T.   *346*

Kaiser, W. C., Jr.   *42, 47, 217,*
    265
Kärkkäinen, V.   *3, 8, 150, 188,*
    211, 357, 361
Kaufman, G. D.   *145*
Kaufmann, Y.   *37, 39, 63*
Keener, C. S.   *165, 303, 307,*
    308
Keil, C. F.   *281, 290*
Keller, T.   *74, 170, 171, 181*
Khodr, G.   *31, 153, 185, 204,*
    205, 206, 207, 224, 225,
    247, 361
Kimball, D.   *346*
Kinnamon, M.   *183, 184*
Klein, W.   *260, 292*
Knitter, P.   *29, 141, 142, 150,*
    152, 153, 154, 155, 156,
    157, 175, 194, 204, 206,
    225, 247, 357, 361
Köstenberger, A.   *34, 79, 267,*
    304, 313, 314, 315, 316, 317
Kovach, S. D.   *315*
Krattenmaker, T.   *346*

Ladd, G. E.   *315, 317, 357*
Lane, W. L.   *308*
Larkin, W. J.   *23, 74, 84, 85, 91,*
    217, 341, 342
L'Engle, M.   *100*
Letham, R.   *222, 284, 358*
Levine, B. A.   *289, 290*
Liefeld, W. L.   *263*
Lightner, R. P.   *123*
Lindsell, H.   *118, 134, 135, 361*

Lints, R.   *261, 272, 273, 274, 358*
Love, R.   *335*

MacDonald, N.   *50, 100*
Macleod, D.   *310*
Marsden, G.   *11, 96*
Marshall, I. H.   *302, 307, 311*
Martens, E. A.   *257*
Mathews, E.   *51*
Mathews, K. A.   *36*
McDermott, G. R.   *3, 7, 77, 169, 337, 341, 358*
McDonnell, K.   *304, 320, 361*
McGrath, A.   *9, 11, 21, 167, 168, 171, 173, 182, 361*
McLaren, B.   *30, 96, 97, 121, 346, 347, 348*
Melick, R. R., Jr.   *311*
Merrill, E. H.   *61*
Meyer, J. R.   *168*
Michaels, J. R.   *114, 165*
Miles, T. L.   *221, 225, 348, 358, 361*
Misselbrook, P.   *266*
Mohler, R. A., Jr.   *97*
Mongeau, L. R.   *1, 2*
Montague, G. T.   *304, 358*
Moody, D. L.   *121, 138*
Morgan, C. W.   *5, 18, 28, 121, 131, 132, 352, 358*
Morris, L.   *165, 278, 302, 308, 314*
Motyer, J. A.   *47, 119, 295*
Mounce, W. D.   *118*

Nash, R. H.   *5, 21, 358*
Needham, N.   *221, 222*

Neely, A.   *138*
Netland, H.   *2, 3, 8, 9, 20, 141, 142, 166, 168, 177, 184, 329, 358, 359*
Newbigin, L.   *172, 173*

O'Brien, P. T.   *108, 310*
Okholm, D. L.   *5, 16, 358*
Ortlund, R., Jr.   *70*
Osborne, G. R.   *31, 260*
Oswalt, J. N.   *295, 299*
O'Toole, R. F.   *267*

Packer, J. I.   *108, 128, 132, 134, 361*
Pagitt, D.   *346*
Panikkar, R.   *29, 141, 144, 145, 197, 358*
Parshall, P.   *335*
Penchansky, D.   *259*
Peterson, R. A.   *5, 26, 28, 71, 121, 126, 352, 356, 358*
Phillips, T. R.   *5, 16, 19, 21, 23, 166, 170, 171, 172, 174, 175, 211, 358*
Pierce, C. S.   *240, 254*
Pierson, A. T.   *138*
Pinnock, C.   *5, 24, 31, 32, 47, 77, 97, 121, 124, 126, 127, 153, 175, 185, 194, 201, 211, 212, 213, 214, 215, 216, 217, 218, 219, 220, 221, 222, 223, 224, 225, 226, 227, 228, 229, 230, 232, 233, 236, 239, 245, 247, 248, 249, 250, 256, 257, 258, 262, 268, 272,*

273, 282, 283, 288, 318, 322, 329, 357, 358
Plantinga, A.   *254*
Plantinga, R.   *16, 18*
Plummer, A.   *263*
Polhill, J. B.   *107, 320*

Race, A.   *8, 16, 149*
Rahner, K.   *29, 31, 153, 185, 194, 195, 196, 197, 203, 358*
Reitsma, B.   *327*
Renz, T.   *73*
Rescher, N.   *169*
Reventlow, H. G.   *267*
Richard, R.   *359*
Richardson, D.   *47*
Ridderbos, H. N.   *268*
Ringgren, H.   *58, 63*
Robinson, B.   *19*
Robinson, G.   *1*
Robinson, J. A. T.   *101, 102, 103, 359, 361*
Rommen, E.   *3, 74, 359*
Rosner, B. S.   *64, 67, 69, 70, 71, 81, 266, 359*
Ryrie, C. C.   *308*

Sailhamer, J.   *36, 62, 280, 281, 291*
Samartha, S. J.   *141, 150, 156, 157, 158, 159, 160, 161, 234, 247, 270, 300, 359, 361*
Sanders, F.   *359*
Sanders, J.   *5, 25, 104, 153, 211, 359*
Sawyer, J. F. A.   *49*
Schemm, P. R., Jr.   *315*
Schleiermacher, F.   *100*

Schnabel, E. J.   *76, 259, 342*
Schreiner, T. R.   *25, 26, 39, 81, 107, 114, 120, 165, 304, 314, 321, 322, 323, 325, 326*
Scobie, C.   *69, 258, 259, 268, 286, 291, 359*
Scott, R.   *335, 336*
Selmanovic, S.   *347, 348*
Sheikh, B.   *335*
Shubin, R. G.   *335, 336*
Sinkinson, C.   *357*
Smith, J.   *79*
Smith, S. M.   *310*
Smith, W. C.   *145, 175*
Sproul, R. C.   *21*
Stackhouse, J. G.   *3, 7, 359*
Staniloae, D.   *222, 223*
Stein, R. H.   *302, 305, 306, 307*
Stott, J.   *101, 121, 126, 127, 131, 134*
Strange, D.   *3, 5, 10, 19, 31, 32, 185, 214, 217, 256, 332, 333, 359*
Stuart, D. K.   *64, 65, 163, 297*
Stuhlmacher, P.   *268*

Talbott, T.   *102*
Taylor, B.   *30*
Taylor, H.   *329*
Tennent, T. C.   *3, 21, 177, 337, 338, 339, 343, 344, 359*
Thielman, F.   *311*
Thiselton, A. C.   *355*
Thornbury, G. A.   *357*
Tiessen, T. L.   *5, 211, 226, 329, 360*
Tilley, T. W.   *142, 350*
Tillich, P.   *28, 29*

Tolle, E.   *141*

VanGemeren, W.   *36, 39, 296*
Vanhoozer, K.   *176, 225, 254,
257, 259, 265, 266, 268,
270, 360*
Van Til, C.   *332, 333*
Vincent, K. R.   *101*
von Rad, G.   *280*
Vos, G.   *47, 258, 260, 261, 273,
299, 300, 325, 326, 360*

Waltke, B. K.   *280*
Walton, J. H.   *279, 280*
Ware, B.   *67, 275, 276, 280,
312, 315, 316, 323*
Watson, D. L.   *101*
Wegner, P. D.   *268*
Wells, D. F.   *11, 329*
Wellum, S. J.   *118*
Wenham, D.   *174*
Wenham, G.   *41, 48, 280, 290*
Wenham, J.   *121*
Westcott, B. F.   *308*
Westermann, C.   *280*

Winter, B.   *3, 80, 89, 355*
Wolterstorff, N.   *254*
Wood, L. J.   *278, 279, 286, 294,
360*
Woodberry, J. D.   *335*
Wright, C. J. H.   *15, 16, 41, 43,
44, 45, 47, 48, 50, 54, 55,
56, 57, 59, 60, 62, 65, 69,
70, 85, 274, 340, 360*
Wright, N. T.   *76, 78, 87, 109,
167, 310, 311, 360, 361*
Wuthnow, R.   *140*

Yarbrough, R. W.   *122*
Yong, A.   *5, 31, 153, 161, 185,
201, 210, 212, 230, 231,
232, 233, 234, 235, 236,
237, 238, 239, 240, 241,
242, 243, 245, 247, 248,
250, 251, 252, 253, 254,
255, 256, 257, 258, 262,
268, 269, 270, 271, 272,
273, 275, 283, 288, 318,
319, 320, 322, 360, 361*
Young, W. P.   *210*

Subject Index

A

annihilationism   *121, 126–133*
anonymous Christianity   *194–195, 197*
apokatastasis   *99, 107*
archaeology   *35, 57*
atonement
  limited   *110*
  universal   *110–112*
  unlimited   *105–106*
avatar   *179*

B

Bible, the   *33*
  authority of   *148–149, 249, 252, 269–272*
  Christocentrism of   *247, 256, 262–269*
  inspiration of   *148, 173, 259, 271*
  unique claims   *182*
  unity of   *259*
Buddhism   *20, 165–169, 189, 207, 256*

C

Canaanites   *44–50, 54, 56, 58, 66*
Christian
  definition of   *9*
  understanding of
    salvation   *13–15*

Christocentrism   *150, 154, 157, 200*
Christology   *223–224, 229, 249–250, 253, 267*
church, the
  age of   *321*
  purpose of   *6*
conditional immortality   *120–121, 126–128*
conditionalism   *121, 126–128, 131–132*
conversion   *237, 243*
craftsmen   *286*
creation   *35–41*
Creator-creature distinction   *36, 177*
crucifixion, the   *133*

D

day of the Lord   *297*
demons   *62–63, 66–67, 81–84*
discernment, spiritual   *239–241*
dreams and visions   *335–337*

E

Emergent Church   *30, 96, 121, 346–349*
Enuma Elish   *37*
Epicureanism   *89–90*
eternal   *129–130*
ethics   *147, 170–171*
evangelical distinctives   *10–11*
evangelism   *5*

ex nihilo 36
exclusivism 3, 16, 19, 28–29
  biblical support 21–26
  theological defense 26–27
exegesis 257
extra ecclesiam nulla
  salus 185, 187, 194, 207,
  245

F

faith 3, 13, 17, 20–21, 41, 111
fall, the 39
figurative language 124
filioque 220–222, 230
foundationalism 254–256

G

Gehenna 123–124
general revelation 330–338
Gnosticism 99
gods 59–64, 69, 79–80, 86,
  162
Gospel Coalition 11–12
gospel, the 2–3, 7, 11–13
  dissemination of 12–13
  Paul's summary of 11
Great Commission 340–341,
  351

H

Hades 123–124
heaven 104, 135
hedonism 89
hell 95–97, 99–104, 120–133
henotheism 59, 79
hermeneutics 176, 251–254,
  260, 274

Hinduism 20, 145, 156, 165,
  168, 189, 338
historiography 225
Holy Spirit
  as Creator 218–220, 236,
  279–283
  blasphemy against 308
  glorifying Christ 3–4,
  277–278, 317–318
  imagination of 253–255
  in church age 321–325
  in Jesus' life 301–312
  in messianic age 295,
  298–300
  in other religions 151,
  154–161, 189–192, 203–209,
  211, 217, 224, 227–230,
  239, 270, 300
  in pluralism 28
  ministry of 3–4, 317–318
  Paraclete 314–315
  power of 151, 292–293
  proleptic work 325–327
  relationship to Word 281–
  282, 294–296, 300
  role in Scripture 269–271,
  273
  special empowerment
  of 285–294
  "touch" of 201
  universal presence 150, 153,
  183–184, 192, 193, 200–201,
  205–206, 209, 217–218,
  223, 226–227, 236–237

I

idolatry 65–66, 70, 145, 179,
  337

in the New Testament   80–86
in the Old Testament   64–72,
    162
Paul on   84–85, 88–89
idols   61, 65–69, 84, 86, 87, 89,
    162
illumination   270
image of God   37–41, 283–284
inclusivism   16–17, 152
    evangelical expressions   210–
        212, 230
    modal   217
    nonevangelical
        expressions   183, 185
    pneumatalogical   211–212,
        217, 230, 232–234, 245–246,
        256–257, 268, 272–273,
        276, 283, 300
inclusivists   3–4
Islam   165, 167, 169, 189, 204,
    227

J

jealousy of God   69–71
Jesus
    baptism of   303–304
    claims of   9
    conception of   301–303
    deity of   79, 149–150
    focus of Scripture   263–268
    incarnation of   300
    life of   180
    lordship of   9
    Messiah   295, 298–300
    ministry of   305–307, 309
    on nature of Scripture   262
    resurrection of   181, 264, 309
    Savior   113

supremacy of   79
temptation of   304–305
uniqueness of   164, 166,
    171–172, 174–175, 180
view of hell   122–123
Judaism   167
judges   286–287, 293
judgment   119–120, 129–131

K

kenosis   309–310

L

liberalism, Christian   100
logos   239
love, God's   102–103, 115–117,
    131, 212–213

M

Melchizedek   46–47
Messiah   265
missions   6, 245, 328–329, 336,
    350–354
monotheism   48–53, 52–53,
    57–60, 78–80, 88, 163

N

nations   73–75, 213–215
new Covenant   237, 252, 291,
    296, 320–321
new heavens and new
    earth   133
New Testament   33–34

O

obfuscation   141–142, 147,
    171–173
old Covenant   291, 300
Old Testament   33–34

omnipotence, God's   *117–118*

P

pagan believers   *215–217*
paganism   *76–77, 86–87*
Paraclete   *314–315*
particularism   *16, 177–178,*
   212, 226
patience, God's   *117–119*
Pentateuch   *36*
Pentecost, promise of   *318–320*
perspectivalism   *139*
pluralism   *29–30, 89*
pluralism, philosophical   *139–*
   140, 182
pluralism, religious   *6–7, 17,*
   34–35, 86, 137
   attacks of   *142*
   authority of Bible   *148,*
      159–160
   call to church   *150*
   Christocentric   *196*
   deity of Christ   *149, 174*
   orientational   *169*
   repudiation of
      Christianity   *166*
   response to   *161–162, 179,*
      181–182
   resurrection   *181*
   salvation   *139, 146, 168–170*
   supporters of   *141*
   theocentrism   *150, 153–155,*
      157–158, 175
   truth claims of   *143*
   Western doctrine of   *167*
   Western value   *140, 275*
   world religions   *144–145*
pneuma   *239, 278, 301*

pneumatology   *194*
   aid to pluralism   *150*
   balance with
      Christology   *153–154, 200,*
      223, 241, 249–250, 253
   biblical   *268*
   discernment of Christ in
      religious practices   *161,*
      191, 200, 208, 212, 235
   foundational   *152, 254–256*
   in theology of religions   *155,*
      185, 204, 235
   in world religions   *194*
polytheism   *59*
postmodernity   *2, 6, 139,*
   175–176
preaching   *12–13*
priests   *38*
proclamation   *12–13, 17*
prophets   *293–294*
protoevangelium   *40, 44*

R

Real, the   *143–146, 166, 172*
reductionism   *141, 143, 165–*
   166
religions   *33–34*
   in Genesis 4–50   *41–48*
   in the Old Testament   *35–70,*
      162
   in the New Testament   *72–*
      94, 162
   of the state   *76*
   Paul on   *87–88*
religious others
   dialogue with   *341–344*
   meaning of   *2*
   sacred writings of   *270, 338,*

340

reminiscent knowledge   *336–337*

repentance   *20–21*

restoration
  cosmic   *105*
  eschatological   *107, 109*
  universal   *104, 107–108*

restrictivism   *16*

revelation, divine   *260–261, 316–317*

Roman Catholic Church
  departure from
    exclusivism   *191–194, 208*
  exclusivism of   *185–187*
  Vatican II   *188–191, 196, 215, 217, 229*

S

sacred writings, non-
  Christian   *336–339*

salvation   *330, 333*
  biblical   *14, 180*
  in world religions   *168–170, 184–185, 190–191, 213, 340*
  nature of   *14–15*
  redefined   *146*

salvation history   *215–216*

salvific desire, God's   *105, 109, 116–117, 127, 196, 200, 213*

Satan   *39, 63, 81–84*

Savior   *16*

Scripture. *See* Bible, the

Shema, the   *50–51, 78*

Sheol   *123–124*

Shinto   *168*

sovereignty, God's   *118*

special revelation   *336–337*

spirit   *278, 301*

Stoicism   *89–90*

syncretism   *57, 163, 179, 243*

T

tabernacle   *38, 71*

temple   *38–39*

theocentrism   *150, 175*

theogony   *37*

theology, biblical   *272–273*
  Christocentrism of   *262–269, 274*
  definition of   *257*
  determination of themes   *259*
  goal of   *257–258*
  relationship to
    hermeneutics   *260*
  relationship to systematic
    theology   *258*

theology of dialogue   *156*

theology of religions   *1, 6, 40, 44, 73*
  biblical   *247*
  categories in   *16*
  Christian   *29, 231, 328–329*
  Christology in   *79, 154, 198, 214*
  in dialogue with world
    religions   *231, 242*
  in Acts   *24*
  inclusive   *212*
  key questions of   *330*
  meaning of   *8*
  need for   *7*
  Paul on   *86*
  pneumatology in   *155, 204, 208, 231, 235–238, 256*
  purpose of   *152*

relationship to gospel   *9, 12*
soteriology of   *18, 231*
themes of   *34*
theocentrism of   *157*
theology of religious
    pluralism   *196*
tolerance   *167*
transformation, spiritual   *295–*
    296
Trinity, the   *28, 38, 78, 115,*
    284–285
"two hands of God"
    metaphor   *224–225, 233,*
    251

U

unevangelized, the   *5, 19*
universalism   *16–17, 100–102,*
    134, 212
    Christian   *98, 102–106*
    history of   *99–102*
    pluralistic   *98*

popularity of   *29, 97*
theology of   *114–119*

W

walk   *42*
world religions   *2, 152, 155,*
    166
    Christian relationship to   *4*
    concepts of God   *167*
    culture   *156*
    differences in   *143–144, 169*
    ethical differences   *147*
    salvific potential   *5, 184–185,*
        189–190, 195–201, 340
    sameness of   *180*
    Spirit in   *157–158, 160–161,*
        227–229, 239
    World's Parliament of
        Religions   *137–138*
    worldviews of   *339*
worship   *71, 162–164, 205*

Scripture Index

Genesis

1   *36, 70, 265, 280, 282*
1:1   *107, 163, 177*
1:1–2   *177, 327*
1:2   *218, 220, 279, 280, 281,*
    295, 302
1:6   *62*
1:14   *62*
1:14–18   *61, 62*
1:15   *62*
1:26   *37*
1:26–27   *37, 283*
1:26–29   *284*
1:27   *38*
1:28   *40*
2:7   *177, 218, 283*
2:18   *38*
3   *40, 120, 333*
3:1   *39*
3:1–6   *332*
3:8   *38, 39*
3:12   *39*
3:14   *39*
3:14–15   *39*
3:15   *40, 44, 300*
3:17–24   *39*
3:22–23   *38*
4   *41*
4:5   *71*
4–11   *42*
4:26   *38, 41*
4–50   *41–46*

5:3   *40*
5:22   *42*
6:3   *279*
6:5   *42*
6:5–6   *110*
6:9   *42*
6:17   *279*
8:20–21   *43*
8:20–22   *43*
9:6–16   *43*
9:12–17   *43*
10   *43*
11   *43, 237*
11:4   *44*
12   *44*
12:1–3   *9, 40, 44, 300*
12:2   *44*
12:3   *44*
12:8   *41*
12–50   *41, 44–47*
13:4   *41*
14:18   *46*
14:18–20   *46*
14:18–22   *41*
14:19   *46, 163*
14:19–20   *47*
14:20   *46*
14:22   *47*
15:16   *45, 119*
17:1   *42*
17:5   *44*
19:1–29   *45*

20   *46*
20:7   *46*
20:11   *41, 42*
20:17   *46*
20:18   *41*
21:33   *41*
22:5   *42*
26:25   *41*
28:18   *65*
29:31   *41*
30:2   *41*
30:22   *41*
31:30–35   *68*
31:32   *61*
35:2   *61*
37:35   *123*
41   *46*
41:37   *294*
41:38   *285, 291, 294*
42:38   *123*
44:29   *123*
45:27   *279*
48:9–10   *9*
49:8–12   *300*
49:9–12   *40*

Exodus

3:1–6   *331*
3–4   *178*
3:14   *52, 178*
6   *52*
6:3–4   *52*
7:15–25   *55*
8:1–14   *55*
8:10   *54*
8:16–24   *55*
9:1–7   *55*
9:8–12   *55*

9:13–35   *55*
9:14   *54*
9:22–26   *54*
10:1–20   *55*
10:13   *279*
10:21–29   *55*
11–12   *55*
14:21–31   *331*
14:31   *42*
15:8–12   *54*
15:11   *61*
18:25–26   *289*
20:2   *49*
20:3   *49*
20:4   *162*
20:4–6   *64*
20:5   *42, 65, 116*
20:6   *116*
20:23   *61*
23:13   *164*
23:24   *66*
23:32   *61*
25:8   *71*
25:18–20   *64*
25:22   *69*
25–26   *38*
25–31   *71*
25:31–37   *286*
28:3   *285*
31:1–11   *71, 285*
31:2–3   *286*
31:3   *281, 286*
32   *57, 71, 178*
32:7–10   *110*
32:31   *61*
34:5   *117*
34:6–7   *116, 117*
34:13   *66*

34:14   *69*
34:26   *163*
35:30–35   *285*
40:34–35   *302*

Leviticus

10:3   *72*
11:1–23   *164*
11:44   *116*
17:7   *64, 70, 163*
18:21   *164*
18:24–28   *45*
18:27–28   *56*
19:4   *61, 66*
19:19   *164*
19:26   *163*
26:1   *65, 66*

Numbers

7:89   *69*
9:18   *302*
11   *289, 293, 297*
11:17   *285, 289*
11:17–29   *288, 294*
11:24–25   *289*
11:26   *290*
11:29   *289, 290, 297, 320*
16:22   *279*
16:30   *123*
19:13   *296*
19:20   *296*
21:29   *59*
23:5   *291*
24:2   *293, 294*
25:2   *61*
27:18   *285, 288, 291*

Deuteronomy

1:29–32   *42*
3:24   *52*
4:15–16   *70*
4:15–31   *65*
4:17–19   *70*
4:19   *61*
4:23   *65*
4:24–27   *65*
4:25–26   *66*
4:28   *68*
4:32–35   *48*
4:32–39   *60*
4:34   *52*
4:35   *53, 61*
4:39   *60, 61*
5:8   *66*
6:4   *78*
6:4–5   *50*
6:13   *305*
6:16   *305*
7:3   *164*
7:7–8   *115*
7:9   *116*
7:9–10   *54*
7:13–14   *54*
7:25   *66*
7:25–26   *69*
8   *305*
8:3   *305*
8:5   *131*
8:19–20   *70*
10:14–15   *115*
10:17   *56, 163*
12:2–3   *66*
13   *56*
18:9–12   *45*
18:9–14   *63*

28:11 *41*
28:18 *41*
28:36–37 *59*
28:49–52 *59*
29:26–28 *70*
32:10–11 *280*
32:11 *280*
32:16–17 *64*
32:16–21 *63, 66, 84*
32:17 *63, 66, 163*
32:21 *66*
32:35 *95*
32:36–39 *55*
32:37–39 *70*
32:39 *63, 163*
33:26 *53, 54*
33:26–28 *54*
34:9 *288*

Joshua

2:11 *56*
23:16 *61*
24:14 *66*
24:15 *61, 163*

Judges

3:10 *286*
6:31 *68*
6:34 *287*
11:24 *61*
11:29 *287*
14:6 *287*
14:19 *287*
15:14 *287*
17–18 *68*

Ruth

1:15 *61*

1 Samuel

1:5–6 *41*
2:2 *53, 60*
2:6–8 *63*
4:1–11 *66*
5:1–2 *54, 59*
5:1–4 *68*
9:16 *292*
10 *290*
10:6 *291*
10:10 *291*
10:27 *292*
11:5–11 *292*
11:6 *288, 292*
11:12–14 *292*
13:8–14 *72*
16:13 *288, 292*
16:14 *288, 292*
17 *292*
17:46–47 *292*
19 *290*
26:19 *61*

2 Samuel

6:6–7 *72*
7 *299*
7:8–17 *293*
7:11–16 *40*
7:12–13 *9*
7:13–16 *284*
7:22 *60*
23:2 *259*

1 Kings

2:4 *42*
2:6 *123*
6:23–28 *64*
7 *38*

7:13–14   *286*
8:60   *60*
11:1–11   *58, 164*
12:25–33   *58*
16:28–33   *58*
16:31–33   *35*
18   *55*
18:20–29   *68*
18:26   *163*
18:29   *163*
20:23   *59*
21:25–26   *58*
22:19–23   *63*
22:53   *35*

2 Kings

1:2–3   *58*
2:9   *294*
2:15   *293*
2:15–16   *294*
5:15   *60*
5:17   *61*
11:28   *35*
14:19–35   *331*
16:3   *123*
17:14   *42*
17:33   *57*
18:33–35   *59*
19:15–19   *69*
21:3–7   *58, 164*
21:6   *123*
23:10   *123*

1 Chronicles

12:18   *293*
15:13   *72*
21   *81*
21:1   *81*

28   *38*
29:11–12   *115*

2 Chronicles

15:1–7   *293*
20:14–17   *293*
20:20   *42*
24:30   *293*
26:4   *72*
26:16–23   *72*

Nehemiah

9:6   *53*

Job

1–2   *63, 81*
9:18   *279*
12:10   *279*
14:13   *123*
15:7–8   *54*
19:17   *279*
26:5   *123*
26:13   *280*
28:28   *42*
31:24–28   *62*
33:4   *218, 280*
34:14–15   *218*

Psalms

7:12–14   *54*
9:17   *123*
16:10   *123*
18:5   *123*
18:13–15   *54*
19   *332*
19:1   *330, 331*
19:1–6   *332*
19:7–11   *332*
29:1   *61*

29:10   *54*
30:3   *123*
31:6   *66*
33:6   *218, 281, 283*
34:6   *14*
34:15–16   *119*
35:10   *52*
36:9   *331*
47:1   *215*
47:8–9   *215*
49:14   *123*
50:1–15   *177*
51:11   *279, 288, 301*
71:19   *52*
86:8–9   *53*
86:13   *123*
89:8   *52, 117*
89:9–10   *54*
93:3–4   *54*
94:3   *132*
95:3   *61*
97:7–9   *61, 70*
99   *14*
103:9–11   *116*
104:3–9   *54*
104:29–30   *279*
104:30   *220, 280*
106   *66*
106:12   *42*
106:36   *69*
106:37   *63*
106:37–38   *66*
111:10   *42*
113:5–8   *52*
115:2–8   *68*
115:3   *117*
135:15–18   *68*
135:17   *279*

136:2   *56, 163*
139:7–10   *288*
139:7–12   *319*
139:8   *123*

Proverbs

1:7   *42*
5:5   *123*
11:10   *132*
15:24   *123*
17:15   *14, 132*

Ecclesiastes

12:13   *42*

Isaiah

6:3   *14*
8:11   *259*
9:6–7   *9, 284, 301*
11:1   *304, 313*
11:1–2   *303*
11:1–5   *9, 40, 284, 298*
11:1–10   *298, 312*
11:2   *299, 302*
13:6   *119*
13:9   *119*
14:11   *123*
14:12–15   *54*
27:8   *279*
28:5   *298*
31:3   *279*
32:14–18   *312*
32:15   *295, 320*
32:15–16   *299*
32:15–17   *299, 320*
32:16–17   *295*
32:18   *320*
34:14   *64*

34:16   *295*
36:18–20   *54, 57*
37:26–29   *57*
37:29–35   *59*
38:5   *163*
40:7   *295*
40:12–14   *280*
40:12–31   *177*
40:16   *67*
40:18–20   *69*
40:19   *67*
40:19–20   *67*
40:22   *67*
40:28   *163*
40:29–31   *67*
41:7   *67*
41:19   *67*
41:21–23   *67*
41:24   *67*
42   *89*
42:1   *298, 299*
42:1–3   *307*
42:1–4   *75, 294, 312*
42:5   *295*
42:8   *70*
43:1–5   *115*
43:9–12   *53*
43:11   *16*
43:28   *295*
44:1–5   *312*
44:2   *67*
44:3   *295, 299, 313*
44:5   *295, 298*
44:9–10   *67*
44:12   *67*
44:15   *67*
44:17   *163*
44:23   *67*

44:24–25   *55*
44:24–45:7   *59*
44:28   *33*
45:5–7   *63, 163*
45:16   *69*
45:18   *163*
45:21   *16*
45:21–22   *163*
46:1–2   *57*
46:6   *67*
46:9–10   *57*
48:16   *298, 299*
49:1–6   *294*
49:6   *23*
50:4   *294*
51:4–5   *75*
51:9–16   *54*
52:13–53:12   *40*
54:16   *67*
55:5   *75*
55:8   *177*
59:15–21   *294*
59:21   *294, 298, 299*
60:2–3   *75*
61   *26*
61:1   *298, 304*
61:1–2   *299, 306*
63:7–14   *280*
63:10–11   *301*
65–66   *38*
66:18–23   *75*
66:24   *125*

Jeremiah

2:11   *70*
2:27–28   *68*
7:32   *123*
10:1–16   *68*

11:10   66
12:1   132
14:22   68
16:11–13   70
16:13–14   71
18:7–8   215
19:6   123
20:7–9   294
23:5   9
23:9   280
30:4   259
31:31–34   291
31:33   321
31:33–34   296
46:10   119
49:1   59
49:19   52
50:44   52

Ezekiel

2:2   279, 294
3:12   294
3:14   294
5:8   59
8:3   70
11:17–20   312
11:19   296
14:14   216
18:23   117
28:12–19   54
30:2–3   119
33:11   115
34:23–24   9
36:22–32   291
36:24–27   312
36:25–27   296, 313
36:27   299, 321
37:1   294

37:1–14   312
37:3   296
37:6   296
37:9   297
37:10   297
37:13–14   309
37:14   297, 299
37:24–25   9
37:24–28   301
39:29   281, 295, 299

Daniel

2:47   56
4:8–9   294
4:18   294
4:34–37   163
5:11–14   294
5:14   294
7:13–14   284
11:36   56

Hosea

2:8   57
2:13   70
2:16   57
8:4–6   68
13:2   68
13:4   16
13:14   123

Joel

1:15   ·119
2   291
2:1   119
2:11   119
2:12–13   110
2:23–26   297
2:27   53, 60

2:28   *313*
2:28–29   *291, 297, 300*
2:28–32   *237, 299, 312*
2:31   *119*
2:32   *25*

Amos

1–2   *59*
5:18   *119*
5:20   *119*
9:7   *215*

Obadiah

15   *119*

Jonah

2:9   *16*

Micah

3:8   *294*
4:4   *259*
5:1–5   *301*
5:12–15   *71*
7:18   *52*

Habakkuk

1:6   *33*
2:18–19   *68*
3:3–15   *54*

Zephaniah

1:14–16   *119*
2:11   *62, 163*

Haggai

2:4–5   *293*

Zechariah

3   *81*

3:1–2   *63, 81*
4:6   *293*
7:12   *294*
12:10   *9*
14:1   *119*
14:9   *51*

Malachi

1:2–3   *115*
1:11   *215*
3:1–6   *301*
4:5   *119*

Matthew

1:1–17   *266*
1–7   *267*
1:18   *302*
1:20–23   *331*
1:21–23   *15*
2:13   *331*
3:1   *20*
3:2   *25*
3:11   *25, 303*
3:12   *125*
3:13–17   *303*
3:17   *303, 304*
4:1   *304, 312*
4:1–11   *82*
4:8–10   *82*
4:10   *82*
4:15–16   *73*
4:17   *20*
4:23   *13*
4:24   *83, 309*
5:13   *349*
5:14   *349*
5:16   *349, 351*
5:17–18   *9, 259*

5:22   *122, 123, 125*
5:27–30   *119*
5:28–29   *122*
5:29   *123*
5:30   *123*
5:45   *115, 330*
6:1–8   *74*
6:7   *73*
6:32   *74*
7:12   *343*
7:13–14   *214*
7:15–20   *229*
7:21   *241*
7:28–29   *309*
8:5–13   *74, 179*
8:25   *14*
8:28–29   *82*
8:28–33   *83*
8:31   *82*
9:17   *128*
9:32   *83*
9:34   *83*
9:35   *13*
10:1   *82*
10:28   *119, 122, 123*
10:29   *115*
10:42   *349*
11:5   *13*
11:18   *83*
11:23   *123*
12:1–8   *267*
12:9–14   *307*
12:13   *99*
12:15–17   *307*
12:17–21   *75*
12:18–21   *308*
12:22   *83*
12:22–29   *307*

12:22–32   *307*
12:23   *307*
12:24   *82, 83*
12:28   *307, 312*
12:30   *345*
12:31–32   *308*
12:39–42   *267*
13:19   *82*
13:38–39   *82*
13:58   *312*
14:33   *79*
15:21–28   *179*
15:24   *75*
16:16   *182*
16:18   *123, 324*
17:11   *99*
17:14–18   *82*
17:14–21   *83*
18:8   *124*
18:9   *123*
23:15   *119, 123*
23:33   *119, 123*
24:14   *13*
24:24   *82*
24:36   *312*
25:30   *122, 125*
25:41   *82, 83*
25:41–46   *119*
25:46   *124, 129, 130*
26:8   *128*
26:13   *13*
26:24   *133*
27:54   *309*
28:9   *79*
28:17   *79, 180*
28:18–19   *75*
28:18–20   *22, 112, 340, 352*
28:19   *6*

28:20   *6, 320*

Mark

1:7–8   *303*
1:9–11   *303*
1:12   *304*
1:14–15   *13*
1:24   *82*
1:32   *83*
1:34   *82*
2:7   *79*
3:5   *99*
3:22–27   *307*
3:29   *124, 129, 130*
5:1–5   *83*
5:1–20   *82, 179*
5:30   *307*
5:34   *14*
7:24–30   *74*
7:25–26   *83*
8:25   *99*
8:32–33   *82*
9:12   *99*
9:39–40   *345*
9:43   *123, 125*
9:43–47   *119*
9:45   *123*
9:47   *123*
9:48   *125*
13:10   *13*

Luke

1:13–17   *303*
1:15   *302*
1:17   *307*
1:35   *302, 306, 324*
1:41   *302*
1:42–45   *302*

1:67   *302*
1:68–69   *302*
2:27–35   *303*
2:32   *73, 75*
2:40   *302, 306*
2:47   *302*
2:52   *302, 306*
3:3   *25*
3:16   *25*
3:16–17   *303*
3:18   *13*
3:21–22   *303*
3:22   *303, 306*
4:1   *304, 305*
4:1–13   *82*
4:13   *82*
4:14   *305, 307*
4:15   *305*
4:17–19   *306*
4:18   *13*
4:21   *27, 306*
4:22   *306*
4:31   *306*
4:31–37   *83*
4:33–35   *306*
4:34   *83*
4:36   *306, 307*
4:39   *306*
4:40–41   *306*
5:17   *307*
6:10   *99*
6:19   *307*
7:21   *82*
7:22   *13*
8:26–29   *83*
8:28   *83*
8:31   *83*
8:46   *307*

9:1   *307*
9:6   *13*
10:15   *123*
10:18   *82*
10:19   *82*
10:21   *306*
10:25   *244*
10:25–37   *244*
10:29   *244*
11:14–23   *307*
12:5   *123*
12:30   *74*
13:10–17   *82*
13:11   *83*
13:23–24   *214*
13:29   *213*
14:15–24   *75*
16:16   *13*
16:23   *123*
16:24   *129*
17:11–19   *74*
20:1   *13*
22:3–4   *82*
22:29   *180*
22:31   *82*
22:31–32   *82*
24:25   *262*
24:25–27   *9*
24:27   *27*
24:31   *263–276*
24:36–49   *263*
24:44   *263–276*
24:44–45   *27*
24:44–47   *9*
24:45   *263–276*
24:46–47   *112*
24:46–49   *340*
24:47   *22, 75*

24:49   *312*
24:52   *79, 180*

John

1:1   *79, 284, 311, 316*
1:1–3   *163, 281*
1:1–4   *29*
1:1–5   *282*
1:3   *79, 177, 283*
1:9   *275*
1:9–10   *73*
1:11   *75*
1:11–12   *111*
1:12   *22*
1:14   *316, 331*
1:17   *155*
1:18   *27, 79, 164, 312*
1:29   *303*
1:29–34   *303*
1:32   *304*
1:33   *317, 318, 320*
1:36   *303*
1:44   *27*
1:48   *312*
3:5   *296, 312, 313*
3:5–16   *323*
3:8   *231*
3:10   *313*
3:16   *11, 22, 73, 111, 115, 180, 315*
3:16–17   *341*
3:16–18   *164*
3:17–18   *232, 322*
3:18   *15, 22, 341*
3:19   *182*
3:34   *304*
3:34–35   *306, 313*
3:35   *115*

3:36   *15*
4   *244*
4:10   *164*
4:13   *164*
4:14   *163*
4:19–20   *165*
4:22   *74, 165, 244*
4:23   *165*
4:25   *165*
4:42   *16, 73*
5:18   *79*
5:20   *115*
5:21–22   *27, 163, 164*
5:21–24   *180*
5:23   *27, 73, 164, 352*
5:24   *22, 111, 180, 352*
5:26   *164*
5:27   *119, 180*
5:29   *111*
5:39   *27, 29*
5:39–40   *266*
5:40   *27*
5:45–47   *27*
6:38   *164*
6:40   *22, 164*
6:48–51   *164*
6:63   *219*
7:7   *73*
7:18   *317*
7:37–39   *164, 312, 313*
7:39   *314*
8:12   *22, 164*
8:24   *111*
8:36   *164*
8:44   *82*
8:48–52   *83*
9:5   *164*
9:38   *79*

10:1–2   *164*
10:9–10   *164*
10:10   *22*
10:25–26   *111*
10:28   *164*
10:28–30   *163*
10:30   *312*
10:35   *259*
11:25   *22, 164*
11:26   *111*
12:20–21   *111*
12:20–22   *75*
12:31   *73, 83*
12:32   *106, 110, 111*
13:2   *82*
13:27   *82*
14:6   *27, 73, 165, 180, 315,*
    321, 352
14:6–11   *164*
14:9   *27, 79, 180, 312*
14:15   *314*
14:15–17   *314*
14–16   *314*
14:16   *314, 315*
14:16–17   *319*
14:17   *73, 314, 315*
14:18   *314*
14:26   *314, 316*
15:4   *320*
15:4–10   *304*
15:9–10   *116*
15:18   *350*
15:26   *164, 314, 316*
15:26–16:15   *317*
16   *315*
16:3   *321*
16:7   *164, 312, 314, 315, 319*
16:7–15   *314*

16:12–13   *168*
16:13   *316*
16:13–14   *277*
16:13–15   *317*
16:14   *4, 317, 321, 327, 352*
17:3   *22*
17:4   *317*
17:8–9   *116*
17:20–21   *325*
17:20–23   *325*
20:28   *79, 309*
20:31   *22, 111, 263*

Acts

1:1   *316*
1:4   *318*
1:5   *303*
1:6   *99*
1:8   *6, 75, 168, 237, 312, 320, 340, 352*
1:16   *259*
2   *236, 324*
2:4   *318*
2:6   *318*
2:14–40   *334*
2:14–41   *264*
2:17   *236, 319, 320*
2:17–18   *320*
2:17–21   *319*
2:21   *22*
2:22–39   *319*
2:27   *123*
2:31   *123*
2:32–36   *9*
2:33   *319*
2:36   *264–276, 343*
2:38   *22, 319*
2:38–40   *20*

2:41   *6*
3:6   *349*
3:12   *312*
3:12–26   *334*
3:15–21   *20*
3:16   *349*
3:18   *259*
3:18–24   *27*
3:19–20   *22*
3:19–21   *107*
3:21   *99, 105, 107, 259*
4:7   *312*
4:8   *321*
4:8–12   *322, 334*
4:12   *20, 21, 22, 163, 164, 180, 231, 322, 352*
4:18–20   *349*
4:24   *115*
4:25   *259*
4:30   *349*
4:31   *322*
4:33   *312*
5:3   *82*
5:31   *16*
6:8   *312*
6:10   *312, 322*
7:25   *14*
7:41–43   *80*
7:59–60   *163*
8   *202*
8:7–13   *84*
8:9–24   *83*
8:12   *349*
8:25   *13*
8:26   *334*
8:26–40   *334*
8:29   *322, 334*
8:35   *334*

8:36–39   *335*
8:39   *334*
8:40   *335*
9:1–8   *334*
9:4   *324*
9–10   *24*
9:10–12   *334*
9:13–14   *334*
9:15–16   *334*
9:17   *322*
9:20   *352*
9:22   *343*
10:2   *24*
10–11   *322*
10:19–20   *322*
10:30–32   *335*
10:34–35   *216*
10:34–43   *334*
10:35   *205*
10:38   *307, 308, 312, 327*
10:42   *119, 352*
10:42–43   *24*
10:43   *27*
10:45   *205*
10:45–47   *326*
11:12   *322*
11:13–15   *335*
11:14   *24, 322*
11:26   *9*
12:2   *80*
13   *23*
13:2   *322*
13:6–12   *84*
13:8   *84*
13:9–11   *322*
13:16–41   *23, 334*
13:38   *22*
13:45   *23*

13:47   *23*
14   *88, 341*
14:7   *13*
14:8–13   *80, 88*
14:8–20   *80*
14:15   *13, 77, 85, 88, 89*
14:16   *88, 93–94, 205*
14:16–17   *85, 216*
14:17   *205*
14:38   *23*
15   *24*
15:7   *24*
15:8   *25*
15:11   *25*
16:6–7   *322*
16:10   *13*
16:16–18   *83, 84*
16:16–24   *73*
16:18   *349*
16:25–34   *334*
16:30   *13*
16:30–31   *22*
16:31   *13, 77*
17   *88, 340, 341*
17:2–3   *27, 88*
17:16   *85, 87, 89*
17:16–18   *77*
17:16–34   *73*
17:17   *89–94, 343*
17:18   *90–94, 94*
17:21   *90–94*
17:22   *75, 87, 90–94*
17:22–31   *216*
17:23   *90–94, 205*
17:23–24   *91–94*
17:25   *91, 177, 218*
17:26   *330*
17:27   *92–94, 331, 333*

17:27–28   92–94
17:28   77, 253, 338
17:29–31   80, 181
17:30   92–94
17:30–31   21
17:34   94
18:28   27
19:1–7   24
19:2   25
19:4–6   25
19:11–34   77
19:13   349
19:13–16   83, 84
19:14–16   83
19:16   205
19:21–41   73
19:23–41   80
19:26   85
20:28   324
20:29–30   142
20:35   343
22:16   22
24:25   119
26:12–18   334
26:16   334
26:17–23   22
26:18   82, 84
26:19   334
26:22–23   27, 264
28:23   27
28:30–31   352

Romans

1:1–3   27
1–2   216
1:4   301, 309
1:15–16   13
1:16   13, 343

1:18   14, 76, 87, 120, 332
1:18–19   87
1:18–20   46, 81
1:18–23   93–94
1:18–32   15, 80
1:19–21   76, 331
1:19–23   77
1:20   87, 330
1:20–21   87
1:21   81, 87
1:21–25   337
1:22–25   84
1:23   81
1:25   177–182, 336
1:32   87, 330
2:1–5   332
2:1–16   46
2:4   110, 118, 330
2:5   120
2:6–16   120
2:12–16   232
2:14   87
2:14–15   331
2:15   87, 330
2:15–16   330
2:16   132, 331
3:9   14
3:11   333
3:23–25   14
3:25   93–94
3:26   132
3:28–30   78
4:21   117
4:25   11
5:6–11   15
5:9–10   14
5:12–21   106, 113
5:17   113

5:18   *106, 112, 214*
5:21   *14*
6:4–11   *325*
6:22   *171*
8:1–4   *323*
8:1–8   *323*
8:2   *323*
8:6–8   *14*
8:7–8   *345*
8:9   *202, 320*
8:9–11   *327*
8:11   *309*
8:14–15   *323*
8:15   *14*
8:16   *324*
8:17   *326*
8:19–25   *325*
8:20–23   *112*
8:22–23   *284*
8:24   *15, 131*
8:30   *51*
9–11   *112*
9:22   *118*
10:4   *9*
10:8–9   *13*
10:9   *105*
10:9–10   *25*
10:9–18   *25*
10:10–13   *232*
10:12   *25*
10:13   *25*
10:13–17   *318*
10:14–15   *335, 352*
10:14–16   *25*
10:17   *26, 334*
11:23   *112*
11:32   *105, 112, 113, 213*
15:16   *324*

15:19   *322*
15:19–20   *13*
15:20   *352*
15:21   *352*
16:20   *82, 83*
16:25–27   *27*

1 Corinthians

1:17   *13*
1:18   *7, 14, 26*
1:22   *179*
1:23   *182, 342*
1:23–25   *179*
2:9–16   *253*
2:10–16   *252*
2:12–13   *325*
4:5   *132*
4:6   *263*
5:5   *82, 84, 128*
5:10–13   *80*
5:17   *325*
6:3   *83*
6:9   *80*
6:11   *323*
6:14   *309*
6:17   *326*
7:5   *82*
8   *85*
8:1–13   *86*
8:4   *80, 86, 205*
8:5   *80*
8:5–6   *86*
8:6   *78, 80*
8:7–10   *86*
8:11   *86*
9:14   *13*
9:16   *13*
9:22   *78, 342*

10   *85*
10:1–22   *86*
10:6–12   *81*
10:14–22   *80, 84*
10:19–21   *84*
10:20   *83*
10:22   *84*
10:23–30   *86*
10:25–26   *86*
10:31   *345*
12:2   *80, 86*
12:3   *241, 295, 318, 323, 345*
12:4–11   *324*
12:12   *324*
12:13   *325*
15   *12, 109*
15:1   *12*
15:1–2   *13*
15:1–4   *21, 26*
15:1–6   *322*
15:1–8   *11*
15:1–19   *12*
15:2   *12*
15:3   *12*
15:6   *180*
15:8   *334*
15:11   *11, 13*
15:12   *13*
15:12–49   *325*
15:14–19   *325*
15:17   *21*
15:20   *326*
15:20–28   *214*
15:22   *108, 108–136*
15:22–29   *105, 108*
15:28   *318*
15:45   *202, 326*

2 Corinthians

1:20   *27*
1:22   *326*
2:11   *82*
2:15   *15, 131*
2:17   *343*
3:3   *326*
3–4   *323*
3:18   *323, 324*
4:1–4   *87*
4:1–5   *182*
4:2   *343*
4:3–4   *26*
4:3–6   *343*
4:4   *7, 82, 84, 323*
5   *113*
5:5   *326*
5:10   *120*
5:18   *113*
5:18–21   *214*
5:19   *106, 113–136*
5:20   *113*
10:4–5   *340, 343*
10:5   *9, 329*
10:16   *13*
11:3   *82, 84*
11:4   *13*
11:7   *13*
11:13–15   *84*
11:15   *120*
13:4   *327*
15:1–4   *22*

Galatians

1:6–10   *26*
1:11   *13*
1:12   *334*
2:2   *13*

3:2   *26*
3:8   *13*
3:26   *324*
3:28   *298, 347*
4:3   *14*
4:4   *267*
4:4–7   *349*
4:6   *324*
4:8   *76, 80*
4:13   *13*
5:19–21   *80*
5:20   *84*
5:22–23   *345*
5:22–24   *324*
5:28–29   *193*

Ephesians

1:4–5   *115*
1:11   *117*
1:12–14   *326*
1:13   *245, 326*
1:19–21   *117*
1:23   *324*
2:1   *26*
2:1–3   *14, 87*
2:2   *14, 81, 84*
2:3   *120*
2:4–10   *15*
2:5   *14*
2:8   *26*
2:8–9   *26, 113, 244, 245*
2:12   *14, 76, 87*
2:13   *325*
2:18   *325*
2:20   *324*
2:22   *324*
3:6   *326*
3:13   *26*

4:26–27   *82*
4:30   *326*
5:5–6   *80*
5:6   *120*
5:18   *321, 324*
5:22–24   *324*
5:25   *115, 116*
6:10   *117*
6:10–20   *82*
6:12   *82*
6:12–17   *84*
6:16   *81*
6:17   *305*

Philippians

1:28   *120*
2:5–8   *309*
2:6   *310–327*
2:6–8   *310–327*
2:6–11   *105, 214*
2:7   *310–327*
2:9–10   *284*
2:10–11   *108, 163*
2:11   *318*
3:19   *108, 127, 128*

Colossians

1:13   *171*
1:15   *27, 283*
1:15–20   *282, 284*
1:15–23   *180*
1:16   *27, 79, 283, 340*
1:16–17   *214*
1:17   *283*
1:19–20   *105, 107, 112, 113*
1:23   *13*
2:3   *339*
2:4   *84*

2:4–23   *180*
2:8   *84*
2:9   *174, 310*
2:14–15   *112*
2:15   *83, 108*
3:5–6   *81*
3:6   *120*
3:16   *321*

1 Thessalonians

1:5   *322*
1:9   *87*
1:10   *131*
2:2   *13*
2:16   *21*
2:18   *82*
3:5   *84*
4:5   *76*
5:3   *120, 127, 128*
5:8   *15, 131*
5:9   *131*

2 Thessalonians

1:5–10   *131*
1:6   *132*
1:6–7   *124*
1:8–9   *124*
1:9   *120, 127, 129*
2:4   *80*
2:8–10   *83*

1 Timothy

1:6–11   *109*
1:16   *118*
1:20   *84*
2:2   *109*
2:4   *117, 213*
2:4–6   *214*

2:5–6   *226*
3:7   *82, 84*
3:16   *309*
4:1–2   *109*
4:1–3   *82, 83, 84*
4:10   *106, 112, 113–136, 214*
5:15   *84*
5:24   *109*
6:9–10   *109*
6:15   *163*

2 Timothy

1:9   *14*
1:14   *324*
2:12   *284*
3:15   *27*
3:16   *29, 148, 259, 294, 305, 331*
3:16–17   *10*

Titus

1:4   *114*
2:11   *106, 114*
2:13   *16, 163*
2:14   *114*
3:5   *14, 114*
3:5–7   *114*
3:5–8   *15*
3:6   *114*
3:7   *114*
3:8   *114*

Hebrews

1:1–2   *79, 337*
1:1–3   *311*
1:1–4   *21, 26, 79*
1:2   *267, 283*
1:3   *27, 163, 283, 284*

1:10   *163*
1:14   *15*
2:1–4   *26*
2:2–3   *112*
2:9   *106, 110, 112*
2:14   *82*
2:14–15   *14*
2:16   *83, 112*
2:17–18   *311*
4:2   *26*
4:12–13   *132*
4:14   *163*
4:15   *311*
5:6–10   *46*
5:8–9   *311*
5:9   *129, 130*
6:2   *124, 129*
6:4–6   *112*
7:23–26   *324*
7:25   *15*
8:1–2   *324*
9:12   *129*
9:14   *308*
9:23   *286*
9:24   *286*
9:26   *286*
9:27   *14*
9:28   *14*
10:19–22   *26*
10:26–31   *112*
10:29   *324*
10:29–30   *120*
11:3   *284*
11:6   *26*
12:2   *26*
12:6   *131*
13:19   *99*

James

1:17   *14*
2:13   *120*
2:19   *82*
3:6   *123*
3:15   *82*

1 Peter

1:9   *15*
1:10–11   *313*
1:10–12   *27, 294*
1:11   *320*
1:12   *13, 322*
1:16   *171*
1:22–25   *26*
2:5   *171*
3:15   *343*
3:18   *309*
3:18–22   *106, 114*
4:3–5   *80*
4:11   *345*
4:17   *131*
4:17–18   *114*
4:17–19   *120*

2 Peter

1:11   *16*
1:20–21   *10, 148, 259, 269, 331*
2:3   *110*
2:4   *82*
2:9–10   *110*
2:12–13   *110*
2:15–17   *110–136*
2:17   *125*
3:7   *110, 127*
3:9   *105, 109, 110, 213*
3:16   *259*

1 John

1:1–2 *311*
1:1–3 *111*
1:7 *111*
2:1 *314*
2:2 *110, 111, 112*
2:15–16 *73*
3:2 *15, 283, 324*
3:8 *83*
4:1–4 *83*
4:1–6 *318*
4:2–3 *229, 241*
4:6 *26*
4:8 *115, 116*
4:8–10 *115*
5:10–13 *111*
5:18–19 *81*
5:19 *82*
5:21 *81*

Jude

3 *8*
6 *125*
7 *124*
21 *116*

Revelation

1:1 *321*
1:6 *117*
1:10 *321*
1:17–20 *163*
1:18 *123*
2:1 *321*
2:7 *321*
2:8 *321*
2:11 *321*
2:12 *321*
2:17 *321*

2:18 *321*
2:29 *321*
3:1 *321*
3:6 *321*
3:7 *321*
3:13 *321*
3:14 *321*
3:22 *321*
4:2 *321*
4–5 *135*
4:8–11 *135*
4:11 *117, 135*
5:3 *135*
5:4 *135*
5:5–6 *135*
5:6 *135*
5:8–14 *27*
5:9 *135, 237*
5:9–14 *135*
6–8 *135*
6:8 *123*
6:10 *132*
7:9 *213*
7:10–17 *135*
8:2–9:21 *120*
9:20 *81, 83, 85*
11:15–18 *135*
12:7–9 *82, 83*
12:7–17 *83*
12:9 *39, 82*
12:10 *82*
12:10–12 *135*
13:8 *263*
13:12–15 *83*
14:6 *13*
14:9–11 *80, 125*
14:10–11 *129, 131*
15:3–4 *135*

15:5–16:21   *120*
16:1–2   *80*
16:5–7   *135*
17:3   *321*
17:8   *263*
18:2–20   *135*
19:1–3   *108, 134*
19:1–4   *132*
19:1–6   *134*
19:1–8   *135*
19:1–20:15   *120*
19:3   *125*
19:10   *321*
19:11–21   *163*

19:16   *163*
20:1–3   *83*
20:4   *284*
20:7–10   *83*
20:10   *83, 126, 134*
20:13–14   *123*
20:15   *125*
21:8   *80, 205*
21:10   *321*
21:22–26   *235*
22:2   *214*
22:12   *163*
22:15   *80, 205*